The University of Chicago
Libraries

THE ASATIR

The Samaritan Book of the "Secrets of Moses"

TOGETHER WITH
THE PITRON OR SAMARITAN COMMENTARY AND
THE SAMARITAN STORY OF THE DEATH OF MOSES

PUBLISHED FOR THE FIRST TIME WITH
INTRODUCTION, TRANSLATION AND NOTES BY

MOSES GASTER, PH. D.

WIPF & STOCK · Eugene, Oregon

Wipf and Stock Publishers
199 W 8th Ave, Suite 3
Eugene, OR 97401

The Asatir
Samaritain Book of the Secret Moses
By Gaster, Moses
ISBN 13: 978-1-62564-867-9
Publication date 1/28/2015
Previously published by Royal Asiatic Society, 1927

IN LOVING MEMORY

OF MY FATHER

THE CHEVALIER A. E. GASTER

1834—1927

AND

OF MY MOTHER-IN-LAW

BERTHA FRIEDLÄNDER

1843—1926

*

PREFACE

A preface to a little book with a voluminous introduction of some hundreds of pages seems a superfluous luxury. I believe, however, that such an introduction is intended to give to a superficial reader a brief indication of what he may expect to find in the book. The scholar requires none of it. In order, therefore, to satisfy such a reader, I will tell him briefly that I am publishing here for the first time a Samaritan collection of Biblical legends, a parallel to the Jewish Midrash and to the pseudepigraphic literature. I claim for the "Secrets of Moses" that it is the oldest book in existence of this kind of literature, and I put the date of its compilation to be about the middle or end of the third century B. C. E. In the introduction the reader will see how I have reached a conclusion as startling to me as probably it will be to him who will take this book for the first time into his hands. It was very slow and uphill work, and I had to cover a wide field, leaving no document unexamined which might help to throw light on the date and origin of this book. I have searched through the entire pseudepigraphic literature, in whatever language it may have been preserved, and I have worked my way up to the Hellenistic literature, to the Sibylline Oracles and Eupolemos. Josephus has attracted me quite specially, and I believe I have been able to put a new complexion on the character and sources of his "Antiquities." The Palestinian Targum has come under minute examination, and in connection with it all the Jewish Midrashim. The Sibylline Oracles have been traced down to their latest development in the Tiburtine, and the mediaeval oracles down to Matthew of Paris, and even to Slavonic and Rumanian texts. In my re-examination of the pseudepigraphic literature I have arrived at conclusions which differ widely from those accepted today. I have drawn attention to affinities with Mandaean traditions, and I have endeavoured to give as literal a translation as was possible of a text so old and unfortunately so corrupt that even the joint wisdom of the Samaritans of today has been unable to solve many of the problems raised by it. A commentary prepared by them has also been added, which exemplifies the exact state of scholarship among the Samaritans of the last few centuries. Brief but I believe sufficiently ample references to the entire literature have been given in the footnotes, and a chapter of the book has been given in transliteration, showing the pronunciation by the Samaritans of the old text. I can faithfully say that I have spared no effort in trying to elucidate a book which, by its character, claims special attention from more than one point of view. The parallelism between Jews and Samaritans in all their mental activity, to which I have referred in my Schweich Lectures manifests itself here again. A Midrashic interpretation of the middle of the third century points to a fixed text of the Pentateuch, already considered as holy and immutable in word and letter. The time is not yet ripe to enquire into the primary source of these Biblical legends. I have endeavoured, however, and I believe for the first time, to lift some of them out of the narrow confines of Palestine, and to join them to the wider cycles of world-legends, and a new view has been advanced, among others, of the origin of the Antichrist legend. It must be left to others to continue this comparative study, and to investigate the closer relations between them, and the mutual influences which they may have exercised upon one another.

It would be ungrateful on my part were I not to mention in the first place the assistance which the Samaritans have tried to give me, especially the late high priest Jacob the son of Aaron, and his son Ab Ḥasda, and to a large extent Abisha the son of Pineḥas. From time to time one friend or another has rendered me valuable help, but a special debt of gratitude is due to Mr. B. Bamberger, who, with sincere devotion and scholarly acumen has assisted me in the final process of shaping the book and reading the proofs while it was passing through the Press. Last but not least I should like to place on record my appreciation of the generosity of the Royal Asiatic Society, which has enabled me to publish the most ancient monument, so miraculously preserved, of the Samaritan literature, truly "a brand plucked out of the fire."

M. GASTER.

London, 193 Maida Vale, W. 9. June 16th. 1927.

TABLE OF CONTENTS

	Page
PREFACE	
INTRODUCTION	1—183
Character and Title of the Book.	1
Detailed Contents	
Sibylline Oracles, Eupolemos and Other Hellenistic writers	9
Abraham and Nimrod Legends	
The Sibyl of Tibur and Other Oracles	42
The Cave of Treasures — Methodius of Patmos	
The Asatir and Josephus	61
The Palestinian Targum	80
Bileam Legends and Antichrist	
The Asatir and the Cycles of Universal Sagas	99
The Universal King — The Return of the Hero — The Child of Destiny — The Antichrist Legend	
The Pseudepigraphic Literature	105
Enoch — Jubilees — Pseudo-Philo — Adam-Books	
Characteristic Points of Difference	120
Astrology — Demonology — Eschatology	
Mandaean Affinities	125
Language and Anti-Jewish Tendency	
Asatir and the Samaritan Literature	134
Markaḥ — Book of Joshua — Ab Ḥasda — El Doweik — Abdalla B. Shalma — Meshalma	
Chronology and Dates	141

Geographical and Others Names: Arabic Glosses   147
    Samaritan Targum — Cryptograms

The Original Language   156

Date of the Asatir and Final Conclusion. . . .   158

The Manuscripts and Edition of the Asatir . .   163

The Arabic Paraphrase.   168

The Pitron: or Arabic-Samaritan Commentary
to the Asatir.   171

Specimen of the Asatir Transliterated According to the Pronunciation of the Samaritans . .   174

Story of the Death of Moses.   178
    The Apocalypse of Moses and Josephus

TRANSLATIONS . . . . 184—321

    Asatir . . . . 184—320

    Pitron or Commentary to the Asatir . . . . 185—301

    Samaritan Story of the Death of Moses . . 303—321

LIST OF ABBREVIATIONS.   322

INDEX   327

THE SAMARITAN TEXTS . . . .   1—59

CHARACTER AND TITLE OF THE BOOK.

The best way to describe the Asatir is to call it a Midrash, Aggadah, or legendary supplement to the Pentateuch. Unlike other Apocrypha—with which it has much in common—the author does not attempt to retail anew the sacred history and to present it in a specific form, and with a deliberate tendency. He is content to leave the sacred scripture as it stands, without meddling with its narrative and without trying to readjust the events recounted therein, according to a certain preconceived system either legal or astronomical. The author takes for granted the Samaritan tradition as he knows it, and does not waste his ingenuity to prove its truth. The following Table of Contents will show the exact character of the book:

Chapter I.
> Division of Earth by Adam (v. 2). Sacrifice of Kain and Hebel on Mt. Garizim (v. 6). Killing of Hebel and the darkening of Kain's spirit (v. 9—13). Various dates (v. 24ff.). Adam separated from Eve 100 years (v. 26).

Chapter II.
> Seth builds Antokia (v. 1). Genealogies and building of towns (v. 2). Twice twelve precious stones (v. 7). Lamech making images (v. 10). Sign of birth of Noah (v. 16). Adam foretells the Flood (v. 17). Children of Lamech and the towns built by them (v. 20). Aḥidan son of Tubal Kain taught by Adam (v. 35). Enoch buried near Mt. Ebal (v. 38). Sanctity of Mt. Garizim (v. 40). Noah studying Adam's Book of Signs (v. 44).

Chapter III.
> Death of Adam in Badan (v. 1). Burial in cave (v. 4). Noah studies the Three Books (v. 9). Aḥidan builds Sion (Rock of Shame) (v. 13). Asur son of Aḥidan marries Gifna (v. 20). The worship of sun and moon in that place (v. 22). Mechanical contrivances (v. 26).

Chapter IV.
> Flood (v. 2). Division of Earth (v. 13). The Three Books (v. 15). Death of Noah (v. 36).

Chapter V.
> Tower of Babel (v. 1). First War of the Nations (v. 11). Nimrod (v. 12). Birth of Abraham (v. 14). Seclusion of Women (v. 20). Death of Haran (v. 28).

Chapter VI.
> Death of Nimrod (v. 1). Two Nimrods (v. 2). Abraham going down to Egypt (v. 10). Fall of idols (v. 11). Punishment of Pharaoh (v. 14). Sorcerer Turts (v. 18). First proclamation of Faith (v. 23). Abraham rebuilding the first altar (v. 27).

Chapter VII.
> Amraphel and Sodomites (v. 1). Turts going from Hebron to Shinear (v. 4). Last Kings of Ham (v. 7). Capture and rescue of Lot (v. 8). Advice to Kedar Laomer (v. 12). Dates of Abraham's movements (v. 13ff.). Abraham in pursuit (dates) (v. 14). Abraham in Salem with Melchizedek (v. 17). Various dates (v. 26).

Chapter VIII.
> Reign of Ishmael (v. 1). Ishmael partner with Esau (v. 5). Kings of Edom (v. 7). Abraham and

wickedness of children of Ashur and Joktan (v. 9). Jacob going to Haran (v. 13). Genealogy of Paraoh (v.14). Pharaoh coming to Egypt (v. 21). Plti the wizard and his prophecy about Moses (v.24). Amram;s greatness (v. 27). Plti prophesies Moses' death by water (v. 35)

Chapter IX.
Moses' birth (day and dates) (v. 1). Moses rescue (v. 4). Killing of the Egyptian (v. 15). Flight to Midian (v.14). God's appearance to Moses (v.21). Dates from God's appearance to Moses to the Death of Arron (v. 24ff.).

Chapter X.
Mertis (v.1). Balak and Bileam (v.1). Bileam's seven gods (vv. 5—7). Bileam's curses frusrated (v. 13ff.). Bileam and the daughters of Moab (v. 18ff.). Stations of the tribes (v. 22ff.). Pinhas and Zimri, miracles (v. 30ff.). War against Midian (v.41). Death of Bileam (v.47).

Chapter XI.
Joshua appointed (v. 1). Death of Moses and his prophecy (v. 20).

Chapter XII.
The Oracle.

The book is called by the Samaritans the "Asatir," or, as it should have been, "Astir." I have translated this title "The Secrets of Moses," thus translating the Samaritan word "Asatir," so pronounced by the Samaritans, in order to distinguish it at once from the other books ascribed to Moses, such as the "Apocalypse" or the "Assumption of Moses." The Samaritans themselves no longer understand the title, and were unable to enlighten me in spite of frequent questioning, but they at the same

1*

time emphatically repudiate the notion that the title may be of Arabic origin. The word is one which has not been taken by them into their language; it occurs neither in their liturgical poems nor in any other book with which I am acquainted, although they are quite familiar with the Hebrew parallel form אסתיר from the passage in the Bible, Deut. 31, 18., to which they attach overwhelming importance. The fulfilment of the threat expressed by that sentence in the Bible, marks according to them the starting point of the Fanuta, the Hiding of God's presence. The Hebrew word has not been retained in its Hebrew form even in the Samaritan Targum to that passage. But in the case of the present book, they have evidently retained the very old name, the true meaning of which they have since forgotten. It is unquestionably the primitive Hebrew name for that literature which has since become known under the two Greek names of Apocryphon and Apocalypse, both meaning something hidden or something revealed in a secret form. A narrower meaning has been attached to the word "Apocryphon," inasmuch as it has been given to a set of books not received in what is called the Canon of the Jewish Bible. Without entering upon any discussion as to the meaning of the Canon of the Jewish Bible, whatever may be understood by it, it is clear that it cannot be applied to any Samaritan writing, since the Samaritans have only the Pentateuch, and outside this the Book of Joshua and some fragments of Judges and Samuel. These latter are treated by them as profane history. The use of the title "Apocryphon," therefore, would have been misleading, and as for "Apocalypse," it could only be applied to the two last chapters, which deal with prophecies connected with the very last hours of Moses upon earth. I have, therefore, as mentioned before, chosen the title "The Secrets of Moses" in preference to any other, for it agrees much more closely with the character of this book; moreover, "Secreta Moysi" ("Secrets of Moses") appears as a title in one of the old lists of books excluded from the Canon by the Church (see Charles, "The Assumption of Moses," London 1897, p. XV). It is not unimportant to mention that in the Hebrew literature a book has been preserved, to which reference will be made later on (p. 52), under the title of "The Secrets or Mysteries of Rabbi Simeon ben Yochai." It is a real apocalypse, and contains prophecies concerning the end of time and various events connected therewith. The Hebrew name of it is "Nistarot," which is precisely of the same root as the Samaritan form of "Asatir."

From the contents, and from the fact that it is ascribed to Moses, the book might also be described as pseudepigraphic. True, it is nowhere in the text expressly stated that Moses wrote it, but his authorship is assumed by the title, and by the tradition still alive among the Samaritans, although in quoting the book, as will be seen later on (p. 137, 140) the various Samaritan writers quote only "the Master of the Asatir," or the "Author of the Asatir" (Baal Asatir). They leave it undecided as to whether Moses actually wrote it, or whether it is a tradition handed down from Moses. Thus the Asatir belongs to the large number of pseudepigraphic writings ascribed to Moses. It differs completely however from the others, inasmuch as it is the only one that starts from Adam and finishes with the Death of Moses. It thus covers the whole of the Pentateuch. The Book of Jubilees carries its story from Creation to the Exodus. The so-called Apocalypse of Moses is in reality an Adam Book. It contains only the story of the going-out of Paradise by Adam and Eve, the various incidents connected with the first man, and closes with the death of Adam and Eve. Another is the "Assumptio" or rather the "Testament" of Moses, which is limited exclusively to the last days of Moses and closes with a prophecy.

The reason why an Adam Book should have been called "The Apocalypse of Moses" has hitherto remained obscure, as no reference to Moses is found in any of the texts, neither in the Greek, Latin, Slavonic, Arabic nor Ethiopian, nor even in the Syriac "Cave of Treasures," which already goes beyond the more limited scope of the others. In the light of the Asatir, this difficulty is now removed, since it explains the reason for that title, as the text here begins with the history of Adam and Eve and finishes with the Death of Moses. The "Apocalypse" may, therefore, have originally belonged to a similar full compilation. In fact, the "Apocalypse" agrees in the main with the first chapters of our book ascribed to Moses (cf. p. 115). From this the "Apocalypse" has then been detached, but retained the old title of the whole book.

The Asatir, then, is accepted by the Samaritans as a book of Moses.

Although those who made copies for me from the older original MSS. differ among themselves in the wording of the title, still they are unanimous in ascribing it to "our Master Moses." So it appears also in the Arabic paraphrase, and in the "Pitron" (Commentary). Moreover, to the questions which I put to the Samaritans I received the unequivocal reply that *of course* the book was written by Moses, and although it did not enjoy the same authority as the Law, none the less the facts which were related in the book were all true and reliable. The old tradition has thus been preserved unaltered down to our very days. One must realise that the name of an author was not considered to be of such a determining value, as it is in modern times. Hence the reason why the same book was at one time ascribed to one author, and at other times to another author. Take e. g. the very same apocalypse being ascribed in turns to St. Paul, St. Peter or the Lady Mary. Most of the apocryphal writings are practically anonymous, quite indifferent to the names which were from time to time attached to them. They are popular literature in the widest sense of the word, and have been treated as such. Originally neither the Jews nor the Samaritans would have enquired too closely about the authenticity of any such legendary writing ascribed to the one or the other of the Patriarchs. So little importance was attached originally to the name of the author that those older writings which were circulating under various names were afterwards gathered under one heading, e. g. the Enoch Books or the Adam Books or the Moses Books. As Moses had written the Law, why should he not have added another book of explanatory tales which completed his narrative and did not affect the Law? The Asatir keeps free of every legal prescription. The people, no doubt, believed that Moses did not limit his work to the Pentateuch. The Jewish tradition goes further. The whole Oral Law is said to have been developed by Moses in addition to the written and not a few very ancient legal prescriptions are described distinctly as Laws (Halaḥa) given by Moses from the time of Sinai. In the Bible itself a psalm is indeed ascribed to Moses. Among their oldest prayers the Samaritans have one ascribed to Moses and also one to Joshua, the former, save for a few words, consisting of verses from the Pentateuch. No wonder that to them many a legend connected with the narrative of the Pentateuch should also have been the work of Moses. Thus we have in our Asatir a book genuinely believed by the Samaritans to be a work of Moses, the only man acknowledged capable of writing such a book and foretelling the future.

That the book was held in very high esteem by the Samaritans, and treated almost as a sacred book is proved by the fact that it has exercised great influence on Samaritan literature, as will be shown later on (p. 134) as well as by another fact, which appears to be very simple, and yet is of great significance. Anyone acquainted with Samaritan MSS. will notice that no profane book, whatever its character may be, has ever been written on *parchment*. This material has been reserved for books of a sacred or a semi-sacred character. It is only the Law, some ancient prayer-book, or some very old philacteries, which were invested with a special character of sanctity, that have been written on parchment, and no other work. I have not found even a copy of Markah's great poems on parchment. The only exception is the Asatir, in a copy which is still preserved among the Samaritans of Nablus. From the end of the fifteenth century they have ceased using parchment because by that time the last remnant of the ashes of the red heifer prepared a few centuries previously, had come to an end. They were therefore no longer in that state of levitical purity to handle and to prepare skins for sacred use. The fact that the old copy of the Asatir was written on parchment, shows the reverence with which this book was treated by the Samaritans, in the belief that it was indeed a work of Moses.

Ever since I discovered the book for the first time among the Samaritans in May 1907 I have endeavoured to trace its origin and to compare it with the existant apocryphal and pseudepigraphic literature. There were, apparently, so many common traits that I felt sure by means of such comparison, to be able to establish its true character and the approximate date of its composition. I did not at first fully realise its high antiquity, although I knew that very little is found in the Samaritan literature written in that language for which some high antiquity could not be claimed. There are, in fact, very few works found written in the pure Samaritan language, and one could *a priori* consider it anterior to the time when Arabic had become the literary language of the Samaritans. It also differed from the language used since the period of the revival in the fourteenth century. This was no longer real Samaritan, but a peculiar Samaritan Hebrew. After a careful examination, one after the other, the pseudepigraphic writings emerged as belonging to a more recent period, than the date of the Asatir, and I was thus led up the stream of the literary tradition to its remotest sources through the Palestinian Targum, Josephus, until it reached the Sibylline Oracles and the fragments of the Hellenistic literature preserved by Eusebius. There seems to be nothing of a high antiquity which could be brought into some relation with the one or the other section of the Asatir, and in the following pages I am now giving the result of that slow and patient investigation which has taken me so many years to complete. The first work to be examined is the Sibylline Oracles. The Sibyl of Tibur, Josephus, the Palestinian Targum follow in the order of their approximation to the Asatir, and then, the apocrypal and pseudepigraphic literature fall into their proper place in their relation to the Asatir.

SIBYLLINE ORACLES, EUPOLEMOS, AND OTHER HELLENISTIC WRITERS.

The Sibylline Oracles are a remarkable product of that Jewish Hellenistic propaganda which flourished as early as the second century B. C. and was continued for a long time afterwards. It is a curious blend of old and new, of pagan prophecies and of Jewish legends. Some of the books are distinctly Jewish, but even here not a little has been borrowed from elsewhere, and incorporated in the collection, not always systematically, and very often in a haphazard manner. Much has been done to elucidate the history of these oracles, the manner of their composition, and to separate, if possible, the old from the new, the Jewish from the non-Jewish. No one, however, seems to have succeeded in finding the sources from which the Sibyl has drawn her materials. The older pagan literature has unfortunately perished, and except a few quotations from that literature, the rest has been guess-work. No better is the case with those portions which are decidedly Jewish in origin, as is shown by the spirit which they exhibit, by their virulent attack against heathen practices and beliefs, by the lavish praise bestowed upon the Jews, and by the glorification of the Jewish faith and hopes. Still, the direct sources have not yet been traced, nor would it be an easy task since the authors of the oracles have covered up as deftly as possible all the traces, and very little, if anything, is known of the contemporary Jewish literature. Some parallelism, no doubt, has been found between the Messianic outlook, or rather the prediction of woe and tribulation, as found in the Sibyl, and that in some of the pseudepigraphic writings. But a diligent search might yet reveal some more points of contact, and this Samaritan text may prove to have been one of the hitherto unsuspected sources of portions of the Sibylline Oracles. The task is not an easy one, for there is profound disparity between these two kinds of writings. The one is a simple legendary complement to the Bible, with no ulterior motive, whilst to the other the Bible is merely a source to be used with very great discretion. Only a few historical points are vaguely alluded to: the rest, however, must have been drawn also from similar legendary elaborations of the Bible, and from the eschatological literature, which had developed from the time of Daniel. It is in books of legends that we have to look for such information as we find in the Sibyl, and we must rest content if under the pagan guise, we shall be able to discover the Jewish original. If, then, we shall be able to establish some parallelism between the general outlines and episodes in the Sibyl, as well as in other Hellenistic writings and the narrative found in the Asatir, and if literal coincidences in expression and thought are adduced, then the question of, at any rate, one source may be considered as satisfactorily answered. Of course, such an investigation must be carried on step by step; small incidents are not to be neglected, and even hypothetical assumptions must be allowed in one case or another, until facts afterwards corroborate the accuracy of such hypotheses.

Among the prominent episodes in the Asatir are the history of the Flood (Ch. IV), the division of the earth by Noah among his three sons, the covenant of peace which he makes with them, the rebellion of Nimrod, who is represented as a giant, and who causes the tower of Babylon to be built (IV, 31, 32) which is afterwards destroyed by winds and storm, his oppression of the other nations, the wars which are initiated by him against seven nations, and their destruction, the rise of Egypt to be the first kingdom after their dispersion, immediately after which there is added a peculiar history of Nimrod (V, 11.12). He, all the time being the hero of this tale, is frightened by a sign which is explained by the soothsayers, that a child will be born to Arpachshad, son of Shem, who will destroy him and his kingdom. He thereupon separates the men from their wives, but his stratagem does not succeed, and Abraham is born, who later on defies his authority, and is therefore cast into the fire and saved by God. This abstract may suffice now for our immediate purpose. In the course of this investigation further variants and parallels from the Samaritan literature will be adduced which complete the tale, such as we find it in the text before us, which unfortunately seems to be corrupt and incomplete. But for all this tale, there are only very slender allusions in the Bible, which have afterwards been worked up until they have assumed this more elaborate form.

Two points may however be noted, for they may be helpful in elucidating the problems before us. Nimrod is practically made contemporary with Abraham, though in fact only three generations separate Nimrod from Noah. This is a serious anachronism, and yet no notice is taken of it. Further, the portion which Noah gives to Shem is in the land of Afrikia, i. e. Phrygia (Ch. IV. 30).

We turn now to the Sibylline Oracles.

Book III of the Sibylline Oracles is universally acknowledged as the oldest in the collection which has been preserved, and is of undoubted Jewish origin. Scholars have been able to establish the fact that the book is of a composite character, some parts being older and others probably of a much later date. But even the latest parts are not later than the middle of the second century B. C., the time of Ptolomaeus VII Physkon. In its present state, it is composed of many fragments which have been joined together, not always very happily, and the book has suffered many interpolations and changes. Moreover, it must be remembered that none of the MSS. of the Sibylline Oracles hitherto known is older than the thirteenth or fourteenth century: no wonder, therefore, at the incoherent character of some parts of its contents. But on one point all are agreed, that the book can be safely divided into three sections, of which the first from line 97 to line 170 or thereabouts, is unquestionably the oldest oracle.

The Fathers of the Church, especially Lactantius and Eusebius, the latter quoting Polyhistor, all show more or less complete knowledge of the first lines of this section. Of real importance for our present investigation is the first section from lines 97—121 and 154—170 (reserving a separate treatment later on for lines 122—153). The former deals with the building of the Tower, the fight of the Titans and the establishment of the first kingdoms, the destruction of the giants, the history of Egypt, the rise of several kingdoms, and an abrupt reference to Solomon. This is that special section which has been quoted variously in olden times as belonging to the Erythraean Sibyl, the Chaldaean or the Hebrew Sibyl. We are, therefore, justified in subjecting that section to a new examination, especially as its Jewish origin cannot be doubted, particularly since it seems also to have enjoyed a very wide reputation as such; for the story of the Tower of Babel and the subsequent fight is not only told by the Sibyl, but we find parallel legends in other writers not of Jewish origin. It is, therefore, obviously a legend which from the time of the Sibyl had become widely known and had been appropriated by writers in various countries, and modified in such manner as to suit local history. This is a process generally followed by all historians of olden times, and greatly favoured by the writers of the Hellenistic period.

It seems, however, that the scholars, while admitting interpolation and amplification in the rest of the book and in the other oracles, have not recognised that we have also here two distinct narratives which have been joined together in a somewhat synchretistic manner. It will therefore be best for the time being, to eliminate lines 122—153 and to join lines 121 to 154, and to treat this as an undivided whole. The flow of the narrative is not in the slightest way interrupted, and in fact, line 154 is a repetition of line 121.

Now, as far as this section is concerned, I am not aware that anyone has endeavoured to elucidate its source or to answer the question as to how on the one hand, it came about that the Sibyl should have woven into her poem the tale of the giants just in connection with the Tower of Babel, and on the other, why the Sibyl should have traced the War of Nations and the origin of the Egyptian Kingdom to the same period.*

The story of the Tower of Babel and its destruction by a wind sent by God or by the gods is mentioned with slight variations by Alexander Polyhistor, Josephus, Abydenos and the Armenian Chronicler Moses of Chorene. In the Hellenistic writings collected by Eusebius in his Praeparatio Evangelica, however, there are only very few

* The literature which has gathered round this portion is so vast that it must suffice to refer to the principal writers where the bibliographies complete one another. (Stählin-Schmidt, in Christs Geschichte der Griechischen Literatur, vol. I p. 609 ff. 612 ff., Munich 1920, Schürer, vol. III p. 571 ff., Gruppe, Griech. Myth., Vol. 2 p. 1483, Krauss in the Jew. Enc., s. v. "Sibyl," Hastings Encycl., s. v. Sibylline Oracles and above all now Rzach in Pauly-Kroll, Enc. Klass. Alt., s. v. Sibyll. Orakel.)

in which the story of the fight of the giants is given with as many details as in the Sibyl. The names of the gods against whom Titan fights are also changed from chronicler to chronicler. Neither do we find in all these any complete coincidence with the Sibyl nor any reference to the beginning of the kingdom of Egypt.

It would be easy to multiply the parallels to this story which, however, as cannot be denied, rests here ultimately on the Biblical narrative. Another version has been ascribed to Berosus, but probably without any reason. There is a confusion somewhere. It is not likely that Berosus, who wished to glorify Babylon and its past would insert into his narrative a tale so destructive and humiliating as that of the rebellious builders of the Tower which was destroyed by the wrath of God. As he is more or less contemporary with Euhemeros, and the latter quotes the Sibyl, the version ascribed to Berosus is probably also of a later date and wrongly ascribed to him. The Bible is the starting point, but we shall have to seek in writings which rest upon it for the primary source of this legend in the form in which it now, appears as well as for the reason why the giants' fight should be introduced here. A glance at the Asatir may now fully solve the problem. I point to the fact that, in its essence, we have to deal here with the Nimrod legend.

A certain Mar Apas Katina, reputed author of the Syriac Armenian Chronicle used by Moses of Chorene, has also a full reference to the building of the Tower by the giants and its destruction and subsequent confusion.* In this version the tale attributed to Berosus by Moses of Chorene has already assumed a totally different colouring. Very little if anything is left of the Greek legends, and although the story of the fight

* Langlois, Collections des Historiens de l'Arménie, Paris, 1867, Vol. I p. 15. Especially note I, where the whole literature is given. By the way, the name of Mar Apas Katina as an author does not occur in A. Baumstark, Geschichte d. Syr. Literatur, Bonn 1922.

between the brothers for the supremacy is retained, other names are substituted and finally the legend is connected with Bel. The Armenian writer whilst reproducing this passage, recognises already that this legend is practically an enlarged development of the story of Nimrod, and he says distinctly that Bel or Nisus, who takes his place later on is none other than Nimrod.* Here we have a writer who is able to disentangle the legends which had been gathered elsewhere and had been changed from writer to writer; for he quotes also Abydenos and others, and reduces the story, as far as his own purpose goes, to the primitive form of the Biblical record.

We have here the reflex of the legend as found in Christian literature, drawing its information not only from the pagan writers, but in all probability also from some of the ancient apocryphal writings, or some legendary history of the Bible; and thus we are brought face to face with the older literature as it has developed in the course of time.

Before proceeding further, it is necessary that the essential points of the legend as found in the Sibyl should be briefly summarized, stripped as much as possible of their mythological garb. The Tower of Babel is built by people who rebel against God and is cast down by the winds. Then, evidently, the surviving king has three children, and in the tenth generation from the deluge (anachronistically) the whole earth is divided into three portions among them upon oath of mutual peace. After the death of the father, Titan rises up and fights his eldest brother, and this is the beginning of war in the world; but peace is established on the condition that all the male children of Chronos are destroyed and they are accordingly torn by the giants. But one male child escapes and is hidden, and afterwards overthrows Titan.

* "Mais je dis que celui qu'on appelle Chronos et Bel est bien Nemrod." (Langlois II, 61).

Then arises the kingdom of Egypt and seven kingdoms are mentioned.

We have now only to introduce the equation Titan = Nimrod, to assist us in solving the problem as to whence the Sibyl has drawn her information as well as the seqeunce of events, for if we follow also the identification of older writers, we see in this the development of a legend whose central figure is Nimrod, for, as indicated above we have here unquestionably the story of Nimrod, which has been greatly developed and to which many incidents have been added not found directly in the Bible, but probably deduced from it by that specific Midrashic exegesis which interprets names and words in a manner of its own. It is well known that one single word of the Bible is often sufficient to become the starting-point for a whole series of legends. This Midrashic exegesis connects the name of Nimrod with the word *'marad'* 'to rebel;' and this was sufficient to spin it out into a long story of Nimrod who is *rebellious* against God. The fact that he is mentioned as King of Babylon is, for the author of the legend, sufficient proof that he must have usurped his power, especially when taken in connection with the history of Noah and his three sons. Of these, Shem is the one appointed king by Noah, and yet we find Nimrod as the first king. Here is again sufficient reason for legendary activity to develop Nimrod's kingship into usurpation or fight. Moses of Chorene does not fail to recognise that the three sons between whom the power is divided, i. e. Zerouan, Titan and Japhetos, are none other than Shem, Ham and Japhet (Langlois II, 59). The fact that Nimrod is mentioned as *'Gibor'* gives him pre-eminence in the eyes of the maker of legends. Why should he be called *'Gibor'* and what is the real meaning of that word? In the LXX to Genesis XVII, 4; X, 8. 9; we already find the Midrashic interpretation. The word is there translated as 'giant.' According to Samaritan tradition 'Gibor' is also the word used regularly for 'giant.' This word is at once connected with the *'Giborim'* in Genesis VI, 4, a further corroboration for that interpretation of the word *'Gibor'* as meaning 'giant,' inasmuch as the *'Giborim'* here mentioned are also translated 'giants' as well as is the word *'Nephilim'* in the same verse.

So deeply rooted had become the conviction that the builders of the Tower were giants, that not only was the translation of the word 'Gibor' as 'Giant' found in the LXX as well as being taken over by the Peshitto and even the Arabic translation, but Philo also accepted it without hesitation and based upon it his own philosophic explanations and discourses in his "Questions" II, 82 to Gen. X, 8. There he not only takes it for granted that Nimrod was a giant, but practically identifies him with Titan, and refers to the war of the Titans with the gods, a parallel evidently to the rebellious action of Nimrod against God, and echoed by the Sibyl. This he further develops in the special treatise upon the giants (§ 14). Here in his reference to Nimrod he says, "This man was a giant upon the earth, the name 'Nimrod' being interpreted 'desertion' (rebellious)." This tradition has been handed down to the writers of the Middle Ages where Nimrod is always described as a giant. It must be mentioned that the Samaritan tradition knows nothing of the fall of angels, nor of their marrying the daughters of men. The "Bene Elohim" are to them the sons of the mighty and their children the all-powerful giants.

Among the Hellenistic writers from whom the Sibyl may have drawn some information, there is a certain Pseudo-Eupolemos, a writer whom Freudenthal (Hell. Stud. p. 82 ff.) has rightly separated from the other fragments ascribed to the genuine Eupolemos, both quoted under one name by Alexander Polyhistor, and hence by Eusebius in his Praeparatio Evangelica. Freudenthal has proved beyond doubt that the author of these fragments must have been a Samaritan and he assigned to him the date ca. 200 B. C. It will be seen later on that Freudenthal's conjecture is fully corroborated by our investigation. Small though those fragments are, they offer important parallels to the Asatir and to some extent also to the Sibylline Oracle. The first fragment runs as follows:

"And Eupolemos in his history of the Jews in Assyria says that the city of Babylon was first built by those that escaped from the deluge; and that these were giants, and dwelt in the tower about which we have spoken. But this having fallen by the act of God, the giants were dispersed over the whole earth. And he says that in the tenth generation in a city of Babylon, Kamarina, * which some call the city of Ourie (which interpreted means 'City of the Chaldaeans'): in the tenth generation, then, there was born Abraham, a man excelling all in goodness and wisdom and who discovered the Chaldaic astrology: and being intent upon piety he found favour with his God. And he having gone to Phoenice at the command of the God he dwelt there, and teaching the Phoenicians the turnings of the sun and moon and many other things he found favour with their king. And later on the Armenians marched against the Phoenicians. And they proving victorious and taking captive his younger brother Abraham together with his household went to the rescue and conquered the captors and took captive the women and children of the enemy. And ambassadors coming to him ordered that he might accept a ransom and release them, he did not choose to trample on the unfortunate, but taking for the feeding of the young men he released the prisoners. And he was entertained with sacred honours by the city of Argarizin (which

* Kamarina i. e. Furnace. Pseudo Eupolemos knows therefore the interpretation of the Hebrew word "Ur" as "furnace" thus being the starting-point of the legend of Abraham and the furnace. At the same time he goes on to say that Ur is the name of the town: true syncretism.

interpreted means "Mount of the Most High" * and he received gifts at the hands of Melchisedek who was a priest of the God and also king."

We have now all the elements required for the reconstruction of the legend as it appears in the Asatir and in the Sibyl. We have then only to identify Saturnus with Noah and Chronos with Shem to see exactly how the story resting upon the Biblical record could assume a Greek form without altering in substance.

Josephus, whose close relation to the Asatir will be discussed later on, has also worked up the subject more completely. According to him, Nimrod is not only the rebellious king, but he and his associates are the builders of the Tower, for he induces and forces the people to build the Tower and thus to defy God (I, 4, 2, 113).

Then follows immediately in the Asatir as well as in the Sibylline Oracles the War of the Nations. Here again we must be guided by the Midrashic exegesis to find in the words of the Bible a basis for this development. We find in Gen. X, 11 "he went forth," which has been taken to mean he went forth to battle against the other nations. Again in the Biblical history (Gen. X, 6), we find that directly after Kush the father of Nimrod, Egypt is mentioned. The fact that Egypt should have been mentioned before any other country, is sufficient for the Midrash to proclaim Egypt as the first kingdom. Thus from a few stray threads drawn from separate words and then woven together, we get a complete history of events for which there is otherwise no warrant in Holy Writ. These legends were evolved to satisfy the curiosity of the listener and no doubt were the origin of many of the legends circulated in Syria, Palestine, and Egypt. In the same chapter in Genesis, seven nations are mentioned, of which no trace could be found and which even the most ingenious

* By calling Argarizin the "Mount of the Most High" Pseudo Eupolemos gives decisive proof for his Samaritan origin.

geographer of the time of the Sibyl could neither identify nor localise. Throughout that period, every translator of the genealogical tables endeavoured to substitute more modern and better known names for those found in the Hebrew text. But no identification had been attempted for the nations mentioned in Genesis ch. X, 13, the Lehabim, etc. They must, therefore, have perished in very olden times, and are described in the Asatir (V, 9) to have been the victims of the war waged by Nimrod.

Josephus, curiously enough, mentions in connection with Nimrod, the disappearance of these very nations, but evidently misled by the word Kush, which stands for Nimrod, he transfers the time of the destruction of those nations to a later period: he connects it with the legend of Moses as told by Artapanos, but in reality the man who is the cause of the destruction is none other than Nimrod. He must have found it so in his original source, as otherwise there is no reason why he should have mentioned their disappearance in the chapter where he deals with the history of Nimrod. (Antiq. I, 6. 2.)

In the light of the Asatir, all that which has been advanced hitherto is now fully corroborated. Chs. IV, 31, to V, 28 gives up a complete parallel in its primitive form, not yet affected by Hellenistic tendencies. No one could otherwise under stand how the Sibyl came to utter prophecies of destruction against seven nations, in this connection. They are the seven nations mentioned in the Asatir, but with the difference that new names had been substituted, in the Sibyl, for the old ones that had entirely disappeared. Otherwise, it would be impossible to explain why these nations should anachronistically be mentioned before Solomon, line 167. It is only in the light of the above parallelism that the disappearance of these nations can be explained.

Even the manner of the Destruction of the Tower, a detail not mentioned in the Bible, which is described in the Asatir as having been shattered, is found in the Sibyl as having been destroyed through the action of winds and storm. It is found in a Samaritan commentary to Genesis by Meshalma, and in the Malif of an unknown author of uncertain date, but perhaps anterior to Meshalma. Although these books are of a more recent origin, they have retained very old Samaritan traditions, and also occasionally, readings of a slightly different recension of the Asatir. In them we are told that God sent violent storms and rains which broke down and destroyed the Tower built by Nimrod and his associates.

That the legend rests upon a Biblical Midrash can also be proved by stray references in various ancient Jewish writings, but it appears almost in its entirety in another book of pseudepigraphic origin, which stands in a peculiarly intimate relation with the Sibylline literature. I refer to the Revelations ascribed to Methodius of Patara, or Patmos (see Sackur, Sibyll. Texte pp. 60—96).

The original source from which Methodius drew the first part of his chronicle of the world—for it purports to be the description of the world from the Creation to the End of Days and Final Judgment—has hitherto not yet been discovered, but the investigations of Sackur have shown that, to a large extent, this compilation (of the fourth or fifth century) agrees with the Syriac "Cave of Treasures," and that it must have been composed somewhere in Syria or Palestine. But it is now evident that the ancient source approximates more closely to the Asatir than to the Syriac text, with which it has only a few traits in common. The history of Nimrod, the building of the Tower, the rise of Egypt, the fight of the Nations, and all the other incidents, so characteristic of the Asatir and of the Sibyl are found in this compilation of Methodius. In the "Cave of Treasures" many of the older details have entirely disappeared. They all have undergone a thorough revision from a Christian point of view.

We have still to deal with that section of the Sibyl, which, for the time being, was eliminated from the present investigation: I refer to the lines 122—153, containing the history of the agreement between Titan and Chronos, the fear of the former that the succession may not come to him, that the descendants of Chronos might prevent him from becoming the ruler of the world, the destruction of the male children, the clandestine birth of the male child, the surreptitious removal of that child, the imprisonment of Chronos and his wife, and later on how the child is destined to destroy the power of Titan. Whence has the Sibyl taken this story and why has she inserted it here into her oracle, where we find it now in close connection with the Tower of Babel?

In the mind of the Sybil there must have been some connection between the Biblical personages and this continuation of the story of the Tower and the fight between the three sons of Noah, in which Kush or Nimrod is represented by Titan. There must have been a legend referring to Shem, or as we are dealing here with two or three generations later, with Arpachshad or Ashur. Pseudo-Eupolemos will now help us to find a guide by which to trace back this story to some old legend connected with Nimrod; for we must not lose sight of Nimrod, who is the central figure of this whole passage. It is noteworthy that the story of the Tower of Babel and the dispersion of the giants precedes immediately without any break the story of the birth of Abraham in Pseudo-Eupolemos, unless we assume, for which there is no apparent reason, that Alexander Polyhistor, who has preserved the words of this writer, has omitted something in between; but in that case, the first section referring to the building of the Tower would also have been omitted. The retention of this otherwise irrelevant first section is clear proof that the combination already obtained in Pseudo-Eupolemos' narrative. We have in this portion of the Sibyl therefore to seek for a parallel to the Abraham and Nimrod legend. After the knowledge of the birth of the male child has come to Titan, he imprisons Chronos and his wife, and then the fight takes place between the members of the family of Chronos and the Titans. This story of the fight and the imprisonment seems to be out of place. Originally, Titan must have imprisoned Chronos and his wife *before* the birth of the child, for safety's sake, and the fight must have been waged quite independently of that imprisonment, and only in order to vindicate their rights and to punish Titan for his violence and cruelty.

Apart from the Sibyl, we have two parallels, one anterior and one long after, the first being ascribed to Euhemeros. His version of the ancient myths of the Titans, borrowed to a large extent from detached fragments from Hesiod has been incorporated by Ennius into his Latin translation and reproduced by Lactantius in his Divine Institutes. (Book I. Ch. XIV.) He does not agree entirely with the Sibyl; the names of the goddesses and the hiding place of the child is different, but he also mentions that Titan encircles Saturn and Ops with walls, and he adds, "the truth of this history is told by the Erythraean Sibyl." This, as mentioned before, was the very name by which our Sibyl was known and obtained currency. In Bk. III, 813 the Sibyl protests against this identification. As Euhemeros distinctly states that he depends on the Sibyl he could not have been the source for the Sibyl and the Jewish character and origin of this story therefore cannot be called into question But, of course, if she were to have any effect at all, the Sibyl could not but assume heathen forms, and was therefore popularly identified with the Erythraean Sibyl, who stood in very high veneration among the various nations. But this does not in the slightest degree affect the *true* origin of this Sibyl, nor would it prevent her from taking some material from the Greek myths in a rationalised form to further her own ends, so long as there was a substratum of Jewish legend to warrant her taking over such material.

In the second account which is a variant ascribed to the Berosian Sibyl by Moses of Chorene, the encircling walls and the imprisonment have already disappeared. It was felt to be incongruous in the place in which it stood, and practically the whole of the remainder of that Oracle, (ll. 150—152), has entirely disappeared. It has already been shown above that no higher antiquity than this Sibyl can be claimed for the Chronicle of Moses of Chorene.

Now in the Asatir, there is what appears to be a complete solution of the whole problem. Let us turn again to Ch. V. 16—29. Here Nimrod, after having captured Egypt, reigns in Babylon. There he is warned by the Book of Signs that out of the seed of Arpachshad, i.e. Shem, a child will be born who will destroy him. He takes the advice of the astrologers and orders that all the male children of Arpachshad should be imprisoned in one place whilst the women should be imprisoned in another, in order to prevent the conception of the child, which, as he is told, will take place within thirty days. His plan is defeated and a child is born. This is Abraham, who is thrown into the fire but who escapes. The story as told in the Asatir, however, is incomplete. The book has evidently been preserved in a more or less fragmentary condition and the rest of the story follows in the main the narrative as given in Holy Writ. Some details found in other variants, may therefore supplement this story, which, as the author himself indicates, runs parallel to that told of Moses. There, the children are killed: Moses is born secretly and miraculously saved from the wrath of Pharaoh. His father Amram is a man of high rank, and afterwards Moses fulfils the prophecy of the soothsayer and not only destroys the idols, but is also able to bring about the destruction of Pharaoh and the Egyptians.

All this has dropped out from the Abraham-tale in the Asatir, but that it must have formed an essential feature cannot be doubted in view of the fact that we find this story with all the details in some Jewish versions. There is first the Jewish-Arabic legend of Abraham among the fragments of the Genizah once in my possession, now transferred to the British Museum. There the story is put into the mouth of Kabelhaber, the well-known companion of Mohammed. He was of Jewish origin and is believed to be the author of many of the Biblical legends alluded to in the Koran and found afterwards in various Mohammedan commentaries. Unfortunately, the beginning is missing in the MS., but what is left is quite sufficient to prove the antiquity of this story. It begins with the wizards and soothsayers warning Nimrod against the descendants of Arpachshad. On their advice, he builds an immense prison where he keeps all the women of Arpachshad's family. Thus far, it is in agreement with the Asatir, but unlike it, they are not imprisoned in order to prevent pregnancy, but to await the time of their child's birth. Every male child is then torn to pieces. The mother of Abraham is able to conceal her situation and when the time of the birth of the child approaches, she quietly leaves the town, hides herself in a cave and gives birth to Abraham. He is miraculously fed by angels. He first goes to the house of his father, Teraḥ, who is an idolater, breaks the idols and also induces others to do likewise, he is then brought up before Nimrod where he defies the latter's claim to be worshipped as a god, is cast into the fire and saved by God.

So far, we have complete identity: the fear of Nimrod (Titan) lest a son be born to Arpachshad (Saturn) who will dispute his usurpation, since Arpachshad, according to the decision of Noah, is to be ruler: the wise men of Japhet advising him to build a prison or erect a wall around the pregnant women of the house of Arpachshad and to kill all the male children born; Abraham (Zeus) is born secretely in a cave, fights Titan and destroys him. The same story occurs in Yakubi's* commentary to the Koran, but it is not of Arabic origin, as is evidenced by the fact adduced here. No allusion is made to it in the Koran, where Abraham is merely described as a friend of God and the only reference made is to the burning of Teraḥ's idols.** But there is a Hebrew recension which agrees in almost every detail with the Jewish Arabic, differing only in those details where that version has assumed a more Arabic character. It is found in Elijah de Vidas, Shebet Musar, *** where the story has been fully expanded with the exuberance of Oriental fantasy, but all the important incidents have been faithfully retained. They are as follows: Nimrod declares himself a god, and demands to be worshipped as such on pain of death. Through his knowledge of astrology he knows that a child will be born who will destroy him. Upon the advice of his nobles, he builds an immense place and orders all the pregnant women to be gathered there. He instructs the midwives to slaughter every male child immediately after its birth, and thus no less than 70,000 male children perish. By a stratagem Abraham's mother is able to allay the suspicions of her husband Teraḥ, and going out into the wilderness, she gives birth to the child in a cave, which at once becomes filled with light. There she leaves it. It is fed by the milk which it sucks from the finger of the angel Gabriel. When the child is twenty days old it is already grown up, then various incidents happen when Nimrod discovers the birth of the child, such as the destruction of the idols of his father Teraḥ, the conversion of the multitude to the belief in God,

* v. Grünbaum, Neue Beitr. p. 94, and also Weil: Biblische Legenden der Muselmännner, Frankfurt a/M. 1845, p. 69.
** See Geiger, Mohammed, p. 22.
*** Reprinted by Jellinek Vol. I p. 25—34, and by Eisenstein, Ozar p. 2 ff. For numerous variants of this legends see Gaster Exempla no. 2 and p. 185 where the literature is given.

the fall of the idols in the palace of Nimrod when Abraham goes to see him, and his miraculous escape from the burning furnace, which is transformed into a beautiful garden. Thus the story stripped of all the other elements. There cannot be any doubt as to the Jewish origin of the story. Not only do we find no trace of Mohammedan legends, or any of the forms which the legend has assumed in the literature of Islam, but almost every one of the essential details is found already in the ancient Pirke de Rabbi Eliezer (Ch. 25), notably the very important fact that the child is hidden in a cave for thirteen years;* the only incidents here missing are the separation of the men from the women and the killing of the male children. Elijah de Vidas had access to a large number of ancient texts,** which he reproduced in this and in his other works, and thus fully corroborates the Jewish origin of the Arabic Hebrew version found in my Genizah fragments. We have here, moreover, a much more complete parallel to the story of the slaughter of the male children in Egypt, with which the author of the Asatir compares it, though in one or two of the details the version of de Vidas differs somewhat from the Samaritan, for in de Vidas the pregnant women are imprisoned, and the children are slaughtered immediately after birth. In the Asatir Nimrod imprisons the women in order to prevent them from bearing children. In both, however, he through his astrological knowledge forsees the birth of such a child. In the main, this version thus agrees with the Samaritan. Moreover, the same story is told in practically the same words as in the Asatir in the Samaritan commentary to the Pentateuch by Meshalma (see notes ad loc). In both Samaritan texts there is a curious anachronism to be noted, inasmuch as the Nimrod of the Tower here mentioned

* For many variants of this tradition vide Lurya ad loc.
** See Steinschneider, Catalogue of Bodleian 932 and Jellinek, Vol. V, Introd. p. XIX.

is believed to be contemporary with Nahor and of course, with Teraḥ. The importance of this is more clearly seen when we compare this story with that told by Pseudo-Eupolemos as quoted above p. 18. Here, as pointed out before, Pseudo-Eupolemos passes immediately from the story of the building of the Tower and the dispersion of the giants, to the history of the birth of Abraham and his further exploits. He thus brings Abraham into direct connection with the giants. Although he mentions 10 (13) generations in between, still, from the narrative, it is clear that the history of Abraham seems to be contemporary with that of the giants, for after mentioning the birth of a righteous man in a town called Kamarine, he then passes on to Abraham's arrival in Canaan the land of the Phoenicians, whom he (Abraham) instructs in the "revolutions of the sun and moon." Then the Armenians wage war against the Phoenicians and capture Abraham's nephew; Abraham goes to the rescue, defeats the Armenians and then the story continues as previously told. Pseudo-Eupolemos, who was not writing a commentary to the Bible but a romantic history of the beginnings of the people of Israel, has substituted the war of Amraphel, king of Shinear, and his confederates, against the Nations of the Plain, for the war of Nimrod against the nations of Palestine and Egypt mentioned in the older legends. He could do it the more easily as none of his readers was interested in the fate of nations the names of which had perished long ago, whilst he had the story of the Bible upon which to rely. He thus could bring in Abraham as the hero of the occasion, and curiously enough hereby entirely agreeing with the Asatir, he places the story of this war and the part which Abraham played before the story of his going down to Egypt and what befel him there contrary to the record of the Bible.

True, there are some points in the Bible which, by a Midrashic exegesis, help in transferring the battle of the Giants to Palestine and making Nimrod contemporary with Abraham. These points facilitate, in a way, the new presentation of it by Eupolemos and by the Asatir, as well as by the Sibyl. In Ch. XIV of Genesis, Amraphel and his associates first wage war against the Rephaim and Zuzim in the northern part of Palestine; and these appear in the LXX and in the Peshitto as well as in other translations depending upon them, no less than in the Palestinian Targum, as "giants and mighty men." If we add that in the Palestinian Targum and also in the later Rabbinic tradition * Amraphel is identified with Nimrod, then we have the same anachronism. The reason for identifying Amraphel with Nimrod may be found in a Midrashic etymology of the name, which is not rare in the Targum. In the last syllable one can easily recognise Bel, and if Nimrod is Bel and Amraphel also Bel, that would explain the appearance of two kings of the name Bel in the Asatir and in Pseudo-Eupolemos. How widespread such a kind of legend was can be seen from Moses of Chorene's Chronicle, quoting Mar Apas Katina, where these legends appear in a new transformation (see above p. 14). Here we have, Haig* rising up against Bel the giant, who has usurped the power after committing acts of violence, and then leaving the country. This is nothing else than another development of the story of Abraham leaving the kingdom of Nimrod and settling elsewhere. Bel afterwards attacks the country where he is living: a messenger comes to warn Haig, who gathers together his small force, attacks Bel near a mountain in a plain and kills him. This is practically the same story as that told by Eupolemos and agrees also in part with the Bible. One only has to substitute Nimrod for Bel and Amraphel, as has been done by the Palestinian Targum, to have the story complete down to the names.

* Talmud, Sefer Hayashar; for references see Seder Hadoroth p. 31.
** Langlois I p. 16 ff.

One might be inclined to see in the story of Aram (Ch. XIII) in the Armenian version a duplication of the same story, inasmuch as Aram fights with giants in the west country, probably Palestine, which country is mentioned afterwards as Little Armenia. Here we have the Armenia of Pseudo-Eupolemos. There is a faint reminiscence of a similar story in the Samaritan literature, which has also some other features in common with the Abraham legend. I refer to the war between Joshua and Shobakh, the giant of the Armenians, as found in the Samaritan Book of Joshua. Joshua and his army are also encircled through magic powers by seven walls, from which they are saved through the advice of Kenas. However, it would lead too far were I here to follow up the question whether there is any closer connection between these various legends.

If we now examine carefully the Sibyl we shall find a remarkable parallelism which shows that the Sibyl must have been well acquainted with Eupolemos' writings. For when the Sibyl refers to the birth of Abraham, the name of the town is identical with that given in Pseudo-Eupolemos, namely, Kamarine (III, 218).

It should be stated, however, that this verse is believed to be peculiarly corrupt. The copyists have evidently not realised that Kamarine is the Midrashic interpretation of the word 'Ur' as meaning 'furnace;' therefore they either substituted another word for it or left it out entirely. So almost every MS. has a different reading or a lacuna. Alexander and others after him, like Opsopeus (Koch) before him, completed this lacuna correctly by inserting the word found in some other MSS. "Kamarine." Geffcken* leaves the lacuna, but on the other hand** he says that the subsequent lines were written to contradict the

* Die Oracula Sibyllina Leipzig 1902 ad loc.
** Komposition und Entstehungszeit der Oracula Sibyllina Leipzig 1902 p. 6 ff.

statement of Pseudo-Eupolemos (Geffcken thus agrees that the Sibyl knew Pseudo-Eupolemos) that Abraham knew the revolutions of the sun and moon.* Geffcken has entirely misunderstod the passage in Eupolemos. The Sibyl vehemently protests only against astrology and all kinds of idolatrous abominations, not a word of which is to be found in Eupolemos. Furthermore we have precisely the same anachronism noticed in the Sibyl as in all the records before and if we carefully examine the texts we shall find the Sibyl like Eupolemos, mentioning 10 generations that have passed between the deluge and the story of the Titans, thus making the Titan (i. e. Nimrod), contemporary with Abraham, whose story is told under the form of a Greek myth.

Gathering up all the threads of the various parallels and comparisons, two points stand out clearly. In the first place there is the closest possible similarity between the essential details in the story of the Sibyl of Titan, Saturn, and Japhetos, of the slaughter of the male children, the imprisonment of the parents, the secret birth and removal of the male child, which is to grow up, avenge the wrong and finally destroy Titan, with the drapings having been taken from Greek mythology as told by Euhemeros, and the story of Nimrod and Abraham as told by the Asatir and the Samaritan commentary on the one hand, and by the Hebrew-Arabic and Jewish-Hebrew legends on the other. Again

* The real character of the statement that Abraham knew the revolutions of the sun and moon, as mentioned by Eupolemos, can be understood only if viewed in the light of Samaritan tradition. Abraham is not credited with any knowledge of astrology, but with a knowledge of the Calendar, which according to the Samaritans, is based on the direct teaching of God, who had communicated it to Adam, and which then had been handed on from generation to generation down to Abraham. The fixing of the New Moon and of the year with them rested upon astronomical calculations, and it is this knowledge which is the basis of the Calendar, and which Abraham possessed and communicated to the Phoenicians and others. (On this point see also further on.)

some of the details, e. g. the place of birth etc., show a thorough acquaintance by the Sibyl with the writings of Pseudo-Eupolemos.

With this, the parallelism is, however, by no means yet exhausted, for besides that in the general outline of the stories there are also some verbal affinities to which attention must now be drawn. (Later on, I will return again to the examinations of the other Sibylline Oracles in their relations to the Asatir.) We find thus e. g. 114 ff.: The earth divided into three portions by Chronos and the father laying an oath of peace on his three sons. So Asatir IV, 14. 36. 140. Phrygia where the child is hidden: Asatir IV, 30. The portion which Noah gives to Shem, which is to be the birthplace of Abraham is Afrikia i. e. Phrygia 155. This was the beginnings of the war: Asatir V, 9. These are more than mere coincidences.

Returning now to Pseudo-Eupolemos, the parallelism between the latter and the Asatir is still more marked than that with the Sibyl. So we find that after having told the story of the fight of Abraham against the Armenians, Pseudo-Eupolemos goes on to tell the story of what happened to Abraham in Egypt. Leaving out the first portion in which he tells of the giants and of the war of Abraham (given before,) he continues as follows: —

"... But when the famine set in Abraham repaired to Egypt, and there settled down with his whole family; and the king of the Egyptians married his (Abraham's) wife, because he alleged that she was his sister: in further detail he records how he found no pleasure in his union with her, and how his people and his household were destroyed; and how summoning his seers, they told him the fact that the woman was not unmarried at all. How also the king of the Egyptians thus found out that she was Abraham's wife and how he returned her to her husband. How also he dwelt among the Egyptian priests in Heliopolis, i. e. The Sun City, and taught them many things and introduced amongst them astrology and other things. He (Eupolemos) says that the discovery of it belongs to Enoch and that he was the originator of astrology, not the Egyptians. For the Babylonians say that Bêlos was the first man (the same is Kronos) and from him sprang a second Bêlos who was Ham and he begat Cham who begat Chanaan who was the father of the Phoenicians and he also begat Chus, who is called by the Greeks Asbolos, the progenitor of the Ethiopians, and a brother of Mestraim who was progenitor of the Egyptians. The Greeks say that Atlas originated astrology, but Atlas is the same as Enoch. The son of Enoch was Methusala who learned everything through the agency of the angels of God and we acknowledge this fact."

Now this story of Abraham's descent into Egypt with all the details contained in Pseudo-Eupolemos is not found in the Bible, neither has Freudenthal nor Beer, who has written a book on all the legends referring to Abraham, been able to find a close parallel in any Jewish Midrash. The nearest approach to this story is the reference to it in Josephus, but Josephus, in his usual way, has enlarged upon the simple story and has omitted one or two of the essential details, such as the peculiar illness of Pharaoh and his household. The closest parallel is now found in the Asatir Ch. VI, 10ff. Not only, as remarked before, do Pseudo-Eupolemos and the Asatir go together in putting the journey to Egypt after the war with the giants contrary to the Bible, but also most of the other essential details given by Pseudo-Eupolemos are set out fully and in a much more coherent manner by the author of the Asatir. The illness of Pharaoh, the calling in of the soothsayers, the pointing out that the woman whom he has taken into his house is the only cause of the plague, then Abraham disputing or discussing with the wise men and proclaiming the faith, are all found there. It may be objected that Pseudo-Eupolemos may have confused the story of Abraham's sojourn in Egypt with the parallel story of his sojourn among the Philistines. In the latter story some of the points to which attention has been drawn, such as Pharaoh's illness, consultation of soothsayers etc., are indeed to be found. How great Pseudo-Eupolemos' knowledge of the Bible may have been would be difficult to say, but this very confusion proves absolutely the close relation, nay, the very dependence of Pseudo-Eupolemos on the Asatir. For if it be a confusion it is already in the Asatir which also contains no mention of Abimelech, and tells the tale as happening to Pharaoh only. The author has gone very far in his Midrashic licence, and here as in other passages, he does not hesitate to deviate from the record of the Bible His was a book of legends, and has to be judged as such and as such it served also as a source to Pseudo-Eupolemos and other Hellenistic writers who did not hesitate to make use of it as far as it suited their purposes, for the book must have been invested with some authority.

There is one notable feature in the Asatir version, and that is that mention is specifically made of a magician (VI, 18ff.), who has studied in the Book of Signs, i. e. the heavenly signs, and who is the man who tells Pharaoh of the importance of Abraham. He explains furthermore the reason for the falling down of the idols at the moment when Abraham enters Egypt: both these incidents are omitted by Pseudo-Eupolemos. What he says about Abraham's teaching the priests of Egypt astrology, must be understood in the same manner as the teaching which he gives to the Phoenicians, where Eupolemos also uses the word 'astrology,' but explains it immediately after by his saying "the science of the revolutions of the sun and moon." In Josephus, Ant. I, 8, we find the same elements, and although they are worked up and amplified to a great extent, one can easily recognise that he must have drawn his information from the same source as Pseudo-Eupolemos and the Asatir. He also makes it perfectly clear that Abraham did not teach *astrology* in the later sense of the word, but he says deliberately that Abraham taught them arithmetic and astronomy and adds that the latter was of Chaldaean origin and that Abraham brought it to Egypt. A characteristic of Josephus and a proof of his later date is that he regularly omits definite details, such as the reference to the magician, to his name, and other similar details. Josephus prefers as a rule a general statement in the rhetorical style of the time.

The stress which is laid in Pseudo-Eupolemos on Abraham as the man who teaches the revolutions of sun, moon, and stars, can only be best understood in the light of Samaritan tradition and by the importance which the Samaritans attach to the determination of the Calendar. Towards the end of that fragment of Pseudo-Eupolemos Enoch is mentioned as the one who had been the first to discover the science of astrology, which is entirely in keeping with Samaritan tradition. According to the Asatir Adam possesses even a higher knowledge, for by certain signs in Heaven he learns the death of Hebel (I, 22, 23) and he also foretells the Flood. Artapanos also in the fragment preserved, states definitely that Abraham was the first to practise and teach the sciences of astronomy or astrology and this statement has afterwards been taken up by many subsequent writers (cf. Fabricius, p. 350 ff.). No trace, however, which could justify such a claim seems to be found either in the Bible or in the Rabbinic literature. The reference in Gen. VX, 5, where God asks Abraham whether he could count the stars, only shows that Abraham is not able to number the stars.

This question, however, assumes greater importance if seen from the point of view of religious practice. To the fixing of the Calendar, the determination of the New Moons, and in consequence of the fasts and feasts, great prominence has been given in the religious life of the Jews, so intimately bound up with the days and months.

This point is one of the principal sources of controversy and strife between Jews and Samaritans. The proclamation of the New Moon was considered by the Jews as a special privilege of the Sanhedrin in Jerusalem, and the method of intercalation was claimed as a great secret.* The Samaritans, in contradistinction to the Jews, did not base the proclamation of the New Moon only on the sight of the reappearence of the sickle of the New Moon, but they declared the calculation of the Calendar to be a divine revelation made to Adam. Gen. I, 14, where the luminaries are set in the heavens to be "for signs, and for seasons, and for days and years," has been taken by the Samaritans to prove that from the very beginning the sun and moon had been appointed as means by which to calculate the Signs of heaven and the seasons of the festivals (the Hebrew word is "*Moadim*," which means "Festivals") and that this knowledge had been imparted to Adam. He was king, and high priest, and with him the science of astronomy or astrology, which were both identical in olden times, really began. He alone possessed the knowledge of that mystery. We find thus in the Asatir, that Adam is the possessor of the Book of Signs. Enoch learns from the Book of Signs given to Adam (II, 7), Adam reads it to his children (II, 12), Aḥidan learns from the Book of Signs of Adam (II, 36), Noah learns the Book of Signs, obtains possession of the Book of Signs (III, 9) and gives it to Arpachshad (IV, 15). All these get the knowledge of the revolutions of sun and moon, i. e., the true astronomy applied in the first place to the regulation of the Calendar. From Arpachshad that knowledge is handed down to Abraham, as the safe keeper of that mystery, to Joseph and to Moses.

Thus we have here the real source of the legend that

* The first act of Jeroboam, when separating the North from the South, was to introduce a new calculation of the Calendar (I Kings XII, 33).

Abraham teaches astronomy to the Phoenicians and to the Egyptians. In the Book of Jubilees it is Noah to whom the secret of the Calendar is revealed (ibid. IV, 17), for with him the new order of the world begins, and Enoch is also mixed up later on with the knowledge of astronomy and astrology, the legend of his translation to Heaven being more fully developed.

It is significant that in the Asatir not a word is found of the late astronomical system of the Samaritans, which rests on the assumed calculation made by Pineḥas, son of Eliezer the high priest, which he made soon after the conquest of Palestine, taking as the basis the meridian of Mount Garizim. So it is already found in the Samaritan Book of Joshua, further in the Tolida of the eleventh century (if not earlier), and it is repeated in every subsequent work of the Samaritans, where they engage in polemics with the Jews on this question of the origin of the Calendar and the method of its calculation and regulation.

Returning now to the story of Abraham in Egypt, we find in the Samaritan commentary by Meshalma not only the same story of Abraham journeying to Egypt, as told in the Asatir, but also the name of the magician and one important detail which approximates his version to that of Pseudo-Eupolemos. He states that the magician had learned from the Book of Signs, which was the work of Enoch. Meshalma must thus have had access to other material, which he used extensively in his Commentary. According to the Asatir, Nimrod also knew of the Book of Signs, and thus far the Asatir indicates that the Book of Signs was in the possession of the Chaldaeans or Babylonians no less than in that of Abraham. This is also stated explicitly in the Malif. This again tallies absolutely with the final portion of the abstract of Pseudo-Eupolemos, where he says that both Abraham and the Chaldaeans trace the knowledge of astronomy back to Enoch.

But there is still one more point in this last portion to which attention has already been drawn before which deserves special consideration. Two men of the name of Belus are mentioned, a first and a second Belus. Some confusion has arisen in the genealogy of these Belus and their descendants, which Freudenthal* attempted to clear up, but not successfully. This confusion is due to the similarity of the writing of the names Ḥam, Ḥun and Ḥush. I have substituted Ḥus for the corrupted Ḥun and then no difficulty remains: this genealogy is then identical with that given in Genesis X, 6. Chronos, of course, stands for Noah, the first Belus is identical with Ḥam and then follows Kush, the father of Nimrod, with whom the second Belus is no doubt thought to be identical. But this mention of two Belus has a reason of its own. There is a chronological discrepancy of hundreds of years, or close upon a thousand years, between that Nimrod who is the son of Kush and the other Nimrod with whom Abraham is described as a contemporary. This anachronism is partly obviated by the Samaritans, who mention a second Nimrod as contemporary with Nahor the father of Teraḥ, just as the first Nimrod is contemporary with the third generation from Shem: Shem, Arpachshad, Ashur. This number "three" is probably the reason why in Pseudo-Eupolemos two readings are found, where Abraham is first described as being of the tenth generation from the Flood and then of the thirteenth. Here the thirteenth (13) is a corruption from the third (3), but the Samaritans felt the discrepancy and thus there appear in the Asatir two Nimrods. The Samaritans endeavoured to explain the number of years which had elapsed between the one and the other by inventing a second Nimrod. Hence the two Belus in Pseudo-Eupolemos. That Belus was meant for Nimrod has already been shown

* Hellenist. Stud. p. 93 ff. p. 95 ff.

above. In another fragment given by Eusebius (fol. 457) we find Abraham also brought somehow into connection with Belus, the builder of the Tower in Babylon. The fragment, however, is too brief for any definite conclusion to be drawn therefrom, except as a further proof that similar legends of an anachronistic type were circulating at an early period, anterior, no doubt, to the period of the Sibyl.

The close coincidences between the Asatir and Pseudo-Eupolemos cannot be the result of mere chance; one must depend on the other, and as the Asatir is free from any synchretistic or Hellenistic tendencies, and as it follows closely the narrative of the Bible, which it attempts to enlarge and to explain, there can be no question as to which is the older and which belongs to the later period. The Asatir unquestionably represents the older source of this tradition, but it is of course, impossible to determine how far back that tradition can be traced in any literary monument of any kind. The Asatir must thus be a product of an exegetical Midrashic interpretation carried on for some time among the Samaritan inhabitants of Northern Palestine. Nor can there be any doubt that the Samaritans who wrote in Greek lived in Palestine and that they started their activity at a very early date. The Jewish Hellenistic literature did not start, as I have endeavoured to show more fully in my Schweich Lectures on the Samaritans, p. 131 ff., in Alexandria or Egypt in general, but without doubt in Palestine. In the Asatir we find corroboration for this opinion inasmuch as those legends which really originated in Egypt, such as those of Artapanos, and possibly also of Eupolemos, are not found in the Asatir, whereas on the contrary, parallels to the Asatir and other apocryphal writings can be found almost exclusively in the writings of Palestinian origin.

A brief reference to Artapanos must now suffice. He is an Egyptian writer but his date is entirely uncertain.* The whole style and the full development of the story of Moses, which becomes a complicated romance, on the contrary seem to indicate that he must have belonged to a somewhat later period, contemporary with Eupolemos, i. e., at the beginning of the third century. Artapanos was unquestionably a Jew living in Egypt, and he wrote the history of the Jews with a definite purpose. He wanted to show to the Egyptians that they owed their science, their political organisation, nay, their very freedom to the activity of Abraham, who taught them "astrology," to Joseph, who divided the land and introduced fair economic conditions, and above all to Moses, of whom he writes a complete romance. The difference between Artapanos and the Asatir is absolute. Moses, in fact, in Artapanos' writings becomes almost the founder of Egyptian religion, and the rod in his hand is the rod of Osiris. He is the teacher of Orpheus, he teaches the art of ship-building, and many other practical sciences. Not a trace, however, is to be found of the story of the birth of Moses, and everything that preceded and followed immediately, nor anything resembling the full history as told by Josephus, of Moses' behaviour when hugged by Pharaoh, whose crown he tramples, and only a faint allusion to the war against the Ethiopians, without ever mentioning the stratagem of Moses, and his subsequent marriage to Tharbis, the daughter of the King of Ethiopia.**

In the same place where Alexander Polyhistor gives the first excerpts of Artapanos in connection with Abraham, he joins to it another excerpt from an "uncertain author,"

* I do not know on what ground Eisler, Orpheus p. 6, n. 6 states that Artapanos must have lived about 332 B. C. E. This, of course, if proved, would make all the parallels much older than has hitherto been assumed.
** Freudenthal, Hell. Stud., p. 143 to 174, and texts 231 ff. V. also Susemihl, Geschichte der griechischen Litteratur in der Alexandrinerzeit. Leipzig 1891/92 vol. II p. 362, 606 and s. v. Artapan in Pauly-Wissowa, Encycl. d. klass. Alt.

marking it off clearly from the former. Freudenthal in reproducing the text (p. 225) has therefore rightly eliminated it from the excerpts of Artapanos. The fragment runs as follows (Eusebios IX. 18. 2. 420):
"We find in writings of uncertain authorship that Abraham went against the Giants. That they inhabited Babylonia but were annihilated by the gods on account of their impiety. That one of them, named Bêlos escaped death and remained settled in Babylonia and that erecting a tower he fixed his seat in it, and that this was called Bêlös after its builder Bêlös. Moreover that Abraham, learned in the science of astrology, went first to Phoinicia and taught the Phoinicians astrology and afterwards migrated into Egypt."

It is clear that this passage could not belong to Artapanos and that it is another variant of the story of Abraham's fight with the giants, of Bel and his Tower in a rather confused way, and of Abraham's teaching the Phoenicians the science of astronomy. It runs parallel with Pseudo-Eupolemos, and is a faint reflection of the fuller story told in the Asatir.

The question may now be asked whether the author of the Asatir borrowed his legend from the Hellenistic writings or whether on the other hand the author of the Sibylline Oracles could use books like the Asatir written in the Aramaic dialect? The answer to these questions, however remote the contingency may be, is very simple. The Sibylline, as well as all the Hellenistic writers, if they did not know Aramaic, may have had access to Greek translations made already in Palestine. Neither the Jewish nor the Samaritan writings in Greek were restricted to Palestine, but circulated far and wide, and in the same manner as the Samaritan translation of the Pentateuch reached Egypt, so also would the legendary matter which had grown up round the texts from a very early period have reached the same place.

The Sibyl would theefore use the legendary matter in such a manner as was consistent with its character and purpose, whilst it would have been impossible for the author of the Asatir to have used the legends in the form which they took in the Sibylline Oracles, in Pseudo-Eupolemos, and other Hellenistic writings. Otherwise, it would be inexplicable why the romance of Artapanos should not have been taken up by the Samaritans. The close connection of the Asatir with the Sibylline Oracles will become still more evident after further examination of the other Sibylline Oracles and primarily that of the Sibyl of Tibur.

THE SIBYL OF TIBUR AND OTHER ORACLES.

The last portion of the Asatir finishes in a peculiar manner. It consists of two parts. The first, Chapter XI, v. 20—v. 42, which I call the Prophecy, contains strong invectives against the Jews; Eli, David, Solomon, Ezra among others are clearly indicated, Samuel and Saul doubtfully and each of them is strongly condemned. The truth of the Samaritan claims will at the end be fully vindicated against the Jews, who will be converted to the Samaritan faith and accept as true the Samaritan Book of Laws, whereupon general happiness will ensue, but not without a period of tribulation intervening. After this follows Ch. XII which I call the Oracle: a list of anonymous rulers succeeding one another. This list finishes with the last prince who will "come with the rod of miracles in his hand" (ibid. v. 24), meaning thereby the Taheb, with whom the period of happiness will begin. It is quite sufficient for our purpose to have before us only the frame in which the prophecy and oracle are set. The form of the distich which prevails in the latter is specifically characteristic of ancient oracles as well as is its deliberate obscurity and ambiguity.

This brings the Asatir into line with other apocryphal and pseudepigraphic writings which also end with prophetic utterances. It is a common feature of this literature which gives to it its peculiar character and importance. The great figures of the past are made to utter prophetic statements intended to lift the veil from future events. The "Assumption of Moses" claims to be such a prophecy; in other works such as "Biblical Antiquities" of Philo and similar writings, this final prophecy also occupies a prominent position; and to a large extent is the one of the reasons for the book's having been written (see anon) Great events of a political character, profound upheaval, stir the imagination and strike terror into the hearts of their contemporaries and the people are anxious to solve the riddle of the times and to obtain some consolation or some warning. How rich that literature has grown can be gathered from the fact that almost at every turn in the history of the world such oracles come to light and are widely circulated. The downfall of the Persian Empire, the conquest of the East by the Romans, the irruption of the Arabs who swept over the whole of western Asia and spread as far as the north of Spain, the earlier invasion of Europe by the Huns, the devastations by the Mongols and last but not least, the conquering march of the Turks up to the walls of Vienna, are each and all reflected in the numerous oracles which have seen the light of day. Merlin's more ancient prophecies may also be mentioned in this context. But the messages from the past have also a polemical character and principally so. Into the mouth of the great prophets or of the Sibyls is put the condemnation of opponents and these denunciations often assume a minatory character. Evildoers are threatened with divine punishment, and reward is promised to the pious. The hope is granted to those who persevere that a time of happiness and peace is in store for them. This applies *a priori* to the largest part of the Sibylline Oracles, for this voluminous propaganda literature is filled with denunciations of the sinners, evildoers, idolators, and wicked emperors. They are threatened and their doom is proclaimed over and over again, and against them is set, especially in the Jewish Oracles, the sublime faith of the Jews and the ultimate salvation of mankind. A reign of happiness and peace is promised at the end, when the Divine punishment has overtaken the wicked. The Sibylline Oracles thus run parallel with this apocalyptic literature.

There is now one peculiar characteristic which one must bear in mind; subsequent oracles are not always new: most of them are simply the older oracles modified, altered and re-cast to suit changed circumstances. Prophecies which events have belied are deferred to a later time, when they are sure to be fulfilled; incidents alluded to are accordingly altered. In the place of old names, new are substituted. But such names are very rarely given. The general rule is that no names are mentioned. At one period (Sackur, Sibyll. Texte, p. 181) the name is referred to by the numerical value of the initials only, leaving the reader to apply it as best he can. Thus the oracle retains its outer form, while the substance is often greatly enlarged by the mixture of two or three oracles, all combined in one form. In this way one can easily trace the successive development in the literature of oracles. The simplest is the oldest and the most complicated the most recent. Most of them retain traces of their ancient polemical origin.

Two streams can thus be detected. Both by the way stand in close connection with the Book of Daniel. In one the symbolical element is predominant: the other is of a more direct and simple character, and free from symbolism. This is probably anterior to the development of the apocalyptic type. To the simple type belong, in the first place, the Sibylline Oracles and all the stages of its development are fully represented by the fourteen Books of the Sibylline Oracles, covering a period of at least 500 years. They are of a minatory and polemical character. The God-fearing Sibyl denounces heathen idolatry and wickedness, threatens divine vengeance and concludes, as a rule, with a hopeful outlook for the future. The Christian writers who worked up the old oracles remodelled them to suit their own purposes. They are no less minatory in their way, but at the same time, they also foretell the future. In the Assumption of Moses, the author deals with local problems, and the minatory character is fully retained, but above all it has assumed a distinctly polemical character. Different, as can be seen at a glance, are the prophecies in the Book of Enoch with their peculiar symbolism, and still more closely following Daniel are the visions in the Fourth Book of Ezra, the Apocalypse of Baruch (X) and the Revelation of St. John. The fusion between these two types will be discussed a little later on.

We now find in the Sibylline Oracles, which are next in order of comparison, in Book VIII in the introduction (1. 4ff.) another reference to the Tower of Babel, the Flood etc., the Kingdom of Egypt, then a description of various emperors of Rome succeeding one another, interrupted however by strong denunciations and long complaints of the wickedness of Rome and of its impending doom. But more important is Book XII (XIV). Here the chief portion of the oracle is filled up with a list of emperors, probably of Rome, who succeed one another. These are designated by the numerical value of their initial letters, but their description is rather vague and no scholar has yet succeeded in identifying precisely the emperors that are meant. As far as the scheme is concerned, it agrees entirely with the Oracle in the Asatir, with a very significant difference, inasmuch as in the Sibyl the rulers are indicated by the numerical value of the initial letter of their names, whilst in the Asatir they are still anonymous. We have in the Sibylline Oracles a later development of a theme which seems to have its oldest representative in the Samaritan text. This bears out the principle laid down that oracles are remodelled, amplified and adapted to altered conditions. The reason for the absence of references in the Patristic literature to Book XII (XIV) of the Sibylline Oracles is no doubt the fact that this oracle contains nothing of a religious character. It is purely secular in its contents and outlook. As to the date, it is not of much consequence to determine the precise period of the composition of Book XII of the Sibylline Oracles in the form in which we find it now, for it rests upon a much more ancient oracle which in the same way as other Oracles has undergone some change in the course of time as shown. The fact that one cannot identify precisely either the names or the order of the emperors, shows that this adaptation is of a later date, and made by a clumsy hand. In its present form, it may belong to the second century, but the original, however, is probably much older. It is, very likely, the product of a Jew of Alexandria before the Common Era, for he looks forward, just like the Asatir, to a time when the Chosen People will live in happiness with all the nations of the world (ibid. vv. 349—360). It may be sheer coincidence but it is no less curious that the number of emperors mentioned in Book XII is 26, precisely the same number which is postulated in the colophon of the Oracle, Asatir Ch. XII. In addition to that, we read in l. 354: There will be at that time an "equal light for the living" almost the same phrase, in the same connection as Asatir XII, 25, "There will be light and no darkness."

We turn now to the Asatir, Ch. XI. This prophecy is of the simplest character. The verses owe their origin not to any Daniel influence, but stand more under that of the Song of Moses, and also of the Blessings of Moses (Deut. Chs. XXXII and XXXIII). To the former profound eschatological importance has been given by the Samaritans; it contains, according to their interpretations, the revelation of the events to come here and hereafter in this world and in the world to come and of the Day of Judgment. Thus the prophecy in the Asatir has a distinctly historical background, quite in conformity with the character of the book; it is purely polemical, directed against the secession which they connect with the name of Eli and concludes with the change of the script which as they say, Ezra carried out by substituting the later Hebrew, or rather Aramaic square script for the ancient Hebrew alphabet retained by the Samaritans. He is, moreover, charged by them with having falsified the text by substituting new readings for the old. One may add that the obscure wording chosen by the author led to an anachronistic and anti-Christian interpretation of Ch. XI. 29 found in the Pitron and elsewhere. But the succeeding verses make it impossible to apply the prophecy contained in v. 29 to any other period than that of Solomon and that in v. 36 to that of Ezra. This will be shown more fully in the notes to the text.

But much closer is the parallelism between the Oracle in the Asatir and the oracle which is known as that of the Sibyl of Tibur.* Sackur (Sibyll: Texte pp. 115—187) who was the first to give us a critical text, traces it back in its original form to the third or fourth century C. E. Unfortunately no Greek text has yet been discovered, but the Slavonic version and the Rumanian which rests upon it, (published by me J. R. A. S. 1910, and now reprinted in my "Studies and Texts" p. 211ff.), leaves no doubt as to the existence of such an old Greek text, anterior probably to all the existing Latin versions. Here the oracle has been thoroughly adapted to Christian conditions and Christian views and the story of the Antichrist has been introduced as a fitting setting for the End of Days. In the Slavo-Rumanian version, this oracle assumes the character of a Biblical apocryphon; inasmuch as the Sibyl is described as the daughter of King

---

* Kampers Werdegang p. 88 ff. and Rzach in Pauly-Kroll 1923 s. v. Sibyllinische Orakel col. 2170 ff.

David, and the whole first part differs considerably from the other Sibylline Oracles. The Sibyl interprets a curious dream of the Senators of Rome, who see one hundred suns, but the Sibyl explains the meaning of only nine suns, representing the constant deterioration of the world. The figure "9," the tenth being considered Christ, is evidently modelled after the type of the ten generations from Creation to the Flood, or the ten generations from the Flood to Abraham, or after the legend of the ten kings who will rule over the whole world, God being the last (see further). In another recension only seven suns are mentioned, and here probably we have the more primitive form of the seven nations that have been destroyed (Asatir Ch. VI, v. 9) and the seven kingdoms substituted for them in the Sibylline Oracles Book III v. 167 ff. which has been treated previously. There is no astrological meaning to be attached, as Kampers assumes. In between, there appears a strong invective against the Jews, whose conversion is forcibly urged and who are to be convinced of the error of their ways when the claim of Christianity will be vindicated. This episode seems to drop out afterwards and after the ninth ruler a list is given of the kings who succeed one another until the time of Antichrist, when the final triumph of Christianity will occur. This prophecy has exercised a profound influence upon the writers and chroniclers of the Middle Ages, and has to a large extent also influenced the revelations of the so-called Methodius of Patara (Patmos, Olympus). It has even been fully reproduced by an old English chronicler towards the end of the twelfth century, borrowed afterwards by Matthew of Paris in his Chronica Maiora and introduced by Archbishop Parker into the second edition of the "Flores Historiarum" (1570) which he believed to be the work of Matthew of Westminster.* In the Sibyl of

* H. R. Luard. Flores Historiarum London 1890 vol. I, XL Band
H. R. Luard. Matthaei Parisiensis Chronica Maiora, London 1872

Tibur, as in the Asatir, the kings are described very briefly, with the only difference that here also as in the Sibyl of Book XII the kings are indicated by the initials of their names, a fact not noticed by Sackur, who has not carried the comparison as far back as the Greek Sibylline Oracles.

The Oriental origin of the Sibyl of Tibur, in spite of its name, may be assumed by the fact that it is the only Sibylline Oracle of which we possess translations into Arabic and Aethiopic.* In these as well as in the Oriental versions the kings referred to are the Arabic Khalifs.

In these recensions and in the Rumanian, the second part, the Oracle of the Asatir is missing, but a portion of the material has been embodied in the interpretation of the nine dreams or nine suns. Yet it can be proved that such a list of succeeding kings must have belonged to the primitive form of this Sibylline Oracle which, in its oldest version must go back in all probability to a Syriac text, resting upon a still older tradition, Greek, Samaritan (Aramaic) etc. It is found, though transformed, in the adaptation to the Italian and Frankish kings, and before that, in the old Latin version and in the Byzantine literature, of which the most famous is the oracle ascribed to the Emperor Leo.**

The existence of such an ancient oracle can best be proved if we turn to the Hebrew literature where we find that the oracle in which the future is described by a

---

p. 42 ff. An English translation of Matthew of Westminster has been done by C. D. Yonge London 1853. Sibyl of Tibur in vol I. p. 69 ff.

* Ed. Schleifer, Die Erzählung der Sibylle, Denkschriften der Kaiserl. Akademie d. Wissenschaften, Philos. Hist. Kl. Band LIII, Abhdlg. I Wien 1906.

** For the Western literature see Gfrörer and for the Byzantine the exhaustive literature in K. Krumbacher, Gesch. d. Byzant. Literatur. 2nd ed. München 1897, p. 628 f. Vassiliev, Anecdota Greco-Byzantina, Vol. I. p. 33—38. Moscow 1893, cf. preface pp. XII—XXV, containing the text of Methodius greatly enlarged and mixed up with the Daniel Apocalypse.

succession of kings has its oldest representatives in the Visions of Daniel. Here chiefly in Ch. XI a succession of kings is mentioned, and at the same time many details are given of an historical character which may fit a time from Alexander's conquest of Asia downwards. At the same time we find in Ch. VII and VIII a series of visions purporting to describe future events. But here the kings, or the empires are described in the similitude of beasts, armed with horns of a peculiar character, and thus these chapters are full of fantastic and allegorical imagery. Of special interest for our purpose is the first class of anonymous kings succeeding one another. The second lies entirely outside our sphere of investigation, although it has had a very great influence upon subsequent writers, especially in the Similitudes of the Book of Enoch, the Vision of Ezra IV, and later, as will be seen, in other productions. The list of kings of Daniel Ch. XI, however, is the one that approximates more closely with the Samaritan Oracle. It would be perhaps an idle question, as far at any rate as our present knowledge goes, to enquire after the source from which Daniel drew this kind of prophetic utterance. In its present form it seems to have already undergone a certain elaboration and development. The primitive form would have been, in all probability, very brief, and not so pointed, for it is the very essence of this kind of prophetic anticipation of the future not to be too definite, but to leave room to the imagination, and for the re-adjustment of interpretation according to circumstances. There is, besides, also some connection between the Oracle in the Asatir, the Sibyl, and the last chapters of Daniel, inasmuch as they all finish with the same phrase of a happy and peaceful time to come, nay, they use practically the same words; and yet with a notable difference. In Daniel we find the hope of resurrection which is missing in the Samaritan Asatir. But leaving aside this point, to which attention will be drawn presently, it is sufficient to have pointed out this parallelism, and how this prophecy may have become the starting-point of a long list of similar oracles not without importance for the history of that literature. In the chequered career of Jewish mystical and apocalyptic literature, it is difficult to follow the slowly developing prophecies of the future through the ages. An intermediate stage is occupied by the Palestinian Targum, to which a separate chapter is devoted in this introduction. There as in the Asatir, such a prophecy is placed in the mouth of Moses towards the end of his life. Similar utterances referring more especially to the woes at the end of time are mentioned in the name of some of the sages of the first century. All this will be elaborated later on.

To this class of similitudes and allegories belongs also the Armenian version of the Daniel Apocalypse called the Seventh Vision of Daniel.* This rests upon a Greek original dating in its present form from the middle of the seventh century, and it deals with the history of the Byzantine Emperors from Constantine to Heraclius. It is a very elaborate counterpart of the Western recension of the Tiburtine. The kings are described allegorically and by name, showing that the old material had been utilised and adapted to the conditions of the Byzantine Empire. Here we have a complete mixture of the ancient Sibylline Oracles, the Daniel Apocalypse, and the Antichrist Legend.

Of a similar character but from a critical point of view of far greater importance is the Jewish-Persian Daniel Apocalypse.** The date of that composition is difficult to determine. Daniel is anxious about the future and God tells him that a number of kings will arise who in turn will do good or evil to the Jews, and that in the

* Kalemkiar in Wiener Zeitschrift für die Kunde des Morgenlandes, Vol. VI, 1892, pp. 109—136 and 227—240. Armenian and German Text.
** Ed. H. Zotenberg in Merx Archiv für Wissenschaftliche Erforschung des Alten Testaments, Vol. I, Halle 1869, p. 385 ff.

end a false Messiah will appear, and a Jewish parallel to the Christian Antichrist and the Day of Judgment is briefly given. Mohammed and his successors, the Khalifs, are clearly indicated in that list of kings, which, however, is not carried down to the destruction of the Abbasid Dynasty. Among the signs which the Jews will ask the false Messiah to produce in order to justify his claim is also the Rod of Miracles of Moses, a point which deserves to be noted, for as Zotenberg remarks, the Apocalypse, though dealing with the events of a later period rests in all probability upon a more ancient recension; and what is still more important is his statement that the Persian is in all probability a translation from an Aramaic text, thus bringing it within the sphere of our investigations. It assists in proving an Oriental origin for the Sibyl of Tibur.

This view is further strengthened by a similar apocalypse, the hero of which is Rabbi Simeon ben Yochai:* he, like Daniel, is anxious to know the events of the future and he also is shown a list of Mohammedan kings. This belongs to the same period as the supposed Aramaic version, and is likewise a later adaptation to actual conditions of a much older text. It goes by the name of Nistarot, i. e. "the Secrets," a word which resembles very closely the Samaritan title of the present work, as mentioned before, p. 5. This title has thus been preserved in its primitive meaning of "secrets revealed." In this connection may also be mentioned the mystical oracle, which, like the Asatir, consists of a number of distichs and is written in very obscure Aramaic. It is known as the prophecy of the young child, Naḥman Ketufa. (Ed. Pr. Amsterdam 1788 and ed. Satanov, Berlin 1793.) The problem of the date of this composition has also remained unsolved, but it suffices to mention that this oracle was already known

* Ed. Pr. Saloniki 1743, rptd. by Jellinek Beth Hamidrash III, 78—82.

to Abraham, son of Maimonides (thirteenth century). The only difference between the latter and other oracles consists in the absence of any kings being mentioned; only a sequence of events is described. I may also mention a similar Hebrew-Arabic prophecy, referring to the time of the Abbasid Khalifs and finishing with the Advent of the Messiah, a fragment only of which has been preserved in my collection of the Genizah documents, now in the British Museum. All these show the continued existence during many centuries of such apocalyptic oracles in the East and among the Jews, no less than among the Christians.

One of these must have been the origin of the oracle which was afterwards known in its western recension under the name of the Sibyl of Tibur. It seems in fact that we have in the latter one of the oldest oracles, inasmuch as with the exception of the initial letter indicating the name of the king, which this Sibyl has in common with the oracle of Book XII (XIV), the rest is very brief, no allegories are introduced and the influence of the Daniel literature has not yet affected this Sibyl of Tibur. If we compare it with the Asatir, the parallelism will in some instances appear very striking. The way in which certain kings are described agrees very closely, but we must remember at the same time that the Samaritan text may have suffered in its long transmission through the obscurity of its language and the vague allusions contained therein.

One has to take into consideration the changes to which all these texts have been subjected in the course of time, and one must also remember that the obscurity of the Samaritan may have caused some words or portions of the text to have been omitted, while some of the verses have also been hopelessly corrupted. Yet in spite of these difficulties, there are too many details which the Sibyl of Tibur and the Asatir have in common to be the result of mere coincidence. It is curious that in the Sibyl only a few kings are mentioned with the number of years of their reign, and the same peculiarity appears also in the Asatir. In the former about five are mentioned out of close upon forty, and in the latter two out of twenty-five.

The corresponding passages are now given in parallel columns, always bearing in mind that the Sibyl has been adapted to Italian and Lombardian conditions and that the simple, vague indication as found in the Asatir has in consequence been amplified and more clearly defined in the Sibyl. We find thus:

PARALLELS.

ASATIR, Ch. 12.	SIBYL OF TIBUR.*
v. 4. A prince will arise strong in truth; in his days the salvation of the community will be great.	After him shall arise a ... king. He shall be very great and very pious ... and ... shall execute judgment and do justice to the poor (Sackur. Sibyll. Texte p. 182).
v. 6. A prince, etc. ... in his days the house of worship(?) shall be built.	After them shall arise, etc. ... He shall build a temple to the Lord (Sackur. ibid. p. 181).
v. 8. A prince, etc. ... mighty in the knowledge of truth: the people will rejoice.	In those days shall arise, etc. ... he shall be very mighty ... and good: he shall do justice to the poor and shall judge rightly. (Sackur ibid. p. 182).

* It is a remarkable fact that in two or three places the version found in the Matthew of Paris recension seems to contain some ancient details missing in the Sibyl of Tibur, Sackur's text; e. g. "barbarians" (Luard, Matthew of Paris p. 46) which is missing in Sackur.

v. 10. A prince, etc. ... rulers will perish in his days in secret; a hundred will flee to the borders of Sichem.	Then shall arise two kings ... they shall be masters of cities and provinces ... All the people of the East ... shall be scattered (Sackur ibid. p. 181).
v. 11. A prince, etc. ... Gog will perish in grief; in his days the people will turn back to sin and they will forsake the covenant.	The sin and punishment indicated in this verse are very fully elaborated and worked out in the Sibyl under the Salic king, "a brave man and warrior and many of his neighbours ... will be indignant with him." (Sackur ibid. p. 183).

Still more striking is the last paragraph in the Sibyl in which the prophecies concerning a number of kings at the end of the list have all been combined in the name of the last, Constans (Sackur ibid. p. 185) (or rather, a play upon the word meaning probably "steadfast")—this suggestion is fully corroborated by the reading in Beda: Nomine Hanimo Constante (Migne P.L. XC, 1183)—and which has undergone a thorough transformation at the hands of the Christian scribe. The last king, Constans, is expected to live 120 years; all the virtues and all the achievments of the last princes in the Samaritan text have been combined together in one; in both cases the final triumph of the faith is proclaimed, and the man to bring about that happy event is described in the Samaritan as holding the Rod of Miracles in his hand (Asatir XII, 24). He is a descendant of the house of Levi (ibid. v. 22) and is probably no one else than Moses Redivivus, who comes back with the Divine Rod. This is the Rod which, according to the Persian Apocalypse of Daniel, the Jews will ask the false Messiah to produce as proof of his

Messianic mission. This also is probably the rod or the wood in the Sibylline Oracles Book VIII, 245 ff., which has been misinterpreted as the Cross. In the Sibyl the Greek Emperor holds the Cross. Again, in both cases the temple of idols will be destroyed, and more significant still, both quote at the end the same verse of the Bible, "Judah will be saved and Israel will dwell securely," taken with a slight variation from the prophecies of Bileam (Numb. XXIV) to which Messianic importance has been attached, as will be shown later on. This striking coincidence shows that there must have existed a very ancient oracle in Aramaic similar to that preserved in the Asatir, which served as basis for the text, upon which the Tiburtine Sibyl ultimately rests.

The Samaritan oracle finishes with the following words, "Happy is he who will see it and reach that time," (ibid. v. 25), which again is absolutely identical with the words in the Sibylline Oracle Books III, 371, and a little more concisely in IV, 192, "Most blessed shall he be who will live to see that time," thus referring to the happy consummation at the End of Days. It agrees with and yet differs from the last verse with which the book of Daniel finishes (v. 12) which runs as follows: "Blessed is he that waiteth and cometh to the one thousand three hundred and thirty five days." It is, therefore, a very significant variant from what must have been once a pious exclamation found, probably, in the oldest form, and is also common to Daniel, the Asatir, and the Sibylline Oracles. This at any rate, is one more proof of the close connection between that literature and the Asatir.

The similarity between the Asatir and the Sibyl of Tibur grows still clearer if we compare these two texts in their formal aspect. In both we have, to all appearance, two sets of revelations; the one dealing with historical events which, more or less, can be clearly understood, and then there follows a list of kings which seems to be suspended in the air. The relation in which these two revelations stand to one another is just as obscure as the language itself. Is the second revelation intended to supplement the former, or is it to cover to some extent the same period as contained in the former? Is it a mere repetition under a different form, or is it to be an entirely independent revelation? It seems as if it were running parallel to the former, and yet quite independent of it; in fact, we have two sets of independent revelations. But whilst in the former the starting-point is quite clear, in the second there is nothing to indicate from which period that list of kings starts, and again, on the other hand, both lead up to the same consummation and happy time following after tribulation. This is very marked in the Asatir. In the Sibyl, the connection is also very loose between the two parts, and although the list of kings is less shadowy, still the same question remains as to the relation between the two parts, all the more so as this whole section is otherwise missing in the Oriental and Slavonic text. This is not a proof for it being less old, for it is an integral part of other oracles. But it evidently has been omitted in those versions where they found its interpretation and application very difficult. The coincidence, however, between the Asatir and the Sibyl of Tibur remains a matter of no little significance.

In view of the difficulty which is thus created by the relation between the Prophecy and the Oracle, the question may be asked whether the latter indeed formed a part of the original composition, or whether it has been appended at a later time. It is true that it is apparently missing at the end of the Arabic paraphrase of the Asatir; but a careful examination of the last portion reveals the fact that the Arabic paraphrast knew it very well, but not understanding the text, satisfied himself with quoting the first and last sentences. It will be seen that on many occasions the paraphrast was not equal to his task, inasmuch as he left also many difficult and obscure words of the Asatir untranslated. None would offer more difficulties to the paraphrast than an oracle replete with archaic or corrupt words. Yet the oldest Samaritan writers, such as Abul Ḥassan in his Tabah (eleventh century) and Tabyat el Doweik (middle of fourteenth century) show full acquaintance with the oracle. The very nature of its form and contents would be different if the oracle really were of a later origin. The similarity with Daniel and the Sibylline Oracles, and above all that with the Sibyl of Tibur, prove the reverse. Both prophecy and oracle conform, moreover, to ancient traditions. Both differ considerably from the rest of the book. The one, (the prophecy), consists of short sentences, sometimes only of three words, or of two hemistichs, although they are written consecutively in the MS., as though they were prose. They are entirely in the form of the ancient pagan oracles, which consisted often of one verse, or at the utmost, of a distich. The same occurs also in some of the old Jewish prophecies, put in the mouth of the high priest, or, as will be seen later, in the mouth of sages of the first century, when foretelling the future. The form of the oracle follows the same tradition which governs the Sibylline Oracles. It is a poem consisting of a number of stanzas, each of two lines and each beginning with the words "A prince will arise."

In this respect there is therefore a remarkable difference between the Oracle and the Asatir itself. The former is a poem whilst the rest of the book is in prose. The beginnings of Samaritan poetry are still obscure. Not a single investigation as to the origin of the Samaritan liturgical poetry—and it is only liturgical, except Markaḥ—has as yet been undertaken. Neither F. H. Gesenius,[*] one of the first to study the Samaritan liturgical poems, nor any of his

---

[*] in his Carmina Samaritana, Leipzig 1824.

successors,* nay, not even Cowley, the editor of the Samaritan liturgy, have as much as uttered a single word on the system of Samaritan poetry and on the poetry of the Jews or the Syrians. The outward form may thus also be a criterion for an old date. The poem consists, as mentioned, of 25 stanzas, each beginning with the words "A ruler (or prince) will arise," giving it a solemn cadence. Each stanza consists of two lines, and each line of two hemistichs. There is occasionally an inner rhyme, but it is not consistent and may be due to accident rather than to design. The poem was no doubt intended to be chanted, as I presume, at the end of the prophecy. Each hemistich seems to consist of four beats. This seems to be the system followed by Ephrem (or Bardesanes), and that system approaches more nearly the Samaritan. It need not be further developed here. It is sufficient to have drawn attention to it, but the Samaritans evidently follow the much older examples found in the two Songs of Moses, in Exod. Ch. XIV, and Deuteronomy Ch. XXXII, which are divided into two hemistichs. The guiding principle is the word-accent, according to Samaritan pronunciation. A verse consists of one line. The text is not divided into stanzas as in the Oracle, where the contents leads logically to such a division into couplets. There is besides another "prophecy" in the Bible: that of Bileam, (Numbers Chapters XXIII and XXIV) And this is written in verse form by the Samaritans in their ancient scrolls, and has evidently exercised a deep influence both on the prophecy and the oracle, no less in the form than in the contents. Thus there are sufficient examples in the Pentateuch to explain the metrical form of this oracle.

The real object of compiling this and similar oracles containing lists of kings is not explained by the simple enumeration of successive rulers. What was the ultimate

* Such as R. Kirchheim, Carme Shomron. Frankfurt a/M. 1851.

aim of those who drew up such lists? They were intended, no doubt, to serve a definite purpose, and speaking generally, they aimed at creating a feeling of hope in times of stress and trouble. They were to give the scheme of the Divine plan according to which the world is guided, and the nations led in a preordained way to a final end, when they will be free from further tribulation. This Messianic outlook, depicted by each sect in its own way, was afterwards mixed up with eschatalogical ideas. The end of the world was not to come without such troubles, caused, to a large extent, by a powerful enemy, but it was also afterwards connected with the Final Judgment and the Resurrection of the Dead. The figure of the Antichrist was later on introduced into these last events, but neither in the Asatir nor in the Tiburtine, do we find anything of those eschatalogical views about the Doomsday and Resurrection. Similarly in the older Sibylline Oracles, the Messianic period is described as a time reached after a period of woe and tribulation and ending without any reference to Resurrection or Day of Judgment. No definite period is contemplated, apparently, in these Hellenistic oracles. We find one, however, indicated at the end of the Samaritan oracle, which is of extreme significance. It says (ibid v. 26) "twenty-six this way and twenty-six that way." Here a definite period is anticipated for the advent of those happy days, and of the man who will bring about those happy times. "Twenty-six this way" probably means that so many generations have passed since the Creation to Moses. He is the one for whose sake the world has been created, and with his appearance the first period in the history of the world has been completed. Another "Twenty-six," a similar number of generations, here represented by kings, must follow, in order to complete again the second cycle, for at the end of it, Moses is again to appear. Just as he completed the Divine plan at the time of his birth, so will he again complete it at the time of his reappearance, and thus finally achieve the redemption of the world from trials and troubles. This is so thoroughly a Samaritan conception, that it puts the final seal on the Asatir. Nothing is as yet mentioned in it of the Day of Judgment or of Resurrection. Here, at any rate, we have a clear plan which guides the author in evolving this Oracle. In later oracles, when a definite term had been mentioned, which passed away without realisation, that point of view was more and more lost sight of, and kings were added, thereby serving immediate dynastical interests. Consequently the Asatir must belong to a much higher antiquity than any other oracles known.

THE ASATIR AND JOSEPHUS.*

The consensus of opinion of almost everyone who has studied the writings of Josephus and more particularly his "Antiquities," is that in addition to the apologetic character which he, of necessity, gave to a book adapted to a heathen or Greek public, he is accused of having introduced many legends and fantastic interpretations mostly of his own fabrication or borrowed from Hellenistic writers, all believed to have been of Egyptian origin. It will now cause no little surprise if we assert that many of these legends, far from being his own invention, were in fact drawn from a source closely approximating the Asatir. It must be borne in mind that there is a profound difference between the work of Josephus and the Asatir. The latter consists mostly of legendary glosses and tales added to the text of the Bible. The Bible is principally supposed to be known to the reader and therefore everything contained therein is entirely

* The literature on Josephus is so vast that it hardly even can be indicated here; it must suffice to refer to Schürer, Leipzig 1901, vol I pp. 100—106; and Hölscher in Pauly-Wissowa, Encycl. Klass. Alt. Vol. IX; s. v. Josephus, Col. 1997—2000.

omitted in the Asatir, as already remarked before, neither is there in it any apologetic tendency, nor the desire of paraphrasing the text in such a manner as to make the story of the Bible more plausible or more acceptable to the Gentile reader. The Asatir has only one aim: to fill up the lacunae in the historical narrative, to supplement with a few more or less explanatory details the lives of the Patriarchs, and to emphasise the truth of the Samaritan claims to be the possessors of the genuine text of the Bible and the strict observers of the Law. With this exception the rest comes within the sphere of Agadic Midrash.

Not so Josephus. He, like many of his predecessors, recounts anew the whole history of the Jewish people from the Creation down to his own time. His book is written for a wider circle: it has an apologetic tendency, since it was intended to present the Biblical narrative to the Gentile reader in the most alluring form, and it glosses over every difficulty so as to make it as readable as could be done by the skill of the writer, who was conscious at the same time that he was performing a sacred and patriotic task. In the comprehensive and consecutive writing which covers the whole period of the Bible and more, Josephus, while following the account given in the Sacred Books, weaves into it a mass of legendary matter. This was done with a definite purpose, and as will be seen, following more or less an older example. The Gentile reader had no necessity to recur to Josephus' works for a knowledge of the Bible as such, since he had at his disposal the Greek translation of the LXX, centuries older than Josephus, and in his time already invested with a special character of authority. Josephus, on the contrary, had another intention; he wanted to make a new presentation in a popular and acceptable form, and in the spirit of his time. At the same time he made use of legendary matter which had already won popularity among his countrymen. Anticipating here already the results of my investigation, I should like to formulate them at once into the statement that Josephus wrote a *Greek Targum* to the Pentateuch parallel to the Aramaic Targum then in vogue among the Jews. From this point of view a new light is thrown on the character of his work, and much that has hitherto appeared obscure and perplexing will be more easily explained, and Josephus' veracity vindicated. It will also explain his relation to the LXX of which he curiously enough makes so little use in the First Books of his "Antiquities." One example will suffice: the Chronology of the Patriarchs, in which he differs from the LXX as well as from the O. T. Hebrew text.* It will also be shown that he also ignores genuine Egyptian Hellenistic literature. Hitherto, the sources of the legends have been sought, and to a large extent in vain, in the extant fragments of that Hellenistic literature. Take for example the parallel story in the narrative of Josephus and that of Artapanos, in the story of Moses, and one can see how great the discrepancies are between the one and the other. They prove unquestionably that Josephus had not borrowed directly from this writer, and even if he did make use of a Greek translation of the Bible, it was not the LXX, which is the one now in our hands. I am speaking, of course, only of the Pentateuch and of the Book of Joshua. The alleged liberties which he took were quite in conformity with the character of his book. In his writings Josephus followed merely the examples set by others who did not scruple to take much greater liberties with the Biblical narrative than he did when they worked with the same apologetic tendency. For example, Pseudo-Eupolemos, Artapanos, and other writers did not hesitate to mix Biblical stories even with Greek myths. Josephus, on the contrary, kept strictly to the Biblical narrative without any such admixture of

* I find now that also Hölscher in Pauly-Wissowa Encycl. d. klass. Alt. s. v. Josephus vol. IX, col. 1953 ff. comes to the same result that Josephus made no use of the LXX.

Greek mythology and without any real attempt at such synchretism. He followed the example set by the synagogue itself. It is well known that long before his time the Midrashic homiletic exegesis was introduced into the public readings and even into the service of the synagogue. Therefore there was no reason for Josephus to refrain from introducing similar legendary matter into his own exposition of the Biblical narrative, which thus made it ever so much more attractive and to a large extent also much more instructive. It also served his apologetic purpose, for the legend always tries to exalt the personage round whom it is woven, and often transforms simple mortals into great heroes.

Whence, then, did Josephus obtain his legendary matter? The difficulty of tracing it back to more ancient sources is indeed very great, inasmuch as no other parallels can be found in the hitherto known literature, but if we turn now to the Asatir, we shall find a surprising number of close parallels between Josephus and the traditions embodied in the former.

It must, however, at once be emphazised that Josephus has not borrowed directly either from a Samaritan source or from Pseudo-Eupolemos the incidents connected with Abraham in Egypt in spite of many points of agreement. Josephus never disguises his profound hatred of and contempt for the Samaritans; it is spread over all his writings, and occasionally he shows his strong bias when he touches upon Samaritan history, for example, in the dispute in Egypt before King Ptolemy, not to speak of other more important occasions (cf Gaster, Schweich Lectures, Sam. p. 118f.). It is, therefore, out of the question that Josephus, writing his Antiquities of the Jews, should have gone to the hated Samaritans for legendary matter. The nearest source would be the Palestinian Midrash, especially the one that flourished in the north of Palestine, in Samaria as well as in Galilea. It is there, no doubt, that much of this legendary matter had been simultaneously evolved, perhaps under the influence of mutual rivalry between the various sects of the community, each one selecting the same weapons for its polemic and borrowing from the armoury of a Midrashic exegesis common to both. This may also point to the original home of the Palestinian Targum, for all go back to the same common anterior source. The value of the Josephus legends, therefore, lies in the fact that we have in a Jewish writing definite proof of the existence of such northern Palestinian Midrash, of which, otherwise, only a few traces have been preserved in Hellenistic writings.

The parallels between Josephus and the Asatir are very numerous. They will be referred to regularly in the footnotes accompanying the translation, but a number of them may be grouped here, since they go a long way to show how close is the parallelism between the two. In some cases, as will be seen, there is even literal agreement, but still more in the general character and in peculiarities which may in themselves be of little consequence, but which yet offer cumulative evidence for the close relation between the Josephus traditions and those embodied in the Asatir and other Samaritan writings.

We find Josephus describing the Patriarchs down to the period of Noah inclusive as *ruling* the world and *delivering* the government to their sons (Ant. I. 3. 4. 83 and ib. 87, cf Asatir I, 1 and passim).

"Astronomical and geometrical discoveries" (Ant. I. 4. 9. 106). This is a paraphrase of Asatir IV 15, where Adam, Enoch and others are possessors of the Book of Signs, evidently astronomical sciences.

"He sent colonies abroad" (Ant. I. 4. 1. 110. 112. As. IV. 26; As. IV. 32 ff.) We may mention here again the whole description of Nimrod which tallies exactly with the Asatir in many details. He is described as the builder of Babel, the man who incites the people to rebel and who raises the Tower. The Geomeria differs to some extent, but there are certain points of similarity.* Notable are the boundaries of Egypt, which he traces quite specially, and the inclusion of the Philistines, to whom prominence is given, thus agreeing in the main with the narrative in the Asatir (Ant. I. 6. 2. 136; As. V, 11). Again, in both narratives the story of the destruction of the seven nations is mentioned in connection with the kingdom of Egypt, and the war to which allusion has already been made before. There the confusion has been explained into which Josephus has fallen.

Josephus (Ant. I, 6. 4. 143. 147) places the sons of Joktan near the Indian Ocean, substituting geographical names better known to him for the Biblical ones. The Asatir (V. 13) also translates curiously the name of the place mentioned in Gen. X. 30, evidently with the desire of avoiding identification of the mountain of the East הר הקדם with Mount Garizim, which the Samaritans call by that name, and substitutes Timnata for it, the place in the South of Palestine, known from Gen. XXXVIII, 12.

Josephus, curiously enough, ignores entirely the legend of the birth of Abraham, and his trial by fire, so fully developed in the Asatir, but both have one feature in common of great importance. Teraḥ is *not* described as an idolator, a theme fully developed in all the Abraham legends both in the Jewish Agada and the pseudepigraphic literature. It is also found so in the Koran. Now this omission is very significant. It is not a mere oversight, but has its origin in the same set of traditions which the Samaritans possess. The Jewish legend which describes Teraḥ as a maker or worshipper of idols rests ultimately on the words of Joshua, where he says (Joshua XXIV, 2)

---

* V. for the whole literature: The Chronicles of Jeraḥmeel, Introduction to Ch. 42; Ad. Bauer and Jos. Strygowski, Eine alexandrinische Weltchronik. Denkschr. d. Kaiserl. Akademie der Wissenschaften Philos.-Histor. Klasse vol. LI, Wien 1905, p. 92 ff., Appendix I.

"Even Teraḥ, the father of Abraham and the father of Nahor served other gods." One might argue that Josephus, for apologetic reasons, did not wish to refer to Teraḥ as a worshipper of idols, but in the Samaritan Book of Joshua this very chapter is entirely missing, and Meshalma, in his commentary, protests energetically against the Jewish tradition which makes Teraḥ an idol worshipper. The parallelism shown by me between Josephus' description of Joshua and that of the Samaritans, finds here again an important corroboration, and on the other hand, indicates the high antiquity of the Samaritan Book of Joshua discovered and published by me. The writer of the Asatir did not find in his source any allusion to Teraḥ as an idol-worshipper. Consequently Josephus also omits any reference to the cause of Haran's death.

The 120 years (Ant. I. 6. 5. 152) mentioned in Gen. VI, 3 before the Flood are thus explained by Josephus that God fixed that number because it was the length of Moses' life. The connection of 120 years with Moses rests on the well-known Samaritan interpretation of the numerical value of the word בשגם (ibid.) which is identical with that of the name of Moses, namely 345. This is absolutely Samaritan.

"Noah departed from the land where he lived," (Ant. I. 3. 1. 74). More precisely given in the Asatir (IV. 1. 3).

"He turned dry land into sea," (Ant. I. 3. 2. 75). "The earth became humid and broke open," (As. IV. 9).

Josephus, in deliberate opposition to the Samaritans, and agreeing with the Palestinian Targum, calls the second month in which the Flood started Marheshvan (Ant. I, 3. 3. 80), but according to the Samaritans it was the second month after Nisan.

"The animals were sent into the ark," (Ant. I. 3. 2. 77). Meshalma's Commentary: God sent the animals into the ark. It is already thus in the Sibyl I, 208. This is according to Samaritan interpretation.

Special stress is laid on the fact that Noah was the tenth

from Adam. (Ant. I, 3. 2. 79). So also in the Samaritan Chain of High Priests.

"Whence it is that they have not written down his (Enoch's) death?" (Ant. I, 3. 4. 85). As the words stand, Josephus may have believed that Enoch died. In the Asatir, the death of Enoch is fully described (As. IV. 32 ff.).

"The ark rested on a certain mountain in Armenia," (Ant. I. 3. 5. 90). Josephus does not mention Ararat, though it is distinctly mentioned in the Bible (Gen.VIII,4). Asatir (IV, 1) also gives a name different from that of the Bible, which is not found in the Samaritan Targum. It is a name which does not agree with that in any of the other Apocryphal books. Here again, Josephus prefers a vague expression to the more definite form of the Asatir, but both agree in so far that neither mentions the Biblical name.

The order of the sons of Noah is Shem, Japhet and Ham (Ant. I. 4. 1. 109). So also the Asatir (IV, 14).

The story of Nimrod, which has already been fully dealt with above, is in complete agreement with the Asatir in the main features, especially in those details where Josephus amplifies the Biblical narrative.

"He (Noah) prayed for the prosperity of his two sons," (Ant. I. 6. 3. 142), cf. Asatir (IV, 33—34), where Noah appoints Shem King giving him the preference in the kingdom.

Abraham was tenth from Noah (Ant. I. 6. 5. 148). The importance attached by Josephus that Abraham was the tenth, agrees with the Samaritan practice down to this very day, so also in their genealogical Chain, where special attention is drawn to the seventh and tenth among the Patriarchs.

Teraḥ hating Chaldaea (Ant. I. 6. 5. 152). The Bible gives no reason for Teraḥ leaving Chaldaea. Josephus says "he hates Chaldaea on account of his mourning for Haran." The Asatir gives the reason for this hatred: he had been imprisoned by Kedar Laomer (Asatir VII, 12) and freed by Abraham.

"(Abraham was) the first to publish this notion that there is one God," (Ant. I. 7. 1. 155). This is not given in the same words in the Bible, although it is implied so; it is, however, specifically mentioned in the Asatir that he proclaimed the faith first before Nimrod (As. V, 27) and later on before Pharaoh (As. VI, 23).

"The Chaldaean and other people of Mesopotamia raised a tumult against him," (Ant. I. 7. 1. 157). Nothing of this is found in the Bible. It is merely a paraphrase of the definite statement in the Asatir, where it says that Nimrod was angered with him and threw him into the fire (As. V, 27).

"Skilful in celestial sciences" (Ant. I. 7. 2. 158) which Josephus mentions in the name of Berosus is another proof that he did not use Hellenistic writings, and as for Berosus, the authenticity of his authorship is open to great doubt. Abraham's knowledge of astronomy, etc. has already been discussed.

"The fame of his wife's beauty was greatly talked of" (Ant. I. 8. 1. 163). "The women saw Sarah and told their husbands of her beauty, who told the king," (As. VI, 13)

The various incidents in Asatir Ch. VIII concerning Pharaoh and Sarah, the specific illness with which Pharaoh is smitten, also Abraham discussing with the priest, see p. 33

It is at least surprising that Josephus should also have been led into confusing the two incidents of Abraham's experience in Egypt and that among the Philistines, in the way he describes it here. Although he mentions afterwards also the incident of Abraham with Abimelech, still he agrees in the former case with Pseudo-Eupolemos and the Asatir. What better proof is there that Josephus did not take his inspiration from the text of the Bible, but that he introduced into his narrative in the most uncritical manner such a legendary combination of two independent incidents? The Asatir as well as Pseudo-Eupolemos offers direct parallels. Josephus may have taken it from the same source as the latter who was a Palestinian writer.

"(Abraham) fell upon the Assyrians near Dan," (Ant. I. 10. 1. 176). Josephus describes this as a spring of the Jordan, but here his geography seems to be wrong. He wishes to combine the name mentioned in the Bible with the Agadic interpretation. In the Asatir "Dan" is not mentioned; but a full description is given of the place reached by Abraham, who comes to the mountains near Kenaret (VII, 13), the lake Genesaret, which is one of the sources of the Jordan.

Josephus here gives two dates not found in the Bible. "On the fifth night he fell upon the Assyrians," and then (ibid 178) — "On the second day he drove them into Hoba." Josephus has evidently confused the meaning of the dates in the text. The "fifth" is either a corruption for the "first" night, i. e., the night of the Sunday, or he has taken the same date as that found in the Asatir, "the fifth" meaning "Thursday," when Abraham returned victorious to Salem (As. VII, 17). "On the second day" is evidently nothing else but the "second" of the Asatir, meaning the Monday (VII, 15). It must be remembered that these are dates of the week and not dates of the month. This is an absolutely decisive proof of the close parallelism between the two, for these numbers could not have been invented independently of one another. On the other hand, Josephus here definitely differs from the Samaritans, by making Salem Jerusalem instead of Sichem (Ant. I. 10. 2. 180).

"Whilst they were feasting," (Ant. I. 10. 2. 181). This agrees absolutely with the Asatir (VII, 19), while none of these events are found in the Bible.

"They (the children of Ishmael) inhabited all the country from Euphrates to the Red Sea, and called it

Nabatene," (Ant. I. 12. 4. 221). This geographical interpretation by Josephus of Gen. XXV, 18 agrees in almost every detail with Asatir (VIII, 23) and shows the prominence given to the Nebaim, after whom, according to Josephus, the whole country was called Nabaoth. This is quite different from the Samaritan Targum which follows the Biblical text.

In the Asatir, the story now passes on rapidly from Abraham to Moses. The stories of Isaac, Jacob and the children of Israel offered very little for legendary development. Josephus also keeps more closely to the text of the Bible, without much legendary addition. With the Samaritans Moses is the hero and centre of the Biblical narrative. For his sake the world was created and many legends and wonders were connected with him even from before the day of his birth.

"The crown (of Egypt) now being come into another family," (Ant. II. 9. 1. 202). Here Josephus explains Exod. I. 8 that the kingdom passed to another family. Asatir (VIII, 14) not only gives the same interpretation of the text but, as usual, is more definite and precise in the details. The LXX translates the verse "And there arose another king," instead of "a new king," in the Hebrew text. The same tradition is also mentioned much later on in the Tr. Sotah fol. XIa, Erubim fol. 53a.

Departing from the brief account in the Bible of the birth of Moses, Josephus has written a romance full of wonderful details. The parallelism between his version and the later Hebrew legends, such as are found in the socalled Chronicles of Moses, the older version of which has been published by me in the Chronicles of Jeraḥmeel, has been noted by various scholars, but Freudenthal in his "Hellenistische Studien" (p. 169ff.) has endeavoured to establish a close connection between the narrative of Josephus and the fabulous romance of Artapanos, as preserved by Eusebius. We are thus again brought face to face with the different ancient Jewish-Hellenistic writings, and it is therefore necessary to establish the relation in which they stand to one another.

Artapanos, according to Freudenthal, is older than Eupolemos, and belongs therefore at the latest to the middle or end of the third century B.C. Freudenthal has pointed out certain similarities in the story as told by Josephus and the romance of Artapanos. On minute examination, however, it will be found that these similarities can be reduced to very few and even Freudenthal (p. 170) was compelled to admit that between Josephus and Artapanos there must have been some modified version by a Jewish writer. It is much more plausible, however, to assume that Artapanos like other writers of his kind, used more ancient Jewish material for the making up of his own fabulous story. Thus the similarity of some details between Josephus and Artapanos should be traced to a more ancient source or to one accessible to both, of which each made use in his own way. Artapanos makes Moses, in fact, one of the gods of Egypt, Hermes-Thoth, and even the founder of the worship of Isis. Josephus shrinks with pious horror from such an idea; to him Moses is the wonderful leader of the people, chosen by God for that purpose.

The parallelism between Josephus and ancient Hebrew writings concerning the birth of Moses is very much closer, and yet some of the very specific details which characterise the narrative of Josephus are missing in the Hebrew versions. If we now turn to the Asatir and to the Samaritan traditions,—and there are a number of writings in the Samaritan literature hitherto unknown, full of legendary matter concerning the birth of Moses and his further exploits,—the parallelism is very striking. Going on now step by step, we find the following passage in Josephus (Ant. II. 9. 2. 205):

"One of those sacred scribes who are very sagacious in foretelling future events truly, told the king, that about this time there would be born a child to the Israelites who, if he were reared, would bring the Egyptian dominion low, and would raise the Israelites; that he would excel all men in virtue, and obtain a glory that would be remembered through all ages." We must remember that Josephus always prefers vagueness, whilst the Samaritans are much more definite in detail. Josephus speaks of a scribe, whilst in the Asatir (ch. VIII, 24 ff.) not only do we learn who the scribe was, but also what was the sight which induced him to make that prophecy and to foretell to the king what would happen. There he sees Amram and the honour paid to him, and he foretells the future in almost the same words as those used by Josephus (Ant. II. 9. 2. 207). In Josephus the king commands that the parents should be destroyed with their children, but in the Asatir (VIII, 42), the women throw themselves (into the water) with their children.

There have also been preserved in the Samaritan literature other traditions concerning the birth of Moses, which go back to very high antiquity. They have been embodied in various writings, referred to more fully later on, such as the poem called the Molad Moshe ascribed to Abdalla b. Shalma, who lived about the fourteenth century. The author explains that he has derived his material from the tradition of the high priests. Another poem by him, containing similar traditions, forms part of the service for the Sabbath during the Tabernacle festival (Cowley, Samaritan Liturgy, p. 746).

The first part of the poem agrees in the main with the Asatir, but adds a few details; amongst them that Amram approaches his wife only after an angel has appeared to him in a vision of the night. He is told that the child to be born is one which will obtain glory and which will be remembered throughout the ages.

The same is found in other Samaritan poems of the fourteenth century, and still more in the Arabic treatise of

Ishmael Rumihi (1537), which is also called Molad Moshe. In all the details they agree with the Asatir: that the scribe Plti, through seeing Amram, recognizes that a child will be born from the loins of that man, who will bring destruction ot the kingdom of Egypt and who will obtain glory and be "remembered throughout the ages." These very words used by Josephus are thus found not only in the Asatir but in the whole cycle of Samaritan writings referring to Moses, and have almost become a stereotyped phrase. Already Markaḥ (of the second or third century C. E.) uses the same phrase, "May his name be remembered for glory *'leolam.'* " This word must be translated "throughout the world" and not "for ever," and so it is repeated in the various Samaritan writings to which reference will be made later on in the chapter on the Asatir and the Samaritan literature.

Ant. II. 9. 5. 226 "(Moses) would not admit of her breast but turned away from it." The same tradition is also found in the Pitron and Molad and other books, and also indicated in the Asatir (IX. 13) by the words "He would only drink of the undefiled milk."

Ant. II. 9. 6. 229. Moses as the seventh generation from Abraham is a distinct feature of Samaritan chronology.

Examining now the rest of the story of Moses with the Asatir and the Samaritan tradition, we find no trace in the latter of the other incidents narrated by Josephus, such as the trampling upon the king's crown and his expedition against the Ethiopians and his subsequent marriage. In the Jewish literature these incidents are fully developed, for they are also an outgrowth of the same exegetical activity, which caused many legends to be invented in order to explain various difficult passages in the text of the Bible. They are, no doubt, later developments, and even Josephus has not recorded them in full; for he leaves out one of the chief reasons for the legend that Moses, while a child, took off the crown of Pharaoh and trampled upon it, and what befell him afterwards. The origin of this legend is to be sought in an attempt to explain how it came about that Moses was heavy of tongue. The Jewish legend goes on to say that when the scribe or sorcerer saw the incident, he advised Pharaoh to have the child killed, but an angel assumed the form of another courtier and suggested that the child should be put to the test of placing before it two plates, one containing burning charcoal and the other sparkling gems. The angel then made the child stretch its hand out towards the coal und put it into its mouth and thus burn its lips.

The story of the Ethiopian war is told to explain the passage in Numbers XII, 1 when Aaron and Miriam complain of Moses having married the Kushite wife. It would be difficult to say how old these legends were. They are independent of Artapanos and may be posterior to the time of the composition of the Asatir. It is also possible, that no Samaritan would introduce into his legendary lore a story which so greatly affected the honour and glory of Moses, for whose sake the world had been created: he was the most perfect of men and a priest among the angels. He could not be described as having any blemish, either physical or moral, and thus nothing that could have detracted from his glory would have found acceptance among the Samaritans. It is clear that Josephus could not even have seen Artapanos' writings, who like the Sibyl, made use of a Palestinian Midrash in a synchretistic manner and wove out of it a romance, which differs in almost every detail from those recorded by the Asatir, Josephus, and the entire Samaritan and Jewish literature. Josephus paraphrases "heavy of speech" by "man of no ability," probably for the same reason as the Samaritans (Ant. II. 12. 2. 271).

The comparison between these various texts brings out still more clearly the fact that Josephus, on the whole, adheres more closely to the Hebrew text, and is in part a

translation and in part contains legendary additions
But he shows at the same time a further stage in the development of that tendency which has its origin in the purely homiletic and Midrashic exegesis of the synagogue. The further the legends depart from the Hebrew text and assume an independent character, the later is the date of the compilation.

Ant. III. 10. 5. 248, 249. Here Josephus seems to differentiate between the Feast of the Passover, which is celebrated on the 14th of Nisan, and the Feast of Unleavened Bread, which, he says, "succeeds it" quite in accordance with Samaritan interpretation, which also differentiates between the Passover and the Feast of Unleavened Bread, which succeeds the former, but is independent.*

The story of Bileam is told by Josephus at very great length; he not only repeats the narrative of the Bible but enlarges upon it considerably, introducing into it many details of a legendary character, at the same time attempting to smoothe away difficulties found in the text of the Bible. Not a few of these attempts are also found in the Asatir, where again the story of the Bible has been developed in a very extraordinary manner, owing to influences to which attention will be directed later on, but of these only a few of the most important points may be considered here.

Ant. IV. 6. 2. 102; cf. Asatir X. 42, where the Midianites call upon Bileam to save them from Israel.

Ant. IV. 6. 2. 105 "willing and desirous to comply with their request," cf. Asatir X. 2, where the text is somewhat obscure.

The whole story of the stratagem of Bileam to encompass the destruction of Israel through the daughters of Moab,

* This explains a command of Hillel (Haggada, special service for Passover night) which hitherto has remained a mystery: to the effect that the Passover lamb must be eaten together with the unleavened bread and bitter herbs. It was meant to be a direct protest against the Samaritan teaching and practice.

which is given so very fully in Josephus, is in its main incidents identical with the story in the Asatir, whereas in the Samaritan Arabic Book of Joshua the whole story of Bileam and all the incidents with the daughters of Moab is told much more fully. It agrees with the version of Josephus. This is of no mean importance, since Josephus also agrees with many other details contained in that version of the Book of Joshua, not only according to the text published by Joynbull, Ch. III and IV, but still more in the other recension found in my MSS. The Arabic version which dates at the latest from the eleventh or twelfth century was made from a Hebrew original, and that Hebrew text draws its material almost verbatim from a version of the Asatir, which at that time was a little more expanded than our present text. But most of the passages agree literally with our text, and contain a few more details which are now missing in the Asatir, but which are found both in Josephus and in the Samaritan Arabic Book of Joshua. The Palestinian Targum to Numb. XXIV, 14 also contains a very brief parallel to the advice given by Bileam to Balak concerning the Midianite women.

It is noticeable that Josephus has a peculiar description of the death of Moses which reads almost like an epic poem, and which is considered to be due to his own literary skill in embellishing the simple narrative of the Bible. In the Asatir the death of Moses is just briefly touched upon (Ch. XI, 18), but in the Samaritan literature a description has been preserved which approximates very closely the version of Josephus. I have printed it on p. 303 from my Cod. No. 1168. The date of the composition of this chronicle is uncertain, but it is, like all the Samaritan chronicles, a mixture of older and more recent material. It contains also the Book of Joshua, to which this chapter forms an introduction, and it is found not only in the Arabic version of the Book of Joshua, but can be traced much farther back (see p. 178—179). This story, then, occurs also in my Cod. 876, a composition probably of the thirteenth century, a in slightly more archaic form, inasmuch as angels are introduced accompanying Moses up the mount and burying him.

If we compare this epic description of the death of Moses with those in other pseudepigraphic writings, we shall find that it differs very considerably from the latter in description and detail. The Hebrew legends lay stress on Moses' ascent to heaven, whilst the tale found in the Assumption of Moses lacks practically all the characteristics of Josephus and of the Samaritan version of the "Death." It is similar to some extent to the Asatir itself, inasmuch as it also contains a prophecy of the events to follow after the death of Moses. On the other hand, Pseudo-Philo keeps the balance between the two. In some sentences it agrees with the Samaritan description of the death of Moses, and it also contains a summary prophecy; but both belong to a later period. They have already been used for propagating certain eschatological views, and ideas of a very late date have been introduced into the prophecy of Moses.

But the version published here can be traced still further back, since it occurs in almost every detail in the last book of Markah, "The Book of Wonders." The author lived in the second or third century. The tradition has thus been most faithfully preserved, and Markah on his part shows his indebtedness to an older source—probably to a more extended form of the Asatir—for he shows undoubted acquaintance with the whole book, and quotes the characteristic sentence with which God adresses Moses, announcing to him that the day of his death has arrived. This proves the contention that the Samaritan chronicles, though compiled at a later age, contain much material that is very old and reliable. They invent nothing.

Further parallels to Samaritan traditions occur in various parts of Josephus' description of the Biblical period from the Creation to the death of Moses. Besides those already referred to above, there is, e. g. Moses' allocution at the account of the revelation on Mount Sinai (Ant. III. 5. 3. 86—87). This passage finds a complete parallel in Brit. Mus. Orient. 5481 where all the Patriarchs are mentioned from Adam onwards, and introduced with the formula, "He who saved Noah from the Flood, etc. He who saved....." There is a late parallel in the Jewish Liturgy in the poem on the Day of Atonement: "He who answered," (Gaster, Sephardic Prayer Book, Day of Atonement Vol. III. p. 12). But more specific, as has been pointed out, is the parallelism between Josephus and the Samaritan Book of Joshua, published by me.

These numerous coincidences cannot be simply fortuitous. Josephus invented them as little as did the author of the Asatir or the authors of other writings such as the Palestinian Targum or Samaritan texts. Nor is it likely to assume that the one borrowed directly from the other. As already suggested before, the Asatir is older by at least two centuries than Josephus, and Josephus would be the last to borrow anything direct from the hated Samaritans. They point to an older source common to both from which they have drawn their material, which was the result of the Midrashic Agadic interpretation of the Pentateuch which flourished throughout Palestine, in all probability in the North as well as in the South. It was the common property of Jews and Samaritans alike. This is why some of the incidents referred to are found scattered throughout the various writings of a later age.

The unexpected result of this investigation is to place Josephus' activity in a new light. The Antiquities, far from being a somewhat enlarged recount of the Pentateuch, resting, as has hitherto been assumed, exclusively on the Hebrew text, is nothing else but an enlarged Targum in Greek of the Pentateuch, drawing its information from Aramaic paraphrases and collections of Biblical legends. Of these the Asatir is a Samaritan representative, thus far the oldest hitherto available. It has still retained the primitive Midrashic character. It consists of the legendary matter only, and is not yet woven into a running commentary accompanying the Hebrew text. The Palestinian Targum has already reached this secondary stage of development, but in Josephus we have an independent work in which the author no longer follows the original scrupulously word for word and verse for verse. It is a consecutive narrative of the Biblical story in which facts and legends have been skilfully blended.

THE PALESTINIAN TARGUM.

The basic principle laid down at the beginning of this investigation that the Midrashic interpretation which clings to the text of the Bible is older than any such Midrashic commentary which departs from it, is further corroborated by the comparison between the Asatir and the Palestinian Targum. Here we have a complete translation of the text, following it word for word; but at the same time a large amount of legendary matter and legal interpretation of the prescriptions found in the text has been added. It is all kept within a comparatively limited compass; the language is purely Palestinian, but like other works of a similar kind it has suffered greatly by changes and interpolations which have been freely introduced into any such book which serves a popular purpose. It is of an educational and at the same time of a polemical character, inasmuch as the author eliminates practically every other interpretation of the text but the purely Jewish. In its legal interpretations this Targum represents very old traditions. Zunz* who has studied this Targum, recognizes

* Die gottesdienstlichen Vorträge der Juden. 2nd ed. Frankfurt a. M. 1892. p. 76 ff.

that in spite of the many alterations and modifications to which it has been subjected, the author has retained some very ancient elements, and that in addition to its being a free paraphrase, the author has also introduced a mass of legendary matter not of his own invention, for which parallels can also be found in later literature. Yet in spite of it, Zunz assigns the book in its present form to the middle of the seventh century. This view rests on a misconception of the character of this anonymous literature. It is due to late interpolations in that MS. from which our text has been printed; his argument that the name of Constantine (i. e. Constantinople)—itself not a very modern name—is mentioned, and that other similar changes of geographical and personal names appear, cannot be taken very seriously. Geiger, however, who had a keener insight into the spiritual forces and sectarian movements at a very early period, emphatically declares in his "Urschrift," for the very high antiquity of this Targum. He asserts that a large mass of extremely ancient material has been preserved in this Targum (ibid. p. 165). Frankel (Einfluss, p. 3ff.), when studying the influence of the Palestinian exegesis on Hellenistic interpretation of the Bible, takes it for granted that such Midrashic or rather Targumistic activity had already existed in Palestine during the early Hellenistic period, and was anterior to the Greek translation of the LXX. He thus clearly assumes the existence of such a Targum in a written form, as otherwise it could not exercise any influence upon a Greek-speaking and -writing author. It is therefore utterly impossible to accept a late date for the Palestinian Targum.

There is now another proof for the high antiquity of the Palestinian Targum, in the fact that already at the beginning of the second century C. E. it was looked upon with serious misgivings by the leading Jewish authorities. So much so, that another Targum was then prepared, which received the official sanction of R. Akiba and his school, and which has hence ever since been regularly associated with the Hebrew text. The number of Biblical MSS. which contain the Hebrew with the Targum known as that of Onkelos is overwhelming, whilst the MSS. hitherto discovered of the complete and fragmentary Palestinian Targum scarcely exceed six in number, some consisting only of a few leaves; in fact the existing text was printed for the first time in Venice in 1591 from an unique MS. and the fragmentary recension which appeared before in the Rabbinic Bible, Venice 1517, also from another unique MS.

The reason for this thorough revision goes to the very root of the matter. Akiba was engaged in preparing with the assistance of his pupil Aquilas a revised Greek translation of the Pentateuch. It was not directed, as hitherto assumed, only against the LXX, which by that time had already been greatly corrupted; but it was intended also to counteract the influence of the Greek Samaritan translation: it was to discredit, as far as possible, any legal interpretation of the text other than the one sanctioned by his school. It was to embody the new principle of exegesis which was evolved in accordance with the doctrine of the synagogue. Every admixture of Agadic or Midrashic element, and still more of such translations in which the LXX seems to have agreed with the Samaritan, had to be entirely erased. Akiba and his school were then guided by the same principles in practically eliminating from the service also the popular Aramaic paraphrase, which in its Midrashic portions lays itself open to misinterpretations, and in some instances seems to favour older and independent interpretations now discarded by that school. Here we have, as Geiger (op. cit p. 163 ff.) has also pointed out the reason for so thorough a revision of the older Targum, which was then replaced by quite new texts intended to serve the interests of the synagogue, no longer open to misinterpretation or capable of being used by Samaritans and other sectarians in their polemics against the Jews. The Samaritans, or as they were then called, the Kutheans, loomed largely at that time before the eyes of the Jews, who were preparing for the great fight of liberation, in which the Samaritans took an attitude by no means friendly to them. Thus we have on the one side LXX, Greek-Samaritan, and possibly Greek paraphrastic commentaries reflected in the Hellenistic literature and in Josephus, and on the other side Aquilas, Theodotion and others who follow the same principles of literary exegesis; then the Midrashic Targum, Hebrew and possibly Samaritan such as the Asatir on the one hand, and on the other, the Targum of Onkelos, in which scarcely a trace of the Midrash has been retained, and the interpretation of the text is as literal as possible and quite in harmony with the legal exegesis of the school of Akiba. There was no intention of suppressing the legends which had grown out of the text in the course of centuries; they had become the common property of the people, and they flourished as independent Midrashim, Agadoth and Maasiyot, to an even larger extent than before; and these are the sources of the whole literature of Apocrypha and Pseudepigrapha. These were now no longer considered as direct commentaries to the text of the Bible. They became the homilies delivered in the synagogues in connection with the reading of the Law. The preacher took his text from a verse of the Bible and then developed the subject freely so as to satisfy the popular demand. Thus arose the large collections known as the Rabboth (Collectio Maxima) and the Pesiktot, i. e. homilies for selected days and occasions. At that time there was no longer any need for such a comparatively simple Targum, and that is probably one of the reasons why it was almost lost. Add to this the peculiar Palestinian dialect of the Aramaic in which it was written, and we see why it remained circumscribed in its circulation, and shared the fate of the Palestinian Talmud, which also was also almost forgotten and preserved in one single incomplete MS. The language is practically the same as the Samaritan. Far, therefore, from being a late composition, this Palestinian Targum must rank as the oldest of its kind and be placed either as a contemporary of Josephus or even of a somewhat earlier date. This conclusion is borne out by the fact that we find in the Palestinian Targum traces of pre-Massoretic readings agreeing with the LXX and the Samaritan, such as the addition in Genesis Ch. IV v. 8, and many other examples. Still more is this the fact when comparing the Palestinian Targum with the Asatir. The agreement between these two Midrashim of the Pentateuch is very close indeed. The notes to the translation of the Asatir will give ample evidence of the thorough parallelism which runs through both; it extends to many minute details, and yet, whilst agreeing in the main, they differ so completely from one another as to prove their mutual independence. They both go back, no doubt, to older sources common to both and they are both expressions of that Midrashic Palestinian exegesis which must have flourished in the country and developed in the vernacular Aramaic common to all the inhabitants of Palestine. Of the numerous parallels between the Asatir and the Palestinian Targum, a few may be cited here.

Twins born with Cain and Abel. Gen. IV, 2. Asatir I. 3.

Date and Place of Sacrifice. Gen. IV. 3 and VIII. 20. Asatir I. 7.

Different Name of Mountain for Ark. Gen. VIII. 4. Asatir IV. 1.

Abraham and Nimrod. XI. 285. Asatir V. 16 ff. Death of Haran. Gen. XI. 28. Asatir V. 28.

Moses Legend. Asatir VIII. 24 ff.; (Wizard foretelling birth of Moses.) Exod. I. 15. Two magicians foretell birth.

Daughter of Pharaoh healed. Exod. II. 5. Pitron. Ch. IX. 9.

Three supreme mornings; four supreme nights Exod. XIII. 42. Asatir IX. 35 ff.

Miracles of Pineḥas Numb. XXV. 8. Asatir X. 33.

Death of Bileam Numb. XXI. 8. Asatir X. 47.

Bileam's evil advice about the daughters of Moab. Numb. XXIV. 14. Asatir X. 18 ff.

Bileam=Laban. Numb. XXII. 5. Asatir XI. 1.

Interpretation of Bileam prophecies (see later on p. 88—90).

Moses Redivivus (see later on p. 97—98).

Besides these agreements there are some points which require fuller treatment.

First special attention is paid to the institution of the Calendar. It is traced back to Genesis, I. 14. It is here set forth fully and runs as follows:

".... and let them be for signs and for festival times, and for the numbering by them the account of days, and for the sanctifying of the beginning of months, and for the beginning of years, the passing away of months, and the passing away of years, the revolutions of the sun, the birth of the moon, and the revolvings (of seasons)."

It is thereby made clear, that the institution of the Calendar in all its details dates from the fourth day of Creation, a point of view with which the Samaritans fully agree. But they add that this knowledge of calculating and fixing the Calendar was revealed to Adam, and thus the counting of years found in the Biblical record starts with Adam. To them, the Creation of the world took place in Nisan, which was the older view among the Jews, against which Palestinian Targum, Gen. VII. 11 declares that the Creation of the world began in the month of Tishri. It will be seen later on when discussing the chronology of the Asatir, what far-reaching importance has been attached to the

Calendar so that it even became a line of cleavage between Jews and Samaritans (referred to above).

We find further in the Palestinian Targum to Deut. Ch. XXXIV, v. 2 ff. a vision seen by Moses from the top of Mount Nebo, in which the future events from the time of Joshua to the final victory over the armies of Gog and Magog and over Armilos, in which the Jews are helped by the angel Michael, are summarily described. It differs from the more vague eschatological interpretation which turns round the prophecies of Bileam, in so far as some of the chief judges and kings are mentioned here by name. This prophecy represents an historical sketch which can easily be verified from the subsequent events, up to a certain point. It loses itself in the indefinite description of the wars of Gog, etc. Slightly different, but not in any essential is the parallel recension in the old Tanaitic commentary to Deuteronomy (second or third century) which goes under the name of Sifre (Piska 357). On many occasion there is a strong affinity between the Sifre and the Palestinian Targum. The Asatir then finishes also with the Prophecy (XI, 20 ff.) which has the same aim, viz. to reveal the future; here also that future is unmistakably described by a series of events in a more precise historical sequence from the death of Moses to a final era of general happiness. The chief figures of Jewish history are all mentioned one after the other the names being veiled by cryptograms and yet sufficiently clear to recognize in them the names of the judges and kings, the building and destruction of the temples, and the exiles and returns according to Samaritan tradition. Ezra is also mentioned (Asatir XI, 36, 37). After this a vague allusion to the time of trouble and ultimate success is appended. It is much simpler and more systematically arranged than in the Palestinian Targum, and it is a bitter pronouncement of hatred and invective against the Jews. In principle the two prophecies run parallel, but each sect uses the occasion according to its own religious standpoint. If we then compare these prophecies with those found in the apocalyptic literature such as the Assumption of Moses (Ch. II, 1 ff.), the prophecy in the Book of Enoch (Ch. LXXXIII ff.) with its allegorical and symbolical figures, the introduction to the Book of Jubilees (Ch. XXIII, 18 ff.) and the prophecy of Pseudo-Philo (Ch. XIX ff.), we can easily recognise that these have entirely departed from the ancient form. These prophecies have been made to subserve a totally different purpose: they are more or less made to point a lesson depicting current events to contemporaries, and the ancient Biblical history becomes a mere shadowy background for the new picture which is now drawn. Thus the Asatir stands at the beginning of that series of prophecies ascribed to Moses.

I now pass on to the consideration of the relation of the last portion of the Asatir, the Oracle of Ch. XII to the Palestinian Targum. I have briefly referred to it before, where I pointed out the parallelism between this oracle and the cycle of the Tiburtine, Methodius, etc. This oracle refers to the events which are to happen at the End of Days. We are dealing here with that period which was afterwards known as the Messianic age. True, there is no eschatology, no mention of the Day of Judgment or Resurrection; only the prophecy that a man chosen by God will return, who is to inaugurate an era of happiness and prosperity. It is unquestionably the most primitive form and represents the Messianic idea in its embryonic state. How far-reaching that idea has been need not be emphasized here. It is written large in the pages of human civilization, and it is not my desire to dwell upon it at any length. It would lead me too far away from the immediate object of this research. But it is of no mean importance to be able to trace it back to its obscure beginnings. It is again in the light of the Midrashic exegesis of the Bible that one may be able to detect the *Pentateuchal* source. The foundations of this belief are not to be sought in the writings of the prophets but must have had their origin in some words or allusions in the Pentateuch; otherwise it could not have been taken up by the Samaritans and have taken there such deep roots as it has done. A careful examination of all the dates available leads to the surprising result that the ultimate sources in the Pentateuch are the prophecies of Bileam, and that a special importance has been attached to Bileam's personality and activity. It has been mentioned before that both in the Asatir (X. 1) and in the Palestinian Targum (Numb. XXII, 5) he is identified with Laban. The significance of this identification will soon become manifest.

From very ancient times the figure and prophecies of Bileam have exercised a deep influence upon Israel. References to him occur in many passages of the Bible, such as Deut. XXIII. 5; Josh. XXIV. 9; Mic. VI. 5; Nehem. XIII. 2; furthermore in the New Testament: 2 Peter II. 15; Jude XI. Revel. II. 14. Quotations from his prophecies (Numb. XXIV. 17) are repeated by Jeremiah (XLVIII. 45/6) and others; and finally a passage in Daniel XI. 30, where Numb. XXIV. 24 is quoted with the same meaning as given to it by Bileam, shows the continued preservation of Bileam and his prophecies in the memory of the people. He becomes the typical antagonist of Israel and he works constantly for its destruction. Jews and Samaritans agree to read the future in his prophecies, but they agree also in the detestation of his person and his works. A kind of saga has been formed round him and, as will be seen, he assumes a most unexpected form in their religious traditions. In the Oracle we can now trace some of that influence and here the Palestinian Targum in its two recensions (A and B) will prove of special importance. Numb. XXIV. 17. "I see him but not now, I behold him but not near" is commented upon it as follows (A) "that there will reign a mighty king from the house of Jacob, and there will be exalted the Messiah and a mighty rod from Israel, and he will kill the rulers of the Moabites and bring to nought all the children of Seth yea, as well as the hosts of Gog that are in array to do battle against Israel and all their carcases shall fall before him (the Messiah)."

(B) "I see him but not now, I behold him but he is not nigh. A king will arise in the future from the house of Jacob, a deliverer and ruler from the house of Israel, who will slay the strong ones of the Moabites and will annihilate and destroy the peoples of the East."

The same interpretation of the verse is found also in Onkelos who translates: ". . . there will arise a king from Jacob and there will be exalted the Messiah (i. e. the anointed, the Christos) of Israel and he will slay the mighty of Moab and he will rule over all men."

Numb. XXIV. 18. (A) "And there will be driven out the Edomites and there will be driven out the sons of Gabala from before Israel their foes, and Israel will be strengthened with their riches and inherit them."

(B) "And the portion of his inheritance will be the mountain of Gabala of their enemies, and Israel will be strong with a mighty host."

v. 19. A) "And a prince of the house of Jacob will arise and destroy and consume the remnant that have escaped from (Constantina) the guilty city and will lay waste and ruin the rebellious city, even Ḳaisarin, the strong city of the Gentiles."

B) "A king will arise from the house of Jacob who will destroy the remnant of the wicked city."

This is thus far the oldest application of the words of Bileam to the idea of a future ruler who will arise from Jacob and Israel. It may be noted in passing the astrological lore has not yet been developed, nay, a different meaning altogether is given to it in the Asatir X. 45

by the "star" being applied to Pinehas. The Messianic import of the whole prophecy has been developed still more in some later Samaritan treatises, like that of El Doweik and others. In the Jewish tradition the Messiah is actually compared with the star, but the rise of a star does not signalize his birth. Akiba applied this prophecy to Bar Kochba, not at his birth, but after his valiant deeds; (T. J.Taanith IV, 5). At a later stage in the Midrash, however, the birth of Abraham is signalised by such a rising of a star, and similarly at the birth of Jesus.*
The Messianic expectation of the ruler, however, was deduced from this prophecy of Bileam. Here we have all the elements necessary for the elucidation of the last portion of the Asatir. So important did these passages appear to the author of the Oracle that in one or two instances he preserved even the Hebrew words of the original, thus leaving no doubt of the connection between this Oracle and the words of Bileam in the Bible. In the Oracle nothing else is evidently expected than first, some trouble with Gog, some invasion on his part, and then some serious wars, which are here described (XII, 21) with the very words of Numb. XXIV, 18, whilst Gog appears also in the Targum to ibid v. 17.

The mention of Gog now is of special importance. Whence did the author of the Asatir obtain a knowledge of the name of Gog, considering that that name never occurs in the Pentateuch — and it is well-known that the range of the knowledge of the Samaritans never went beyond that of the Pentateuch? Still more surprising is it then to find Gog here in connection with troubles of the end of time. But a careful examination of the Samaritan recension of the Pentateuch will solve the mystery. We must first turn now to another prophecy of Bileam: Numb. XXIV. 7. Here the Samaritan reads Gog instead of Agag

* v. Wiener, Realwörterbuch II. p. 524; Strack and Billerbeck, Kommentar N. T. Vol. I (Mathäus), p. 76-77.

in the M. T. This reading is corroborated by that of the LXX, which has also replaced Agag by Gog, and by the way it is inserted under the form of Gog by the LXX, Numb. XXIV, 23; and it may thus help to explain the use which has been made of it by the prophet Ezekiel.* Frankel (Einfluss p. 182 ff.) has rightly drawn attention to this interpretation in the LXX, in which he recognises the effect of Messianic anticipations connected with the prophecy of Bileam. This form of Messianic hope in the LXX, as well as in the Asatir, represents unquestionably the oldest phase of that belief, for it clings closely still to the text. This is the only standard by which Biblical legends can be measured according to age and origin. Frankel and those who followed him, being under the impression that the LXX was of Egyptian origin, believed this Messianic interpretation of the Biblical text to have been adopted and developed in Palestine at a much later time subsequent to the LXX. But the whole apocryphal literature is an eloquent testimony to the existence of such beliefs in a very early time in Palestine. The Samaritans also cherished such beliefs in very early times. They expected the advent of a Messiah or a Taheb, as did the Jews, and the Samaritan woman meeting Jesus speaks plainly of this expectation of a Messiah (John IV, 25). And they also derived this belief from the same passages in the prophecy of Bileam. Among the latest to testify to this interpretation, which runs through the whole Samaritan literature (Merx, Taheb), I quote the letter of the High Priest to Huntingdon in 1671 ed. Schnurrer, Eichhorn Repertorium, IX, 1781, p. 27 and de Sacy, Notices et Extraits, p. 198 ff), who refers to the coming Messiah as the one predicted by this prophecy. But his coming is to be preceded by troubles and wars, from which Israel will issue victoriously. These wars and troubles are derived

* It is significant in this connection that Gog is introduced in an eschatological sense in the rendering of the LXX of Amos VII, 2.

from similar prophecies, in the first place, in the above mentioned reference to Gog, which as Frankel has pointed out, was brought here into close connection with the Messianic expectations. Gog appears here both in the Samaritan recension of Numbers XXIV. 7 and in the Asatir. This is not the place to discuss the possibility of the prophet Ezekiel having also read in his Pentateuch Gog instead of Agag. It belongs to the wider problem concerning the background of the prophecies of Ezekiel. Gog together with Magog already appears in the Sibylline Oracles III. 319 as the adversary to be annihilated before the Messianic age.* The description differs considerably from that given in Ezekiel XXXVIII and XXXIX although the origin of this portion of the Sibyl is to be traced back to Ezekiel. These ideas have been greatly developed and exaggerated in the pseudepigraphic literature and worked into the Antichrist legends, to which reference will presently be made.

In the Asatir, there is still another close parallelism with the Palestinian Targum in the mention of "Gabala" in Ch. XII v. 21, where the destruction of Gabala is anticipated. This is exactly the same name which occurs in the Palestinian Targum as the translation of the Hebrew "Seir" (Numb. XXIV. 18). The subjugation of Edom and the occupation or destruction of Mount Gabala will be the outstanding signs of Israel's doing valiantly, as foretold by Bileam in that verse. Round this Gabala a whole literature has grown up,** but few have recognized its importance for these oracles connected with the Messianic Age. This interpretation and translation of "Seir" as "Gabala" is constant in the Samaritan Targum, with the one exception of this passage, where the Samaritan Targum substitutes "Esau," as is found also in the LXX.

* V. full parallel literature of Messianic woes, Bate, Sib. Or. ad loc.
** Josephus Antiq. II. 1.2.6. Gabalitis part of Idumea. This form agrees absolutely with the Samaritan form in Asatir.

This proves that the Asatir represents an older text than the present Samaritan Targum. The destruction of Gabala was one of the premonitory signs of the Advent of the Messiah. It recurs in the Talmud as one of the oldest traditions. R. Gamaliel II (first half of second century) is reported to have said "that before the Advent of the son of David ... Galilee will be deserted, Gabala destroyed and the men of Gaulan will wander from town to town." This tradition was handed down in numerous variations with many additions giving a full description of a complete state of demoralisation, of poverty or infamy, shamelessness and cruelty.*

From the above investigation, it is now clear that the stories of the Messianic Age and of the preceding periods of trouble and woe have their origin exclusively on the soil of Palestine, and flow directly from the Agadic interpretation of the prophecies of Bileam. The course of the Messianic troubles and woes is thus traced here directly to Gog, whose enmity against Israel is like that of Balak, the king of the Moabites, who, according to Numb. XXIV, 17 will be the first to suffer by the onslaught of Israel. It was natural at once to connect these

* This prophecy of R. Gameliel II of the destruction of Gabala, Gaulan, etc., is reported by R. Jehudah with further additional details in T. B. Sanhedrin 97a, where other signs premonitory to the advent of the son of David are given, full of awe-inspiring details. Slightly different is the recension in Derech Ereṣ Zutta ch. 10, by R. Simeon and again differing slightly in Midrash to Esther ch. 2. v. 13. Much fuller is the version put into the mouth of Eliezer of Mosin in the Mishna Sotah IX. 15. Wagenseil, Sotah, Altdorf 1674, p. 973, translates this passage differently and he refers to Pugio Fidei of Raymundus Martinus II. 37, c. 16, who has a different reading. The Jewish literature on these woes of the Messiah is best given by Hamburger, Realenzyklopaedie f. Bibel und Talmud, II, Leipzig 1883, p. 735ff. W. Bacher, Agadah der Tannaiten, Leipzig 1884, Vol. I, p. 97; Schürer, Gesch. d. Jüd. Volkes, etc., II, Leipzig 1886, p. 440ff.; Hühn, Die Messianischen Weissagungen des Israelitisch-Jüdischen Volks, Freiburg 1899; Weber, Jüdische Theologie, Leipzig 1897, p. 374ff. and finally Charles, Eschatology, London 1899, who has dealt exhaustively with the pseudepigraphic and Christian literature.

Messianic wars with Bileam, the false prophet and arch-enemy of Israel. He is supposed to lead the hostile army and he is the enemy of the Messiah. The Greek translation of the name of Bileam is ’Ερεμηλάος in accordance with the ancient Jewish interpretation already found in the Palestinian Targum. Numb. XXII. 5, where Bileam's name is explained as "Bal‘ + ‘am;" i. e. "the one who is destined to destroy the nation," (so also in Talmud Sanhedrin 105 b). This gives us a final solution of a problem which has hitherto baffled the scholars in their endeavour to explain the name "Armilos." It has nothing to do with "Romulus," but is simply the above-mentioned Greek translation of "Bileam" who, as I have endeavoured to show, is the sinister prototype of the Arch-enemy of Israel, the antagonist of the Messiah. "Armilos" occurs in the Targum to Isaiah XI. 4, ascribed to Jonathan, first century, in connection with the Messianic interpretation of that chapter, and in the Palestinian Targum Deut. XXXIV, 3, as the enemy who at the end of days will incite the nations against Israel and against the Messiah, who will be defeated by the latter.* The fact that this name occurs already in the Targum of Jonathan without any further explanation justifies the assumption that the name as well as the character of Armilos was already then widely known, and the people at once understood the whole implication which that name carried. The idea that it is an interpolation is not likely to prove correct, since it occurs in the old Codex Reuchlinianus under the form Armalogon as in the Palestinian Targum in the Editio Princeps (Venice 1517). I must, however, state that in some of the MSS. hailing from Yemen this word is missing. It is very likely that it has dropped

---

* After writing this I find that Prof. Graetz had suggested the identification of Bileam with Eremilaos (Levy s. v. Armilos) but has drawn no further conclusion and made no attempt to explain this identification, nor has anyone followed up this clue. My conjecture, however, of this identification is thereby corroborated.

out in a country where the reference to Armilos had lost its meaning, though not so in the West, where the word was still pregnant with deep significance. It recurs in all the legends connected with the Messiah, such as the Nistaroth of R. Simeon ben Yochai, Tefillath R. Simeon b. Yochai, Pirke Elijahu, or Pirke Mashiah, and in the Sefer Zerubabel, the latter in all probability the oldest and one which stands in some relation with Ezra IV. "Armilos" is also found in the Midrash Vayosha which, by the way, is a Midrash on the lesson of the seventh day of Passover, the Song of Moses (Ex. XIV), whilst the chapter of Isaiah in which the name of Armilos occurs, is the lesson from the prophets for the same day. Hence probably the Armilos legend in this Midrash; there is no better proof for the high antiquity of Armilos in the Targum, as otherwise no such name would have occurred on that occasion.*

The recognition of the identity of Armilos and Bileam was only possible after the foregoing investigation concerning the character with which Bileam had been invested in the course of time, when from a mere soothsayer hired for the purpose of cursing Israel, he had developed into the type of arch-heretic and arch-enemy. It is not a mere coincidence that both Bileam and Armilos are regularly called "the wicked ones." There occurs now in the Haggada (the Passover service) a peculiar sentence which seems straightforward, but which in the light of this comparison assumes a deeper meaning. Laban is mentioned there as the archenemy who wants to destroy the whole nation. No reason is to be found in the text of the Bible; but this reference may find a satisfactory solution if under the enigmatic name of Laban the people were reminded of Bileam, with whom he is identified by the legend, and so stands throughout the ages as the arch-enemy of the Jews, and of their

* Fuller literature: Ginzburg, Jewish Encyclopaedia Vol. II, p. 118, s. v. Armilos.

Messianic hopes; the latter which are intimately bound up with the Passover festival.

Thus the Armilos-Bileam Legend prepares the ground for the monstrous figure of the Antichrist; for just as he is to the Jews the enemy of their Messiah, so does he become in the eyes of the Christians first the source and instigator of the anti-Christian heresy, and then he is the Antichrist himself. Moreover, in a Jewish legend, Bileam is identified with Jesus, the latter being considered as a false Messiah, just as the Antichrist is the false Christian Messiah who claims to be the true one. Therefore in the N. T. times the apostles after the appearance of Christ stigmatised the claims of the sect of the followers of Bileam as preposterous and blasphemous. Later Christian writers easily enlarged upon that theme and thus the grotesque figure of the Antichrist as he appeared in the legends of later ages slowly took form. That the origin of the Antichrist Legend is an offspring of the Bileam legend is, as I believe, now fully substantiated. This result runs counter to the hypothetical solution attempted by Bousset and others.* One may hazard a conjecture that the Beliar (Sib. Oracles III, 64: v. Bate. Sib. Or. Lit. ad loc.) may be no one else than Bileam, whose name has been travestied to "Beliar" meaning "Evil Tempter" and "Wicked Sorcerer," although by some commentators he is identified with Simon Magus, Acts VIII. 9; but the description of that Simon fits entirely that of Bileam. The name appears also in the Ascensio

* Bousset, The Antichrist, trans. Keane London 1896, p. 121ff., who has collected a rich parallel literature from the Sibylline Oracles has been able to trace the Antichrist Legend of Methodius as far back as the writings of Ephrem Syrus of Nisibis (died 373) and to Jerome in Palestine (died 420). Bousset seems to have overlooked the Talmudic and Agadic literature although mentioned by others, but not in this connection. In consequence he has been led astray in his conclusions as to the origin of the Antichrist legend. Hühn has already disposed of his attempted identification of these troubles with the ancient Babylonian Tiamat or Dragon legend.

Jesaiae I. 8, and in the Testament of the XII Patriarchs (see Index II in Charles' edition, London, 1908). I have discovered that this name is used by the Samaritans for the designation of the Evil One who tempted Eve.

Bousset (loc. cit. p. 123 ff.) raises the very interesting point that "the one premonitory sign which recurs in nearly all the sources" is the fall of Rome. This contrasts curiously with the favourable disposition towards Rome displayed by the Fathers of the Church. Bousset cannot find sufficient explanation, but our text now gives this explanation. Whilst Gog is taken to represent the Greek Empire, after whose destruction the Messiah will come, Edom and the people of Gabala are mentioned in the Palestinian Targum as those with whom the war will have to be fought and with whose fall the victory of Israel will be complete. The LXX and Samaritan Hebrew, as already remarked, substitute "Esau" for "Seir." Now Esau and Edom were the old enemies of Israel. So we have here the ultimate source of the belief that the fall of Rome, i. e. Edom and Esau, must precede the fulfilment of the last words of Bileam's prophecy, Numb. XXIV. 19, which has been retained in the original Hebrew in the Asatir.

The picture of these eschatological events is rounded off by the Oracle (XII. 22). To this a close parallel is again found in the Palestinian Targum XXXIII. 21, which reads as follows: "... For there was a place (B. a place for a sepulchre) a place laid out with precious stones and pearls, where Moses the prophet (and scribe of Israel) was hidden (B. buried) who as he went in and out at the head of the people in this world, will go in and out in the world that cometh; because he wrought righteousness before the Lord and taught the orders of the judgments to the house of Israel his people." The two Targumim are practically identical, with the slight and yet not insignificant difference that in version A Moses is described as hidden, whilst in B he is buried. Here we have a complete parallel to the Samaritan doctrine of Moses Redivivus, he who will return at the end of days and go in and out at the head of the people. This doctrine differs entirely from the Jewish conception of the life and death of Moses and could only have been retained in the Palestinian Targum as the remnant of a very ancient legend when the Davidic origin of the Messiah had not yet taken deep root in the consciousness of the people, or at any rate had not yet met with universal acceptance. We find that strange doctrine already modified in the parallel passage of the Sifre ad loc., since it did not seem to agree any longer with current ideas.*

No room is left for doubt in the Asatir that Moses is meant. Stanza 24 of the Oracle, which follows, distinctly states that he will come and bring in his hand the Rod of Miracles, i. e., the wonder-working Rod of Moses. This is the sign of the genuine Messiah as already mentioned before on p. 55—56, which the Jews will ask of him who comes to them and demands their recognition. This close parallelism between the Asatir and the Palestinian Targum cannot be the result of mere coincidence, as it affects fundamental principles, and there is no apparent reason why such identical legendary interpretations should be deduced from the simple text of the Bible. All this points again to the fact that the Palestinian Targum and the Asatir have drawn from older sources common to both, i. e. the Midrashic exegesis of the Bible in Palestine. Yet, each one has used that midrashic material in his own way, independent of the other.

Attention may now be drawn to another survival of the Bileam legend in the Asatir; for at the time when the Asatir was composed Bileam was already regarded by the Samaritans as the chief sorcerer and wizard, the one who possessed magic powers; for we find in the

* Ed. Friedmann, Vienna 1864, par. 355, f. 147 b; see also T. B. Sotah f. 14 a.

prophecy one of the men described as "he who will use the witchcraft of Bileam," (XI. 30). According to my interpretation of the prophecy, this refers to King Solomon, differing from the anachronistic one given by the Samaritans, who apply it to Jesus (cf. Pitron ad. loc.). The importance of the application of the wizardry of Bileam to Solomon lies not only in the fact that we have here a survival of the continued consciousness of the part played by Bileam, but still more that it is the first reference made to Solomon in which he is described as a wizard using magic powers. It is in this character that he appears in all the legends of the East. He is master over the world of demons and performs many wonderful acts, almost as a magician. To the Samaritans, Solomon is not endowed with divine wisdom and power, as in the Jewish tradition, but on the contrary, acts like Bileam, and even introduces the worship of strange gods, for he is the builder of a vile temple. Thus the legend of Bileam continues to work and it furnishes us here with the key to the origin of the legends of Solomon, the magician of later literature.

THE ASATIR AND THE CYCLES OF UNIVERSAL SAGAS.

Having arrived so far, it will not be amiss if another survey is taken also of the various legends treated hitherto. Thus far my aim has been to discover, as far as possible, the probable date and origin of the Asatir, by comparing it more or less minutely with Hellenistic literature, with Josephus, the Palestinian Targum, and with the literature of Oracles of a later date. Important as these investigations may have been from a literary and historical point of view, they do not entirely exhaust the interest which these legends claim. On the contrary, by these investigations, they come into clearer relief. They take their place now in the greater world of myth and legend; not limited to one nation, but international. Certain primitive types now can be evolved for cycles of legends which are traceable from age to age. Each of them in its turn stands at the head of a long series of developments, and each of them has exercised an extraordinary influence upon the imagination of mankind in the whole western civilisation. Their real value, therefore, will lie in the fact that we have in these Samaritan legends the oldest prototypes, or, at any rate, the oldest yet recovered, for these different tales and legends.

(A) There is first the Nimrod Saga and the subsequent legend of the Universal King. This legend, which, as mentioned, is the starting-point of a whole series of similar conceptions of world-empires and world-rule, and of a king who in time even claims to be worshipped as a god, is found also in the Jewish literature. The ten kings who mark the ten periods of the world's existence are enumerated as follows in that old collection of Jewish legends published in my "Exempla." Here we read (No. I) that Nimrod was the first king over the whole world after God, and further on among the next seven we find also Nebuchadnezzar, Cyrus, and very significantly Alexander the Great. The ninth king will be the Messiah, and after him the rule will return again to God, who will be the tenth. Of these Nebuchadnezzar appears as the emperor of the world in the legend of Babylon; and in another set of legends, instead of Cyrus, we find Chosroe, not only as the king who aspires to imperial rule, but who evidently also claims to be worshipped as a god, for when Heraclius has defeated the latter's grandson, it is said that he destroys a colossal statue of Chosroe, who is sitting on a throne surrounded by pictures of the sun, moon and stars, in a building looking like a temple. Here again we find first in the Asatir the description of a temple built in a similar manner, adorned also with the sun and moon, and apparently it is a woman that occupies the throne and is the object of worship. The language is very obscure, but it refers, no doubt, to a similar building. What is mentioned here about the temple built by Aḥidan (Ch. III. 20 ff.) is found, curiously enough, in almost identical terms ascribed to Nimrod, in the old version of the Abraham legend found in my "Exempla" (No. IIa.) Nimrod also claims to be worshipped as a god, and sits on a throne or in a temple similar to that of Chosroe. In the Jewish legend there appears also another king who wishes to be worshipped as a god, and tries to imitate the order of the world over which he rules. It is the Hiram legend (Exempla No. 4), which runs as follows: "Hiram, king of Tyre, made seven artificial heavens placed on pillars of iron, first of glass, sun, moon and stars. Second of iron, with a lake of water in it; third of tin with precious stones rolling over it (thunder). Fourth of lead, fifth of copper, then silver and gold and on the top a couch of gold and precious stones and pearls. By moving it he produces scintillation (lightning). The prophet Ezekiel carried up to him tells him that although he has been promised long life he will not live for ever."

In all these versions we have the same idea of a king ruling the whole world, or who in himself represents the god who rules it. It is the same idea which we find already dimly represented in the ten kings of the Sibyl of Tibur, more pronouncedly afterwards in the West, in Imperial Rome, in the Emperors of Byzantium, and in those of the Western Kings, who also dreamt of becoming Emperors of the world, or who considered themselves heirs to the Empire of Rome of the West, or Rome of the East. The globe, the sceptre, and the star-spangled mantles represent in a symbolical manner the orb of the world and the star-spangled sky.

(B) There is a second cycle of legends to which I now turn, that of the exposed child-hero, or the child of destiny.

The central idea of this cycle of legends is that a king is warned against his offspring. His child or grandchild, and sometimes the child of another woman will in time rob him of his power. He tries many devices to destroy that child, which is often secretly born, then exposed to wild beasts, or left in a cave or forest to die. But somehow the elements and animals are friendly to the child; it grows up, is exposed to various dangers, such as being cast into the river, or by some stratagem is cast into a burning furnace, when by some change or substitution the hero is saved, and the old prophecy comes true. Here we have all the elements found in the Abraham legend: Nimrod is warned that a child will be born, which in time will destroy his claim to be worshipped as a god, and rob him of his power. He tries to prevent the birth, but does not succeed, the mother is able to conceal her situation, the child is born and is hidden in a cave. It is miraculously protected, grows up, confronts as a man the king, who tries to destroy him by casting him into a furnace; but Haran, his brother, is burned by the flames, Abraham is saved, Nimrod's claim destroyed, and later on Abraham defeats him in battle. The birth in the cave and the mysterious death of Haran are best understood if both are taken as attempts on the part of Nimrod to destroy Abraham, in which he fails, so that Haran becomes, as it were, the substitute for Abraham destined to be burned in the furnace. This story is duplicated, with some slight change of detail, in the Asatir in the legend of the birth of Moses. In this wise these legends of Abraham and Moses contain all the details found in the innumerable variants of this cycle of legends. The stories of Yima, Cyrus, Oedipus, Siegfried and Romulus will at once be remembered in this connection; also the no less numerous legends throughout the world literature of the child willed by fate to obtain possession of a throne or another man's property, and which is connected with the third type of tales of the man sent to be burned in a furnace or to be destroyed in some way or other by a message, which he is expected to deliver, but who is saved by the enemy who forestalls him and suffers the death which is intended for the hero.*

(C) The third cycle to which attention may now be drawn is that of the return of the lost hero, or rather, of his coming to life again.** Towards the end of the Asatir we gather that the expectation of the future happiness, of the inauguration of an era of peace and joy is made to be dependent on or coincident with the Advent of the Taheb, described so that in him one can easily recognize Moses Redivivus. Moses cannot really die, but he is hidden away until the time destined for his reappearance. He will then come back with the insignia of his Messiahship. In the Jewish tradition this idea of a hero Redivivus is expressed in a slightly different form in connection with the Pineḥas saga. He is also destined not to die, and he reappears under the name of Elijah, who also does not die, but is translated to heaven in a miraculous manner. Yet he will reappear at the end of days, to fight the false Messiah, and then help to inaugurate the time of universal peace and joy, when the Messiah will obtain rule. Whether Ezekiel contemplated also a David Redivivus must be left an open question. I have shown elsewhere Ezekiel's connection with the northern tribes of Israel, (Gaster, Schweich Lectures on the Sammaritans pp. 12. 15) and also with reference to Gog (above p. 90—92). He, in any case, speaks emphatically of David, the king (Ezek. XXXIV, 23. 24 and XXXVII 24—5) as living, as it were, and in the last mentioned verse, as living for ever. He is thus not only

---

* It is quite sufficient to refer here to the literature of the exposed child in the table given by Dunlop in his "History of Fiction," 2nd edition, and to the immense literature of parallels collected by Bolte and Polivka, "Annotations to Grimm" I. No. 29 p. 278 ff. and finally V. Tille in "Zeitschrift d. Vereins für Volkskunde" 1919 Berlin p. 22 ff.

** See also H. Schmidt, "Der Mythos vom wiederkehrenden König im Alten Testament" p. 28.

Redivivus, but is a king for ever at the end of days. With this utterance of the prophet runs parallel the idea of the second Advent of Christ. This idea of the hero disappearing for a while, and then reappearing with might and glory, and ushering in the long-expected time of happiness is found afterwards also among many nations. It may have been first applied to Alexander, but curiously enough it was then transferred to Nero, so already in the Sibylline Oracles (cf. Bate. Sibyl. Oracles p. 39ff.); not to speak of many prophets and Law-givers, who for a time disappeared, and then came back with a new revelation, such as Zoroaster, Zalmoxes and others. It is sufficient here to refer to the story of Arthur in Avalon and of the Emperor Frederick Barbarossa in the Kyffhaeuser.*

(D) The last, and not the least important cycle, which is intimately connected with the preceding one is the Antichrist legend, that curious figure of a monstrous being endowed with witchcraft, and capable of leading the world astray, which will arise at the end of time and endeavour to obstruct by every means the Advent of the true Messiah and the salvation of the world, as well as the proclamation of the True Faith. How profound the impression has been which this arch-enemy of God and man has produced upon the mind of the world can scarcely be exaggerated. (See Bousset, The Antichrist Legend, London 1896.) To have traced it to its possible ultimate source, and to have realised that it was the outcome of a growing development of a legend the centre of which was the wizard and old arch-enemy, Bileam, is to have added another contribution towards the history of this remarkable conception.

Four cycles of legends have thus been evolved out of the narratives in the Asatir: the universal king, the exposed child, the return of the hero, and finally the Antichrist. Incidentally reference may be made to the possible start-

* See Kampers, "Kaiseridee," and the same "Werdegänge;" Eisler, "Orpheus," p. 354.

ing point found here of the belief that King Solomon possessed magic powers.

One more word may finally be said about Josephus. He must now be lifted out of the narrower sphere of a mere interpreter of the Biblical narrative, and placed at the head of a whole cycle of literary developments of no mean importance. With him begins the literature of the Historiated Bible, which in the course of time was to appeal to the popular taste more strongly, if possible, than the simpler narrative of Holy Writ. His example was imitated, his work enlarged upon or abbreviated, and much of the legendary matter was taken over into other writings and widely circulated. In the Jewish literature we have a parallel to Josephus, in the often-mentioned Sefer Hayashar, and in the more loosely connected legends in the Chronicle of Jeraḥmeel. In the Greek I refer to the Palaea, from which translations have been made in very early times into Slavonic and later on into Rumanian, and have found their way into the versified Biblical stories in popular Greek by Chumnos. In the Latin I mention Petrus Commestor's Biblia Historiale and it is impossible even remotely to delineate the influence which these works have exercised upon the mind of the Middle Ages in literature and art, especially in the Biblical Mystery Plays of France, Germany, and England. It is an uninterrupted chain which stretches through the centuries, and it is of no little interest to follow it up link by link from its latest development to its remotest source. This gives to the Asatir its specific additional value.

THE PSEUDEPIGRAPHIC LITERATURE.

It will now be more easy to define the relation between the Asatir and the pseudepigraphic literature. From the above investigations, no doubt can be entertained as to the high antiquity of the Asatir. It precedes by a very long time, not easily determined, any of the other pseudepigraphic writings hitherto known. Scholars differ among themselves as to the date to be assigned to each of these. No wonder, as no real starting point for this kind of literature has as yet been defined. Allusions of a very vague nature, dark prophecies, not one of which has been as yet absolutely verified, have guided these scholars in suggesting the age of the composition, and I venture to add, an ill-applied interpretation of alleged sectarian disputes, the reflex of which was believed to have been found in these writings, as well as the confused historical background, have contributed to prevent scholars from arriving at definite conclusions. The real starting-point, however, should be as I have endeavoured to show the relation in which each of these pseudepigraphic writings stands to the text of the Bible. So long as they present the character of a pure commentary, though embellished by many legends and tales, they must be considered as old. But as soon as their character changes and they are used as a mere vehicle for the propagation of new ideas, not seldom subversive to Judaism, they proclaim themselves to be the product of a later age. The conditions under which they were originally written, had by then been entirely changed. This can best be proved by a careful analysis of the peculiar character of those pseudepigraphic writings, which have not been preserved in their original Hebrew or Aramaic language. Every one of those now found only in Greek or in other versions depending upon the Greek have travelled far away from the original form, whilst those preserved in a Semitic tongue (Hebrew, Aramaic, Samaritan and even Syriac) have retained to a large extent their ancient character. The degree of change, however, in the former varies also considerably.

These have been worked over, changed, mutilated and above all have now become purely and simply part of a definite propagandist literature. They serve as a cloak for polemical invective, sheltering themselves behind old and venerated names. None of these books, could therefore be directly compared with the former class except in so far as they have some Agadic material in common; they start only from one portion or another of the Bible narrative, and use old legends and Midrashim. They no doubt had recourse to the same sources of popular and Agadic exegesis which lie at the root of the Asatir and of the other writings hitherto mentioned, such as the Hellenistic literature, the Palestinian Targum and Josephus.

The comparison with the other pseudepigraphic writings will not detain me, therefore, very long. The differences between the Asatir and these writings are far more pronounced than the agreements.

In order to elucidate the true relationship of the Samaritan book to the extant pseudepigraphic writings, I have chosen the Book of Enoch as the first in point. It is believed to be the oldest of its kind, yet no pseudepigraphic book shows more clearly the profound difference between the Asatir and the other works of a similar character than this book. I have chosen it deliberately for comparison in order to determine more sharply the specific character of the Asatir in contradistinction to the rest. If, as is assumed, the date of the various fragments out of which the Book of Enoch has been compiled, ranges from 160 B. C. E. to 64 C. E., then they must be the result of a lengthy development which had taken place a very long time before the date assumed by scholars. But this assumption will have to undergo a very serious revision, the discussion of which lies outside the sphere of this investigation. The apocalyptic visions in the Book of Enoch, as well as the allegories and symbolical pictures, are far removed from those found in the Book of Daniel. The description of Hell and its punishments, the Fall of Angels, the demonology and astrology are so fully developed that it would be impossible to ascribe to them any great antiquity. Even the interpretation of the prophecies contained therein, in the light of certain events, is a matter of hypothetical speculation, and does not prove contemporary origin. These prophecies are subject, as a rule, to constant changes and modifications, and are often so worded that they can easily be applied to changing conditions. There is, moreover, one item in the Book of Enoch on which special stress is laid. I refer to the calculation of the Calendar. This seems to have been a burning question which agitated all the sects in Palestine to a very high degree. It is the pivot round which the Book of Jubilees turns, as will be seen p. 110—112.

If one turns now to the Samaritan Asatir, one cannot imagine a greater contrast. It is sober and simple; there is no trace of the Fall of Angels, no demonology, no apocalyptic vision of Hell, and no exaggerated conception of Enoch. There is no translation to Heaven, no symbolical or allegorical vision and parable. Yet there is some common ground on which they both meet; viz, the origin of the Calendar. The Samaritans also accept it as a divine revelation, and the astronomical calculation dates from the beginning of time, with the difference, however, that this revelation has been made to Adam, who is represented as being the first high priest and king (see above, p. 36). He observes the march of the planets; he possesses the Books of Astronomy, which he communicates to Enoch and Noah; he foresees the Flood, whilst Noah, who is studying these books, teaches his contemporaries and warns them of the consequences of their evil ways. The prophecy is here fittingly relegated to the end of the Asatir and put into the mouth of Moses, to whom alone these "Secrets" are revealed. Enoch to the Samaritans is a human being like all the rest and he dies, but at an early age. What a difference between the exuberant fantasy of the Book of Enoch and the sober legends told in the Midrash of the Asatir! If, as scholars (Beer and

Charles*), suggest, the origin of the Book of Enoch or some portions of it, is to be sought in Northern Palestine, the very place where the origin of the Asatir is also to be sought, then the difference between these two is still more striking, and one is driven forcibly to the conclusion that the one belongs to a much higher antiquity, when such mystical speculations did not exercise any sway on the minds of the people as was the case in a much later period, when such fantastic speculations were the order of the day, and assumed such an extraordinary shape as in the Book of Enoch. Here we have the two extremes of Midrash and myth, even if it should be the case that they belong to two different sects. The one represents the ascetic Essenes, with their contemplative life and theosophic speculations on the banks of the Jordan, and the other, the people in general who frequented the houses of learning and worship, and enjoyed the legendary interpretations and the embellishments of the sacred text. A portion of the Book of Enoch has, in fact, been discovered by me to be nothing less than the "Logos Ebraikos" in the magical papyrus of Paris (Gaster, "Studies and Texts" p. 356 ff.). It shows that a certain sect made use of the Book of Enoch for magic purposes, owing, no doubt, to the numerous names of angels and demons that occur therein. I have taken this book as an example in order to show the profound difference between the Asatir and the pseudepigraphic literature, and to measure the distance of time which must separate the one from the other. If the Book of Enoch should really belong to the year 160 B. C. E., it would be very difficult to determine the century to which the Samaritan book would belong.

The relation between the Asatir and other pseudepigraphic books is, however, much closer intendency and form, than that between the Asatir and the Book of Enoch,

* The Book of Enoch. Trsld. from the Editor's Ethiopic Text. Oxford 1912.

which represent the two extremes. Next in order of antiquity is believed to be the Book of Jubilees, which contains not a few elements found in the Asatir. The legendary matter, however, has grown to such an extent that it is no longer only a small addition or interpretation of the narrative, or simple glosses on the text of the Bible. It is, on the contrary, quite an independent work, in which the Biblical record has been greatly overlaid by legends and tales. But what characterises the Book of Jubilees especially is, that it has become a book *with a purpose*. It is intended to inculcate a new lesson, not even hinted at in the Bible, and to propagate new theories. A new Calendar is being evolved and recommended as a divine revelation made by the angel to Moses. The history is arranged according to Jubilees, and care has been taken by the author to give the exact dates, especially the years in each Jubilee when the events recorded in the Bible have happened. In addition, we find also genealogical information, such as the fictitious names of the wives of the Patriarchs. The book, moreover, contains a number of very rigorous legal injunctions for the strict observance of the Sabbath and the festivals; for all are preordained and observed already by the first Patriarchs. We find here a long story of the fight of Jacob and his sons against Sichem (ibid. Ch. XXX) and then against Esau and his children (ibid. Ch. XXXVIII). This may be a proof of its late origin, for under the form of an ancient story a real chapter of contemporary history may have been told. It may be a reflection of the wars between Jews and Samaritans and also with the Edomites. If we then find, as is the case, a Hebrew parallel of this ancient story with the name of Herodion in it, it is obvious that we are dealing here with a legend which has its origin in the history of the death of Herod the Edomite. In the Book of Jubilees there is also a brief chapter on the birth of Moses (Ch. XLVII). It is idle to speculate as to the origin of the book, as various scholars have done, ascribing it in turns to the Ḥasidim, Essenes, Pharisees, Saducees of various shades and degrees, and even to the Samaritans themselves; not to speak of the other theory, advanced by Singer,* who ascribed to it a Christian-Pauline origin. And yet, in spite of such conflicting views, and on the slenderest of grounds, the Book of Jubilees is still believed to belong to the middle of the second century, B. C. E. The very character of the book, the expansion of the legends, the insistence on a Calendar according to the solar year, the Messiah from Levi, the era of the Jubilees; all these, whilst showing in many minor points similarities to Samaritan traditions, can only belong to a period of great political unrest and religious upheaval. The system of counting by Jubilees insisted upon by the author points moreover in that direction. It must have been written after the Destruction of the Temple in Jerusalem, when the Jewish Calendar could no longer be fixed by an existing authority on the first sight of the New Moon, and the Sanhedrin had ceased to function. The era of the Creation, on the other hand, had not yet been adopted, and the Seluecidan was probably not allowed. The difficulty thus grew how to establish the Calendar without having recourse to the official proclamation of the New Moon and the interpolation of the months, according to the old method. But by the new solar Calendar of the Jubilees the feasts and fasts would become definitely fixed The author would thereby also meet the claim of the Samaritans, whose Calendar rests on astronomical calculation and the readjustment of the solar and lunar year. The scant references to the Temple form part of the archaic colouring. It was at the end of the first century that the fixing of the Calendar became a burning question. Nobody would have troubled about it before, so long as the Sanhedrin existed, and the same, as

* Das Buch der Jubiläen o. die Leptogenesis, Stuhlweisenburg 1798.

will be seen presently, is the case with a Hebrew book of the same period, the Chapters of Rabbi Eliezer. Thus the distance between the Book of Jubilees and the Asatir is very considerable; nor do we find so many points of contact between these two books as one would otherwise expect, if the Book of Jubilees were as old as is alleged. We find in consequence also that the Book of Jubilees has very little in common with the older Hellenistic literature, i. e. Josephus and also with the Palestinian Targum. There are, however, some details in which Asatir and Jubilees agree; these are referred to in the notes accompanying the translation.

Concerning the Biblical Antiquities of Pseudo-Philo, limiting myself to the Pentateuchal period, we find they agree, in some details, with the Asatir. This book belongs, in a way, to the class of the Historiated Bible mentioned before. It resembles the Asatir in so far as the author refrains from repeating the Biblical story. He gives instead many legends of a very curious character, numerous names of the children of the first Patriarchs, and geographical names of the divisions of the land, not easy to find elsewhere. I must refer to the elaborate discussion of this book in the introduction of my edition of the Chronicle of Jeraḥmeel p. 40, where I suggestad Samaritan affinities, and since then to the English translation by M. R. James, London, 1917. The book, preserved in archaic Latin, is a literal translation made in the third or fourth century from the Greek, which in its turn rests upon an older Hebrew or Aramaic text, probably dating from shortly after the destruction of Jerusalem. There is moreover, one parallel the importance of which cannot be exaggerated. It throws light on the history of the Farewell Oration and Death of Moses, (ibid. ch. XIX) as it appears in many apocalyptic writings. I am publishing here a Samaritan version of this episode, and it will be seen how close the parallelism is between Pseudo-Philo and the latter.

The parallelism is so close that it cannot rest on mere coincidence and strengthens again my surmise that the author of Pseudo-Philo stood in some close connection with the Samaritan tradition. True, in Pseudo-Philo the story is much more fully developed than in the Samaritan, and yet it finishes there also with a prophecy which resembles that contained in the Asatir.

The points of contact are besides this not very numerous. The legends are entirely different from those found elsewhere, such as the story of Abraham in the furnace (ibid. Ch. VI, 13 ff.). All the parallels are given in the notes. A few characteristic ones, however, may be mentioned here, such as the restraint of men and women in Egypt (IX. 2) the peculiarly long genealogies of Caleb and Joshua (Philo, XV. 3), which reminds one of the long genealogies of Pharaoh (Asatir, VIII. 15), and Bileam (Asatir X, 1) in the Asatir Bileam's advice concerning the Moabite women (Bibl. Antiq. XVIII, 13), and that remarkable story of the peculiar twelve precious stones (ibid. XXV. 12 ff.), which remind one of the twenty-four stones in Asatir II. 7. A reference may be made here to Rev. XXI. 19. 20. Altogether it is a book which stands alone and represents an independent development from the same simple sources and running on parallel lines. It requires still further study.

The "Testaments of the Twelve Patriarchs" is already an entirely different work, and more akin to the Book of Jubilees. It has very little in common with the older traditions in the Asatir.

If we now pass on to the Adam Books, there is curiously enough the Syriac "Cave of Treasures," which shows much more agreement in detail with the Asatir than any of the preceding writings. In its present form this book has been compiled somewhere about 450 C. E. It is entirely changed and has become a thoroughly Christian legend. But the story of the Patriarchs down to Moses has suffered comparatively less from the hand of the Christian manipulator than the succeeding parts. It rests ultimately on a text resembling the Asatir. The similarity of language may have facilitated this appropriation of the older material for the new compilation. The Samaritan language differs very little from the Aramaic, and so also from the Syriac. And perhaps another consideration may have weighed with the author of the Cave of Treasures, inasmuch as it was not a book written by Jews, but by a dissenting sect of which Jesus had spoken in friendly terms. Goetze, who has made an independent study of the book, has come to the same conclusion, viz: that the first portion of the "Cave of Treasures" is nothing more than an ancient Midrash embodied in that book by the author of the "Cave."* He was unaware of the existence of the Asatir, by which his conclusions have now been corroborated. He then followed up his study by an investigation into the influence which the "Cave of Treasures" has exercised on subsequent writings. Of these I quote now at once the Revelations of Methodius of Patara or Patmos (treated more fully previously). There are, however, in the latter, many details not found in the Cave, but in the Asatir, and although this writing also belongs to a later period, probably to the time of Heraclius (Sackur, Sibyll. Texte, p. 122), still, it shows much greater affinity with the Asatir, especially in the first part, than with the "Cave." It was compiled originally in Persia or Babylonia. It was a purely Oriental compilation, and the author, therefore, could have used a version of the Asatir, or a similar work of which he has made ample use. The Asatir seems to be thus far the only source known to us for many of the details found in the last two books, since they are absent from the other apocryphal and pseudepigraphic writings, which are all ultimately of

* A. Goetze, Die Schatzhöhle. Sitzungsberichte der Heidelberger Akad. d. Wiss., Philos.-hist. Bd. IV, 1922. Idem "Die Nachwirkung der Schatzhöhle" in Zeitschrift f. Semitistik u. verwandte Geb., Bd. II, Heft 1, Leipzig 1923.

Jewish origin. References are made in the notes throughout to every one of these writings, thus showing the connection which may have existed between them and their mutual interdependence. If we now turn to the other Adam books, there is first the so-called Apocalypse of Moses, published by Tischendorf,* like all the others from late Greek MSS. Here the story is strictly limited to the creation of Adam, his life, penitence and death. It has undergone a similar thoroughly Christian revision, although it ultimately goes back to a Jewish original. I have already drawn attention to the fact that this story must have belonged at one time to a larger book (see above p. 6) which contained the whole Biblical history from the Creation to the death of Moses, and must have contained an apocalypse of the latter. Hence the names; for otherwise the title "Apocalypse of Moses" given to a story limited to the life of Adam and Eve would be inexplicable. At one time or another the first portion became detached, and the old title was retained. In a few points, the "Apocalypse" and the Asatir agree, but these points of resemblance are very slender and few. The same may be said of the rest of the Adam-Books, which have departed more and more from the ancient original, and have become thoroughly Christianised legends.** In each of these one finds reminiscences of old traditions.

* Apocalypses Apocryphae Leipzig 1866, pp. 1—23, and completely by Ceriani in "Monumenta sacra et profana" tom I, fasc. 1 (Mediolan. 1861) pp. 55—64.
** Such as the Ethiopic Book of Adam (ed. by Malan, London 1882). The Latin Vita Adae et Evae (ed. W. Meyer, Abhandl. d. Münchener Akad., Philos.-Philol. Kl. Bd. XIV, 1878. German Translation E. Kautzsch, Pseudoepigraphen des Alten Testaments, Tübingen 1906, II, p. 506 ff. English in R. H. Charles, Apocrypha and Pseudepigrapha of the Old Testament, Oxford 1913, vol. II, p. 123 ff.). The Syriac and Arabic (ed. by Renan in Journal Asiatique, cinquième serie, tom II, 1853, pp. 427 ff.). Armenian (German transl.: E. Preuschen, Die apokryphen gnostischen Adamschriften a. d. Armen. übers. u. unters., Giessen 1900. English transl. by Conybeare in Jew. Quarterly Review VII, 1895, p. 216ff. Old Slavonian (ed. Jagic, Denkschrift

8*

I have left now for special consideration the greatly mutilated Assumption of Moses (ed. by R. H. Charles, London 1897). A careful examination reveals here again only stray resemblances to the Asatir. The apocalypse has become also a definite pronouncement from a special point of view, a kind of party pamphlet, but I submit that the conclusions which have been drawn as to the time of the composition and the circumstances alluded to are not a little rash. On the one hand, our knowledge of the situation which prevailed in Palestine before the Maccabean period is almost nil. The relation between Jews and Samaritans and the continually growing feud between these two sections has not yet been sufficiently realised, and still less the influence which it exercised on the contemporary literature. Moreover, the fluidity of prophecies and symbols, and their easy application from one set of events to another apparently similar, is constantly occuring. One has to follow up only the transformation (referred to above p. 43—45) of the Sibylline Oracles in the course of ages from the third and eighth book to the Sibyl of Tibur and then to the mediaeval oracles, in order to realise the ease and frequency of those changes and how difficult it is to determine the persons and situations found in one book or the other. They may be much older, and often are indeed much older, since they have been taken over bodily and transferred to a much later compilation, in the hope and expectation that readers would apply them to the new conditions that had since arisen.

Turning now to the Hebrew literature, with the exception of the Palestinian Targum, with which I have dealt previously, only a few writings can be mentioned, which contain legends running parallel to those in the Asatir.

d. Wiener Akademie d. Wiss., phil.-hist. Kl., XLII, 1893). Rumanian (Gaster, Literatura Populara, Romana, Bucaresti, 1884. For the whole literature see Schürer, Gesch. d. jüd. Volkes, III, 397 (4th ed.) and R. H. Charles op. cit. II, 133.

The first book to be mentioned in the Hebrew literature, which stands in some close relation to the Asatir, is "Pirke de Rabbi Eliezer" or "Chapters of Rabbi Eliezer." This book resembles much more the Book of Jubilees, inasmuch as it is a kind of elaborate commentary on Genesis and some parts of Exodus. It is more disjointed in its composition, and contains a number of legends similar to those found in the Asatir. The character of the book, however, is more that of a homiletic commentary on certain sections of the Bible, and it thus belongs to the much wider class of Midrashim which have grown up round the text of the Bible. It is replete with direct quotations of verses from the Bible, which are used as props to the legends. Here also we find that special attention has been paid to the problem of the Calendar. In the details, however, there is some parallelism between that book and the Asatir. At the same time the difference between the two works is sufficiently great to show their absolute independence of one another.

In the further course of this Agadic activity we also find in the Hebrew literature that, like in the above-mentioned, certain episodes of the Biblical narrative have been developed more fully, and have started on an independent life, separated from the main body to which they may have originally belonged. We have thus a certain number of independent Midrashim, some preserved in a fragmentary form, others more fully expanded, such as the Book of Enoch, the Life of Abraham, the Chronicle of Moses, the Life and Death of Aaron, and others of a similar character. These have been strung together by Jeraḥmeel in his Chronicle (see above p. 7). This book constitutes a chain of legends from Creation down to the period of the Maccabees and later. Here we find the best and oldest recensions, and these offer parallels to the Asatir, although they have now become fully elaborated stories and romances. One has only to compare the story of Moses in Josephus, which approximates more closely to the Asatir, with the elaborate Chronicle of Moses, to realise at once the distance which separates the one from the other; and yet, even these Hebrew Midrashim belong to a very high antiquity. It is very difficult to define exactly the time of their composition, but they must belong to the first century C. E., seeing that the old legends thus far preserved only in the Hellenistic literature inclusive of Josephus, are the nearest parallels to the older Hebrew and Samaritan texts, which are the basis for the more elaborate Hebrew versions of a later age. The Greek texts of the Pseudepigrapha, as already pointed out before, are as a rule translations and modifications of previous or contemporary Jewish writings. These had not perished, and they reappear in the above-mentioned Hebrew texts thus far preserved. Finally, another book, similar to the Chronicle of Jeraḥmeel, is the Book of Yashar.* Written in the same pure Hebrew language as the other Midrashim, this book is a continuous legendary companion to the text of the Bible. Whilst the Midrashim have still their individual character as independent writings, or are simply strung together in chronological order by Jeraḥmeel, their individual character has been entirely obliterated in the Book of Yashar, and they have all been unified and rewritten into a continuous legendary story from Creation to the time of the Judges. The author of this book had at his disposal not only the Midrashim hitherto quoted, but also a large number of other legends not found elsewhere in the Jewish literature. The legends woven into this book are in all probability of very old origin, and in many details they approach much more closely those found in the Asatir than any of the others hitherto mentioned, as will be seen from the notes. Moreover, neither in the Chronicle of Jeraḥmeel nor in the Book of Yashar is there any specific tendency or propaganda. Both agree in the desire of enriching by legend the story of the Bible, without introducing any-

* Ed. Pr. Venice 1613, transl. into English by Donaldson, New York 1840. French transl. in Migne, Diction. des Apocryph.

thing of a legal character. The stories are not to be used either for propagating a new Calendar, or for insisting on the strict observance of this or that ceremony of Law, or reward for the pious or punishment of the sinners, nor is any man or family singled out for special praise. The Messianic question is not even touched upon. The story moves within a strictly limited circle of Biblical legends. Therein both Yashar and Jeraḥmeel have followed the same lines as the author of the Asatir, but each one in an independent manner. The ultimate source from which they drew some of their material must be the same as that used by the previous writers. In the notes which accompany the translation of the Asatir, special attention has been paid to the parallels which can be gathered from all these writings, and care has been taken to give the references as fully as possible. The conclusion which must be drawn from this comparison is obvious; that the Samaritan Asatir is entirely independent of any of these writings, be they Hellenistic, be they Greek, or be they Jewish; and although there are many points of contact between them, their differences are far more profound than their agreements. The Asatir serves no tendency, propagates no special doctrine, and serves no direct purpose.

There is a collateral result arising out of this investigation which is as unexpected as I believe it to be important. The pseudepigraphic writings can now be definitely divided into three groups: first is that one which clings to the text of the Bible, and is preserved mostly in Hebrew and Aramaic writings, such as the Asatir, the Palestinian Targum, Josephus, whom I count also as a Targum, although written in Greek; furthermore Jeraḥmeel, Yashar and all the other Jewish Midrashim, no less than the various Samaritan writings on the birth of Moses (Molad), the poems of Jacob ha-Rabban and his contemporaries, the commentary of Meshalma, the Malif, and not a few of the poems of the Samaritan liturgy, containing legendary and eschatological matter. The second group, which is sharply distinguished from this first one, is the literature chiefly preserved in Greek and Latin translations, and those derived from them, like Ethiopic, Arabic and Slavonic. To this group belong such writings as the Adam-Books in their multifarious variety, the Book of Enoch, Jubilees, the Testaments of the Twelve Patriarchs, and all the Moses Apocrypha. To an intermediate third group, which may serve as a link between the other two groups, I would assign those writings which do not claim Biblical personages for their authors, such as the Sibylline Oracles, the Tiburtine, the Cave of Treasures, the Revelations of Methodius, and, above all, the Antiquities of Pseudo-Philo. This classification may tend to modify to some extent the conclusions at which scholars have arrived from the study of the second group only, in their endeavour to reconstruct the spiritual life and the strivings of the so-called sects during the period ascribed to them. Far from representing the real state of things prevalent at those assumed periods, they have departed very considerably from those times, and are the echoes of voices raised under totally different circumstances. They do not represent the views of a class or a consensus of opinions prevalent among the masses. They are, on the contrary, the personal views of the anonymous authors who used the great names of the past to further their own purposes. No reliable conclusion can therefore be drawn from these pseudepigraphic writings belonging to the second group, whereas the first group gives us a perfect idea of the true religious tendencies moving the mind of the people during those centuries.

CHARACTERISTIC POINTS OF DIFFERENCE.

I have hitherto endeavoured to establish the relation between the Asatir and the other apocryphal literature, and to find the parallels between the former and the latter, and also occasionally the differences between the Asatir and each of them separately. It now remains to group together those distinctive features in which the Asatir stands quite alone, and which prove, therefore, its entire independence from the others. There is no mystical cosmology, such as is found in Enoch, Ascension of Isaiah, or again no visions as seen by Ezra IV, Baruch and others. There is no apocalyptic Ascent to Heaven or Descent to Hell as in the Jewish Assumption of Moses, and no Visions of Heaven and Hell like those of Peter, Paul etc. There is no trace of asceticism like that of the Essenes, who lived an exceptionally pure and secluded life. There is no demonology, and consequently no soteriology. There is no trace here of any legends connected with the Sethians. Much has been made of this alleged sect, in the various studies concerning the Adam-Books, where some of the legends of the "sons of God" mixing with the depraved daughters of Cain, have been taken as the basis for part of the Adam-Books, and the origin of these legends has been connected in some way with these followers of Seth. In the Asatir, Seth plays no distinct rôle, neither do we find any distinct reference to the mixing of the children of Seth with the children of Cain, nor, which is more important, any allusion whatsoever to the legend of the Fallen Angels.* These are the result of a literal interpretation of the words of the Bible (Gen. VI. 2). Bene Elohim, as "the sons of God," are taken as a metaphorical application to angels. This is found fully set out in Enoch, and in the literature into which it has passed, as well as in the Jewish legend of Shemḥazai and Azael, the latter being afterwards identified with the Azazel of the Bible.

We have then in the Asatir a curious history of the bulding of the Tower and the subsequent wars of the nations and a genealogy of the first Pharaoh. Of the

* See L. Jung. Fallen Angels in Jewish, Christian, and Mohammedan Literature, Philadelphia 1926.

former only faint traces have been found in the Sibylline and in Methodius, but nowhere a parallel to Pharaoh's genealogy. Of the history of the birth of Abraham, of the segregation of the women, of his battle with the kings, of the illness and cure of Pharaoh, which is peculiar to the Asatir, only fragmentary parallels can here and there be found elsewhere. There is still that distinctive feature of dates for minute events, so that even the day of the week on which certain events have happened is given. These are not found anywhere else. In the Book of Jubilees, and in the "Cave of Treasures," the year is given, and sometimes the month, but nowhere the day. Whether these dates were once in the lost chronology of Demetrius, of which only a fragment[*] has been preserved, must remain a matter of speculation.

The history of the birth of Moses, and the incidents connected therewith, differ considerably from all the other versions of the birth of Moses. Only Josephus shows in part closer agreement with the Asatir; none other.

Turning now to the Bileam episode, it differs entirely from all other legends and traditions, and even in some details from the Biblical narrative. The names of the idols which Bileam is said to have worshipped, the mystical names and groups of letters, which find their parallel only in ancient Samaritan writings like the phylacteries, mark a profound difference between the Asatir and all the other writings. Whether they have been drawn from the magical writings of Bileam, mentioned in the Talmud, must remain an open question. In any case, there are no parallels. In the story of the death of Bileam, of which only a faint trace can be found in the Palestinian Targum, the Asatir stands quite alone.

There remains now one point in which the difference is fundamental and yet not obvious, since it has been almost

[*] Freudenthal, Hellenistische Studien page 35—82. M. Gaster, Studies and Texts, p. 650.

obliterated; it is in connection with the Sethian legend mentioned before. In almost every one of the Adam-Books, the dwelling place of the children of Seth is described to have been "on the top of the mountain." It is a Holy Mountain near the Gate of Heaven, or near Paradise, and the Patriarchs are incessantly warning their children not to descend to the valley below. Where was that mountain? In Jewish and in Christian Adam-Books, it is either left vague, or in some way identified with Mount Moriah, i.e. Mount Zion. But this is evidently not the original form, since in all the Adam-Books it is said that when Adam dies he wishes to be carried to that Holy Mountain. But if he lived there, how could he be carried thither? The transference of Moriah to Golgotha or later on Hebron, which is *not* the Holy Mountain, is the result of manifold manipulations and adjustments. But if we compare these legends with Samaritan tradition, the whole problem is easily solved. The Holy Mountain of the legend is none other than the Holy Mountain of Gerizim. It is there that Adam dwells when he is sent out from Paradise, there he offers sacrifices, and there he erects an altar, as do Noah, Abraham and Jacob after one another. The latter says distinctly "This is the Gate of Heaven:" (Gen. XXVIII. 17), it is where the Ark finally rests. There Adam dies, and then according to his wishes, is carried not *to* the Holy Mountain but *from* the Holy Mountain, to a distant place differently named, and finally identified with the cave of Machphelah. There cannot be any doubt, that in the primitive form of the legend, the Holy Mountain was none other than Mount Gerizim. It became, however, subsequently clear to the Jewish and Christian writers that they could not very well maintain the claim of sanctity for Mount Gerizim. They were conscious that they would be playing into the hands of the Samaritans, and thus the name of the place was omitted. But the tradition of a Holy Mountain had seized the minds of the people so strongly, and had become such an indissoluble part of the legend, that it could not be entirely obliterated, notably since the play upon the name of Jarad, one of the Patriarchs, which was interpreted to mean "to descend," had been so closely woven into the legend of the "descent" from the mountain of the pure Sethians that the "mountain" had to be retained, but the geographical location was then entirely omitted.

The Holy Mountain was also believed to be the centre of the earth, the "Omphalos:" not only by many other nations, but also by the Jews, to whom Mount Moriah was the centre or navel of the earth. Precisely the same belief was held by the Samaritans, with regard to Mount Gerizim.

I am quite aware that the Babylonian legend of the Holy Mountain on the top of which the god lives, and of the fact that the Zigurat* is claimed to be an imitation of that Mountain. But it remains open to doubt whether those ancient Babylonian beliefs of a Holy Mountain were still strong enough at the time when these legends were compiled to influence the authors of the apocryphal literature to see in Mount Gerizim a similar Holy Mountain.

Finally, attentio nmust be drawn to the peculiar use of numerous cryptograms throughout the chapters of the Asatir. Personal as well as geographical names appear in cryptic forms, for the extraordinary use of which there seems to be no apparent reason. One might understand it in conection with the prophecy of Chapter XI of the Asatir. The author refrains from putting into the mouth of Moses well known names, thus giving a mystical character to this vaticination. By there is no obvious reason why geographical names should be treated in a similar manner. This problem still awaits solution.

* As to Zigurat see Kampers "Werdegang;" for Jewish parallels; see Wensinck.

MANDAEAN AFFINITES.

Through the publications of Petermann and Lidzbarski we are now practically in possession of the whole extant Mandaean literature. Until recently only the Genza was accessible, and then in an unreliable form. It is the chief work of the Mandaeans, the "Treasury" in which many of the ancient legends and traditions have been preserved. First published in an incomplete form by Norberg,* Petermann produced a critical one** and a new exact translation by Lidzbarski has since appeared.*** On the basis of the Genza W. Brandt† tried first to give a description of the Mandaean doctrines and practices, and later on he published a translation of about one fourth of the whole book,†† having chosen those portions which appeared to him to be the most characteristic; and a succinct summary then appeared by Brandt in Hasting's Encyclopaedia.††† No one could fail to recognize the close similarity between the Mandaean and Manichaean doctrines, and this has become still more manifest through the publication of the "Book of John the Baptist" § and to a large degree by the "Qolasta" the funeral dirges and hymns constituting the most important part of their liturgy. §§ Reitzenstein §§§ endeavoured to piece together from the portions of the Genza published by Brandt, a kind of Apocalypse of Adam, or rather a brief abstract of the history of the world from Creation

---

* M. Norberg, Cod. Nasaräus liber Adami appellatus. Lund 1815 to 1816.
** Thesaurus s. liber magnus vulgo liber Adami appellatus opus Mandeorum, Leipzig, 1867.
*** Ginza, Göttingen und Leipzig 1915.
† Die Mandäische Religion, Leipzig, 1889.
†† Mandäische Schriften, Göttingen, 1893.
††† E. R. E. Vol. VIII s. v. Mandaens pp. 380-393.
§ Lidzbarski, M., Das Johannesbuch der Mandäer, Giessen 1915.
§§ Mandäische Liturgien, Abhandlungen d. königl. Ges. d. Wiss. Götttingen, Phil.-hist. Kl., Neue Folge, Bd. XVII, 1, Berlin, 1920.
§§§ Das Mandäische Buch des Herren der Grösse, Heidelberg 1919.

to Doom, as taught by the Mandaeans. He felt himself justified in so handling the material, as the Genza itself, from which these fragments are taken, is a compilation made probably as late as the fourteenth century, but the compilers have used in a most uncritical manner fragments of the old literature which had survived up to their time. It is of a most heterogeneous character and a most exasperating type of syncretism: an almost hopeless medley of old and new and of the most contradictory elements drawn from different sources; for the Mandaeans followed no visible system in their compilation, but tried to keep together everything that had remained of their old literature. Out of this they made their sacred book. Now at the hand of this complete material and with the invaluable assistance of the Mandaean Grammar of Th. Nöldeke,* which had been to the scholars the key by which to open the door to the understanding of this peculiar literature, it has become possible to determine with greater accuracy the date and origin of the Mandaeans.

The result to which scholars have unanimously arrived now is that the origin of the Mandaean doctrine is to be sought in the northern part of Palestine, and still more exactly by the banks of the Jordan. The language is distinctly Aramaic. It has been compared with the Aramaic of the Babylonian Talmud, but a closer observation will convince those who have the opportunity of examining the dialects of Palestine, that the language resembles much more closely the Aramaic of Galilee, slightly changed owing to the Mandaeans leaving Palestine at an early time and settling in Babylon, where their language was subjected to local influences. As to the date, it is now being assumed that some of the Mandaean doctrines took their rise at the time of the appearance of John the Baptist; and Lidzbarski as well as Reitzenstein assert that the Mandaean teaching is the direct offspring

* Mandäische Grammatik, Halle 1875.

of the teaching of John the Baptist, further developed by his followers. This does not exclude profound Gnostic and Manichaean influences and it is to these influences that the strong anti-Christian bias is ascribed which pervades the teaching of the Genza. It is surprising, however, that neither Lidzbarski nor Reitzenstein, should have thought of the Samaritans, the most powerful sect which at that time dominated the spiritual life of the inhabitants of Galilee. Our knowledge of the sectarian movements in Palestine at the beginning of the first century is very scant, but that there must have been such dissenting sects in great number can be gathered from the somewhat confused references scattered throughout the pages of Josephus' works in his "Antiquities" as well as in his "Wars." The rise of the Essenes alone would suffice to prove the existence of a strong religious sectarian movement in its widest sense, not to speak of the Ophites, Theraputes, Haemerobaptists, and the followers of many prophets who arose at that period. It would have been much more natural to seek parallels between the Mandaeans and the Samaritans before going farther afield to the Manichaean fragments from Turfan or from other Manichaean teachings, which, as Scheftolowitz has shown, are of a much later date and have been borrowed from the Mandaean and not the reverse. On the contrary, the most characteristic principles of Manichaeism find their source in Mandaean, Babylonian and early Jewish teachings.

It is not here the place to discuss the theology of the Mandaeans, since it lies outside thesp here of our investigations. I must limit myself only to such points as are covered by th contents of the Asatir. In the first place attention must be drawn to the phonetic and orthographic peculiarities of the Mandaeans. Characteristic of the language of the Galileans from very ancient times is the lack of distinction between the gutterals. Ḥeth and Ḳoph, Ain and Aleph are often used one for the other, both in Samaritan and in Mandaean, a feature peculiar only to these two among all the Aramaic dialects. The lexicon also approximates very closely to the Samaritan and as for the orthography, both use with predilection the Scriptio Plena, i. e. making full use of the letters of the alphabet for designating the vowels. This is so well known for the Samaritan itself that it only requires mentioning; they have even gone so far as to introduce these vowel letters into the Hebrew Pentateuch. More important, however, are the parallels between the Mandaean and the Samaritan teachings. There is, in the first place, the common enmity against Jerusalem, which has been built by Rûha and the Planets against the order of Enoš (Messias) and from which proceed afterwards all the perversions and lies. The Jews come and settle there and later on kill the 365 pupils (of the prophet); Enoš destroys the town or Temple which he describes as the "house without virtue" and finally he kills Christ. (Reitzenstein p. 33—34, who also gives the literature.) This agrees entirely with the Asatir; the building of the temple of idol-worship, and the name of the House of Shame given to it (ibid. III, 13): the burning of the Temple at the end of the Prophecy and the final victory of Kushṭa. In the latter part of the Mandaean text I see a reflection of the Antichrist legend in its more primitive form, but which has not been recognised either by Lidzbarski or by Reitzenstein.

One of the most important elements in the Mandaean doctrine is that of the Manda de-Ḥaya, which as Lidzbarski (Johannesbuch pp XVII and XVIII) has shown, must have had its origin in Palestine, and has become a stereotyped term in that Palestinian form. It belongs to the oldest elements and has given the name to the sect. The meaning of it is the Gnosis or Knowledge of the Life. With the Mandaeans it has become the name for the Supreme Being.

No real explanation has been given for this term; it is simply taken for granted as meaning the Knowledge of the

Life. I translate it the "Gnosis" or Knowledge of the Life, taking the last word to be a substitute for the Name of God; in fact I have not found in the Mandaean any word for God.* On three momentous occasions in the Asatir, we find then the peculiar expression Ḳol Ḥayyeh or Ḥayyah, a "Voice of the Living," i. e. the Voice of God, (X. 28, X. 51, XI. 17). Here the word Ḥayyah means the 'living' or the 'life,' precisely as in the Mandaean, and is used exclusively for the designation of the deity. This seems to be the expression used by Jesus (John XIV. 6): "I am the way, and the truth, and the life." No commentator, as far as I am aware, has realised the real meaning of this expression and has simply taken it literally as standing for Life Eternal, which is not warranted by the context. In the Bible, the combination 'living God' is often found, but nowhere has the word 'living' been substituted for God. At a later time there appears the Bath Ḳol, as the mysterious voice, by which divine commands are communicated to mortals, but nowhere do we find anything to be compared with this use of the word Ḥayyah or Ḥayyim. The identity of the word and its significance in both Samaritan and Mandaean cannot be a simple coincidence, since it affects the fundamental doctrine of the Mandaeans, and is equivalent there to Divinity or Deity. As already remarked above, this technical term must have been adopted by the Mandaeans while still in Palestine and retained by them henceforth in the original form.

Two more words now may be mentioned which play an important rôle in the Mandaean system—Ḳushṭa and Shekina. Though they occur only seldom in the Asatir, they are very often referred to in the Samaritan literature and everywhere a particular meaning has been attached to them which seems to stand in some relation to the meaning given to these words by the Mandaeans. 'Ḳushṭa,' originally meaning Truth, is, in the Asatir (XI. 28) the thing

* "Elaah" occurs sporadically, but is not used specifically as the Name of God.

to be desired as the highest ideal before the restoration and the coming of the happy days, i. e. "the True Faith (cf. John XIV, 6) and 'Shekina' has throughout in Samaritan the simple meaning of 'temple' or 'dwelling;' unlike the later Hebrew where 'Shekina' has become synonymous with the Name of God.* The Mandaean here as throughout represents in its terminology a further change from that of the Samaritans. Ḳushṭa means now with the Mandaeans: 'Belief,' 'Faith;' and 'Shekina' is the dwelling place of the Celestial Beings.

The peculiar tendency, so characteristic of hostile sects, of depreciating the names and objects considered holy by the others, appears also in a marked degree in the Mandaean terminology. Thus, Ruḥa becomes practiccally an evil spirit.** To the Mandaeans Ruḥa has become the embodiment of evil. She is assisted by her seven sons, the planets, who are also represented as evil spirits or demons. In three places in the Book of John, we even find Ruḥa d'Ḳudsha, which literally translated should mean 'holy spirit,' but in reality, it means 'unholy demon,' so that the word Ḳadosh has assumed a meaning contrary to that which it has in the Hebrew.

The importance of this fact is be to seen if we turn to the chapter in the Asatir on Bileam. Here (X. 6) Bileam is represented as worshipping five or seven elements, or rather, the demons of the elements. In Samaritan, however, there is no demonology with the exception of Belial mentioned above. They follow the example of the Bible, in which the objects of the worship of the heathen

* The same development has taken place in post-Biblical Hebrew also with the word "Makom." Originally it meant merely "place" and became afterwards a metaphorical synonym of God. Both developments run on parallel lines. The Samaritan, however, has retained the old meaning.

** It is noteworthy that the word Ruaḥ in the meaning of 'spirit' occurs only three times in the Pentateuch, and then the word is connected exclusively with Elohim and not once with the Tetragrammaton.

nations are also designated as 'strange Elohim.' The Samaritans use here also the name of 'El' for "strange god:" In the Samaritan Pentateuch, a slight change has been introduced in all the passages in Numb. XXIV, wherever the Hebrew text has "and God spake to Bileam;" the Samaritans could not accept the fact that God should speak to a heathen worshipper of idols, so they inserted the word 'angel' before 'God' in each one of these passages (Numb. XXII. 20; XXIII. 4. 5. 16). These 'angels' became afterwards gods of elements, worshipped by Bileam. This worship of the elements was anterior to the astrological worship of stars and planets which was of Babylonian origin. In the Asatir we are therefore meeting with a much older stage. Bousset has dealt fully with the worship of the elements in his work on the fundamental principles of Gnosticism. (Hauptprobleme der Gnosis, p. 233 ff.) He finds the oldest reference to this worship in Herodotus in connection with the worship of the Persians.* It had been transferred to them from the Babylonian worship of the planets, whence it has entered into the Mandaean doctrine, which has been the source of the Manichaean (Scheftelowitz) and it is therefore the oldest of these various systems. The elements mentioned in the Asatir are precisely those which we find in the more ancient documents as the objects of worship. Especially noteworthy is the worship of the winds, and in all probability that of fire, for I translate the word 'Ur' as 'fire' and not as 'light,' inasmuch as the luminaries which are the source of light are mentioned separately. Among these gods of the elements there appears now curiously enough also an 'El Haḳadosh' which if literally translated would mean 'a holy god,' or 'holy El.' This would be contrary to the whole idea that Bileam worshipped false gods. Now, as already remarked above, we find exactly the same

* Bousset follows it down to some of the Gnostic and Manichaean sects referred to by Epiphanius, Hippolytus and Augustinus.

word in the Mandaean system, with the only difference that 'Ruḥa' stands for 'El,' but in both cases, among the Mandaeans and in the Asatir, the word 'Ḳadosh' means 'unholy' and not 'holy.' It is difficult to reconcile this meaning given to the word 'Ḳadosh' in this connection, with the usual meaning of 'holy' given to it by the Samaritans. The Samaritans always use 'Ḳadosh' (קדש) in the meaning of 'holy!' Be it as it may, this parallelism is certainly remarkable. I have consulted them on that point, but they have not been able to give me a satisfactory explanation, except to say that it was the name of one of the idols worshipped by Bileam. We must assume, therefore, that we have here in the Asatir remnants of a very old tradition, which may have its roots in some such Persian system as that mentioned by Herodotus. Bileam is the wizard who comes from the East, and it would not be very difficult for the writer of the Asatir to credit him with the worship which he knew to be practised in that distant country, identified by him with Babylon or Persia.

A peculiar passage may now be mentioned which carries us back again to the Bileam legends so often referred to before. A passage in the Genza (Brandt, p. 45.) reads as follows:—

"There appears the Messiah (Christ) the prophet of the Jews. He calls the Seven Planets and makes them serve him. Each one fights for him. And these Seven lead astray all the children of Adam. The first of these demons is called Sames, the second Ruḥa d'Ḳudsha, and the third Nbu." Then follows a description of the benefits bestowed by each of these demons upon those who worship them. The demon of Ruḥa d'Ḳudsha brings folly, adultery, frivolity, lewdness, passions, songs and witchcraft into the world. The demons of Nbu-Mshiha (with whom Christ is specially identified) attack the people and spread perfidy among them.

The Mandaeans here consider Christ, the prophet of the Jews, as a false prophet, and we have here again the same beginnings of an anti-Messiah Legend. Everything that is of Jewish origin or is sacred among Jews and Christians is turned by them into an element of evil. Here Christ takes the shape of Bileam, as a wizard and false prophet, the embodiment of evil advice and the man who teaches immorality and gives a bad example. So is Bileam depicted in Rev. II. 14, and in other passages of the N. T., to which reference has already been made. Everywhere Bileam is the arch-type of wickedness, leading people astray to fornication and the worship of idols, and in the Samaritan tradition he also worships stars and planets and invokes their assistance, like Jesus in the Mandaean text. This identification and substitution of the one for the other must therefore have taken shape in Galilee at the time when the Mandaean sect embodied it in their teaching. The Mandaeans thus represent a further stage in the development from more primitive types found among both Samaritans and Jews in the first century. In the Asatir as well as in the Mandaean we find now the Ruḥa d'Ḳudsha and El Haḳadosh as evil powers, demons or false gods worshipped by Bileam as well as by Christ. Only an intimate relation between the various sects in Galilee and especially between them and the Samaritans can explain this remarkable parallelism. The Samaritans were the oldest sect. The difference however between the Mandaean and the Samaritan is sufficiently great to allow us to assume that the Samaritan did not borrow from the Mandaean; the reverse is much more likely to have been the case. Mandaeans and Samaritans held in common the hatred of the Jews and Jerusalem; they both had peculiar views about the Torah; the Samaritans alleging the text held by the Jews to have been falsified (so Asatir, XI. 36); and to the Mandaeans it was a book altogether filled with false doctrines given by Adonai to mislead the world. This attitude was adopted afterwards by various anti-Jewish Gnostic sects.

There are besides many more parallels between the Samaritan traditions and ceremonies and those of the Mandaeans, but they lie outside the sphere of this investigation. They all, however, point to one result, that the Mandaean doctrines, legends and traditions have originated in Palestine under very strong Samaritan influences. The geographical proximity, the possession of a language common to both and also their opposition to Judaism and later on to Christianity, drew them closely together. As the younger sect, the Mandaeans leaned upon the Samaritans as the older and borrowed from them much of the material which formed the basis of their own distinctive creed.*

ASATIR AND THE SAMARITAN LITERATURE.

The destruction of the Samaritan literature makes it very difficult to trace the influence of the Asatir on the Samaritan literature farther back than the tenth or eleventh century. This is the date to which the oldest Samaritan writings thus far known belong. One has also to remember that when the Samaritans copy an older text, or embody it wholesale into their own writings, notably if it is anonymous, they never quote the source from which they have taken it. It is only in comparatively recent times, from the sixteenth century on that here and there the name of an older author is mentioned, especially by Kabasi. Still, the subject matter of the Asatir, which was the only source of information, can be traced amongst almost every one of the prominent writers and poets whose works have been preserved from the tenth to the nineteenth century.

Very little has been saved from the period before that date. The writings of Marķah, who is anterior to that

* The arguments by which Dr. Pallis, in his "Mandaean Studies" Oxford 1926, p. 115 ff., denies the Jewish influence upon the Mandaean doctrine and literature, and ascribes the references to the O. T. to Christian influences, rest upon absolute misconception of the history of religious movements in Palestine, and complete ignorance of the various sectarian developments which have taken place there. As shown above, the contrary is the fact.

period, have unfortunately not come down in a complete form. There must have been a first book of his poems, now lost, which contained a description of the Birth of Moses. The parallelism between Markaḥ and the Hellenistic poet Ezekiel on the one hand, and the appearance of a series of compositions from the thirteenth or fourteenth century downwards, all having as their subject the Birth of Moses, strengthen that contention. It is furthermore corroborated by the analogous fact of the story of the Death of Moses, the text of which is published here, which rests ultimately on the last poem of Markaḥ: the latter is the intermediate link between the Asatir, and the later literature, represented by the above mentioned text. Markaḥ, referring to Moses on two occasions, uses some peculiar phrases such as "His name will be remembered for blessing forever" (Asatir IX, 1), and the words (Asatir Ch. XI. 18) with which God approves of the work of Moses. They are so characteristic that they could not have been coined independently. Markaḥ must have borrowed them from the Asatir.

The next oldest reference thus far available seems to be the Tolida (ninth or tenth century) where, speaking of Akkoh, the author remarks: "This is the town built by Kenan, the ancient." * In the Asatir (Ch. II) we find thus far the oldest source for connecting the building of towns with the first patriarchs.

The next to be mentioned now is Ab Ḥasda, the author of the Tabaḥ, (Gaster Encycl. Islam s. v. 'Samaritans') the oldest and most important work of the Samaritan literature. The author lived not later than the beginning of the eleventh century (ca. 1030 if not earlier). The book is a collection of laws and discussions of legal questions. There is scarcely any legendary matter in it. Still, a few details agree with the Asatir very closely, such as Moses copying the law in the

* Chronique Samaritaine ed. by M. Ad. Neubauer, Paris 1873, p. 24.

course of the last month of his life (Asatir Ch. XI. 3—15). On the very last day he is called by God to go up Mount Nebo. The people are informed of his death by the host of angels which surrounds the Mount and who have come to pay honour to him. There are moreover two passages in the Tabaḥ in which the author seems to be entirely dependent on the Asatir. The first is when, interpreting the blessing of Moses of the tribe of Zebulun (Deut. XXXIII. 18 ff.), he distinctly states that these blessings refer to the Taheb and to the Return of the Time of Favour (Asatir XII. 20). Still more close is the similarity with XII. 19. which refers to the burning of the temple by fire, brimstone and salt. The very wording is identical (cf. notes ad loc.).

Far more extensive use of the Asatir has been made by the author of the Samaritan-Arabic book of Joshua. Here we find the story of Bileam, his visit to the king of Moab the advice he gave, the manner of his death, all of which are taken almost verbatim from the Asatir.* We find furthermore two variants of the "Death of Moses" which agree in the main with the description given in the Asatir, yet with some additional touches taken from Markaḥ or another similar source.

The next work to be mentioned is Ghazal (Tabyah) Al Doweik, probably of the thirteenth century. Two treatises are ascribed to him, one a brief commentary on the Blessings of Bileam, and the other on the Second Kingdom. In the former he interprets the "Blessing," in the main agreeing

* This is of no mean significance since it bears on the problem of the genuineness of the Samaritan-Hebrew Book of Joshua; for it proves that a book of such high antiquity as is assumed for the Asatir had been the direct source of an Arabic version or paraphrase, and that the author of the Arabic Book of Joshua has taken his materials from an anterior Hebrew-Aramaic text, even then when he does not mention the source, as is here the case. The discovery of the Asatir removes every doubt and this will furthermore be proved in time, by means of other ancient documents which have since come to light. They will be treated much more fully in the new edition of the Samaritan Book of Joshua, now being prepared by me.

with the Asatir, though less fully, and without referring to the gods worshipped by Bileam. On the other hand, he also gives an eschatological interpretation to Bileam's prophecy, but only tentatively, and prefers the interpretation found in the Asatir. Bileam is for him the son of Laban, according, as he says, to tradition (which, no doubt, refers to the Asatir). For Al Doweik is the first to mention the Asatir by name and goes on to say that it is the work composed by "our Master, the Messenger," i. e. Moses.

In the second treatise he adduces from the Scriptures ten arguments to prove that a time will arrive when the kingdom will return to Israel. It is thus a treatise on the Advent of the Taheb. In the IVth Proof he gives us again the same interpretation concerning the star as in the previous treatise, and a little more fully, but agreeing with the Asatir. At the same time he gives in Proof VI a similar interpretation to that given by Ab Ḥasda, which agrees with Asatir XII. 19. 21.

The Birth of Moses is the subject of many writings, dating from the end of the thirteenth century or beginning of the fourteenth century. There is first the poem ascribed to Jacob ha-Rabban, probably the high priest in Damascus, who died in 1347, and all the important incidents therein are those found only in the Asatir. There exist besides three more poems of a similar kind. I have not been able to discover the name of the author, but he is a contemporary of Jacob ha-Rabban, whom he mentions with great respect, and also Pineḥas, the son of Joseph, the high priest (1308—1362). The author must have lived before 1347, the year when Jacob ha-Rabban died.

The first of these three poems is a peculiar astronomical piece in which the author endeavours to trace the origin of the Samaritan Calendar to Adam, and its further transference to Moses and Pineḥas, son of Eleazer, son of Aaron. The poem is also of a mystical character, inasmuch as the Mystery of the Calendar is founded on the Divine

Name engraved upon the rod of Adam. This rod afterwards comes into the possession of Moses. These details are partly borrowed from the Asatir, especially the references to the rod of Adam and Moses, and to the book of knowledge and astronomy possessed by Adam. Of special importance, however, are the mystical names of God found in this poem, made by permutations and substitutions of the letters in the true cabbalistic manner. They resemble strongly the mystical names of the gods of Bileam (Ch. X. 7). It is the same system and the same principle in both writings: the Asatir, however, is older and agrees with the Shem Hamitfaresh.*

Still more complete is the agreement in the second poem with the narrative of the Asatir. It contains the full legendary history of the Birth of Moses. Many of the incidents in the poem can be traced directly to the Asatir. No other source so old as the Asatir is thus far known to exist among the Samaritans for these Moses legends. The poem is more elaborate than the short narrative in the Asatir, and a few more incidents have been added, but there cannot be any doubt of the dependence of the poem on the more primitive Asatir.

The third poem, which is much longer than the previous ones, contains all the details found in the Asatir, including the name of the wizard Plti, and other details found only in that book.

Besides these there is still a fragment of a poem in this collection, no doubt by the same author, which contains an allusion to the last scene of Moses' life and to the future of Moses' children, who, according to Samaritan tradition (Pitron XI. 2) were there and then separated from the rest of the children of Israel and preserved to the end of days in a state of absolute purity. In the Asatir this legend, well known in the Jewish literature, is also briefly alluded to

* See Gaster. Samaritan Phylacteries and Amulets, Studies and Texts p. 465 ff.

(Ch. XI. 2). The author of this Fragment must therefore have had access to the Asatir and used it as one of the sources for his composition.

A similar long poem, very fully elaborated, and reminding one strongly of the style of Markah, is ascribed to a certain Abdalla ben Shalma. There is no further information about him except that he may have lived about 1400 C. E. He states distinctly that he has taken his material from the writings of his ancestors, who had obtained it from the tradition of their forefathers. He refers thereby, no doubt, to the Asatir, being the translation handed down in the name of Moses; for we find him absolutely dependent on the Asatir. He is moreover the author of a poem for the days of Succoth (Cowley p. 746 ff) in which occur a few more incidents taken from the Asatir. They are all referred to in the notes to the text.

Before proceeding further, Abisha son of Pinehas, the foremost poet of the Samaritans, must be mentioned, especially his famous Vision (Cowley p. 511 ff.), in which he described the future, the Advent of the Taheb, etc., fully agreeing with the Asatir. He also knows of the altar being built on Mount Garizim (ibid p. 512.)

Abraham Kabasi (fifteenth to sixteenth century) the author of the "Secrets of the Heart," has also some allusions to legends found in the Asatir.

In the year 1537 his pupil and friend, Ishmael Rumihi, at the request of another high priest of the same name, Pinehas, composed in Arabic a versified life of Moses, known as "Molad Moshe;" every incident narrated therein is found in the previous poems and above all in the Asatir. This is the only composition in Arabic, whilst all the others hitherto mentioned are in Samaritan. In some of them reference is also made to the Bileam episode, showing their utter dependence on the old book.

At the end of the seventeenth century, or the beginning of the eighteenth, a certain Meshalma the Danafite composed an elaborate commentary on Genesis. This was afterwards completed by Ibrahim ben Jacob. Meshalma is the second to quote the book under the name of the author of the Asatir, "Baal ha-Asatir," El Doweik being the first to refer to it thus. He gives literal references which are of the utmost importance, for he must have had access to a slightly different recension or to a somewhat more accurate ancient copy. I have, therefore, given all his references in full in the notes, whenever they present variant readings.

Abraham ben Jacob (eighteenth century, Cowley 623 ff.) includes in a poem some incidents from the Asatir and from other traditions, e. g. Adam keeping away from his wife for 100 years (As. I. 26); Amram keeping away from Jochebed until ordered by the angel; Moses hidden in a fiery furnace and saved; daughter of Pharaoh healed from skin-disease (cf. Pitron to XI. 9 and XII. 5.)

Finally, the book is again quoted very fully in the Malif, a kind of catechism for the instruction of the Samaritan children in Biblical history and precepts. In reality it is, however, chiefly a collection of Biblical legends and directions for prayer, and a large number of the legends have been taken verbatim from the Asatir. The book is incomplete, and is written in Arabic by an unknown author. A copy of it was made by Pineḥas, the son of Amram, who died 1897. His son translated it for me into Samaritan from the Arabic, and it consists of 230 questions and answers. The parallels are quoted in the notes by the number of the question. The author was fully conversant with the Samaritan traditions, and he incorporated them into his book. An edition of the Samaritan version is being prepared by me. It is unique in character and value.

None of these writers ever called into question the authority, authorship, or antiquity of the Asatir. It is an essential part of the Samaritan Biblical legendary literature, and its most important source.

CHRONOLOGY AND DATES.

Among the many peculiarities which this little book offers there are the dates on which events have happened, which are here minutely recorded. There must have been a special reason for working out these dates and for introducing them into the book. At one time chronology was the first occupation among the prominent scholars of the various nations. It was a reaction against the arrogant claim of the Greeks of being the masters of civilisation. They would derive everything from their own alleged intellectual superiority, and depreciate as much as possible the civilisations of the East. To this, the latter replied by producing chronological lists of kings and emperors who had ruled the world thousands and tens of thousands of years before the Greeks had ever existed. Their own civilisation was so immensely superior and so much more ancient, that it was claimed that whatever the Greeks possessed was simply derived from these ancient sources. I have mentioned before the claim that Adam had been the divinely inspired author of astronomy, and, in fact, of all the sciences. Berosus for the Babylonians, Sanchuniaton for the Phoenicians, Manetho for the Egyptians; all put forth such long lists. The Jews, for their part, produced the Bible, and told the history of the world from its very creation. Out of the pages of the Bible a special chronology has been evolved, and every minute allusion that could be found in the text has been used for that purpose. As far back as the third century B. C., if not earlier, Demetrius (Freudenthal, Hell. Stud. 35 ff.) with great ingenuity prepared such a chronology, (Gaster, Studies and Texts p. 650). Unfortunately, only a small fragment has been preserved. Another fragment is a further attempt at a chronology which is to cover the whole period of the Biblical history. It was in that atmosphere that search was made also for special chronological data.

There was an additional reason for such a search. The daily Calendar of ancient nations was not merely a record of days and months, but also a record of important events. Based upon one calculation or another the Calendar contained the dates of festivals and of other ceremonial observances. In addition to those mentioned in the Bible, other commemorative days were entered. The people observed these days either by fasting and mourning, when they referred to tragic events, or by rejoicing and revelling, when they brought back the memory of happy occurences in the life of the nation. Astrology brought in its train also the belief in lucky and unlucky days, on which work should or should not be undertaken, best fitted for joy and mourning. These were deftly blended with historical occurrences, so that a day on which some calamity had overtaken the nation, or a great man had died, became afterwards an ill-omened day, on which the people refrained from any joyful activity. On the other hand, the lucky days would be made to coincide either with the birth of one of the great men, or some signal victory or other happy event. From this point of view, the importance of inserting and retaining the memory of single minute dates can easily be understood. This probably is the reason for the dates given in the Book of Jubilees in which, however, with rare exceptions, only the months and years are mentioned. On two or three occasions only do we find the day mentioned, but this must be understood to mean the day of the month, not the day of the week. In the Asatir we find, on the contrary, the larger figures entirely omitted, with two or three exceptions, which will be mentioned presently, and sometimes also the day of the month. Herein lies the difference between this book and the Book of Jubilees. In the Jewish literature we find a host of similar Calendars, in which the days of the month are specially singled out. There is in the first place the Scroll of Fasting

(Ed. Pr. in Seder Olam Rabba, Mantua 1513) with the list of days for the twelve months of the year on which fasting was not allowed. They commemorate days of happy events of the Maccabean period. We see from this fact that popular ceremonies and festivals, which may even have had a totally different origin, obtained an historical justification and backing. There exists also another list of days which is usually joined on to that Scroll of Fasting. Various events which happened on the twelve months of the year are noted down. They are taken mostly from the Biblical period. Not a few of these, as shown in the notes, coincide with the Samaritan dates. Other similar lists are found in other Jewish writings, the dates of which are uncertain, as well as in "Albiruni" translated by Sachau.

Not a few of the dates given in the Asatir, however, are difficult to verify, nor is it clear upon what they are founded. The starting-point of the chronology is here the era of the Creation of the world. There is no trace of counting by Jubilees, although this counting was not unknown among the Samaritans. It appears already in the oldest portion of the Tolida which is not later than the eleventh century. The era of Creation is taken for granted in the Asatir. No question is raised as to whence it came. It is the one found in the Bible, and therefore of divine origin. No other era is even contemplated. At one time the Samaritans started a new era, that of the Entry of the children of Israel into Palestine under Joshua, but they kept to the era of Creation. The author of the Asatir, indeed, seems to be unaware of the era of the Entry. He does not betray any knowledge of a different era from that used by him. The scanty remnants of Samaritan literature cannot help us to determine the time when the era of the Entry was introduced. I have been able to discover a third era from the time of Jezdegerd, and to this they added later on the Mohammedan era. But in some Biblical fragments of the eleventh or twelfth century I have found that the era of Creation and not the Mohammedan has still been used in their colophon.

To the author of the Asatir the world is to last 6,000 years, after which, without saying it clearly, will be the Day of Judgment. This event, however, is not connected directly with the Advent of the Taheb, who is only once mentioned (Asatir XII. 24). He is to bring back the Days of Divine Favour, lost from the time when God "hid" his face, and turned away in anger, owing to the schism of Eli. Then the holy vessels of the Temple on Mount Garizim were hidden in a cave and the period of the "cursed" Fanuta began, which has brought so much misery to the people.

The years of the patriarchs agree, to a large extent, with the readings in the Samaritans recension of the Pentateuch. There is a slight difference, in the case of Seth, (II. 26) due probably to the copyist's mistake. Other slight differences will be seen from the comparative table reproduced later on from Geiger.

It is one of the peculiarities of the Asatir not to use the words "he lived so-and-so many years." Instead of this he says "he learned (or taught) אלף," meaning thereby he learned from Adam or he "ruled." So specially in Ch. II, where the whole list of the first patriarchs is given.

The date of Moses' death agrees entirely with the Samaritan computation found in all their writings, and on two occasions the number of years mentioned as past agrees with the general assumption that the life of the world can only last 6,000 years. Thus at the calculation of the Flood, where the 6,000 years are distinctly mentioned (IV. 20ff.), and so finally for in Prophecy of Moses (XI. 20). It is to be fulfilled at the end of 3,204 years, which added to the 2,796 years, assumed as the date of Moses' death, complete 6,000 years. This must be taken as another proof of the independent Samaritan origin of the Asatir. The

Jews have also endeavoured on their part, to establish the chronology. The Seder Olam Rabba, or the Order of the World, is thus far the oldest book of that kind found in the Hebrew literature. Josephus also uses practically only the era of Creation for the Biblical period. It may be that the Samaritan chronology was directly or indirectly the stimulus to the compilation of a Hebrew chronology. The Samaritan always has a polemical character, and the Jews, no doubt, reacted to it, or the case may have been vice-versâ, the Jews taking the initiative and the Samaritans following suit; cf. the old Chain of the High Priests (ed. by Gaster, J. R. A. S., April 1909, rptd. in "Studies and Texts" p. 283 ff.), and the genealogical lists, each one trying to prove thereby the accuracy of his own tradition. Among the Jews other works have followed in the course of time, like the Yuḥasin by Abraham Zakuto (Ed. Pr. Constantinople 1566, ed. Filipowski, London 1857) the Chain of Tradition (Shalshelet Haḳabalah, Ed. Pr. Venice 1587) by Gedalyah Aben Yaḥia; and finally all these various calculations have been co-ordinated by Yechiel Heilprin in his Seder Hadorot, to which constant reference has been made in the notes.

It may not be out of place if a brief reference is made to the scant allusions of an eschatological character, which are after all bound up with the limit of time. At the end of a certain period something is expected to happen. I have on sundry occasions drawn attention to the simplicity and vagueness of the eschatological outlook in the Asatir. It has not yet moved far away from the Bible. The only points occurring here seem to be the expectation of a Day of Punishment and Reward, and the very curious statement in connection with the burial of Enoch. He is buried near the Holy Mountain and it is stated that those who are buried within a radius of 2,000 cubits will so be exempt from the "burning" (As. II. 41). Nothing further is added to explain what is understood by this "burning." It may mean the burning of the wicked in a kind of Hell, immediately after death, or it may mean their burning after the Day of Judgment. But nothing definite is mentioned of either the character of the Day of Punishment and Reward or the time when it is to happen, nor is anything said of resurrection and immortality. The only allusion to the Day of Judgment is found in the passage of the Three Nights (IX. 37). From other writings of the Samaritans, I gather that these eschatological notions are derived from Deut. Ch. XXXII and XXXIII (The Samaritans like the LXX read ליום נקם "day of punishment," instead of M. T. "mine is punishment" in Deut. XXXII. 35); to the Samaritans Deut. Ch. XXXII has become the ultimate source of their eschatology. It is the result of an early form of exegesis which keeps strictly to the letter of the Law.

COMPARATIVE TABLE OF THE CHRONOLOGY OF THE FIRST TEN GENERATIONS.

(From A. Geiger, Jüdische Zeitschrift für Wissenschaft und Leben, Vol. I, 1862, p. 176.)

	MT.	LXX	Joseph.	Sam.
Adam before begetting Seth	130	230	230	130
Adam after begetting Seth	800	700	—	800
Sum	930	930	930	930
Seth before begetting Enoch	105	205	205	105
Seth after begetting Enoch	807	707	—	807
Sum	912	912	912	912
Enoch before begetting Kenan	90	190	190	90
Enoch after begetting Kenan	815	715	—	815
Sum	905	905	905	905
Kenan before begetting Mahalalel	70	170	170	70
Kenan after begetting Mahalalel	840	740	—	840
Sum	910	910	910	910

	MT.	LXX	Joseph.	Sam.
Mahalalel before begetting Jered	65	165	165	65
Mahalalel after begetting Jered	830	730	—	830
Sum	895	895	895	895
Jered before begetting Chanoch	162	162	162	62
Jered after begetting Chanoch	800	800	—	785
Sum	962	962	962	847
Chanoch before begetting Metushelach	65	165	165	65
Chanoch after begetting Metushelach	300	200	—	300
Sum	365	365	365	365
Metushelach before begetting Lemech	187	167	187	67
Metushelach after begetting Lemech	782	802	—	653
Sum	969	969	969	720
Lemech before begetting Noah	182	188	182	53
Lemech after begetting Noah	595	565	—	600
Sum	777	753	777	653
Noah before begetting children	500	500	500	500
Noah at the time of the Flood	600	600	600	600

Asatir agrees in the main with the Samaritan recension.

GEOGRAPHICAL AND OTHER NAMES.
ARABIC GLOSSES.

The geographical and personal names found in the book, no less than the Arabic equivalents, presented a problem which was not easy to solve. Taking first the geographical names, we find a number of towns built by men of the first generations. Some of them are names of towns found in the Pentateuch, such as Riphat, Rechoboth, Bosra, and others well known to belong to the Palestinian area. Others, on the contrary, are absolutely unknown, for instance, Badan, where Adam lived (I.23) and died. (III.2). For a long time I was inclined to identify it with the Biblical "Padan," in spite of the fact that everything pointed to Palestine, and still more to the neighbourhood of Mount Garizim. By mere chance I found the name in one of the Samaritan chronicles in a totally different connection. It was there described as a place near Sichem, but which had disappeared long ago Strange also are the names of the countries divided by Noah among his children after the Flood (IV) Still more surprising, unless due to corruption of the text, is the description of the boundaries of Palestine as seen by Moses, (Asatir XI.4 ff) though it rests ultimately on the text of the Bible (Numbers XXXIV). Again in the case of places like Adar Shgg (IV. 1) the dwelling-place of Noah, every attempt to identify it has utterly failed, and why Hebron should be called twice Eyul Mṯḥ (III. 3 and IV. 38) is a question no answer to which can be found. The same is the case with Adrms, the place where Adam worshipped first (III. 14), Sursn (III. 19), and many others. I have searched in vain through all available sources; the Bible and Josephus, Eusebius and Jerome (Onomasticon), mediæval travellers and modern geographers of Palestine down to Smith's Historical Geography of Palestine. There is no doubt that some of the names are cryptograms, the result of permutation and combination of letters, as is the case with the personal names, to which reference will be made presently. On the other hand these old names have also undergone the same process of being, as it were, modernised, such as happened notably in the ancient Geomeria, or the division of the land by Noah. The Book of Jubilees also contains such extraordinary names, like Elda, (III. 32) the place of the creation and death of Adam, and also the names of the countries given by Noah to his children. I have shown in my introduction to the Chronicle of Jeraḥmeel that from very early times more modern names were substituted regularly for the older ones found in the Bible. The Palestinian Targum, no less than Josephus, and a host of other subsequent writers, does not hesitate to give the current name of the town or of the nation, better known to their readers than the obsolete and long forgotten. But this substitution has been effected gradually. It took time before the old name was entirely eliminated. It was done first by the way of interpretative glosses inserted in the text. Side by side with the old stood the new name, first as a marginal or interlinear gloss. It was then inserted into the text by the later copyist, and finally retained in lieu of the old, which was then discarded. It is precisely the same process through which the geographical names found in the Asatir have passed. But here they are still in the second stage in which the old name has been retained, and the Arabic equivalent, or reputed equivalent, is added. But this process has been continued in the Arabic paraphrase, where, for instance, when Sifra (a curious form retained integrally as a proper name without re cognition of the *He locativum*) is explained as beingidentical with Sichem, the Arabic paraphrast of the twelfth or thirteenth century straight away substitutes Nablus for Sichem, and so in other places. Meshalma, in his quotations from the Asatir, often altogether omits the Arabic equivalent, for it evidently was not in his copy, or he gives sometimes other equivalents.

I draw special attention to this fact, for the appearence of these geographical names might create the belief that the book is of a more recent origin. How little justified such a conclusion would be is shown not only by the fact that there is no consistency in the equalisation, but by the more important parallelism with the Samaritan Targum.

This Targum is not later than the second century C. E., and it even may be older. In that Targum, a number of words were discovered which had a strange appearance and which no one was able to reduce to any known root. The result was that for a long time they were believed to be survivals of the language of the mythical "Kutheans" brought as colonists into the land by the Assyrian Kings. It was the merit of S. Kohn,* however, to prove beyond cavil or doubt that many of these strange words were nothing other than Arabic glosses to obsolete Samaritan words that had been introduced into the text for explanatory purposes; but they had become so corrupted by constant use that they could no longer be recognized easily. It is precisely the same with the Asatir. Obsolete words, the meaning of which the people had forgotten, were explained originally by Arabic glosses. At one time or another glosses have been introduced, but happily they have been limited to geographical names, and have not affected the personal names, which remain unchanged, except on one or two occasions, like Bab El Abwab (Asatir IV. 27. 29). which, in itself, is not a real geographical name. Cod. A., which has been taken as the basis of the present edition, offers another and if possible more decisive proof for the late insertion of glosses, since Arabic glosses are actually written between the lines above some obsolete words. A careful examination of the text reveals the fact that except for these geographical names, there are only two or three words which seem of doubtful Arabic origin. Such, for instance, is the word "ngmut," (III. 9), translated by me "astrology." But this also seems to be a gloss probably inserted simply to explain the meaning of the "Book of Signs," i. e. that it was the book dealing with the signs of Heaven, with the revolutions of the sun, moon and stars. The word "ngm" is considered by the

* Zur Sprache, Literatur und Dogmatik der Samaritaner, Leipzig 1876; Abhandlungen für d. Kunde des Morgenlandes, vol. V, no. 4.

Arabic lexicographers to be a foreign word, and it may well be of Samaritan or of other North-Semitic origin. The other word, found in Arabic, but also unquestionably of foreign origin, is "fngl", (III. 26), which I have translated as "cup" or "dome." Both are technical terms, and have unquestionably been introduced as explanatory glosses.

A comparison with the Samaritan Targum here again will prove fruitful from more than one point of view. In the Samaritan Targum we find not only explanatory glosses, but real substitutions of new names for those found in the Hebrew original of the text. The translators were not satisfied with merely adding the modern equivalent, whilst leaving the other in its original form, as the author of the Asatir does, but he or those who copied or revised the Samaritan Targum from time to time went one step further. The old Biblical names were entirely eliminated, and their place was taken by modern names, and this, in spite of the fact hitherto not sufficiently recognized, that the Samaritan Targum has also been subject to constant revision and assimilation to the original Hebrew text, just as happened with the LXX and the Jewish Targum. In this respect Gen. Ch. X is highly instructive. As a rule the personal names of the nations are retained in the Targumim in their Hebrew form. But in vv. 11 and 12 there occur the names of the towns built by Ashur. For each of these Biblical names the Samaritan Targum has totally different names. Even the name of Babel (XI. 9) has not escaped the hand of the Targumist. In the Samaritan Targum לילק, read as לקל, as it is a cryptographic permutation, has been substituted for בבל. In Gen. X. 30 the translator misunderstood the Hebrew name Mesha מששא reading it as if it were מִמָשָׁא, he translated it ממסכל which makes no sense. In the Asatir, on the contrary (ch. V. 13), it has been translated in an entirely independent manner reminding one of the Palestinian Targum. The

Samaritan Arabic translator has done precisely the same as the Samaritan Targum. Some of the personal names have not been changed, whilst many of the geographical names have been replaced by more modern equivalents (so Gen. X. 1, X. 11 ff.). In the Asatir we have both names. The Hebrew has been preserved whilst the Arabic has been added. It is noteworthy, however, that these new Arabic equivalents in the Asatir differ both from the Samaritan and Arabic Targumim being independent of both. Furthermore in Gen. IV. 16, the name of the place to which Kain had gone is in the Hebrew מן קדמת עדן. For this the Samaritan Targum has כלי מרנעה עדן. In the Asatir (II. 9) the name of the place is "Ḥanoḥiah," which, by popular etymology and through Samaritan pronunciation, has been changed in one place into "Antokia" (II. 1) thus differing again from the Targum. It is not unimportant to mention in this connection that the proper names in Gen. XXV. 2ff. (the sons of Abraham and Keturah) remain unchanged in the Targum, whilst the Arabic translates most of these as well as of those in vv. 13—15 into better known names of Arabic tribes and clans.

In Gen. XXV. 18 the geographical names which occur also in the Asatir have remained unchanged with the exception of אשורה for which the Arabic has מוצל (=Mosul). Most of the rulers (אלופים) in Gen. XXXVI. 40ff. have also been changed in the Arabic, whilst the Targum has preserved them unaltered. There is still one passage in the Pentateuch to which reference has already been made, viz: Numb. Ch. XXXIV, the names of the boundaries of Palestine. These have remained unchanged in both the Targum and in the Arabic. But most of these names are greatly changed in the Asatir (Ch. XI. 4ff.), and thus again the Asatir is independent of either, and no doubt represents the earliest stage in that slow transformation and introduction of Arabic geographical names. A glance at any Samaritan MS. with Aramaic Samaritan texts will show that this practice has been continued throughout the ages. There are numerous marginal and even interlinear explanatory glosses in the oldest collection of hymns, the "Kenosh," among my Samaritan MSS. In the same way also glosses are found in MSS. of the poems of Markah. Nay, even in the margin of the marriage contract of the high priest Ishak (in "Studies and Texts" p. 139ff.) the Arabic name of the bride is added. The Samaritans, like the Jews, in Hellenistic and later times have often two names, a Hebrew and an Arabic name. The former is, as it were, the holy name and the other the profane or secular name. The Hebrew name of the young woman is duly entered in the text and the Arabic "Kunya" figures as a marginal gloss. These glosses cannot, therefore, be invoked as a proof for the late age of the Asatir, but they are on the contrary one of the best proofs for its high antiquity; for had the book been of late origin, it would be absurd to imagine that the author would have gone out of his way to use apparently old and by then no doubt already forgotten names, and to insert them into his writing. He could at once have used names better known to his contemporaries, as Josephus, Targum, etc. have done. There would then have been no necessity to add the presumed Arabic equivalent, or to substitute altogether a new name for the old one. Arabic explanatory glosses have only been introduced chiefly into old writings for the purpose of elucidating the meaning of an obsolete word, or for the identification of an ancient long-forgotten place-name. Thus these Arabic glosses, like those in the Samaritan Targum, testify to the high antiquity of the Asatir, and the veneration in which it was held throughout the ages. They can only assist in determining the date of the archetype from which the two existing codices are the only extant copies. Nor will this be an easy task, for only a few of the geographical names here mentioned can be identified.

We turn now to the personal names, and here we are also confronted by the fact that names of persons are mentioned in the Asatir of whom nothing is known elsewhere. They were certainly not invented by the author, but whence did he get them? Occasionally one might suggest that symbolical names have been invented, as has been the case elsewhere, e. g. Avan (sin) Azurah (forbidden, restrained), in the Book of Jubilees, IV. 1, as the names of the sisters of Cain and Abel, these names being nothing else than the Hebrew words occurring together in Isaiah I. 13, a fact hitherto unrecognized. Another example is the peculiar genealogy of Haman found in Targum II to Esther (II. 6) in which P. Cassel* recognizes the names of Procurators and Emperors that had been hostile to the Jews, and who were therefore held up to execration as the progenitors of Haman. But no such explanation can be found for the names and genealogies found in the Asatir except e. g. the names of Gifna (leprosy) or Maktesh (disgrace) (III. 13) made by a slight change of letters from the word Makdash (sanctuary) given to Sion and the Temple by the Samaritans. There is no suggestion of anything wrong in the names of the two sisters of Cain and Abel, Al'alah and Makeda (I. 3), or in the very curious pedigree of Pharaoh from the Kittim (VIII. 15). Neither the lists of Manetho and Syncellus nor modern Egyptology have helped in solving this problem. The same is the case with the genealogy of Bileam (X. 1) where he is traced back to Laban. In the Jewish literature Bileam is identified with Laban (see above). The only paralls for these kind of fictitious genealogies I have hitherto found in the pseudepigraphic literature are the two genealogies of Joshua and Caleb in the Pseudo-Philo Antiquities, XV, 3 ff. Great importance was attached to the line of descent, especially at that period. The very lists in the Books of Ezra and Nehemiah and

* II. Targum z. Buche Esther, Leipzig u. Berlin 1885, p. 40 ff. and p. VI.

Chronicles, as well as the Chain of the high priests among the Samaritans, no less than the genealogy of Jesus, in the Gospel Matthew I, show what great value was placed on records of pure and direct descent from great ancestors. One cannot here forget to mention the genealogical list of the Exilarchs in Babylon in Seder Olam Zuṭṭa and that produced by the Karaites, in favour of Anam, the founder of their sect, published in the Notitia Karaeorum.* So strong must that feeling have been that in consequence thereof such fictitious genealogies were invented in order to trace the evil fruit from an evil root. The habit of tracing the pedigree, especially of rulers, as far back as possible, and recording them on their monuments and tombstones, can be seen constantly in the numerous North-Semitic inscriptions (as well as in Arabic and probably also in Babylonian and Assyrian ones). It is curious that this habit should have been preserved among the Samaritans and have become here a regular practice. The author of the Asatir has also taken some liberties with the names of the Kings of Edom and their places of origin (VIII. 10f.) differing from the statements in the Bible (Gen. XXXVI) and also from the Samaritan Targum. Again at least two wizards are mentioned here, one, Plti (VIII. 24), in the time of Moses. (The names are all reproduced here and in the book exactly as they are written, without any vocalisation, unless they are well-known Biblical names.) This name occurs in the Pentateuch, Numb. XIII. 9, as Palti, son of Raphu of the tribe of Benjamin. The name again occurs in I. Samuel XXV. 44, as the man to whom Saul gave to wife Milkah, David's wife. It is not the habit of the Samaritans, however, to give Biblical names to wizards. The name "Palta" or "Palti" occurs as the name of a person in an Aramaic papyrus of the second century B. C. E. found in Egypt (Cowley,

* Ed. J. C. Wolfius, Hamburg 1721, דוד מרדכי Wien 1830, fol 4b ff.

Proc. Soc. Bibl. Archaeology, November 1915). Then there is a name written both Mertis (X.1) and Turts (VI.18). One of these forms is evidently corrupt. We have then the story of Aḥidan (II. 35, III. 13 ff.) the son of Tubal Ḳain, with its distinct virulent attack on Sion and the Sanctuary of which no other parallels are known.

All these peculiarities point to a purely Samaritan origin, which is furthermore corroborated by the fact that we find in the Asatir a number of cryptograms also of personal names which may be the required clue for the identification of the various names occurring in the genealogies mentioned above. Most prominently is this the case in the Prophecy (Ch. XI. 20 ff.) where all the proper names are concealed in cryptograms. This proves again the entire independence of the Asatir from any other pseudepigraphic or Midrashic writing which has thus far come down to us.

THE ORIGINAL LANGUAGE.

The only question that could arise under this heading is as to whether the book was originally written in Samaritan Hebrew or in the vernacular Samaritan. A Greek original is utterly excluded. On many occasions, especially in connection with my studies on the Testaments of the Patriarchs (*loc. cit.* p. 69ff.) and Tobit (*loc. cit.* p. 1), now reprinted in "Studies and Texts," I have endeavoured to show the utter impossibility of a Greek original for Jewish Apocrypha. No trace of Greek idiom has yet been found in these texts, whether preserved in Hebrew or in Aramaic. On the contrary, the Greek texts abound in Hebraisms; even the Assumption of Moses can best be understood when retranslated into a Semitic tongue. There is besides the inherent improbability that a Jew or a Samaritan would recognise as genuine or of any value a book ascribed to Moses and yet written in Greek. However ignorant and credulous—and these books were not written only for the ignorant and credulous—the reader would still know at least that the language used by Moses could only be Hebrew, or at the worst, Aramaic.

The author of the Asatir knew the Pentateuch very well, so much so that he was able to read into the text some allegorical explanations, and to add to the narrative legendary amplifications. In the story of Ḳain the passages from Genesis and in that of Bileam the passages from Numbers are given verbatim in Hebrew (see notes ad loc.). If the book had been written in Hebrew, there would have been no reason why the translation should have retained a few Hebrew quotations, whilst translating all the rest. These quotations are not even indispensible for the elucidation of the legend. It is quite different if we assume an Aramaic original and not a translation. Then the author would give the Biblical passages as quotations to distinguish them from the rest, which was written in the vernacular.

No old Hebrew Samaritan writing is known to exist except the Book of Joshua and a few fragments belonging to the Joshua literature. On the contrary, all the oldest writings—Targum, Marḳaḥ, Nana, Amram Dahra and the oldest prayers—are in the Samaritan language. If this Asatir was to serve a popular purpose either in conjunction with the Targum or independently of it, then it must have been written in that Aramaic vernacular in which it has been preserved to this very day. The Prophecy (Ch. XI) and the Oracle (Ch. XII) with their peculiar syntactic construction, could not have been translated from the Hebrew, besides the obvious obstacles of rendering literally and yet faithfully so obscure a text as this is.

Moreover, neither in Greek nor in Hebrew is there a book completely corresponding to the Asatir of which the one might be deemed the original and the other the translation. It is evident that we have in the Asatir a compilation *sui generis* unlike any other Biblical Apocryphon. It does not follow any known writings, nor is there any one known similar to it.

DATE OF THE ASATIR AND FINAL CONCLUSION.

After this survey, sometimes more elaborate, at other times more restricted, but yet covering a wide field, it is not very difficult to fix the date of the composition of the Asatir. It is obvious that it must be anterior to the date of Artapanos and Eupolemos, and to the third book of the Sibylline Oracles. It is very much older than Josephus and the Palestinian Targum, and the differences between the Asatir and all the other pseudepigraphic writings are so profoundly marked that a long space of time must have elapsed before the simple tales or brief allusions could have been so fully developed as found in the latter writings. I have already pointed out that the Prophecy, properly interpreted, does not carry us down further than the time of Ezra, and the erection of idols or statues on Mount Garizim. Too little is known of the post-Biblical history and of the time when such an event could have taken place, to allow us to draw any definite conclusion from this faint allusion. The Samaritans themselves have lost every knowledge of the meaning of this allusion, and the various interpretations published show how hopelessly they are at a loss. Their interpretations are contradictory and anachronistic, mere guess-work of no value. It is significant that the Taheb is only vaguely referred to and that the whole eschatology is of a most primitive character; it is almost a starting point of the application of Bileam's prophecy to future events. There is no reference to the Resurrection of the Dead in the Prophecy itself, or even to the Day of Judgment, although the world is reckoned to come to an end after 6,000 years. The only outlook on the future is to a time of peace and happiness; of great joy, of intense study of the Law, and of the recognition of the Samaritan claim. All this is of very archaic character, and could not have been compiled at a date when all these ideas had become, in a more fully developed form, the common property of the inhabitants of Palestine. If, as has been assumed, e. g. the Book of Jubilees and the Book of Enoch, etc. are as old as the middle of the second century B. C., astrology and demonology of a very elaborate character must have been rampant at that time. Yet there is no trace of it in the Asatir, whilst the picture of the happy times following upon the Advent of the Messiah, on the one hand, agrees with the last chapter of Daniel save in the reference to the awakening of those "who slumber in the dust," and still more closely with the Sibylline Oracles.

Attention must be drawn in this connection to the remarkable fact that not the slightest allusion is made to the Maccabean period. The Samaritans, as well as the Jews, were deeply affected by the action of the Hellenizing king Antiochus, and Josephus (Ant. XII. 5. 5. 257 ff.) did not hesitate to accuse the Samaritans of bowing their knees to the heathen worship; and yet, not a trace of the terrible persecution to which the Samaritans were exposed is mentioned either in the prophecy or in the oracle. And still more significant is the complete silence about the Destruction of the second Temple. The existence of that second Temple had been the cause of the most virulent contention between the Samaritans and the Jews. The former would have gloated over its destruction, and would not have failed to point to its fate with the utmost satisfaction. On that occasion the Jews again accuse the Samaritans of having acted treacherously towards them. Not only, it was said, did they side with the enemy, but they took an active part in bringing about the destruction of Jerusalem and the burning of the Temple. Such an event, which deeply stirred the feelings and imagination of the people, could obviously not have been passed over in complete silence; yet there is no reference in the prophecy and the oracle to anything beyond the Destruction of the first Temple and the time of Ezra. All these are so many proofs that the composition of the Asatir was anterior to the Maccabean period.

There is, furthermore, no reference to Pineḥas establishing the Calendar, and as for the kings enumerated in the oracle (Ch. XII), the reference is so shadowy and so artificial that no historical conclusion of any value could be drawn from that list. There is no period in history to which it could apply, or there are too many to which, by some ingenuity, the list could not be made to fit; that it is very old, however, has been shown before.

There is one more argument from the language. All the existing Aramaic works belong to the first, second or third centuries of the common Era. Not a single book has been written in pure Aramaic since. The literary revival among the Samaritans from the fourteenth century downward shas only helped to re-establish the use of that peculiar Hebrew which is of a strictly Samaritan colour.

These and many more arguments which arise from the minute comparison of the Asatir with all theo ther documents mentioned hitherto, all point in the same direction, and justify us in assuming that this book could not have been compiled later than between 250—200 B. C. E.

Having thus determined the approximate date of the Asatir, some important conclusions may be drawn from this result. They are of a threefold character: philological, Biblical and exegetical. The book is unquestionably the oldest monument of the Samaritan literature hitherto recovered. It contains already all the peculiarities of this specific Aramaic dialect, and it proves thereby that it must have been the language in general use among the Samaritans at that early date, also for their literary productions. It was not only the spoken, but also the written language: nor was its use limited only to the Samaritans. Aramaic was the lingua Franca of the Persian Empire. It must have been in use long before the beginning of that kingdom. Jews as well as Samaritans and other nations in the Persian Empire spoke and wrote Aramaic. It was also the official language. The decrees of the kings in Ezra and Nehemiah differ little from the Aramaic portions in Daniel, and from that of the contemporary papyri of Assuan. It was the language best understood by the people. This corroborates the interpretation which has been put upon the action of Ezra, who caused the Law to be read to the people both in Hebrew and in the vernacular. We see now in the Asatir the result of a parallel movement among the Samaritans, the outcome of which was the Midrashic expansion and the interpretation found in the Targum, and in the legendary additions to the Biblical narrative. Hitherto the Samaritan Targum was considered to be the oldest work written in Samaritan, followed by Markah, whilst some of the liturgical prayers and hymns were supposed to be older. Now the Asatir easily claims the prerogative of being the oldest specimen of Samaritan in its phonetics, accidence and syntax, not to speak of the vocabulary with its truly archaic character.

Of special importance is the Biblical aspect. We have in the Asatir the oldest references to the Bible; for it a book which rests in all its details upon most minute points in the Bible. It serves exclusively the purpose of supplementing the Pentateuch from beginning to end. No historical incident of any importance is omitted, no apparent gap which this book does not intend to fill, and what is still more interesting, it shows the existence of the Samaritan recension of the Bible already in the hands of the Samaritans as far back as at least the middle of the third century. All the points of difference between the Samaritan and the Jewish recension are already in that text; nay, the polemical part of the Asatir is nothing but an elaboration of these points of difference which rest upon the Samaritan recension. The polemical character of the Asatir has already been referred to before, and it draws its inspiration from the divergence between the two recensions. All the important dogmatic principles in which the Samaritan recension differs from the Jewish are emphasized here, and justified by Agadic interpretation. The holiness of Mount Garizim, the Chosen Mountain, and the hatred against the Temple in Jerusalem, as well as the execration of Eli, Solomon and Ezra, all are prominent features of this text, the author of which displays, by the way, a good knowledge of Jewish history from Joshua to Ezra. The importance of this fact cannot be overestimated, since it leads to a further result viz., the high antiquity of the Midrash, that exegesis of peculiar character, connected with the Bible. The value of it lies not only in the fact that by means of the Asatir one has been able to trace the beginning of this activity as far back as at least three centuries B. C. E., but also in the no less important fact that it contributes to establish the existence of a fixed Biblical text of at least some centuries before that period. As I have shown in my Schweich Lectures on the Samaritans (p. 122), a long time must elapse between the fixing of a text and the endowing of it with a sacred character, and the Agadic interpretation which rests often upon the minutiae of such a text. It must have been considered as holy for a long time, and every word and letter so fixed that legends could be evolved out of these words and letters once definitely fixed. There would have been otherwise neither a basis nor any reason at all for developing a text still fluid. The exegetical Midrashic activity lies also at the root of the Hellenistic literature. The writers in Greek were not the first to evolve these legends, nor are they works, at least in their majority, of an Egyptian or Alexandrian origin, as has hitherto been assumed. On the contrary, as is shown by the Asatir, they rest ultimately on Agadic compilations of Palestinian origin, written in the vernacular Aramaic. These were the primary sources which the Hellenistic writers occasionally embellished by the addition of extraneous matter, but in substance they followed faithfully the old Aramaic original. From all these points of view this Asatir is unquestionably an invaluable addition to the scanty literature of the Samaritans, and a valuable aid towards the elucidation of many problems which have hitherto baffled the investigator.

THE MANUSCRIPTS AND THE EDITION OF THE ASATIR.

Of the Samaritan text only two copies are in existence, one written on parchment (B), which I discovered among them on my visit on the 12th of May, 1907, with which the Samaritans refused to part; and another (A) on paper which turned up a little later, and which they also declined to sell. In consequence of that refusal I induced them to provide me with copies. I asked the priests Ab Ḥasda son of Jacob, and Abisha son of Pineḥas, to make two independent copies of the older MS., whilst Abraham son of Pineḥas provided me with the copy of the more recent MS. In time, I was able to obtain possession of the original paper MS. (A). Of the copies from the older MS., the one made by Ab Ḥasda, son of the late high priest Jacob, is very well executed. It is a fine piece of Samaritan penmanship most calligraphically done, in uncial characters on forty pages with the original pagination, 25 lines to the page. All the quotations from the Pentateuch are written in red ink. The figures in Ch. XII are also marked by red ink. The whole text is written without any break. Punctuation, in the use of which the Samaritans differ entirely from other well-known systems, is freely introduced. Here and there signs above the letters are used to differentiate between words written in the same letters, but having a different meaning. The colon(:), does not mark the end of a sentence and often denotes that the preceding letters are numerals. A peculiar sign which sometimes resembles a semi-colon (⁏) marks an abbreviation, but unfortunately is it more often omitted than retained, causing thereby great difficulty and confusion.

Not satisfied with this one copy of the old MS. I asked Abisha to make me another copy, in order that these two should check each other, so that the chances of mistakes should thereby be greatly reduced or eliminated. This copy consists of thirty-seven pages, with twenty-five lines to the page, written less beautifully than the previous one, in cursive writing called by the Samaritans "half letters." The original punctuation also has been preserved faithfully by Abisha. By collating the two copies I have been able to obtain a reasonably accurate copy of the ol doriginal.

The more recent is the Codex on paper mentioned before. Originally I had to content myself with a transcript made by Abraham, son of Pineḥas the Kahen. A few years afterwards the original came into my possession. I call it Cod. A. It is not dated. It is a rare occurrence that the copyists of Samaritan MSS. should not append their names and the dates when they had completed their work. But judging from the internal evidence and by comparison with other MSS.,—though Samaritan palaeography does not exist—one is safe in assign it to the sixteenth or the beginning of the seventeenth century. A later owner has written a few lines with his name across the back of the last page, but someone has rubbed out the date. The MS. consists of 24 leaves of thick yellow Oriental paper measuring 16.7×14.1 cm.

There are 27 lines to a page, except in Ch. XII. which is written in short distichs, the page being divided into two columns. It is written throughout by one hand in black ink, without any break in the text. The punctuation is used regularly, the colon after the letters denoting numerals and at the end of the sentence are sometimes three dots (∴). Occasionally the sign of abbreviation is introduced, but it is more often omitted, and caused thereby no little difficulty in the understanding of the text. This is a peculiarity in which A and B agree, showing thereby that they are derived from the same common prototype; but the writer of Cod. A has sometimes given the words in full, although he had to compress the text within a comparatively narrower space. For that reason he also wrote in small cursive type, and cramped the writing. Still in spite of it the writing is clear, and what is more the text is in many passages more accurate than in B. Besides a few omissions in the one or the other due to carelessness of copyists, to homoioteleutera and other scribe's errors the two MSS. differ also slightly in the orthography.

Cod. B shows a more thoroughgoing obliteration of the gutturals, or rather, graphic unification, than Cod. A. The different gutturals are treated a little more carefully in A. On the whole both represent the Samaritan phonetics with even greater consistency than is found now in the Targum. Both codices represent, however, one and the same text, and both go back to the same original. Both have in common all the difficult and corrupt passages. The Arabic glosses and geographical identifications and all the proper names of men and gods are the same in both, just as they are also found to a large extent in the Arabic paraphrase and in Meshalma. The scribe seems to have revised his MS., and on not a few occasions he has inserted missing words, and also occasionally a whole sentence. A subsequent owner of Cod. A, to whom the language appeared difficult, or who wished to help a reader no longer quite familiar with the Samaritan, started inserting Arabic glosses. Over every scarce word he wrote—between the lines—the Arabic translation, and he numbered the seven gods worshipped by Bileam (Ch. X. v. 7). Probably finding the work too difficult, or for some other unknown reason, he discontinued these Arabic glosses after a few pages. They henceforth appear only sporadically. These Arabic glosses differ, as far as I have been able to ascertain, from the corresponding words used in the Arabic paraphrase.

The state of the text found in these two MSS. is, however, far from satisfactory. In the course of time, it must have suffered from careless copyists, and a few passages which may have been originally in the Asatir have been omitted, and others so greatly abbreviated that they became mere allusions, such as the story of Aḥidan (Ch. III.) the Wars of the Nations and Nimrod (Ch. V); the reference to the children of Moses (XI. 2) and many other passages that are found more fully in the other Samaritan literature which has drawn its material from the Asatir. A slightly different text was probably in the hands of Meshalma, and here and there one can observe in the Arabic paraphrase slight variants which may be due to the Samaritan text used by the paraphrast, unless indeed they belong to the additions which he so freely made. It shows however that at his time in the twelfth century the text had already suffered corruption and mutilation.

As basis for the present edition I have taken Cod. A as containing, on the whole, a text which has been better preserved. This text has been carefully collated with Cod. B in the two copies, and wherever there seems to be a definite lacuna, a word omitted or a form entirely mutilated by the scribe A, I have corrected and completed the text by the readings of B. Orthographic variants have been ignored. Important variants found in Meshalma have however been set out in full in the notes to the translation. I have transliterated the Samaritan into modern Hebrew square script, but I have retained the punctuation and the few graphic signs found in Cod. A. With the help of the two MSS., abbreviations have as far as possible been completed, so as to reduce the difficulties of the text. The text has then been divided by me into chapters and verses. The MSS. offered no guide, the text being written continuously but for the purpose of annotation and reference I considered it indispensible to divide it into smaller sections. The chapters have been made to correspond, more or less, with definite episodes in the Biblical narrative. The verses contain detailed incidents. Chronological and genealogical data, however small, have been counted as single verses, to facilitate reference.

A Samaritan-Hebrew commentary (Pitron) to which reference will be made later, has been printed under the text, and as far as possible I have tried to make these run concurrently. This, however, was not always possible owing to the prolixity of the latter. Both text and commentary have been *literally* translated. The translation which accompanies the Samaritan text has proved the most arduous part of my work. Difficulties abounded on every side. As mentioned before, the text itself, owing to its great age, has suffered in many places. Small portions have undoubtedly dropped out, thus rendering the meaning of the passages very obscure, or reducing them to mere allusions. There was scarcely anything which could help to nterpret them satisfactorily. In addition there was the archaic language, so old indeed that the Samaritans themselves have given up the attempt to explain it. Already the Arabic paraphrast of the twelfth century, and the latest commentators in the Pitron, have either passed them over altogether, or simply left them untranslated; and whenever they did attempt a translation it was quite fantastic, and did not do justice to the text. Again many words were written in an abbreviated form, and as often as possible, the sign which marked the abbreviation had been omitted, so that it took me a very long time until I discovered the fact that the words which had baffled me were simply abbreviations or cryptograms. Added to this was the peculiar orthography, which follows strictly Samaritan phonetics. All these combined to increase the difficulty of giving as faithful a rendering as was necessary for any study of the text, its sources, parallels, origin and date. The translation is as literal as possible, retaining occasionally the ambiguity of the original. And yet with all these endeavours, I must humbly confess that all the obscure passages have not been cleared up, and that the manifold problems connected with this ancient book have not been entirely solved. The last word has not yet been spoken and it is for other scholars to continue and complete my labours in this direction. But this work would have been incomplete without also adding references to parallels from the Samaritan as well as from the other pseudepigraphic literature. I have therefore added ample annotations in which I have adduced as many parallels as seemed important, to throw light on the relation in which the Asatir stands to that literature. In these notes I have moreover taken care to give in the first place as many parallels as possible from the Samaritan Literature. They are often given in full, since the whole material is otherwise practically inaccessible and the information assists greatly in the interpretation of the text. The references to the other literature could have easily been multiplied; but that would have merely meant a repetition of what others have done so well in their editions, references to which must therefore suffice.

THE ARABIC PARAPHRASE.

The Samaritans possess two Arabic translations of the Asatir, one more ancient and one of more recent date. I am dealing now with the first. I have two copies of it, one written by the late high priest Jacob, and another more recent copy. In the British Museum there is an older copy. These copies represent, as far as I have been able to ascertain, one and the same translation of the same original. In the Introduction the anonymous author, after praising God, says that he is translating the work of the Master Moses; but without giving any title of the book he at once starts to translate the text. This translation is anything but literal. There is scarcely a single passage in it which has not been greatly enlarged. In the last chapter the translator is not satisfied with a verbal rendering of the Prophecy of Moses, but adds also an historical explanation, which is of no value, since it is full of anachronisms and misunderstandings.

This Arabic text is characteristic of the manner in which such translations have been made from Samaritan originals. They took every possible liberty with the text, introduced new matter, and omitted old. These Arabic translations are not the work of skilled scholars, and give a wrong impression of the old original. It is evident that this translator, like others who have translated from Samaritan into Arabic, had no other purpose than to relate the old story in a popular manner. It was not intended to be a literal translation. We find in addition that he either did not understand the Samaritan text, or willfully passed over every difficult passage in his translations. He simply left it untranslated and reproduced it in the Samaritan script. He also left all the proper names in the original Samaritan, but often added the Arabic equivalent as now found in the Samaritan text; and so also with the mystical names of the gods worshipped by Bileam, where he ventured on an astrological explanation, a later attempt to explain those seven idols.

The translation is evidently made for Samaritan readers only, otherwise the very numerous Samaritan words and even phrases would not have been allowed to stand. The author follows, in a way, a general practice. When Samaritans write in Arabic, they always quote the Biblical references in the original and write these passages in the Samaritan script. But then they are quotations from the Bible, whilst in the Asatir they are integral portions of the original text which the author fails to translate. They were a stumbling block to anyone unacquainted with Samaritan, and they have proved such to the late Dr. Leitner, who published a German translation of the British Museum MS. in Heidenheim's Vierteljahsresschrift Vol. IV, Zürich 1871 p. 187ff. The result has been most unfortunate, for the book seems to be quite unintelligible. Every proper name is missing, the most important passages are omitted, not a single sentence is completed, and the meaning is rendered absurd or entirely inaccurate.

The reference to Maimonides gives us a clue to the probable date of this paraphrase and also to the home of the author. The virulent tone adopted against Maimonides shows the bitter hatred against a man with whom the Samaritans must have come into some personal conflict. This could only have taken place in Egypt and probably at a time when Maimonides took up a very strong attitude against the Karaites. Nothing is known of his attitude towards the Samaritans who were then numerous in Egypt. The bitter tone used by the author might be an indication of Maimonides' relation to the Samaritans (v. Paḥad Ishak s. v. Kuthim). To the Samaritans in Nablus Maimonides' opinion or action was a matter of little or no concern. Not so to the Samaritans in Egypt, which thus must have been the home of the author; and the date of this work then could not be later than the end of the twelfth or beginning of the thirteenth century. This date agrees entirely with that given tome personally by the Samaritans who assert that the author lived not much later than the twelfth century.

It is then not a little surprising to find that by that time the knowledge of the old Samaritan should have dwindled to such an extent that a man who undertook to paraphrase a book ascribed to Moses could no longer master it sufficiently. Overladen as this paraphrase is with additional matter, it is not easy to separate that which he took from the Asatir and those portions which he took from elsewhere in order to embellish his paraphrase. But it is evident that his text must have been similar, if not identical, with the text which is now in our hands. At this time already the text had become obscure and many of the corruptions were already found in it; they must therefore be of a much more ancient date. Difficult as the book itself proved to be, the difficulty was immensely increased to the translator when he reached the Oracle. Here he was entirely baffled, and did not even attempt any translation. He simply condensed it into a few sentences.

In the material used by the author to embellish he narrative there is also the episode of Shobakḥ and his mother, the sorceress, taken from the Book of Joshua. It is of special interest to show the inter-relation between these two Arabic works, which both rest on more ancient Hebrew-Samaritan originals. On the one hand, the author of the Book of Joshua takes the story of Bileam among other incidents from the Asatir and the Arabic translator takes episodes from the Samaritan Arabic Book of Joshua. It helps to determine the date of the latter which, belongs probably to the eleventh century, if it be not older.

THE PITRON: OR ARABIC-SAMARITAN COMMENTARY TO THE ASATIR.

Of special interest, no doubt, from many points of view is now the second commentary originally composed in Arabic, the date of which is uncertain; of this commentary, a Hebrew-Samaritan translation has been prepared for me. It appears now in this book. No name of an author is mentioned, and none has been given to me in spite of repeated enquiry. The Samaritans only assert that some scholars, together with Abraham, son of Amram, the high priest, since deceased, had composed it. It is an attempt to provide at any rate a commentary independent of the older one. In it they make no use whatsoever of the older Arabic paraphrase. They knew the latter well, for I obtained a copy of it from them. It is just because of their endeavour to do their very best that this commentary is characteristic and interesting. It shows their scholarship and literary capability at a very low ebb, for it reveals how little the Samaritans themselves understand the Asatir. Obscure and difficult passages remain just as obscure and difficult as they were. No attempt at elucidation is made. The legendary matter is, however, more expanded and in the history of Moses they use those other Samaritan compilations dealing with the Birth of Moses mentioned before, in order to complete the narrative in the Asatir. The interpretation of the final Prophecy of Moses differs from that in the previously mentioned Arabic paraphrase. It is full of anachronisms and contradictions; moreover, it is anti-Christian. It is curious to find among the Samaritans some of the legends concerning the birth of Jesus, against which the Fathers of the Church protested so vehemently, branding them as hostile fabrications. They occur also by the way in the old Samaritan chronicle. Similar legends have found their way also into the older Jewish literature.*

This commentary might be called an Arabic Targum of the Asatir, were it not that this application of the word "Targum" to an Arabic explanation of an Aramaic text would appear incongruous. As stated, it was originally written in Arabic, and has then been translated at my request into Samaritan-Hebrew. Owing to this fact the original quotations from the Asatir in the Arabic Pitron have been retained in the Hebrew, and appear to be a tautology. This can be understood easily when one remembers that in the Arabic the translation precedes the Samaritan text, and is therefore repeated now, when the Arabic text has been translated into Samaritan.

* See S. Krauss, Das Leben Jesu, Berlin 1902.

In my MS. the Arabic and Samaritan are written in two parallel columns on 171 pages. The MS. is very carefully written in the uncial character, like that of the Bible codices, with the usual Samaritan punctuation and occasional diacritical signs. The copy was made by Ab Ḥasda, son of the then living Jacob, son of Aaron, the high priest, on the eighth of the fifth month in the year 1328 Hedg. There are 25 lines to the page from 1—159 and thence to the end 33 lines to the page. The author has divided the Pitron into 144 paragraphs up to verse 6 of Chapter XII. They are of unequal length. They evidently appeared to him logical divisions of the contents and each of these small divisions begins with a slight indenture of the opening line.

The quotations from the Asatir are written in red ink, as is often the practice of the Samaritans of writing quotations in different ink. I have now published this Hebrew-Samaritan Pitron with the Asatir at the foot of the text. Towards the end when the author tries to explain the fifth name on the list of the Oracle, he repeats much of the matter referring to the Birth of Moses, found already in Ch. VII. 27 ff. The text has been divided by me in accordance with the original division, but I have given in the Hebrew text also the pages of the original. In the translation, however, I have divided the commentary into chapters and verses corresponding to those of the Asatir whilst preserving at the same time the division into sections and the pagination of the original for easier comparison. To the translation (see above) I have also given the literary parallels, whenever the Pitron contains additional matter not found in the Asatir. It is noteworthy that the Pitron offers only a commentary to Ch. XII from vv. 1—6, a very lamentable exhibition of ignorance. Here also, except for an attempt to explain the first six names of the kings of the Oracle, which proved very unfortunate, the rest has been left without any commentary.

SPECIMEN OF THE ASATIR TRANSLITERATED ACCORDING TO THE PRONUNCIATION OF THE SAMARITANS.

The Samaritan Aramaic is also written without any vowel signs, in fact with fewer signs than used sporadically in the Hebrew Samaritan text. The pronunciation is then simply a matter of oral tradition. No one, as far as I am aware has as yet tried to obtain details of that pronunciation. Thanks to H. Peterman* we have a fair example of the Hebrew phonetic transcript in Latin characters of the whole of Genesis published in his book. He was helped by the high priest Amram. We are therefore in a better position to judge the system of their pronunciation and how it compares with the phonetics and the grammar of the Hebrew of the Jews. No doubt it represents an ancient tradition. A phonetic transliteration of the Ten Commandments and of the Samaritan marriage-contract has been published by me in the Nöldeke-Festschrift, and in the Monatsschrift f. Wissenschaft des Judentums, both reprinted now in my "Studies and Texts," p. 614 ff. and may be considered as a further contribution towards the elucidation of their Hebrew pronunciation. Nothing, however, has been done in order to obtain from the Samaritans any information of the manner in which they read their Targum and the Samaritan hymns of their liturgy. These texts have occasionally some diacritical signs, but they are so sparingly used that they are of no help whatsoever. I have therefore endeavoured to obtain a transliteration of the Targum to Gen. Ch. I and of a portion of the Asatir. The former was dictated to me by the priest Isaac, son of Amram, and the latter by Abisha, son of Pineḥas (son of Amram). I could take it down only with great difficulty owing to the rapidity with which they

* Versuch einer hebr. Formenlehre nach der Aussprache der heutigen Samaritaner, Leipzig 1868.

read the text and the reluctance they felt to see it set down in strange characters. I am giving it here as a further addition to this publication of the Asatir.

I have kept strictly to the manner in which the text was read, also when words were combined, and which were not mere enclytics. I have marked also occasionally the accent, and I should like to mention that the accent lies almost invariably on the penultimate syllable. As far as the pronunciation is concerned, it may be added that besides the indiscriminate obliteration of the gutturals, ג is almost regularly pronounced as כ and ו very often interchanges with ב, the final ר becomes inaudible on most occasions, and the final ן is pronounced often as ם. I have refrained from introducing any diacritical or other signs for the missing gutturals. My desire was to have a faithful picture of their pronunciation of the Samaritan Aramaic.

I may add here a few words about the pronunciation of the Aramaic by the Jews, as the form in which the Targum appears now in our printed Bibles is thoroughly misleading. In the Yemenite MSS. alone the older tradition has been preserved with the so-called supralinear vocalisation best fitted for that pronunciation. It is now being recognised that when the Oriental MSS. reached Europe the current vocalisation or the Tiberian, had been substituted for the other more ancient vocalisation, and the old pronunciation had been still more obliterated by the attempt to subject the vocalisation to rules of the Massorah which affected only the Hebrew. But not only was the vocalisation thus changed, but also the accentuation. The accent of the Hebrew text had been bodily transferred to the corresponding word in the Targum and placed there according to the rules of Hebrew pronunciation; thus modifying the character of the vowels and also introducing the Daggesh for which originally there was no use. Nothing can therefore be learned from the present form of the Targum, unless we go back to the Yemenite tradition and use it with very great caution. The Samaritan specimen may therefore be of additional service.

Whilst reading the text, Abisha at the same time added some explanations, which are here reproduced as footnotes, and in some passages he gave interpretations of words of the prophecy which agree with those found in the Pitron; I am giving them here also in the footnotes. The text chosen is Asatir XI. 13 to the end of the chapter.

(13) Unaat nebya raba baado uvzoa * (14) aadi ami tuba dara ** umaasec etlitu alal *** le (15) ou emsheri embeyer arauta † alyom hashelishi umasel le abyom arebi (16) ummiyal le elgo mashcana beh (17) unafa ulayeya †† mem anan kabuda (18) ªyesha fūāla kashira tuna yoma e'baaª meyacum dareya maetgala moshe nebeyah raba mima darashta mare (19) ukenama utemunat shema yabet (20) uamar maate atit al ªkemanⁿ alafenª uᵇrish udālat sheninᵇ ke tolēdu banem ubāni banem resh fanuta tera [mekodaya] mikeyata (21) ªam ††† kaba lebaa usherho azrezª bafani urish annaute bede (22) umakdasha yesof abyoma (23) zaru adesh ebraute yalef faleke rami elcoala sedar fanu (24)

* shashon.
** mimhaaraz.
*** mabo.
† torah.
†† idnoa (?)

Verse 18. a—a. if they do the thing properly, then it will be well with them at the end. This is the translation suggested by Abisha, which is absolutely wrong. The first part contains the approving word of God to Moses and the following three words mean: This is the last day, i. e. of Moses.

Verse 20 a—a. 3,000 years. "keman" is the Samaritan name for the third letter of the alphabet and agrees much more closely with the name of the Greek γ (gamma), i. e. "gaman." b—b. 204 years.

††† gaba.

Verse 21 a—a. There will come a man from the tribe of Levi and his name will be Azrz = Eli: b—b and the first of punishment (zeal) will be through him.

Verse 22. and the sanctuary will come to an end in his time.

rashu maklat binyamem bemon yibini (25) rashot edbet yauda balof (balom²) exerate yebatelum (26) shema shema ol yeuda (27) megdol gifna yibne (28) beme² al yai bai eshta (29) yetalasun bar moled edishu (30) yae asami balam (31) ebyamo tashmesh elui nikraya tikoman (32) eksibed* yomem makdash zaruta yetfaka ebyed goe āzfānem (33) udebet sheme udebet faneya evdor bara** el uashamo dar tetiyon beskamo reba (34) al yae [mekbi] emkebi*** lannoote yetabet ara boraya elyence yasenun (35) shadak yae balama bor il iuar uāyem aftab (36) ubataken illof katab yetabet (37) millen hateten umilko† atek yafeen (38) ualinek shēma aleak lara yaratu†† abatak utinadinnē (39) luza tibni (40) ªyobel baado fenuª tinyane teum (41) teu bame nei††† titami balabon yomeya (42) ªadesh kabata yaderª saorren usalamen feru.

Verse 25. ª4637 years from the creation of the world: this will happen up to the day of Solomon. This is the same interpretation as found in the Pitron, see there. The letters of the words "Balom" are read backwards from left to right, as if they were numerical figures and the decimals reduced to units. This is quite a modern way of calculation and follows the ordinary use of figures; otherwise the word "balom" even read backwards would be forty+six+thirty+seventy. The same is the case with the word "beemek" (verse 28) where the letters are read backwards as numerals and units, otherwise it would be following the same order: 100+40+70+2.

Verse 28. ª1472ª the time of Jesus from the Entry of the children of Israel into the land of Canaan.

Verse 30 Abisha read: "mimzar benazanoth."

* Abisha does not know the meaning of this word, although it is a well known Aramaic word, sometimes written צבחר i. e. in one instance, shortly.

** 2127. The same as on previous occasions, but here the letters are counted from right to left in the regular order of Hebrew reading. This gives 2+1+200+70 if taken in their real numerical value; they are, however, to be taken as units and simple numerical figures. Needless to say that all those calculations do not fit.

*** mafek = מהפך change.

† Pronounces it "go."

Verse 38. ªGod will help himª.

†† = yarashu.

Verse 40. a—a. The jubilee will be observed with joy.

††† = tahor.

Verse 42. a—a. The hill will be glorious.

STORY OF THE DEATH OF MOSES.

In addition to the above two texts of the Asatir and Pitron I am publishing here also a Samaritan description of the last scenes at the Death of Moses. The number of such Apocalypses of Moses and of stories depicting in a graphic manner the last hours of Moses' life upon earth is so great that it is sufficient to refer only to this fact (v. Schürer and especially Charles Apocalypse Intr. and the Hebrew tales of the Ascent of Moses to Heaven. J. R. A. S. 1893 (p. 407—424) now reprinted in my "Studies and Texts" p. 124). Of special interest, however, is it to follow the traces of this legend also in the Samaritan literature. The text which appears here for the first time bears out the contention that such an elaborate story of the Death of Moses must have been known also among the Samaritans from a very early date. This story forms the first chapter of a Samaritan Chronicle in my possession (Cod. 1168). The date of its compilation is uncertain. It is probably due to a modern compiler. He has used, however, very old material for his work. This chapter is written in the pure Samaritan Aramaic and differs somewhat linguistically from the rest of the book. At a close examination I discovered it to be a variant of the last poem of Marḳaḥ, omitted by Heidenheim but edited by M. Hildesheimer.*

Those who have no access to the Samaritan original of Marḳaḥ will now be in a position to compare these two versions. It will be found that a considerable portion of the first section of that poem has been embodied in this legend, and on the other hand, there are some additional elements wanting in Marḳaḥ, especially the details about the copying of the law, the placing of it in the Ark, etc. Thus we are carried back at once to the second or third century and to genuine Samaritan literature. But we can carry our

* Des Samaritaners Marḳaḥ Buch der Wunder, Berlin 1898.

story still higher up. Not a few incidents, nay, the very dramatic setting, the gathering, the speeches, and the final scene of the covering cloud are all found in Josephus (Antiq. IV. 8, 45, 309 ff.). Here again the similarity between Jewish and Samaritan tradition is very striking.

There is here then another witness to the extreme antiquity of this story of the Death of Moses, which moreover supplies some details missing in Josephus and found in the Samaritan text and vice versâ, thus completing one another.

The poem of Marķaḥ itself does not seem to be the starting point or the ultimate source of this legend as found in the Chronicle, for it has already been shown that the agreement with Josephus is so close that we must look for a more ancient chronicle as the real source both for Josephus and for the Samaritan. In fact we find a similar description with all the essential details already in Ch. VI of the Arabic chronicle known as the Book of Joshua (ed. Joynboll) which, although a little shorter than the version in the chronicle, agrees, however, with it in every important detail and shows that it must go back to that very old chronicle of the Samaritans which started with the history of the Death of Moses, and then incorporating the Book of Joshua, was continued generation after generation, each subsequent writer adding the events of his time. The author, therefore, of the present chronicle has merely followed the older example, though influenced no doubt to a great extent by the form which the legend had taken in the poem of Marķaḥ. The tradition is, however, a continuous one, and therein lies the importance of this text for the history of the Asatir. Going outside the immediate Samaritan literature, we turn now to Pseudo-Philo's Biblical Antiquities.

There (Ch. XIX) an elaborate description is given of the Farewell and Death of Moses. Sentences occur therein which agree almost literally with our text and with the Asatir, and what is more, reference is made to the rod of Moses and to other details which connect that version closely with the Samaritan and with Josephus. It contains also a much fuller intercession of Moses with God and an eschatology which completes the picture and explain ssome obscure allusions in the Asatir.

There can be no doubt as to the extreme age of this story, and it proves moreover that a very ancient text can be found embedded in a comparatively recent compilation. The date of a Samaritan MS. is no argument for the antiquity of its contents or of the elements which have been used in its compilation. In addition to the Samaritan original I have given also an English translation and in a few notes I have drawn attention to the parallels in the above mentioned works of Josephus and Pseudo-Philo, as well as to parallels in other apocryphal writings.

I have left for the last the comparison of this Samaritan Assumption with the well known pseudepigraphic Assumptio Mosis (ed. by R. H. Charles) which has been preserved in a fragmentary condition and in a late Latin translation. This goes back to a Greek original which in its turn rests upon a Semitic text (Hebrew or Aramaic). It is curious that not one of the numerous scholars who have studied the Assumptio Mosis has recognised the close relation of that book to the narrative in Josephus and the portion referring to the Death of Moses in Pseudo-Philo, not to speak of course, of the Samaritan literature which was not inaccessible, considering that the Arabic Book of Joshua had been published as far back as 1847 by Joynboll and the poem of Markaḥ by Hildesheimer in 1898. The parallel between the Samaritan text and the Assumption is absolutely striking even in minute details. I am referring, of course, to the framework of the last scenes in the life of Moses, his discourse with Joshua, and his lamentation and farewell speeches, and not to the vatication. Unfortunately, the Latin text breaks off in the middle of the last scene, so that it becomes very difficult to reconstruct it.

From ancient quotations a dispute between the Archangel Michael and Satan for the body of Moses is said to have been found in that final portion. This, of course, could not form part of the Samaritan legend, and it is missing as well in the other texts hitherto known. But with the exception of this incident the Samaritan seems to have retained a full description down to the final disappearance in this version of the Death of Moses. The last incident of the sepulchre is found also in the Palestinian Targum (see above). The central portion, Ch. II. 3 to Ch. X in the Assumptio, shows us the manner in which the ancient legends had been utilised for entirely different purposes. But the statement that Moses foretold the future events up to the time of Solomon, or to that of the Messiah, seems to have been the original form and agrees mainly with the Asatir in the general outline. All the rest in the Assumptio is the result of deliberate manipulation. The setting belongs to the wider circle of those legends which deal exclusively with the Death of Moses of which the Jewish parallels have been studied by M. Rosenfeld.* But curiously enough the Jewish texts differ in every detail from the Death of Moses as found in Josephus and in the Samaritan versions, whilst the agreement between these latter is very close indeed. Moses is the intercedor, the people weep at his departure, he takes leave of them one by one, he is met by angels and he disappears in a luminous cloud. Such must have been also the ending of the Assumptio, and these together with Pseudo-Philo and the Samaritan Arabic Joshua form thus one group of identical traditions which must be at least older than the time of Josephus. Here we have a definite *terminus ad quem* below which we cannot place the date of this Assumption. No doubt Josephus and this story of the Death of Moses have borrowed their material from the same more ancient source, which also served as ultimate source for the Samaritan group.

* Der Midrasch über den Tod Moses, Berlin 1899.

This Samaritan Death of Moses in its turn shows in many details also close acquaintance with the Asatir. The latter is so concise in form that the legends are mentioned very briefly. It must remain however an open question whether the author of the Asatir was satisfied with merely referring to the legends as being well known, or whether, as I am inclined to believe, he presents the oldest stage in the development of these legends. Be it as it may, the Samaritan story of the Death of Moses is a welcome addition to the scant literature of Samaritan Apocrypha. It may prove, I venture to think, together with the Asatir a further contribution to the study of the pseudepigraphic literature.

TRANSLATIONS

II.
TRANSLATION OF THE ASATIR.

[In the name of God we begin:]
This is the Asatir of our Master Moses upon whom be the peace of God.

Chapter 1. [Ḳain and Hebel.]

1. Praised be God who made the world and established Adam the ancestor and his sons Ḳain and Hebel like unto him.
2. And he gave to Ḳain the West: and he gave to Hebel the North and the South.
3. And he gave Al'alah the twin sister of Ḳain to Hebel to wife; and he gave Makeda the twin sister of Hebel to Ḳain to wife.

Ch. I.
(1) Adam Ruler and King: Samaritan Chain of High Priests. Samaritan anonymous poem. Abdalla ben Shalma: Cowley p. 522ff passim Samaritan Literature. — Josephus, Antiqq. I. 3. 4 (83); I. 3. 4 (86.87).—Adam King and Priest: Schatzhöhle, (Bezold) p. 4.— Adam as King: Kebra, Chs. 3. 5. etc.
(2) Samaritan Arabic: Suria and the coast lands.—Meshalma, folio 122a: Gave to Ḳain the West, and to Hebel the East.— Gen. Rabba XXII. 7. (Aptowitzer p. 15.): The earth divided between Ḳain and Hebel by agreement: One the earth and the other the movable things.— Yashar I, 14: Adam gave them possession in the land.
(3) Great divergence in these names in later literature. A few are given here. Samaritan differs from all.—Meshalma (quoting Asatir): Hebel married Al'ala sister of Ḳain, who married twin sister of Hebel, Makeda. f. 122b. —Samaritan Arabic: Balala. —Josephus I. 2. 1 (52), speaks only of two sisters, and so Pal. Targ. to Genesis IV. 2 and Gen. Rabba Ch. XXII. 7. (Aptowitzer, p. 20ff.) and Pirke de Rabbi Eliezer, Ch. XXI. Twin sisters were born: Kebra, Ch. 4 (Bezold). Makeda, the name of the twin sister, is the name of the Queen of Sheba in Kebra, Chs. 26 ff. and 85 ff. It occurs as a local name in Joshua three times 10. 10; 12.16; 15.41.— Jubilees Ch. IV. 1. 8: Awan and afterwards Azûrâ, not twin sisters of Ḳain and Hebel. For the origin of

III.
PITRON OR COMMENTARY TO THE ASATIR.

I.
[Ḳain and Hebel.]

In the name of the Lord the All-merciful. Saith our Master Moses, [may the peace of the Lord be upon him.] (1) I begin with the praises and exaltations unto the mighty God, who created Adam above all creatures. And he made and appointed him father to all flesh—praised be God who made the world—and established Adam (man) as the root. And when the Lord—may He be exalted—desired that generations should spring from Adam, he created for him Eve as wife, and gave him from her two twins, each of them a male and female. The eldest was Ḳain and with him a female whose name was Maḳeda, and he married the sister of one to the other. And he divided the earth between them. And he gave to Ḳain the West and he gave to Hebel the North and the South. And this fact is proved by his saying—peace of God be upon him—"and his sons Ḳain and Hebel were like him"; (2) and he gave unto Ḳain the west, and he gave to Hebel the north and the south. (3) And he gave El'alah, the sister of Ḳain to Hebel to wife, and he gave Maḳeda, the sister of Hebel to Ḳain to wife. And the division of the earth between him and his sons was in the month of Abib.

And Ḳain began to build a place called Nikl and this is proved from his saying—upon him be the peace—(4) "and Ḳain began building a place called Nikl," (5) "and he divided the earth in the month of Abib."

And it was at the end of days that Ḳain brought an offering and Hebel also brought a sacrifice. And he built an altar at the foot of Mount Garizim the Holy, between Luzah and Mount Garizim. This was the first altar which

4. And Ḳain dwelt in the midst of a city which was called Nikl.

5. And he divided the earth between him and his sons in the month of Abib.

6. And it came to pass after a number of days that Ḳain brought an offering and Hebel a sacrifice.

7. And the first altar was in the precincts of the holy place between Luzah and Mount Garizim: and the one was opposite the other.

these names see Introduction—Malalas ed. B. G. Niebuhr Bonnae 1831 p. 13: Adam two daughters: Azura and Asua. Ḳain married Azura and Seth Asua.—Eutychius I. 14: Ḳain and Azizun (corrupted fr. Azura).—Jeraḥmeel XXIV. 1: Ḳain and Kalmana.—Schatzhöhle, p. 8: Ḳain and Lebhuda, Hebel and Kelimath, twins. Ḳain takes violently his own sister to wife.—Methodius: Ḳain, Kalmana; Abel, Labora.—Malan Book of Adam, p. 93: Luluwa and Aklemia. H. Rönsch, Das Buch d. Jubiläen, Leipzig 1874, gives the whole list, p. 373.—Gedalyah in Shalshelet: Ḳain and Kalmana. (Amsterdam 1697, folio 74b.)—Abar Banel to Genesis IV. 1: Names of twins Ḳain and Kalmana, Abel and Balbira. of Seder Hadorot, p. 18.—Pseudo-Philo II. 1: Ḳain 15 years old married Themech.—Ḳain 30 years old when Hebel and his twin sister born. Armen. Adam Schr., p. 33. For further literature see Sackur, p. 60, note 4.—Urim ve Tumim: Ḳain born on 3rd and Hebel on 4th of the month.

(4) Meshalma f. 123 a.— Samaritan Arabic: "he built a city called Nikl."

(6) Samaritan Arabic: "At the end of days." "At the border of the holy mountain." First three words in text identical with Samaritan Targ. Gen. IV. 5.

(7) For the Samaritans, Mt. Garizim is the holy mountain; for the Jews Mt. Moria.—Meshalma f. 123a: Hebel built the altar in that place.—Samaritan Arabic: "he was the first to build the altar."—Altar on Mt. Garizim Abisha ben Pinḥas (Cowley p. 512). —Adam offering sacrifice first Jubilees Ch. III. 27.—Josephus Antiq. I. 13. 2 226 identifies place of sacrifice of Isaac, Moria with Zion, anti-Samaritan.—The first altar made by Adam. In the same spot, Noah, Ḳain and Hebel sacrificed on the Holy Mountain. Pal. Targum to Genesis VIII. 20.—Pirke de R. Eliezer Ch. 31, T. B. Rosh Hashana, f. 26a, Aboth de Rabbi Nathan Ch. I: Adam, Ḳain, Hebel, Noah, Abraham, built same altar. —Maimonides Mishneh Torah, Hlk. Beth Habḥira Ch. II § 1. 2: Adam made on the spot from the same earth where Isaac was to be

was built, and this is proved by his saying—on him be the peace—(6) "and it came to pass at the end of days that Ḳain brought from the fruit of the earth an offering to God, and Hebel brought a sacrifice." (Gen IV. 3.) And the first of the altars was at the foot of the sanctuary between Luzah and Mount Garizim. And the two brothers were facing one another at the time when they made the offering and the sacrifice, according to his saying, (7) "and this one was facing that one." And when Ḳain and Hebel sacrificed, it was the course of twenty days from the month of Abib, according to his saying, (8) "and when Ḳain and Hebel sacrificed, it was on the twentieth day of Nisan." And when Ḳain saw that his offering was not accepted, for he knew the sign of acceptance from the offerings of his father Adam, for Adam was the first to bring offerings and his sons learned from him, according to his saying—on him be the peace—(9) "and when Ḳain did not see his offering accepted as he had been taught and he had seen the offering of his father;" now when he offered and saw not the sign of acceptance, he knew in his soul that he was of no account, and the world grew dark before him and his spirit grew angry; according to his saying—upon him be the peace—"he knew that it was unfit and when he offered, and his spirit his face became troubled." And another explanation is that when he offered the world was darkened and his spirit, i. e., when the world got dark, through this his spirit became anguished; but God alone knows. And on the day (10) "on which Hebel offered, there were two turnings [of God]; (11) the Lord turned to Hebel and to his offering, while to Ḳain and to his offering he did not turn." By the first turning [away], Ḳain saw that his offering was not accepted, and his wrath kindled and grew strong, and he could not hide it. And he returned to his country and stayed there four years, and he did not see his father Adam nor his brother Hebel, according to the

8. And it came to pass when Ḳain and Hebel brought the sacrifice it was on the twentieth of Nisan on the first day (Sunday).

9. When Ḳain saw that his offering was not accepted as he had been taught by seeing the offerings of his father he knew that it was unfit and when he offered [his face] and his spirit became troubled.

sacrificed. There Ḳain, Hebel, Noah, Abraham, David, Solomon built the altar i. e. the threshing-floor of Aravneh.—Also Midrash Tadshe. Ch. 20: Altars of Noah, Abraham, David, Solomon all on Mt. Moria.—Paradise on top of Holy Mountain from which Adam and Eve descend. Schatzhöhle, p. 8.—Adam and Eve, Ethiop. Ed. Malan, Bk. I. Ch. LXXXVIII, p. 98: "on the mountain."
(8) Samaritan Parallels. Marḳaḥ fol. 57a (Heidenheim, Bibliotheka Samaritana. Bd. III Heft 5/6 p. 20) gives following events which happened in Nisan: Creation, Flood, Tower of Babel, Message to Abraham about Isaac, Destruction of Sodom, Blessing of Jacob, beginning and end of Ten Plagues. Also f. 58a (Heidenheim ibid. p. 21): It is also the date of the Advent of the Taheb v. F. 62a (Heidenheim ibid. p. 22).—Sam. Ar. Josh. p. 36: Following events happened at the same period 14th Nisan: Creation, Noah going out of the Ark, Sodom destroyed.— Samaritan tradition anon. poem: in the month of Nisan Creation of World, Going out of Egypt, Future Redemption.—Meshalma f. 123 a: 20th Nisan.—Meshalma f. 123b: Fire from God consumed Hebel's sacrifice.—Malif. Q. 55. —In Pal. Targ. to Gen. 4. 3: The date is given as the 14th Nissan Creation of Adam, Pesaḥ, and Advent of the Taheb all in Nisan. Tabya b. Isḥak ca. 1750? Cod. 845. ff. 28b and 30a. —The date of sacrifice differently interpreted in Rabbinic literature. Gen. Rabba XXII, 4.— Chs. of Rabbi Eliezer XXI: 14th Nisan date of Passover.—A complete list of events which happened on Passover, Jewish Hymn in the Haggada or Passover Night Service.—Urim ve Tumim. On the 5th day of the month Ḳain brought sacrifice.—See Aptowitzer p. 37 for other Rabbinic traditions.
(9) "Offering by his father." Malif Q. 54.—Chs. of Rabbi Eliezer ch. XI: Adam offers praises to God immediately after Creation.—B reads צלמה. This agrees more with the Biblical Text. I have translated it accordingly, not "world" but "countenance."—Philo Questiones I. 63: His countenance fell "tristitia enim invasit eum et concidit vultus eius".—So Samaritan Arabic: "His soul was filled with terror and fear."—Meshalma f. 123 a: Ḳain and Hebel brought sacrifice when Adam was 30 years old.

saying of the prophet—on him be the peace—(12) "and
Ḳain when he saw the first turning and he did not see
acceptance, (13) then Ḳain grew angry and he returned
to his country, (14) and stayed there four years, and saw
neither Adam nor Hebel."

(15) Now Eve loved Ḳain, while Adam loved Hebel. (16)
And when Eve saw that the son Ḳain did not come to
her, she longed for him, and she took permission from
Adam and went to see him alone. When Hebel saw her
rising up and going alone, and that the place whither she
was going was distant, then he got up quickly and went
with her. (17) And she found Ḳain gone from the place
where he was dwelling at the beginning, to a place which
was afterwards called 'Arafat. When Ḳain saw his brother
Hebel, he thought in his heart to kill him. But the Lord,
blessed be He, before whom nothing can be hidden, and
who—exalted be He—knows the evil inclinations of the
hearts of his creatures, (18) said unto him, "Surely, if thou
wilt kill Hebel, there will be requital (i. e., return) for it."
The meaning of "surely" is that there will be requital for
the blood, and an avenging of it from him; see what is
written in the book of Genesis, Chapter IV, verse 6, "And
God said unto Ḳain; why art thou wroth and why did thy
face fall; if thou art good, thou shalt be accepted, and if
thou art not good, then at the gate the sin is crouching;
and thou shalt rule over it." The explanation of this is as
follows: Behold this thing is in thy hand as thou wishest,
good or evil. And nothing [is mentioned in the Bible of
what happened], except that Ḳain said to his brother
Hebel: "Rise, O my brother, let us go into the field."
And both went together. And it was as they were in the
field that Ḳain rose up against his brother Hebel and
slew him. (19) And when he had slain him and shed his
blood, his spirit was distressed and the earth cried out
and would not receive the blood of Hebel to drink it
until commanded by God; and the earth trembled, and

10. And on the day when Hebel sacrificed

11. Twice (three times) God turned favourably to Hebel and to his offering, but he did not turn favourably to Ḳain and to his offering.

12. When he perceived from the first the turning, that to him He did not turn,

13. Then Ḳain was wroth and he returned to his land

14. And he tarried four years without seeing Adam or Hebel.

15. And Eve loved Ḳain but Adam loved Hebel.

16. And when she saw that Ḳain did not come, Eve took council with Adam and went to him and Hebel went with her.

17. And she found him removed to another place which was called afterwards Arfat.

18. And this is the word spoken to Ḳain: "to thee is the return" and what follows (up to): "let us go into the field" and there he shed the blood of Hebel.

(11) In the wording Asatir M. T. and Samaritan Targum agree. Onkelos רעוה (Gen. IV. 5) Pal. Targ. differs (ibid.).

(12) לומח the word does not exist in Samarian, evidently a graphic mistake for לותח.

(15) Meshalma 122b: His mother loved Hebel and his father Ḳain.—Kebra Chap. 3: Hebel beautiful, beloved by Adam. —Adam and Eve: Ethiop. Malan I. ch. LXXVIII, p. 97: Eve hated Ḳain.

(16) יחן read חון another reading is עשׁי—Samaritan Arabic: instead of "took leave of," reads "saw his mother go."—Eve going to the west to visit the children: Vita Adae ch. 18.

(17) ערפאת Cf ריפת IV, 1. probably a name disguised by a permutation of letters: to the Pitron and the Arabic the identity is also unknown: they preserve the same form of the name. Meshalma f. 125b: "The name of the place is Id'unt and she brought him back, then he killed Hebel. And that day was the 16th Shebat."—Malif. Q. 56: "Paran."

(18) "And what follows," means rest of the quotation in the text Bible (Genesis IV, 7). Wrongly paraphrased in Samaritan Arabic.—Urim ve Tumim:

the light of the sun and of the moon was darkened, at the time when Ḳain slew Hebel.

Now Adam dwelt in Badan. (20) And when Adam saw what had happened in the world, the darkening of sun and moon and the trembling of the earth, then he was greatly frightened on that day. And that day was for him like unto the day when he and his wife ate of the fruit of the tree which is in the midst of the garden. (21) And Adam went up from Badan to Sifra, and that is Sichem, to see the Book of the Wars of the Lord, [the Stars,] (22) and he saw the rising of the days so that he should understand what had happened in the world. (23) And he saw that of his two sons, only one was still on the earth: one was slain and the other had fallen through his own sin which had seized him. Then Adam understood that this was the cause, and he returned to Badan. (24) And from the day of the creation of Adam, until the day Ḳain killed Hebel, there were thirty years; and the slaying of Hebel happened on the sixteenth day of the month of Tebet. (25) God created Adam on the sixth day, and at the sixth hour, and Adam and his wife dwelt in the garden eight days and he did not know his wife Eve to lie with her in the garden. And their knowledge was changed through the speech of the serpent, and they were driven out of the garden in the same hour at which Adam had been created; he went out from the garden in that self-same hour. And after Ḳain had slain Hebel and Ḳain had been driven away, Adam learned of his sin, and no seed remained to him for his inheritance to be his successor to inherit the command of God.

(26) Then Adam sought repentance and separated himself from his wife for one hundred years, and did not know her during this time, until God received his repentance. (27) And after that, Adam knew his wife, and she conceived and bare Seth, the master of the settlement [of the world]. And he saw the Image [lighting up] his face and

19. And when he shed the blood of Hebel his spirit grew troubled and the earth was in ferment and the seas were moved and the sun was dimmed and the moon darkened.

20. And Adam was frightened with a great fear on that day as on the day on which they plucked the fruit.

21. And Adam lived in the country of Ḥohmata which is called Sifra in the Book of the Wars of the Lord.

22. And he saw the planets (horoscope) of the days: and seven were fighting one another.

Hebel killed on the 7th day of the month.—Ḳain killed Hebel in order to marry Hebel's sister. T. B. Sanhedrin f. 101a.

(19) Samaritan Arabic "and all the living things groaned."—Meshalma f. 125b: identical except that he omits the "sea."—Malif. Q. 57: "It is said that the world was shaken and the creatures were frightened and the mountains and plains all trembled and the light of the sun and moon was darkened and Adam was sorely frightened as on the day when he ate of the tree of knowledge." This description of the upheaval of nature is not mentioned anywhere in connection with the murder of Hebel. It occurs, however, fully developed in that of the wars of the end of time; see Charles, Eschatology passim and Weber, Eschat.

(20) Meshalma adds: "And when they were driven out of the garden" folio 125a.—Apocalypse of Moses (Adam and Eve). The whole story is told differently Ch. 2, so also Vita Adae Ch. 22. 4.

(21) Sifra, so pronounced by the Samaritans, and identified with Sichem, is the name in Gen. X. 20, which is placed near הר הקדם; the Samaritans take it to mean "ancient mount," i. e. Mt. Garizim.—Samaritan Arabic omits "Ḥohmata" and "Book of Wars of the Lord," and identifies Sifra with Nablus.—Meshalma f. 129a. explains Sifra as "Shechem which had then not yet been built." —B. of Jubilees Ch. III. 32: Adam born and died in Elda.

(22) Samaritan Arabic: "And he saw in the Book of the Wars the horoscope of the day." And adds "one was no longer upon the earth." ·Meshalma does not mention anything of Adam looking at the stars. Adam removes after death of Hebel.—Fully set out in a Samaritan poem that Adam was taught science by God. Zohar I. 118a, II. 55a.—The Samaritan traditions about Adam's knowledge of the Calendar see Introd. To the references already given there add—Calculation of Days given

from this Adam knew that this was the mystery of the chain: and in proof of this, see what the Lord—may He be exalted—said in the book of Genesis chapter 5, verse 3: "And Adam lived an hundred and thirty years, and begat a son in his own likeness, after his image; and called his name Seth." Note the significance that it is not said at the time of the birth of Kain and of Hebel, "in his likeness" and this image is the luminous image of Moses—peace of God be upon him—which was transmitted from man to man.

II.
[Ten Generations.]

(1) And in the days of the life of Seth, Kain went to the east to the town which his son Enoch had built; and this is Antokia which in the Syrian language is also called Antokia; and Kain ruled the mountain and the plain and the sea 100 years.

(2) And Seth begat Enosh and he built a town and called its name Pilona in the name of his son Enosh. (3) And Enosh begat Kênân and Seth built a city and he called its name Damascus. (4) And Kênân begat Mahalalel and he built a city and he called its name 'Atrot Shfim.' (5) And Mahalalel begat Jared and he built a city and called its name Ja'azer. (6) And Jared begat Enoch and built a city and called its name Shalem the Great.

(7) And when Enoch grew up and when the days of his life had reached thirteen years, he began to learn in the Book of Signs which had been given to Adam; and this book was copied on the four and twenty precious stones. Of these twelve are for the time of Favour and twelve for the choice of the families of the children of Jacob, and to the generations of the servants of the Most High God. And the Lord knows whether the twelve stones in the breast plate of Aaron the Priest were those for the choice of the families of the sons of Jacob and for the servants

23. And he saw that one of them was no more. And he removed and dwelt in Badan.

24. And he (Adam) counted thirty years when Ḳain had killed Hebel on the 16th of Tebet.

25. Adam was created on Friday. And Adam and Eve tarried in the garden eight days and he did not know Eve. And their minds were turned by the word of the serpent.

26. And after the death of Hebel Adam separated himself one hundred years.

by God to Adam and handed on to Enoch, Noah, etc. Pirke de R. Eliezer, Ch. 8.—Zohar: Sifra de Adam Kadmaah, book given to him. I. 181 etc. (cf. Zunz Gesammelte Schriften. Breslau 1885 vol. I, p. 13). Wisdom of Solomon Ch. 10. 1 ff., "wisdom" i. e.: profound knowledge is given to. Adam and handed on in the same way to Moses, except that Lot is substituted for Isaac.—Sepher Raziel Introd. Ed. Amsterdam 1700 mentions also mystical books given to Adam by God.— Adam taught astronomical calculation by God. Yalkut I. 41. — Vita Adae 22. 4, Apocalypse of Moses 2. 2: Adam and Eve saw in a dream that Ḳain would kill Abel.—

(23) Meshalma f. 129a: (Adam) removed to Badan and there worshipped God facing Mt. Garizim.—So Malif. Q. 58.

(24) Hebel 22 years old when killed. Adam 30 years; Vita Adae 23. 2.—Adam 30 years old at birth of Ḳain and sister, and 31 at birth of Abel and sister. Ḳain killing Abel, 100th year of Adam. 100 years; so Methodius. Ch. I.— Samaritan Arabic.: 10th Shebat. (Probably misread.)—Meshalma f. 126a.; 16th Shebat.—Ps. Philo Ch. 2. 3: Ḳain fifteen years old.

(25) Tishri first month of creation according to one tradition, according to another Nisan. cf. T. B. Rosh Hashana ff.11a, 27a.—According to one opinion Eve created a week after Adam. Ibid.—Adam created in Tishri, was judged, repented, and received back all in Tishri; Zohar III. 100 B.—Urim ve Tumim: On the first day of the month Adam created.—Seder Hadarot, p. 17: First day of New Year Adam created.—Gen. Rabba XVIII. 9: Adam six hours in Paradise.—Pesikta R. Kahana. 150b: Driven out of Paradise on the 12th hour of the 6th day 1st week.—Jubilee Ch. III. 15: Seven years in Paradise.—Schatzhöhle p. 7: 9 hours.

(26) The Samaritan suggests that Adam lived as a Nasirite; Kabasi Sir al Kelb. p. 91.—Adam separated from his wife 100 years after having left Paradise; Poem Abraham b. Jacob (Cowley p. 625).—Meshalma f.131b: Adam

of the Most High God; for upon them were copied the generations of the servants of the Most High God. And the twelve stones of which he said that they are for the time of Favour, these are hidden away as a secret for the last generation.

(8) And the children of Ḳain were born in their dwelling places. And they corrupted the world from one end to the other, until Ḳain begat Enoch and Enoch 'Irad and 'Irad Meḥuyael and Meḥuyael Metushael and Metushael begat Lamech. (9) And in the fourteenth year of the days of his life he went away from Ḥanoḥiah, the town of Enoch. And he built 'Anah and Barah and Nisah and 'Adah, small towns. (10) And he killed Ḳain; and he built an idol and the explanation of it is: an object of worship whose name was Padraid Ṭns in the land of Shinear, and the Lord knows.

(11) In that time Adam went up from Badan to Reḥobot a town of worshippers of idols. And it is said that it is the large city found in the country of Al'ns of which it is said in the book of Genesis, chapter 10 v. 11. "Ashur went out and he built Niniveh and the town Reḥobot and Chalah and Resin." And the cause for mentioning idols is that Enoch (Lamech), the son of Ḳain, made there two idols of gold. And it is said that he called their names, one Lefes and, the other Leḥaburati.

Said our Master Moses—peace of God be upon him—in the book Asatir, (12) "and Adam read Niss before his sons;" that is he read in the Book of Signs before his sons from the seed of Ḳain and he remonstrated with them for these evil deeds; and they would not accept the remonstrance.

Know that the reason for Adam's going up from Al Baadan was that at the time when he heard of the deeds of his sons which were from Ḳain he went to them in order to remonstrate with them. And it came to pass when he met them that he read a part from the Book of

27. And after that he knew his wife and she begat Seth.

Chapter II. [The First Ten Generations.]

1. In the days of Seth Ḳain went to the East where Enoch had built a town whose name was Antokia. And Ḳain ruled one hundred years over the seas and over the dry land.

2. And Seth begat Enosh; and he built a town whose name was Pilonah in the name of Enosh.

3. And Enosh begat Kênân and Seth built a town and called it Damascus in the name of Kênân.

4. And Kênân begat Mahalalel and he built a town whose name was 'Aṭrot Shfim.

spent 100 years in repentance.—
—T. B. Abodah Zarah fol. 8a, T. B. Erubim 18b: Adam fasted 130 years.—Zohar I, 55a, II. 231a. —Chapters of R. Eliezer, Ch. XX: Seven weeks of days (or years).— B. of Jubilees IV. 7: Mourned four weeks of years. This brings us exactly to 130 A. M. and agrees with Asatir, since Adam was thirty years old when Hebel was killed (v. 24).—Schatzhöhle p. 8: mourned 100 years.—Penitence of Adam forms the chief element of the Adam Books e. g. Apocalypse of Moses, Penitence of Adam, Ethiopic Book of Adam etc. see Introd.—Arm. Adamsschr. p. 36: Adam separated from Eve 3 years. Another version 120 years. (Ibid. p. 42.)

(27) Urim ve Tumim: Seth born on 11th day of the month.—Algazi f. 2a: Name of Seth's wife was Azura. Evidently the Azura: v. 3.

Ch. II.

(1) Anṭokia probably corruption from older form Ḥanoḫia, the town built by Enoch, and changed by popular etymology, especially as Ḥ is not pronounced by the Samaritans, as correctly later on v. 9, appears the correct name Ḥanoḫia.—Meshalma f. 129a. has instead "Hdšh." "Some say Enoch built it. But it was Ḳain who built the town".—Belief that Biblical personages built towns: T. B. Sotah. f. 34b. Aḫidan built Anat, Gheshai built Alesh Salmai built Talbush.— T. B. Yebamoth 62a.

(2) Algazi: Toledot Adam, Venice 1600. The name of wife of Enosh was No'am.

(3) Meshalma f. 134a: Seth built Pilonah and Damascus.— Algazi: Name of Kenan's wife: Mehalalot.

(4) Tolida Neubauer, p. 24:

Signs. And the meaning of it was that when he had opened the Book of Signs he informed them and said unto them that unless you return from your evil ways you will all die. And they did not hearken unto him and they were not afraid of his words, so he went away from them and returned to his place in Badan. (13) And it came to pass when Enoch, the son of Jered, heard of the deeds of the sons of Ḳain he was very wroth against them, and he separated himself, and Enoch walked with God; and at that time the days of his life were [three hundred and] sixty-five years. And he walked in the fear of God, (14) and Enoch rebuilt the altar of his forefather Adam (15) and he begat Metushael and Metushael begat Lamech, and Lamech begat Noah; P. 21. and the birth of Noah was in the month of Nisan. (16) And it came to pass on the fourth day from his birth a sign appeared in the heavens and when the creatures of the world saw it, there fell upon them the fear of God and they came to Adam to Badan in order to ask him about this sign which had been seen in the midst of the heavens. (17) "And Adam rose in the height of his wisdom and he foretold the Flood saying that so long as Enoch was alive it would not happen." P. 22. After this Adam—on whom be peace—saw by the holy spirit the destruction of the whole world, and he was telling of the Advent of Moses—upon whom be peace. And when Noah was born, Adam was comforted through him and he knew that he would be the master of the settlement and that no one would be saved from the Flood save Noah and his three sons. And Adam told his sons about this, and this is shown from his saying in the Asatir, "for he saw signs and he told his children." P. 23 And perhaps there is found in it a mystical allusion to Abraham; for the numerical value of the word "Nḳms" is that of "Beabraham:" 250. And Adam alluded in this to the fact that the peace and salvation is in Abraham. (19) And when Noah—

5. And Mahalalel begat Jered and he built a town whose name was Ja'azer.

6. And Jered begat Enoch and he built a town [whose name was] Shalem the Great.

7. And when Enoch was thirteen years, he learned the Book of Signs which was given to Adam. And these are the twenty-four precious stones, twelve for the time of Divine Favour and twelve for the chosen heads of the sons of Jacob and to the descendants of the servants of the high God.

Kênân builds Akhah.—Meshalma 134a: 'Atroth Shfim.—Algazi ibid: Name of Mahalelel's wife Dinah.
(5) Meshalma f. 134b adds: "These are the places rebuilt by tribe of Gad."—Algazi ibid.: Yered's wife Berakha daughter of Daniel.
(6) Meshalma f. 134b. adds: "which is Sichem."—Samaritan Arabic.: "This is Nablus."—Algazi ibid. Enoch's wife Edna, daughter of Azariah.
(7) Meshalma f. 134b reads. "Deyatebo," i. e. which was composed by our Master Adam. Asatir reads Deyahabo, which means "Which was given to." Asatir is the more correct.—Meshalma ibid. (quoting Asatir): "and he learned to know the twenty-four. These are the twelve stones on the breast-plate, the like of which will come back at the time of the return of the Divine Favour. Meshalma omits: "Descendants of the servants of the high God." Samaritan Arabic has here some interpolation: Instead of "Book of Signs," "Book of Wonders."—Eupolemos. Eusebius Prep. Ev.

Book 9, Ch. 17, F. 481 c ff. Enoch first to discover knowledge of astrology i. e. Calendar. Eupolemos probably Samaritan. 2nd century B. C. See Introduction.—Adam taught by God the calculation of the Calendar; Chs. of Rabbi Eliezer, Ch. 8.—Geiger Mohammed p. 106.—Jubilees IV. 17: The first to write and learn wisdom. Contrary to Apocalypse of Enoch. He is not translated to Heaven, and he dies like everyone else.—48 precious stones wherewith the priest was adorned. Evidently twice the 24 mentioned here; Revelations XXI, 19, 20. II Baruch (Syriac Apoc.) Hitherto no one has explained these stones and their number.—Ps. Philo Ch. XXV, 11 same as Jeraḥmeel. —Jeraḥmeel (Gaster) ch. LVII vision of Kenaz: 24 stones, twelve for breastplate now and twelve hidden away for later. Evidently refers to renewal of tabernacle priesthood and recovery and replacing of the breastplate. This version unquestionably is directed against the Samaritan tradition and gives it a very hostile interpretation.

upon whom be peace—grew up, his father brought him to Adam that he might teach him his Writing. And when Adam saw him, he said "This one will comfort us from our deeds and from the sorrow of our hand upon the earth, which the Lord hath cursed." Gen. V. 29). For he was good from his birth; and this was shown in that the light was revealed (P. 24) on the day of his birth, a great light in the midst of the heavens. And this is shown from his saying—upon whom be peace—" And he was good from his birth" or that there was light in his face. (20) And Lamech built a town and called its name Rift and that is the hill which is overshadowed [by clouds] and is on the north side of Mount Garizim. Let us now return to the record of Lamech, who was one of the children of Ḳain, (21) and let us say that three sons were born unto him and one daughter. And the reason for the mention of the daughter in the Asatir is that from her time the evil deed became manifest. P. 25. And now let us mention the first son in the Asatir, viz: Tubal Ḳain; and the reason for his being called by this name is because he was born unto Lamech at the time of the killing of Ḳain.

(22) The second Jubal built Mesdah the Great One. (23) The third Jabal built Kenaz. (24) And Tubal Ḳain built Skips, whose name is Albaṣra. And he made in it a workshop for the production of copper and of iron and he it was who created this kind of work. And the sister of Tubal Ḳain was Na'amah since she was from the same mother, for Lamech married two wives. And this Na'amah was she who established the rock in the town of Jerusalem by means of witchcraft, and God knows. (25) And these are they who were instructed in the books of truth. Adam taught Lamech one hundred and eighty years, (26) his son Seth one hundred and five (? 605) years, (27) Enosh eight hundred and five years. (28) Kênân learned nine hundred and ten years, (29)

8. Meanwhile children were born to Ḳain in various places and he roamed about the world in tribulation, until Ḳain begat Enoch and Enoch begat 'Irad and 'Irad (begat) Meḥuyael and Meḥuyael (begat) Metushael and Metushael (begat) Lamech.

9. In the fourteenth year Lamech went from Ḥanoḥiah and built 'Anah and Nisah and 'Adah.

10. And he (Lamech) killed Ḳain, and he built a place of worship whose name was Padrai Ṭns.

11. And when Adam went up to Rechoboth 'Ir he (Lamech) made (two?) golden images (called) "Iefis'i uleḥaburati" (to my pain and to my wound).

(8) Algazi ibid.: Metushael's wife Edna daughter of Resuyah.—Urim ve Tumim Lamech born on the 9th day of the month. —Seder Hadorot p. 18: Eccles. Rabba: Ḳain had 100 children.

(9) עדה is the name of the wife of Lamech, Gen. IV, 19. עדה and ענה are names mentioned in connection with Esau (Gen. 36, 2). Samaritan Arabic.: Has for Brh (Pitron) "Hazisa"; for "Nisah" "Islands;" and for "Adah" "A region close to the Euphrates."— Algazi ibid.: Brunnish daughter of Barakhael, Lamech's wife.

(10) Sam. Arabic reads: "Madrai Tafs" simply due to Arabic transcript.—Samaritan Arabic adds: "This is the country called Irak."—Lamech kills Ḳain. Yashar Ch. 2. 26.—Schatzhöhle p. 11: Full details.—Ethiop. Adam Book Bk. II Ch. XIII (Malan p. 122)—Methodius Ch. II— Greek Palaea. Jerome, Syrus, Ta- bari; see Grünbaum, Neue Beitr., p. 72. Ḳain lived 800 years; (ibid. p. 43) Chumnos p. 12f.—Eutychius I: Ḳain 730 years old.—Arm. Adamsschr. p. 35, see Ch. I: Lamech wounding Ḳain.—Jeraḥmeel Ch. XIV, 3: Death of Ḳain by sons of Lamech.—Gedalyah Shalshelet f. 74b. —Seder Hadorot, p. 20: Lamech killed Ḳain.— Aptowitzer p. 59 ff.: Jewish parallels.—Other tradition, Genesis Rabba XXII, 12 and Exodus Rabba Ch. XXXI 17. Nahmanides to Gen. IV. 15: Ḳain died in the Flood.

(11) רעי i. e. Rehobot Ir (cf. Pitron) Gen. XXVI, 22, the place named so by Isaac. Sam. Ar. has entirely misunderstood this passage.—"Made images" Ps. Philo, Ch. 2. v. 9: Tubal, in time of Lamech, did so.—Palestinian Targum to Gen. IV. 26: In the time of Enosh images were first made.—In the time of Enosh the first images made; Gedalya

Mahalalel eight hundred and ninty five years, (30) Jered eight hundred and twenty seven years, (31) Enoch three hundred and sixty five years, and all the days of Enoch were three hundred and sixty five years. [The Lamech whom we mentioned is of the sons of Ḳain and the proof is that Aḥidan learned from Adam: similarly, Lamech, who is the forefather of Aḥidan, learned from Adam. This is the truth]. P. 27. And he (Enoch) died and this is what is recorded about him in the Asatir on the day of his death: (33) "On the day when Enoch died, came all the children of Adam to Sifra to hear Adam lament over him." And his death happened on the fourth day (Wednesday) in Badan. And they carried him to Sifra to hear Adam lament over him: (34) and there were Adam and Seth and Enosh and Kênân and Mahalalel and Jered and Metushael (Metushalem) his sons who were dwelling in Badan. (35) And the weeping over him was very great until the report of it reached Aḥidan, the son of Tubal Ḳain P. 28 who was dwelling in Hebron; and he was the first in power and was the leader of all the children of Ḳain (36) who had there learned the Book of Signs from Adam.

(37) And when all had gathered together they asked of Adam that he should (tell them) where to carry him into the secret (cave of burial): and Adam carried him in it. (38) And Enoch was buried therein opposite Mount Garizim in a cave which is called Maḥaneh (39) and the mount is called the Mount of Ebal, for they buried Enoch therein. And the explanation of the name of Mount 'Ebal is the Mount of Mourning. (אבל).

And in the Mount 'Ebal, were made many graves, (40) as Enoch had said, "This is the burial place," for it is near Mount Garizim which is the Gate of Heaven. (41) And any faithful one who is buried at a distance of 2,000 cubits round about will not be touched by the fire . . . For it is the refuge for those who flee in consequence

12. After that Adam started reading Nisis [the Book of Signs] before his sons.

13. And when Enoch heard it, he prayed unto God and he was sixty five years old. And Enoch walked with God.

14. And he (Enoch) rebuilt the altar of his forefather Adam.

15. And he begat Metushelah and Metushelah Lamech and Lamech Noah in (the month of) Nisan.

16. And on the fourth day of his birth was seen a sign in the middle of the heavens and all the inhabitants of the world were frightened and they came to Adam.

17. And Adam arose in the height of his wisdom and he foretold the Flood, and he also proclaimed the statement that so long as Enoch was alive it would not happen.

Shalshelet fol 76b.—The two words from Gen. IV, 23 usually translated "to my pain and to my wound," are taken by the Asatir as being names of idols, differing from Samaritan Targum.

(12) Samaritan Arabic quite different.

(13) Sam. Ar.: "he sought his son, and he was 75 years old."

(14) Sam. Ar. adds: "on the 14th of Nisan."—Meshalma f. 135a: "He built the altar and he brought sacrifices." He adds, "and he was called Enoch the prayerful." Meshalma refers to the Jewish legend that Enoch is still alive, and there follows a long polemic and very interesting detail.

(15) Meshalma f. 137b: Noah born in Nisan.—Malif. Q. 61: Noah born on 4th of Nisan.—Algazi ibid.: Amor'a, daughter of Barkhiel, Noah's wife.—Seder Hadorot, p. 22: Noah born in the year 1056 Era Mundi.

(16) Malif. Q. 62. A big sun appeared in the Heavens.—Gathers the people; Apoc. Moses. Ch. 5. 1 ff.—Vita Adae Ch. 30.—Meshalma f. 137b: Sign appeared in the land of Shinear; so also Sam. Arabic.

(17) Meshalma 137 b (Sam. Arabic.): Adam foretells Flood.—Malif. Q. 62: Adam foretold the Flood.—Joseph. Antiq. I. 2.3,(70). —Clements Recogns. I. 47.—Kenan perfect in all sciences foretells Flood; Josippon II. 11. Seder Hadorot, p. 19. Yashar II. 12.

of their guilt, and is the Rock of Salvation. And the meaning thereof is that everyone who believes in Mount Garizim and is buried near it within 2000 cubits will not be touched by the fire of burning. And both the meritorious ones, our father Adam and Enoch—upon them be peace—have testified to its truth. (42) And Metushael (Metushalem) learned seven hundred and twenty years (43) and Lamech learned six hundred and fifty three years, and Noah learned and read in the book of Adam which he was taught six hundred years.

III. [Aḥidan.]

(1) And then the days of Adam grew near to die and he was subjected to the word "and thou shalt surely die." And these were the days of the life of Adam: nine hundred and thirty years, (2) and all his sons came to his place in Badan. (3) And he commanded them that they should carry him to [Iyul Mṭh] which is the valley of Hebron. (4) For he had seen in his wisdom that it had been created that in it should be gathered the generations of the meritorious ones. It was created at the time of the creation of the Tree of Knowledge— P. 31 (6) and it was built in three sections: the first, for those who came out of the Garden; the second, for those who came out of the Ark; the third, for those who came out of the circumcision. (7) And its name was called Machpelah, (8) and Noah became king in the place of Adam after the death of Adam. (9) For seven years Noah learned in the Books of Creation i. e., the Book of Signs, and the Book of Astrology and the Book of Wars. These are the Books of Adam.

This is the book of the generation of Adam.— (10) Who is like unto Thee among the mighty, O Lord? (11) Who is like unto Thee, the God of beginning and the Judge on the day of vengeance! The Lord is one!—This expression "the book of the generation of Adam," P. 32 refers to the Tolida which has been mentioned before.

18. And Adam was comforted by beholding the prince (head) and seeing his sons.

19. And when Noah was weaned Lamech brought him to Adam to Bispara (Sifra) and Adam said, "This will comfort us for he was good (perfect) from his birth."

20. And Lamech built a town in his name and its name was Rifat which is Gibeon which is situated on the south of the sanctuary of the Mount Garizim.

21. And Lamech begat six sons. Tubal Ḳain was then born [through whom] he (Lamech) killed Ḳain.

22. Jubal built Meseda which is called Rabta.

23. Jabal built Kenaz which is Nisbor.

24. Tubal Ḳain built Skips whose name is Albaṣra. He forged all manner of brasswork.

25. Adam taught these. He taught Lamech one hundred and eighty years in the Book of Truth (i. e. the Law).

(18) Sam. Arab. adds: "Until the life of the righteous one had come to an end."—"there will be no Flood in his days" refers to Enoch.—נקמם probably refers to Noah; the Pitron identifies him with Abraham.

(19) Meshalma 138a: Name of place not mentioned.—Seder Hadorot p. 18: The place of murder of Hebel two days' distance from Hebron, and there also the place of burial of Adam.

(20) ריפת name of a nation and region sprung from Gomer (Gen. X, 3). Meshalma 138b: Riphat. ". . . and that is Gib'␣t, and others say this is Gibat Alma, the Everlasting Hill."

(21) v. II. 10.—Book of the Bee ch. XIX. p. 30.

(22) Sam. Ar.: "Meseda" = "Terikia," probably "Afrikia." רבתא probably the capital of the Ammonites, like Syriac "rabta."

(23) קנז name of one of the descendants of Esau. Gen. XXXVI, 11.—Meshalma f. 131a: "Tubal Ḳain built Knt (or Knd) and its name was Knz; he also built Albṣrh.—Samaritan Arabic: has "Bagdad" for "Nisobar."

(24) אלבצרה probably Basra. Samaritan Arabic omits: "Skips."

(25) In the Asatir we find אלף (he taught or he learned) instead of "he died." May be that is taken from אלוף (Gen. XXXVI. 15ff.)

(12) And after Adam was buried, Noah and all the sons of Adam returned to their places. And the people grew numerous and they grew very powerful. (13) And Aḥidan, the son of Bared, the son of Tubal Ḳain, went and built Sion, whose name is called Gifna, which means house of Mktsh. And the explanation of the word Mktsh in the Hebrew language is 'plague.' And he erected therein a very high stone (pillar) and he called it a place of worship like unto the place called Adrms, which was the first place of worship of Adam. For Adam had brought out with him a stone from the garden, and he made it a place to worship God, may He be exalted. P. 33. And he placed the stone which he had brought out with him from the garden in the house of worship which he had made. And he called the name of that place Adrms. This is shown by the saying in the Asaṭir of Moses: (14) "Like the city whose name has been called Adrms, which is in the place where Adam had bowed down in worship for the first time when he was driven out of the Garden." And the explanation of Adrms is "place of weeping;" and God knows it. For Adam wept there for his going out and being separated from the garden, or its explanation may be "the place of learning or, of desire and study" where he learned in the Books of Creation. P. 34. And it is said in the Asatir concerning the stone which Aḥidan had erected and the worship thereof, (15) "That is the rock in which they trusted," (Deut. XXXII. 37) because they were led astray thereby. (16) And the evil grew for six hundred years, for since Aḥidan made the stone and the place of worship, the nations began to follow and to believe in it, and the transgressions grew and they continued the work of sin for six hundred years. And after this he said, "and they turned to that which did not exist" and its explanation is the worship of strange gods in which there is no substance; and when their sins grew, God caused the Fanuta (i. e., turned away his favour) to the last of that generation.

26. His son [Seth] learned (ruled) one hundred and five years.
27. Enosh learned (ruled) eight hundred and five years.
28. Kênân learned (ruled) nine hundred and ten years.
29. Mahalalel learned (ruled) eight hundred and ninety five years.
30. Jered learned (ruled) eight hundred and forty seven years.
31. Enoch learned (ruled) three hundred and sixty five years.
32. On the day when Enoch died came all the children of Adam to Sifra to hear Adam lament over him.
33. On the fourth Enoch died and he was carried to Sifra.

which could then be translated "He ruled," but as the years given cover the whole period from birth to death this translation offers the same difficulty as the former. סיפרה דקשטה "agrees with the Mandaean terminology Sifra dekusta" cf. Introduction.
(25 to 31.) Josephus Antiq. I. 3. 4 (83—88): A similar summing-up of the genealogies, with the dates corresponding to the birth and death, sometimes confused; but following in the main Gen. Ch. V. —Seth's age ought to read 905. See Comparative Chronological Table Intr. p. 146—147. Samaritan recension where dates agree generally with Asatir except Seth and Jared.—Samaritan Arabic: Lamech 180.

(26) Samaritan Arabic: Seth 165.
(27) Samaritan Arabic: Enosh 808.
(32) Meshalma f. 135a ff.: has here a curious Enoch legend hitherto unknown and makes deliberate protest against Jewish tradition of Enoch being translated to Heaven alive, as found in the Apocalyptic Literature. (Another account found ibid. fol 137a). Death of Enoch also assumed by Josephus I. 3. 4. 85, whilst LXX translates Gen. V. 24 "God translated him."—Arabic Samaritan Book of Joshua contains full description of death and burial place of Enoch. Cod. Gaster.—Samaritan Arabic substitutes: Nablus for Sifra.

P. 35. (17) For at first God—may He be exalted—forebore lest they repented, but they did not repent but they multiplied the sins and the earth became full with violence. (18) At that time was born to Aḥidan a son, and he called his name Asur. (19) And he built also the town, Ṣruṣ, a town which is called Ṣion Talah; and that is Ṣion the Hanging. And he placed therein the stone which he had made and he delighted in dwelling therein. (20) And he sent and brought Gifna, the daughter of Na'amah from Babylon, who was accustomed to worship the idolatry of Lamech and she was a witch skilled in the art of witchcraft. P. 36. And she invented the art of music. And because of this, Aḥidan sent for her and brought her to his house. And he gave her unto his son as a wife, so that she should assist him in the performance of witchcraft. And after the arrival of Gifna, he made a great nigug and its explanation is, an idol (21) and it was on four statues; one of gold, and one of silver, and one of brass, and one of olive wood. (22) And he made a sun and a moon in the midst of the four to give light. And he placed in the midst of the sun a luminous cup of gold, (23) and he placed in the midst of the moon P. 37 a precious stone Shoham. (24) And he said unto Gifna, "This beacon is the first which has been made in the world." (25) And Gifna appointed a host of four hundred servants and twenty eunuchs who ministered to her. It is said in connection with it in the Asatir, "Mighty, holy are the words which were on the staff of Adam," which is the staff of God. The explanation of this thing—and God knows—is that the deeds which have been revealed of these sinners, are fittingly rebuked by [the writing on] the staff of Adam. (26) And after this, Gifna made a nigug which is called Fingal through which the wind passed from all sides, whereby when the wind passed through it, it emitted a sound (27) and it continued for one hundred and ten years. And a son was born to Asur from Gifna and he called his name [Itno] (28) and to Itno

34. And they wept over him, Adam and Seth and Enosh and Kênân and Mahalalel and Jared and his son Metushelah who was living in Badan.

35. And they tarried with the weeping until the news reached Aḥidan the son of Tubal Ḳain who was living in Hebron, and he was the head of the army of Ḳainites.

36. And he had learned there in the Book of Signs before Adam.

37. And when they came, they asked Adam that he should read to them the Law (nims) and he read it (or, Adam should proclaim the faith and he proclaimed it).

38. And Enoch was buried in the neighbourhood of Mount Garizim in the place which is called Jskr.

39. It is called Mount Ebal where they hid Enoch. And there are built in it many tombs.

40. As Enoch (Adam) had said, "This is the place of worship for the God of the world and above it is the Gate of Heaven."

(34) באדאן a place once close to Sichem which has since disappeared. Adam's death and burial mourned and lamented by his sons. Yashar Ch. 3. 15; for according to Jewish tradition Enoch did not die.

(37) נימס probably the procedure of order of burial as this was the first burial which had taken place since the death of Hebel, the method of his burial being unknown; it is an obscure word left untranslated also in the Pitron; it is not likely to be the Greek νομος as no Greek words occur in the book.

(38) יסכר [Onamasticon] probably identical with the village Askar near Sichem, still in existence in the XIth Century. It was the birth place of Ussuef el Askari, the author of the Book of Laws (1040).

(40) Holy Mountain Gate of Garden of Eden; Meshalma 145b. —See Introduction.

a son was born and he called his name Serikah. (29) And Gifna used to call the sun and the moon which Aḥidan had made, and they would go with her whithersoever she desired. (30) And when the whole world saw these deeds they rejoiced and they were anxious to bow down to them. And all bowed down and worshipped them. P. 39. And the earth was filled with violence and wickedness.

Chapter IV. [Noah.]

(1) And it came to pass that the lord Noah admonished and taught in the world, but no one listened to him. And he saw that all the creatures had gone astray and that dwelling in the midst of the wicked would not cause him to prosper, so he went out from Rift and he went to the mountain whose name is ['Adr Śhgg] whereon he made the Ark for Seth had told him of the advent of the flood. (2) And Noah started looking into the secrets of the Book of Signs and he saw the obliteration (i. e. the hiding away) of the children of Adam and he found therein the direction concerning the Ark. (3) And at the time when he left Rift, God revealed a great sign in the place P. 40. where he was residing. (4) And Noah was greatly frightened and Noah continued in prayers and praises one hundred years after his begetting Shem, Ḥam and Japhet; but daughters were not born unto him by the love [of God] for him. For the Lord knew of the advent of the flood. (5) Shem took the daughter of Seth to himself to wife] and (6) Ḥam took [Shkh, the daughter of Jared] (7) and Japhet took [Mḳisthe, the daughter of Lamech]. And at the time when the sins of the creatures had been completed and reached the time of destruction (8) the Lord told Noah to make the ark and P. 41. he made it and completed its making on the tenth day of the second month. (9) And after four days more died the last of the pious ones who was Metushelaḥ. For the flood did not occur except after the death of all the pious

41. For the fire does not touch those who are buried in a distance round about Mount Garizim of two thousand [cubits]. This is called the Shelter for the Fugitive, the Rock of Salvation.

42. And Metushelah learned (ruled) seven hundred and twenty years.

43. And Lamech learned (ruled) six hundred and fifty-three years.

44. And Noah learned (ruled) six hundred years, and he read in the Book [of Signs] which Adam taught him.

Chapter III. [Aḥidan.]

1. And as the death of Adam drew near, then he bethought himself of the words "and thou shalt surely die." And these are the days of Adam: nine hundred and thirty years.

2. And all his children came to him to Badan.

3. And he commanded them to carry him to 'Eyul Mtḥ which is the valley of Hebron (which means) place of joining,

(41) Meshalma f. 145a: Whoever buried within 3,000 cubits from Mt. Garizim the burning fire on the day of requital will not touch. Such is the reward of the repentant and pious. So in Sam. Arab. B. of Joshua Cod. Gaster 9. Sam. Hillukh. Book of Oral Law.—T. B. Zebahim f. 113a: Whole of Palestine untouched by Flood.

(44) Meshalma 138b: "And Noah learned from Adam before his death the true calculation; i. e. Calendar cf. III. 9.—See Introd. —Zohar I. 58b.

Ch. III.

(1—7) From the conflicting traditions concerning the burial of Adam, found already in the various Adam Books and in the legends of the Cross (Story of Golgotha) a few of the less well known are added here.—Meshalma fol 139b: ". . to the place called the oak of Hebron, for that is the place for the gathering of the generations of the meritorious ones, which is called Kiryatarba," i. e. the town of the four, for therein were buried Adam, Noah, Metushelah and ones. And Metushelah no longer lived; and from the holy Law it is shown that Lamech and Metushelah died in the same year and God knows whether Lamech died first. And after the death of Metushelah, whose death was on the fourteenth day of the second month, the earth was humid (10) and three days after were broken up all the fountains of the mighty deep and the windows of the heavens were opened. And the rain was upon the earth in the second month, on the seventeenth day of the month. On the third day (Tuesday) and that is proved from the saying of the messenger in the Asatir [on the fourth the earth was humid and was broken open; and on the thirteenth were opened the windows of heaven]. And the end of the coming down of the rain was on the day of the Sabbath on the sixth hour of the night; and that is proved by his saying [and the time of completion was the sixth hour of the night of the seventh day, the Sabbath, then the decree was completely finished.] The coming down of the rain came to an end on the sixth P. 43. and the rest of the thing is clear. And I have seen some who wish to explain it differently like this. [In the seven hundred and nintieth year, it came to an end in the sixth hour of the night of Sabbath.] And this comes out from his saying seven hundred and ninety, and God knows whether this explanation is according to the truth, though it differs from our interpretation.]

And now let us return where we left the remembrance of it, and let us say with the author of the Asatir—on whom be peace—that Noah's going out from the Ark was on the Sabbath.

On the second and third day he P. 44 (11) built an altar and he sacrificed upon it an offering to God according to his saying, and it was on the seventh [and on the first that Noah went out from the Ark and on the second he built an altar and he brought a sacrifice.] And after the completion of the flood, and of the death of all living on the

4. Which he had seen in his vision as having been made for the gathering of the righteous generations created on the day in which the tree of knowledge was planted.

5. And this was that there be fulfilled "for surely thou wilt die."

6. And there are three divisions in it, one for those who went out of the Garden, one for those who went out of the Ark and one for those who came of the circumcised of the flesh.

7. And this was called "Machpelah" (manifold).

8. And Noah settled in the place of Adam after the death of Adam.

Lamech.—Malif. Q. 114: The following buried there: Adam, Enosh, Lamech, Noah, Abraham, Isaac and Jacob, Sarah, Rebecca and Leah.—Schatzhöhle p. 9. Very close similarity. Calling the children together, praying, and ordering burial in the cave, (centre of the earth).—Malan, Adam and Eve, Ch. IX. p. 116: Adam died 15th day of Barmudeh, the 9th hour of Friday, the day when he was created and the hour when he came out of the Garden.— According to Ephrem Syrus and Christian tradition in general, Adam was buried at Golgotha; See the Legends of the Cross, Gaster, Literatura Populara.—So also Eutyctinus.—Ethiop. Adam, Bk. II Ch. X (Malan p. 116): Adam died in the Cave of Treasures.—Book of the Bee, (Budge) p. 34—5: Shem took the bones of Adam to the place of buriel.—Eutychius I. p. 36. Adam's body carried from Holy Mountain;—Armen. Adam. Schr., p. 45: Adam and Eve buried in cave of Bethlehem. —According to Arabic tradition, Adam buried in Jerusalem; v. Grünbaum, Neue Beitr. p. 78—79.—Jewish tradition, only four couples buried there. Adam and Eve and three Patriarchs with their wives.—T. J. Taanith IV. 2.—T. B. Erubin 53a.—Pirke d. Rabbi Eliezer Ch. XX. Gen. Rabba Ch. 28,3.—Yashar Ch. 3.14: Buried in the cave of which God had told him. V. above Ch. I. 22.— Zohar IV, 164.—Jalkut to Gen. XXIV. 2.—Seder Hadorot p. 20: under the year 930. Adam was buried with royal honours by his son Seth, his grandchildren, in the cave of which God had spoken.—

(5) Gen. II 17.

face of the earth, there did not remain but Noah and those who were with him in the Ark. And Noah was frightened and he thought and said in his heart lest the flood should return a second time upon the earth; (12) and God knew what he thought and he said to his (Noah's) heart, I will not smite any more the whole of the living and he made with him the covenant of the bow (rainbow). He made him P. 45. a faithful promise to the end of the generations and the making of this covenant with him was in the seventh month, and Noah dwelt in Aḥilah which is on the eastern part of the town of Babel. And he taught his sons' and the first thing he taught them was the confession of the unity of God and that God is one alone and there is no second to him. This is proved from the author of the Asatir [and he taught his sons the principles of the confession of faith] (13) and after sixty two years since the flood he divided the earth among his sons. (14) [To Shem three portions and to Japhet four. And to Ham four. P. 46. And Elam and Ld and Aram and Ashur four portions, and Arpachshad one portion.] These five sons are the children of Shem. (15) [And he gave the Book of Signs to Arpachshad. And he gave the Book of Ngmut (astrology) to Elam. And he gave the Book of Wars to Ashur.] (16) And Shem and Arpachshad and Elam and Ashur were great and holy and the leaders over all his sons (17) [And he made unto Japhet four portions and they are Gomer and Magog, Madai and Javan Tubal and Moshek. And Tiras one portion] (18) And he made for Ham four portions and for Kush one portion and Miṣraim one portion and Fuṭ one portion P. 47, altogether twenty two portions. And he separated (or, singled out) the sons of Shem by his gift to them of the Books of Creation for he was the first-born, and he left for himself two portions. At the time of his death we shall refer to them again and their division. (19) And when Noah had completed his work and the division [he found from the

9. In seven years he learned the three Books of Creation: the Book of Signs, the Book of Astrology (astronomy, ngmot), the Book of the Wars which is the Book of the Generations of Adam.

10. "Who is like unto thee among the mighty ones, O God."

11. Who is like unto thee the God of the first ones and He who declares the righteousness of the latter ones. The Lord is one! He helped Noah.

12. And all the sons of Adam grew numerous [in the world] and powerful.

13. And Aḥidan, the son of Barad, the son of Tubal Ḳain, started and built Ṣion which is called Gifna (i. e. house of leprosy) which is Beth Machtesh (i. e. house of shame).

14. And he placed there a stone suspended (in the air) for worship like that in the town which is called Adrms which is on the place where Adam had bowed down [in worship] for the first time when he was driven out of the Garden.

(9) Gen V, I. Meshalma 140b: Noah started the collection of the three books of Creation, Book of Signs etc., 7 years after Adam's death.

(10) Exodus XVI II. Pious exclamation inserted by the author when mentioning the wonders of God.

(13) Gifna. Curiously enough, there existed a strong hold in Samaria not far from Sichem, called Jufna = Gopha of Josephus; George Adam Smith, Historical Geography of the Holy Land, 20th Edition, London, p. 351.

(14) Cod. A reads בן, but B, Pitron and Samaritan Ar. all read אבן evidently scribe's error in A. It must mean stone. The image of a god suspended in the air drops down at the death of Tammuz. Maimonides' "Guide of the Perplexed," III, 29—Hanging stone: Chwolson, "Die Sabier u. d. Sabismus, St. Petersburg 1856, II. p. 205: Norden, Die Geburt des Kindes p. 50. Kampers Werdegang, p. 52. Cf. the late legend of Mohammed's coffin floating in the air, in the Byzantine Chronicle of Chalkocondylas. ed. Niebuhr.

calculation of the Calendar that there were still 4,300 years less seven years after the flood, (20) for from the beginning of the days of Creation to the end there will be 6,000 years.] And the explanation of this is: — from Adam unto the Taheb will be 6,000 years and the seventh thousand will be the Jubilee P. 48. (21) And from the day God created Adam until the flood happened were 1, 307 years! (22) And from the day of the division by Noah unto his sons unto the building of Babel and their scattering by the Lord upon the face of the whole earth were 493 years; and that is proved from his saying in the Asatir (23) [from the day of Noah's division unto his sons until the day of their visitation, from generation unto generation 493 years] and Noah—on whom be peace—divided his kingdom among his sons [320 years] after the flood.

(24) P. 49. And on the day when Noah divided the earth among the eldest of his sons [he was] 930 years. (25) And he divided the earth unto his three sons on the tenth day of the month of Elul, (26) and he sent messengers among his children that each one should go unto his place (27) and they dispersed from him.

[And Elam and Ashur went to the north of Ur Kasdim: the town is now called by us by the name of the Gate of Gates]. (29) And Gog and Magog were on the other border of the Gate of Gates. (30) [Ld and Aram went and settled in the province (or town) Kuth]. P. 50. And this is a great town called The Black Pool which is called the Gezirah in Afrikia. (31) And Arpachshad dwelt in Ur Kasdim Brkṭrs, which is called by the name of Romeia.

And Kush begat Nimrod and when he grew up, he became king over the children of Ḥam, and he was a mighty man in the land. (32) He gathered them together to build Babel the Great, and they built it for him out of fear of him.

And Nimrod was the first giant who appeared upon the earth after the flood.

15. And that is "the rock in whom they confide," the rock upon which they relied.

16. And the evil increased six hundred years, and they turned away and yet the Lord did not cause Fanuta to happen.

17. But at the end of the generation when turning away and oppression increased, the world was full of men.

18. And Aḥidan begat a son and called him Asur.

(15) Deuteronomy XXXII 37.

(18 ff.) This story of Aḥidan, of the temple which he builds destined for idol worship, the reference to the image in it and to the stone suspended in the air, together with the other details borrowed from extraneous sources, is intended to vilify the temple of Jerusalem, and to declare the worship therein as idol worship. I have dealt with it and its probable sources and parallels in the Introduction, where I have also pointed out that the story of the stone suspended in the air and worshipped by the people must be one of the legends connected with the Eben Shetiyah, the stone of foundation inside the Holy of Holies in the temple of Jerusalem. I found only one parallel in the Samaritan literature. It is that given in Meshalma f. 138b; as it is an important variant I am publishing it there in full. "And in those days there appeared a man whose name was Aḥidan son of Barad son of Tubal Ḳain, and he built Ṣion, whose name is Beth Gifna (house of shame) and this is Beth Mactash (house of leprosy) and he erected there a statue and suspended there a stone in the air without pillars, and men came and wondered at it, and this is called (?) 'The stone in which they trusted.' (Deut. XXXII. 37.) This Aḥidan begat a son and called him Asur, and he built a place called Ṣion Tlh, and the Gentiles (Christians) and Mohammedans call it Shion, and that is El Ḳmamh. And they call it also Hḳiamh. And the Jews believe in it. And in what they believed to be the true copy, it says, 'Let their true Torah come out of Ṣion, and let the Torah of Moses be annulled.' (This sentence is borrowed from the Arabic paraphrast who writes: 'Son of Maimon.' See Introduction p. 170.) May God punish them according to the arrogance of their deeds, and for this word, and for what they speak concerning the Toroth, written by the hand of Ithamar, for they have hidden it in that place, and kept it secret. When Asur had completed it, he sent men to Babel, and he brought Gifna, daughter of Na-'amah, sister of Tubal Ḳain (and

(33) And when the days of the life of Noah were 945 years, Nimrod appeared, and he heard of him and of his evil doings. (34) [And his son Shem was the one whom he had placed on the throne of the kingdom because he was the first born]. And the explanation of it is, his son Shem kept his covenant, and when he grew up his father Noah appointed him to the kingdom.

(35) And in those days, Shem sent for his five sons [Elam and Ashur and Arpachshad and Ld and Aram] and he brought them to him, and they came to him and they built P. 52 Nineveh, Reḥbot Ir (or, the town Reḥbot), Klh, Resen, which is a great town between Nineveh and Klh, and it is said about it in the holy Torah [it is a big town.]

(36) And when the days of our master Noah grew near to die, he sent and called his three sons unto him, unto Shalem the Great, and they built an altar. [And they brought upon it thank offerings] and praises and exaltations unto the living God Who never dies. (37) And when Noah had first divided the earth into 22 portions, he left for himself two portions; and at the time of his death he gave Shem one more portion and Japhet another portion, and he divided whatever he still possessed of his kingdom of the world between them. And he set Shem above Japhet for he was the first born and was his successor, and was the owner of the three-fold holiness; but to the children of Ḥam he did not give anything on that occasion, for he had done the thing which is mentioned in the Torah; when Noah had cursed him he had said (Gen. IX. 25), "Cursed be Canaan, a slave of slaves shall he be unto his brothers." And Ḥam is the father of Canaan, and for this reason he did not obtain any further inheritance from his father on that occasion.

And know that from this it is proved that the infidel P.54. shall not inherit the faithful, and the faithful shall not inherit the infidel. (38) And Noah died,—on whom be

19. And he built Ṣrṣ a place called Ṣion Telah (the hanging rock Ṣion) and he gave it to him.

20. And he sent and brought Gifna the daughter of Na'amah and brought her from Babel, who was one of the wicked worship of Lamech. And he gave her as a wife to Asur and he made a high tower (nigug).

21. And it rested upon four statues, one of gold, one of silver, one of copper, and one of olive wood.

he married her to his son). And he made four statues, one of gold, second of silver, third of copper, and the fourth of wood. And he made the images of sun and moon and he put inside the moon the stone of Shoham (onyx) and he gave them to Gifna, the daughter of Na'amah. And she made therein a kind of lighthouse, which she placed upon the four corners, on the four statues, also the images of the sun and moon. And she appointed 400 ministers, and Gifna used to call the sun and moon. And they walked with her. And many people came and worshipped what she had made. And wickedness grew in the world." Thus far Meshalma, who apparently had also somewhat misunderstood the text. He did not realise that the building was to be a kind of temple in which Gifna was sitting and worshipped as a goddess, such as was the case with Nimrod, Chosroe. (See Introduction.)

(19) Sursn, so in Codex B. "Surs" in A and Pitron cf. Zarethan Joshua III. 16. 1 Kg VII. 46.—Sanchuniaton (Eusebius, Prep. Ev. I.) tells of Astarte who picks up a stone fallen from heaven and places it on the holy island of Tyre. —In Book of Heavenly Halls (Pirke Hechalot ed. Wertheimer Jerusalem 1910). VI. 4: R. Ishmael sees the crown of David, adorned with sun, moon and stars.—Tubal Kain. Rashi to Gen. IV. 20 quotes an Agadic Midrash to the effect that Jabal built temples for idol-worship and his brother Tubal invented musical instruments to play therein.

(20) "Nigug" is translated by me "tower" or "lighthouse." The Samaritans translate it (Pitron) "menorah" which is equivalent with Arabic "minaret" (lighthouse: tower).—See legend of Chosroe's throne, Kamper's Werdegang, p. 38—43. Gaster, Exempla IVa. 2a: This kind of temple has been dealt with fully in the Introduction, where the literature is given. Nimrod's throne Ginzberg Leg. of the Jews, vol I, p. 178.—Maybe we have also here an echo of the Semiramis legend.

peace—when he was 950 years old. And his sons carried him and they buried him in the Cave of Machpelah in which Adam had been buried, as he had commanded them. And each one went to his place.

Chapter V. [Nimrod.]

(1) And it came to pass after the 493 years, which had been prophesied by the master Noah, that there was the gathering in the town of Babel in their moving from the East—and this is the place called Maṭlon in the East—to Babel. And they found a wide valley P. 55. in the land of Shinear, and they settled there (2) and it is a valley like the valley of Sichem, and this is Elon Moreh, and next to it is a mountain like Mount Garizim. (3) And one said to his neighbour, "Let us go up this mountain and let us build unto us a high building, a town and a tower, lest we be scattered over the face of the whole earth." (4) And they went up the mountain and built upon it first a beacon where light was seen from the four corners of the earth, (5) and they called its name Sham. And this is the word they said, "Let us make ourselves a Sham." (6) And they finished the building P. 56. but their desire was not fulfilled by God. For He destroyed the building and the children of man were scattered over the face of the whole earth, (7) and not one of them knew the language of his neighbour. (8) And this was the origin of the wars. As it is said in the Book of Asatir (9) And this is the origin of the wars, which were [six] for the dying and the seventh for the living. His saying: "wars for the dead" means, the war of the dying (or, those destined for death. 'The' dead' means these are the sinners, who are empty of virtue. It is said about them, "the living, are like unto the dead." And his saying the other word, 'the seventh for life' P. 57. means that through the wars which will happen at that time, the holy family (chain) will be oppressed and they will suffer great violence at

22. And he made a likeness of the sun and the moon of crystal and he put into the sun a golden luminous cup.

23. And he put inside the moon a precious stone (shoham).

24. And he said unto Gifna "Behold, let thy worship begin here." (or, "let thou be worshipped first here.")

25. And Gifna appointed quickly four hundred servants and twenty ministers. Mighty is the holiness of the proclamation of faith on the rod of Adam which is called [the rod] of God.

(22) The author must have borrowed this imagery from an ancient pictorial representation of the Heaven with the sun, moon, and stars, probably in some heathen temple or anyhow connected with idol worship. I have not been able to trace it. The notion of the sun with a cup travelling through heaven is found in Greek mythology; See Gruppe: Griech. Myth. p. 380 for literature. It has of course nothing to do with the Christian Iconography, which besides offers no real parallel.

(24) In Pitron this verse has been differently translated.

(25) This is a pious exclamation in which the author indulges when referring to idol worship us it to avert an evil omen. It interrupts in a most disconcerting manner the course of the narrative, and has caused me great confusion until I realised its character.— The following legend is found in the Malif, Q. 49: "The rod of Adam has many secrets. Among them that the "Messenger" performed through it the miracles. And it is said that there was written upon it the true calculation (Calendar), the Book of Wars, the Book of Signs, and the Book of Astronomy. And Noah took out these three books from the rod seven years after the death of Adam. And these Books and the rod remained with Noah till his death. And then he gave it to the sons of his son Shem to Arpachshad, to Iram, Ashur. And this rod remained in the possession of Arpachshad and it was handed down (transferred) through the holy chain until it came into the possession of Jethro where it was kept up to the time when the Messenger came, u. w. b. p., and took it from him, and all this (was done) for great purposes. These three books were preserved by Laban until the time when the "Messenger" came, when the Law was brought down. They disappeared slowly with the exception of just a little of the astronomy and the true

the hands of the Nimrods. So, for example, Teraḥ, when they took him and put him in prison, his son Abraham, whom they threw into the fire, and whose wife, Sarah, they took from him twice. They also waged war against him (Abraham), the wars mentioned in the book of the holy Torah.

Know that every one of the Meritorious Ones had to suffer great troubles in his lifetime. These were trials from God to purify them from the sins of the world. P. 58. Then he accepted their repentance and made them great in the world to come. Perhaps the letter ז is the initial of the word זכרון, remembrance, that there shall be knowledge and reputation of them. And our master Marḳah—may God's favour be upon him—speaking of the Meritorious Ones, said, "The dead are like unto the living." And this is his saying, "Remember unto us the covenant of the dead like that of the living." And God knows.

And another explanation of the letter ז (this is seven) is that Sabbath is the seventh (day), and that the observance of it will purify man of his sin; and perhaps the explanation be that he is recounting the wars which happened in the days of the Meritorious Ones and the troubles which happened, came upon them to purify P. 59. them, just as the Sabbath purifies those who keep it. And God knows. And this explanation will agree with the opinion of the masters of knowledge. It says in the Book Asatir, [the beginning of the wars of the dying with the living,] were the beginning of the wars, because the Lehadim, Enamin, Naftoḥim, Patrosim and Kasloḥim gathered together with the others. (10) And they chose for themselves a leader whose name was Giṭṭ the first born of the Lehadim, which were called by his name, Gibṭai. (11) And they went from Philistia and made war first with the Canaanites and Perizites, and took the kingdom from the hand of Nimrod, and ruled P. 60. from the land of Egypt unto the river of Kush. (12) And Nimrod went

26. And he made an open nigug in such wise as is called fngl (i. e. dome or cupola) which when the wind passed through it from the four corners emitted a sound.

27. And it lasted one hundred and ten years. And Asur begat a son from Gifna and his name was Itanu.

28. And Itanu begat a son and called him Shriḳh.

29. And when Gifna called the sun and the moon which Aḥidan had made, they walked with her.

30. And when she did this, the people wished to worship them and the world became evil and all flesh corrupted its way upon it.

Chapter IV. [Noah.]

1. And Noah left Rift and he dwelt in the mountain called 'Adr Shgg. This is the place of the Ark.

calculation of the Calendar which is in our hands. And as for the rod, it was placed in the tent and will be there until the Taheb will come. And one of the signs will be that he will bring it."— cf. Chapter IX. 22. Rod of Adam and Moses.—Origin of these legends must be traced back to Exod. IV. 20 where Moses takes the "rod of God" in his hand. The subject has heen so often treated that I refer here only to Jeraḥmeel. Introd. p. XCI, and literature from there.—Gressmann in Zeitschrift für Kunde des Morgenlands 1913, p. 18 ff. points out that in Babylon rods were engraved with the image of the god.—Pesikta f. 140a: Name of God engraved in the rod of Adam. "Mighty is" etc. A pious exclamation on the part of the author when mentioning idolatry.

(26) Arabic glosses it all over: "He put a dome on the top of the tower" cf. the singing obelisk of Memnon.—Moved by the wind; See Kampers Werdegang, p. 41 see further X. 27.

(27) Have we here perhaps the origin of Joniton, the reputed fourth son of Noah in Schatzhöhle and Nephodins? (see Sackur Sibyll. Texte p. 14—16).

Ch. IV.

(1) ריפת cf. above II, 20, but more likely it is identical with I, 17: ערפאת—Cf. B. of Enoch LXV. 2:

and pitched his camp against Gitt, and he asked the children of Joktan to help him against the children of Misraim and his seed. (13) And the children of Joktan turned away and did not listen unto him, and went away until they reached a place for camping, of which it is said, "from Mesha until thou comest unto Sifra of the mountain of the East,) that is Timnata, whose name was called Yemen, Sifra, the mountain of the East until Timnata." (14) And Gitt died in the land of Misraim, and when Nimrod heard of the death of Gitt, he rose up to fight the inhabitants of the town of Ashur, and that is the place called Almosa; and he ruled over it, (15) and when he became king over it, P. 61. he rose up and made war with Nahor.

(16) And Nimrod did unto Arpachshad just as Pharaoh did unto the Hebrews. For at that time, they had seen in the Book of Signs which had been handed down to them, that there would arise a man who would smite everyone who worshipped idols, and he would destroy them. (17) And he gathered together all the wise men from the children of Ham and the children of Japhet. And he asked of them, that they should tell him of the day of the birth of that man; (18) and they told him that within forty days his mother would become pregnant with him. (19) Then the Nimrod commanded that every man of all the sons of Arpachshad, P. 62. should keep himself separated from his wife for the number of forty days. (20) And they imprisoned all the men in one place and the women in another place separately. (21) And it came to pass after thirty of the above mentioned days that the Lord revealed a sign in the land of Shinear, and it was a pillar of fire which came down from heaven to earth. (22) And all the inhabitants thereof were frightened with a great fear, and they made prayers in the house of their worship unto the idols, and they went out unto a field outside the town and they remained there three days, and the

2. And God announced to him the news of the flood and Noah started to examine the Book of Signs, and Noah saw therein the obliteration of (the children of) Adam, and the protection of those who were to go into the Ark.

3. And it came to pass at the time when he left [Rift] that there was a sign in the land.

4. And Noah feared a great fear and he continued unceasingly with prayers and hymns one hundred years after he had begotten Shem, Ham and Japhet.

5. And Shem took Shrit the daughter of Seth to wife.

Noah went to the end of the earth (to seek Enoch).—Place of the Ark means probably place where Ark rested afterwards. There are different traditions about that place.—Meshalma 141a: "Rift which was built by Lamech."—Pal. Targ. to Gen. VIII. 4: calls it Kadron. Onkelos ibid. has Kardu.—Josephus Antiq. I. 3. 1 74. Josephus Antiq. I. 3. 5. 90: does not mention name of mountain on which Ark rested.—Jubilees V. 28: Ark rested on Mt. Lûbar.—Chronicon Paschale ed. Niebuhr Bonnae 1832; vol I, p. 45: Noah lived on Mount Lubar.—Schatzhöhle p. 17: Built from the wood of the Holy Mountain.—Theophilus III. 19: Arabia, probably Ararat.

(3) Josephus Antiq. I. 3. 5. 89: "When God gave the signal (or sign)."

(4) Sibyl. Or. Bk. I. 47 ff.: Fear and admonitions.—Theophilus III. 19: Noah praying and foretelling the Flood.—T. B. Sanhedrin f. 108b.—Gen. Rabba 3, 33. Eccles. R. to 9. 14.—Prayed 100 years. LekahTob, ed. Buber I. p. 36: Noah worked at the Ark 120 years.—So also Tabari, Grünbaum, Neue Beitr. p. 79.—Noah admonishing and teaching. Often in Koran. e. g. 7. 57—63; 10. 72—75, etc. cf. Geiger Mohammed, p. 110. Schatzhöhle 17 and 18: Three sons born in 100 years. So also T. B. Sanhedrin 108b.—Meshalma 140b: Five hundred years teaching and preaching to the people. Mistake of scribe. Read 100.

(5) Josephus Antiq. I. 3. 1. 77: No name. He also mentions here the wives of the sons of Noah.—Yashar V. 35: The wives of the sons of Noah took three sisters, daughters of Eliakim, son of Metushelah. Algazi ibid.: Shem's wife, Mahlah daughter of Baun. Gen. Rabba XXX., 31.

name (of God)—may He be exalted—gave them work and they forgot the imprisoned ones P. 63. (23) And in that time the master Teraḥ went by a vision of the Lord and slept with his wife, and she conceived (24). And when Terah had slept with his wife, he returned to the prison and the sign was lifted.

And when the wizards saw that the sign had been lifted, they said: "The child hath reached the womb of its mother;" and they told Nimrod so. (25) And he said, "Bring out all the prisoners unto their places." And they did so, and every man went to his place as he had commanded.

(26) After this was born our master Abraham—on whom be peace—by the might of the All-powerful. And it came to pass when he grew up, P. 64. that Nimrod took him and placed him under his command, and he was among those who stood before him, to wait on him. (27) And after that, he took him and cast him into the fire, but the fire could not burn our master Abraham, for God protected him, for the sake of the master of the flesh who was to come out of his loins, and also for his great righteousness. Behold what God said unto him, "I am the Lord, who brought you out from Ur (furnace) Kasdim."

(28) When he saw that the fire had no power over him, Haran said, "He is a great wizard and his witchcraft prevents the fire from burning him." Then the fire came out and consumed Haran. P. 65. See what is said about him in the Holy Law, "And Haran died before the face of his father Terah in the land of his birth, in Ur Kasdim! (Gen. 11. 28.) And when Nimrod and his company saw that the fire had come forth and had consumed Haran, the fear of God came upon them, and they were frightened lest it should come out upon them and consume them also. And the Nimrod commanded that the master Abraham should come out—Praised be He, Who performeth signs and wonders, the One Who keepeth the Covenant and the mercy to those who love Him!

6. And Ḥam took Skh the daughter of Jared to wife.

7. And Japhet took Mkisth the daughter of Lamech [to wife].

8. And when God said unto him (Noah) that he was to make the Ark, he made it and he finished it on the tenth (twelfth?) of the second month.

9. And on the fourth (Wednesday) the earth became humid and broke open.

10. And on the third (Tuesday) were opened the windows of Heaven. And on the seventh (Sabbath) was the end of the decree in the sixth hour of the night of the seventh. And on the first [of the month] Noah went out of the Ark.

(8—10) Gen. VII, 11 has the date of the month (17th of the second month). Here the days of the week are given. But may also mean 1st day of the of the week (Sunday). On the Sabbath, the Flood began and terminated. Samaritans have given the word היה a numerical value i.e. the 7th as the meaning of the words "this day" is otherwise obscure; This phrase occurs twice in Gen. 7. 11 and 13.—Malif. Q. 70: The animals came of their own free will into the Ark. cf. Sibylline I 207 ff.—Meshalma 153a: Started from end of the month of Iyar (Siban).—Meshalma f. 154a quotes Markah to the effect that the Flood did not cover Mt. Garizim.—Arab. Book of Joshua p. 11: According to Samaritan tradition, on the 14th Nisan or rather, on the Festival of Passover, God created the world Noah went out, Sodom and Gomorrah were burned, Exodus Israelites occupied Mt. Garizim. God hid the Temple (2nd day) the curse will be removed, Sanctuary will be re-erected, the Taheb will appear, and the truth will be established. —Josephus I. 3. 3. 80 and 81: Flood begins on 27th of 2nd month called by the Hebrews *Marhesvan*—against Samaritans, contrary to one Jewish tradition; T. B. Rosh Hashana 11b.—LXX. to Gen. VII. 11: says 17th.—Jubilees V. 22: Noah started building the Arkon the New Moon, of the first month 1307 A. M. entered New Moon of the second month 1308 A. M. ibid. 23. Flood begins 17th.—Ibid. V. 29: On the New Moon of the fourth month Flood stopped. — Schatzhöhle p. 21: Flood began Friday the 17th of Iyar. — — B. of the Bee Ch. 20. p. 32: Flood on Friday, and the Ark remained upon the waters until the 20th Tishri.—Albiruni (Sachau), p. 25: Flood began

Chapter VI. [Abraham in Egypt.]

(1) And it came to pass seven years after this occurrence that the Nimrod died and with him was completed the number of the kings P. 66., who reigned from the children of Ham. (2) Through a Nimrod it began and through a Nimrod it came to an end, and from the first Nimrod to the second Nimrod were 1,020 years. (3) The first Nimrod was from Kush and the second Nimrod was from the Kaftorites.

(4) And it came to pass after the death of Nimrod that Terah went out to go into the land of Canaan, which was outside the kingdom of Nimrod, for he was afraid lest other Nimrodim would appear and do unto him as had done the above mentioned Nimrod. (5) And his son Nahor dwelt with Kedar Laomer and Tidhal, King of Goyim. P. 67. (6) And it came to pass when they heard of the going out of Terah, they sent men against him to prevent him from going away, and Kedar Laomer went to plunder and kept Terah prisoner in Haran. (7) And Abraham went out to meet Kedar Laomer in Ur Kasdim and to prostrate himself before him [with the request] that they should release his father, Terah, from the prison. (8) There God called him and commanded him to go out from Haran. And he came unto the land of Canaan, and Lot the son of his brother with him, and they dwelt in Elon Moreh. And now behold, O my brother, how great was the obedience of our master Abraham to his God, for he went from his land P. 68., and from his birthplace, and he forsook his father in the house of prison, for he was afraid to rebel against the command of God.

(Happy are those who are beloved of God, and woe unto them who hate God!) And from this thing it is known that Terah died and Abraham, his son, was not with him, and it is said that his son Nahor buried him. And this is proved by his saying—may He be exalted—

11. And on the second he built an altar and he brought a sacrifice.

12. And God made with him the covenant of the rainbow on the seventh. And Noah dwelt in 'Iṭh at the rising of the sun (East) in Babel and he started teaching his children the principles of (the confession of) faith and the testimony.

13. And after sixty two years he divided the earth among his sons Shem, Ḥam and Japhet.

14. And to Shem he gave three portions and Japhet four and Ḥam four; [Shem divided his portion, giving to] 'Elam, Ld, Aram and Ashur four portions and Arpachshad one portion.

15. And he gave the Book of Signs to Arpachshad, and the Book of Astronomy to Elam and the Book of the Wars to Ashur.

on Friday night in year 2,226; 23 days and 4 hours from death of Adam, according to Anianus.—Urim ve Tumim: Noah started building the Ark on the 10th of the month.—Seder Hadorot p. 23. Flood in year 1656; p. 24. Noah entered the Ark on the fourth, Wednesday.—The "first" in verse 10 may also mean New Moon, although the numbers always refer to days of the week; cf. Gen. VIII. 13.

(11) Meshalma 155a: "Altar on Mt. Garizim,"—Jubilees VI. 1. 4. 11: A covenant on the same day.

(12) Meshalma f. 140b: Teaching the people to walk in the way of God (see below v. 38).—Ethop. Adam Books Bk III Ch. 13 Malan Teaching his children p. 160 ff.—Kebra Ch. 7: Teaching his children to beware of going with the children of Ḳain.—Armen. Adamschr. p. 40: Noah descended from mountain and lived in Akor.

(13) Sibyll. Or. III. 110 ff earth divided among three sons. —Schatzhöhle p. 30.—Langlois Vol. I. ch. V (p. 19 ff): Division of the land by Noah.—Syncellus 80b: Division of the land by Noah among his three sons in 2504.—Malalas (ed Niebuhr) p. 13: Noah calls his three sons and divides the land among them.—Chs. of Rabbi Eliezer Ch. 23: Noah divided the earth among his three sons.

(14 ff.) Evidently two kinds of divisions are confused, one in the lifetime of Peleg, whose name has been etomologically confused with

"And Terah died in Haran " And do not consider his saying. "And Terah died in Haran," before the saying, "Get thee from thy land, from thy birthplace," because the history begins with the second section concerning Abraham, in order that it should be set down without interruption. And there are a large number of similar statements (i. e., not in chronological order) in the Torah. P. 69. And therein is no contradiction according the men of knowledge and understanding.

And Abraham dwelt in Elon Moreh, being shown thither by God—may He be exalted!—for He said unto him; "Go unto the land which I will show thee." And the 'Showing' meant that he should reach Elon Moreh, for he knew that this was the place to be sought for. And he rebuilt the altar of his forefathers Adam and Noah. (9) And after that he went up Mount Garizim to the East of Bethel. And he bowed down and prostrated himself there before God. And he worshipped and went down.

And it came to pass after these things that there was a famine in the land of Canaan, (10) and Abraham and Lot, the son of his brother, journeyed with him from Elon Moreh, and they went P. 70. down to Egypt. (11) And when they reached the boundary of Egypt, there was a great shaking in all the houses of worship which were in Egypt. And all the dwellers of the houses of worship were frightened.

(12) And Abraham encamped in a place called Hrif. And it was in those many days that the women of Egypt went out into the field to the place Hrif. (13) And they found Sarai the wife of Abraham, and they saw that she was of a beautiful face and of a beautiful countenance. And it came to pass that when they returned from the field in the evening, they praised her before their husbands, until the word reached the minister of Pharaoh, who praised her unto him. And it came to pass when he

16. And he made them the foremost of all his sons.

17. And Japhet divided the four portions, among Gomer, Magog, Maddai, Javan, Tubal, Meshech and Tiras each one portion.

18. And Ham divided his land into four portions, Kush one portion and Miṣraim one portion, Put one portion and Canaan one portion.

19. And when Noah had finished the division of the land by the astronomical calculation of the day, he found that there were still four thousand three hundred years less seven years to come after the flood, of the six thousand from the beginning of the creation and three hundred and seven since the flood.

20. For from the beginning of the days of Creation there shall be 6,000 years,

21. From the day of creation until the day of the visitation of the generations (through the flood) were one thousand three hundred and seven years.

"division."—The countries occupied by Noah's three sons and their descendants, see Jeraḥmeel Ch. XXVIII and introduction ad loc. for full literature, to which I may add the exhaustive annotation pp. 234—249 in Vol. II to Chronicon Paschale Vol. I 43—63 ed Niebuhr, Bauer and Strygowski, Alexandr. Weltchr. (see Introd.— Algazi ibid.: Name of wife of Arpachshad, Resuyah, daughter of Sason.

(19) So Malif. Q. 63: Flood in year 1, 307 from Creation.

(20) Duration of the world 6,000 years; T. B. Hagigah 113a v. Ch. Cf. note XI. 20, and Introd.

(21) Flood was in the year 1, 307. A. M. probably the date of the Flood according to Samaritan calculation.—Hebrew Bible 1: 656 years.—LXX. 2: 262 (2: 242?) years.—Josephus Antiq. I. 3. 3 82: gives 2,662 from Adam. Another reading of Josephus 1,656 seems to be the more primitive one. Julius Africanus Chronology 2,263. (Sackur Sibyll. Texte p. 63.)—Methodius places it at the end of the second millenium. 7 years after the date of Schatzhöhle.—

(Pharaoh) heard the report about her, P. 71. that he brought her into his house and he took her. And Abraham went with her but he could not do anything. And Pharaoh gave him many gifts and was kind to him for the sake of Sarai and Abraham went out from Pharaoh with a broken heart and a weeping eye. And he prayed unto God to save his wife Sarah from the hand of Pharaoh; and God hearkened to his prayer, (14) and God plagued Pharaoh and his house with great plagues. (15) And the plague was on the privy parts and Pharaoh was like a stone. (16) And he called all the wizards of Egypt and its wise men and he gathered them together and (18) there was among them a wizard and his name was Ṭurṭs, who had studied in the Book of Signs. He had learned that book in from Enoch, the son of Ḳain, (19) and he strengthened himself in Ḥanoḫia and said, "There is in this place a woman, who is a faithful one, believing in God, and all these visitations one for her sake."

(20) And when our master Abraham—on whom be peace—heard what had happened to Pharaoh and to his house, he rose up and lifted up his face unto heaven and praised God, and he thanked Him and he sanctified Him for all the good He had done him, in that He had preserved unto him Sarai his wife from defilement.

Then it became true and known unto them that this had come through the evil deeds which had been done by Pharaoh. P. 75 (mistake in original pagination). And no man could look on Sarah and no one could see her face. On her face the light was shining strongly. This is proved by his saying, (21) "And they were freed (i. e. from the plague) and they saw that the whole palace was lit up from the appearance of the face of Sarah, and there was great fear." (22) And thereby it became known that Sarah was the wife of Abraham. And Pharaoh begged relief of him, and gave back his wife Sarah, and he went away in rejoicing and in peace, with the innocence of his

22. And from the day when Noah made the division among his children, until the day of the visitation of the generations were four hundred and ninety three years.

23. And he divided his kingdom to his three sons in the year three hundred and twenty.

24. And Noah was on the day when he divided [the land] among his sons nine hundred and thirty years old.

25. And he divided the land among his three sons on the tenth day of the month of Elul.

26. And then he sent proclamations to his sons that each one should go to his country.

27. And they took leave of him and Elam and Ashur went to the north of Ur Kasdim, which is called by them the place of Bab el Abwab (Gate of Gates),

28. And which is on the border of Elam and Ashur.

29. And Gomer and Magog were from Bab el Abwab and onwards.

30. And Ld and Aram settled in Great Kutah whose name is Charassan the Black which is called Algezirah in Afrikia (Phrygia).

Seder Olam Ch. I: Date of the Flood 1656.
(23) Meshalma 171a: 12th of Ellul.' Malif. Q. 80: 'In the year 329" after the Flood.
(26) Josephus Antiq. I. 4. I. 110. Noah sends the children to the various countries.
(27) Jubilees VIII. 12 ff.
(29) Gog, Magog—Herodot III. Pliny VI. 11. 30. Strabo XII. 1. 7.

Polybius V. 44. Hecateus Frag. 71. Ptolemaeus VI. 2. Caspian Gates already mentioned by Josephus, see Marquart Eransahr Berlin 1901, p. 101 ff.
(30) "Algesira" i. e. "island" in Arabic, is the name of the country between the Tigris and the Euphrates.— Meshalma f. 171b: has the following: Arpachshad settled in Laban (white)

wife. And he stood before God and prayed for Pharaoh and for his house. (23) This is the first prayer which our master Abraham prayed. And this is the whole of what he said in his prayer, "O Lord, the God of Heaven and the God of the earth, All Merciful, be merciful." (24) And God healed Pharaoh and his house, and then Pharaoh believed in the truth of the faith of Abraham, since his prayer was received and his God was the God of Gods and the Lord of Lords, and He performed wonders for Abraham's sake. And he knew that his prayer before the idols had not cured him from the plague which he had, but that only the prayer of Abraham to his God had cured him. At that time he commanded the destruction of the houses wherein the idols were, P. 76. and the breaking of the idols and the destruction of all the pillars, and he commanded that those who worshipped them should be killed, as there was no use for them, and whoever prostrated himself before them, became worthless in this world and a sinner at the end of days. And all this is made evident from his word in the Asatir. "And all the houses of worship were destroyed and all those things (i. e., the idols) before which people prostrated themselves fell down and could not be raised up."

(25) And the wizard Ṭurṭs went up from there, when he saw what Pharaoh had done to the houses of worship and to the idols and to the pillars; for he could not stay in Egypt any longer. And he went up thence and he went to Hebron.

(26) And afterwards Pharaoh commanded men from among his people and he said unto them that they should go with Abraham and lead him to the place which he would choose. They were not to forsake him and anyone who would do anything to him or to his wife should surely die. And they did as Pharaoh commanded them and they came with him and with Lot, his brother's son, with their

31. And Arpachshad settled in Ur Kasdim in Brkṭrs (Bactria ?) whose name is Romi. And Nimrod began to rule over all the children of Ḥam.

32. And he built great Babel and they gathered themselves all together and they went to build it, and Nimrod started to walk as a giant in the land.

33. And Noah was nine hundred and forty five years old when the report of it reached Noah.

34. But Shem his son was the one whom he had placed on the throne of the kingdom because he was the firstborn.

Kasdim, in the place called Great Romiah, and Elam and Ashur dwealt on the border of Laban (Tiras) in a place which is called "the door of the gates," Kasdim. Five years before the death of Noah appeared Nimrod a giant in the land, and he became king over the children of Ham, and children of Great Babel. And they gathered themselves together to build it.—Malif. Q. 82: Shem settled in the towns of Afrikia, to which belonged the land of the Kasdin.—Sibylline Oracles III. 140: Shem in Phrygia. See Introd.

(31) ברקטרם probably Bactria: this in Samaritan Chronicon Parshag l.c.—Malif.Q.83.—Urim ve Tumim: Nimrod born on the 6th of the month.—Grünbaum, Neue Beitr., p. 91 ff. Oriental legends of Nimrod.

(32) Josephus Antiq. I. 4. 2. 114, Nimrod built Babel.—Meshalma f. 171 b. Nimrod King (cf. note to IV. 31.— Pirke de Rabbi Eliezer Ch. 29. Nimrod King builds Babel.—Seder Hadorot p. 26: Nimrod King builds Babel.— נבר Giant, so in the Arabic paraphrase and in constant use among Samaritans. See Samaritan Joshua. —Jeraḥmeel 27. 4: Nimrod a proud giant. Nimrod a giant; Adam and Eve Ethiop. ed. Malan Bk. III. Ch. XXIII. p. 173. Methodius Ch. III "Nembrod gigans." Philo (see Introduction), Eusebius, Prep. Ev. Bk IX, ch. 182 Nimrod (Bel.) (420 b) giant.— Tuch, Kommentar über die Genesis, Halle 1871, p. 181: Nimrod King of Egypt. Old tradition.—The Samaritans call every giant Nimrod.

(33) Complete נב טק.

(34–36) Noah appoints son to be ruler: Josephus I. 3. 4. 87. Josephus I. 6. 3. 142: "He prayed for prosperity to his other sons." —Malif, Quest: 85 made covenant of peace.—Meshalma 171 b: Calling Noah's sons together to Shalem the Great which is Sichem. Offerings. Commanded them to observe the laws pleasing to God, and made them take an oath. Placed Shem higher than Japhet, and Japhet higher than Ham.—

flocks and with everything which they possessed, (27) until they reached Elon Moreh, the place of the first altar. P. 77. And Abraham built up the above mentioned altar, and he brought up sacrifices unto God, who had saved him from the hand of the Egyptians. And Abraham and Lot dwelt in the land of Canaan one year.

Chapter VII. [Abraham and Battle of Kings.]

(2) In the month of Nisan Abraham came from Haran, and in the month of Iyar he went down to Egypt, (3) and in the month of Nisan Lot separated himself from him and dwelt in Sodom one year.

(1) It came to pass in those days that Amrafel ruled in the land of Shinear. (4) In that same year in which Lot dwelt in Sodom, the above mentioned Ṭurṭs went from Hebron to the land of Shinear to Amrafel and to Kedar Laomer, and he foretold to them that they would kill many people. P. 78. And he told them what would happen to them in the later days. (5) And Kedar Laomer knew Abraham—on whom be peace—and he did not turn to listen to the saying of the wizards, (6) but he began to kill everyone who stood before him, and he slew the inhabitants and captured the town called Kadosh; (7) and they were the last of the kings over that country from the children of Ḥam.

And it came to pass that Amrafel, King of Shinear, Arioch, King of Elasar, Kedar Laomer, King of Elam, and Tidal, King of Goym, had imposed tribute upon Bera, King of Sodom and with Birsah, King of Gomorrah, Shinab, King of Admah, und Shemeber, King of Zeboim and the King of Bela, (the same is Zoar). P. 79. And these four kings used to send tribute and gifts to Amrafel and unto the kings who were with him, for twelve years, and in the thirteenth year, they left off and did not send anything, and in the fourteenth year came Kedar Laomer and those who were with him, to wage war against them.

35. And Shem sent also to Elam, Ashur, Lud, Aram, and Arpachshad and they came and built Niniveh and Calah, Rehoboth Ir, and Resen which is the big town.

36. And the day drew near for Noah to die, so he sent and called Shem, Ham and Japhet, and they came to him to Shalem the Great and built an altar and they brought upon it thankofferings.

37. And he completed his division and gave to Shem six and to Japhet six, and he made Shem greater than Japhet.

38. And Noah commanded them the keeping of peace and died. And his children carried him to Eyul Mth which is Hebron and they buried him in Eyul Mth and each one returned to his place.

Chapter V [Nimrod.]

1. And they gathered themselves in Babel when they journied from the East and they found

Jubilees VII. 20.—Urim ve Tumim Noah blessing his children on the 14th day of the month.— Jubilees X. 14: Shem beloved by Noah.—Pirke de Rabbi Eliezer Ch. 42: blesses his sons, expecially Shem all the pure descend from him.

(35) Cf. Gen. X, 12 for all these names.

(38) דשלמ May also be translated "and he took leave." cf. however Introduction to Sibylline parallel; in the Pitron the passage is left unexplained Meshalma 172a: Eyul Mth which the cave of Machpelah.—Malif. Q. 85: Only Hebron and Cave of Machpelah mentioned.— Schatzhöhle p. 9: Burial of Noah exactly like burial of Adam ibid. pp. 26—27. Noah's death and Shem's mission.—B. of Bee ch-20 p. 33: Noah died on Wednes. day, Nisan 2nd, second hour of the day. Shem embalmed him, his sons buried him, and mourned over him 40 days.—Armen. Adamschr. p. 40: Noah buried in a place called Nahidžewan.

Ch. V.

cf. Genesis XI, 2. 4. differs from Samaritan Targum ad. loc. (1) The story of Nimrod as giant, the birth of Abraham, the wars of the nations have been fully discussed

And there was war between them (8) and they took Lot captive and all his possessions, he who was the son of the brother of Abraham. And Lot sent and told his uncle Abraham what had happened to him. (9) And 'Aniram and Eshkol and Mamre P. 80. were the confederates of Abraham, (10) and he told them what had happened to Lot, his brother's son, and he asked them to go with him to Sodom and they complied with his request and they, the above mentioned, went to war with him; (11) and when Kedar Laomer reached the kings of the Amorites, he waged war with them and defeated them, and he carried them off captive, and with them he also took Nahor, the brother of Abraham. (12) Then he, (Nahor) sent messengers to tell his brother Abraham what had happened to him. (14) It was then the eve of the incoming Sabbath. So he, (Abraham) and the men who were with him, slept the Sabbath night in Dumh which is Ṭbris, (15) and at the going out of the Sabbath after the setting of the sun P. 81. on the night of the first day (Sunday), Abraham went out to the palmgrove; and on the second (Monda) he reached them before the setting of the sun. And he found them encamped in the valley of Ḥobah (16) and this happened on the twenty second day of the month of Elul, and on the first of the month (new moon) in the valley of Ḥobah which is on the left side of Damascus; and the proof of it is the statement that the time when Abraham reached them was after the setting of the sun and "he smote them in the night," and he returned all the spoil and he returned also Lot his brother, and his goods, which is found in Gen. 14, 15, where it says, "he divided against them by night, he and his servants, and he smote them, P. 82. and he pursued them until after Ḥobah, which is the left side of Damascus." (17) And on the fifth of the lunar month he went up to Shalem the Great, and there came out to honour him, for they were frightened of him, the King of Sodom and King Nahor, and they came be-a plain in the land of Shinear and they dwelt there.

2. And it was like [the plain of Sichem and a mountain like] Mount Garizim.

3. And they said one to the other who beheld the land: "Let us go up here and let us build a high building so that we may not be scattered abroad upon the face of the earth."

4. And they built a tower on top of the hill, and they placed upon it a lamp and the light of it could be seen from the four sides.

5. And they called it Sham and that is the word which is said "and let us make a Sham."

6. And He put an end to their building and the building was shattered and the children of man were scattered abroad upon the face of the earth.

7. And none did know the language of his neighbour.

8. And then was the beginning of wars which were fought [seven] for death and one for life.

I am giving here therefore a few additional notes with reference to some passages not touched upon in the Introd. and the parallels from the Samaritan literature. I must mention at the same time that Meshalma agrees entirely with the Asatir.—Malif. Q. 86. Koran Sure 26. 129. Reference to Nimrod. Sure 11. 62.

(4) Nimrod equal to Amrafel (Introduction) T. B. Erubim f. 53a Yashar XI. 6 ff.

(5) Identifies the word שם (Gen. XI. 4) which he reads שָׁם, with the lighthouse, as otherwise to make oneself a name would not prevent people from being scattered. The P. T. interprets it as Idol which was to fight for them against God. Tower שם translated as "lighthouse" already in Samaritan Targum to Gen. XI 4. —Arabic "minaret" has the same original meaning "lit-up Tower."

(6) Meshalma 179b: "And God sent against them storms of wind and water."—Sibylline Oracles III. 98—103. Quoted by Josephus Antiq. I. 4. 3 (118).—VIII. 8 ff. Jubilees: Play on the name Peleg. X. 26. Overthrown by mighty wind.

(8—9) נוסים beginning or starting point. cf. ניסרום the starting point fore him to Shalem the Great. And King Nahor had made a league with them, (18) and when they saw the might of Abraham—on whom be peace—then they bent the knee and prostrated themselves before him, and they praised the high God. And someone among them, told what God had done to Pharaoh for the sake of Sarah and that they had seen him (Abraham) pray to the one and only God, and that he had pursued the mightiest of kings with three hundred men. P. 83. And then they recognised the truth that there was no man who could have power over him and that his God was greater than all the others. So they went forth to meet and greet him, (19) and the first who started was Melchizedek, the king of Shalem; and he brought out unto him bread and wine and he blessed him for all which he had done to them and for all his mercies and lovingkindness, for he had returned unto him all the captivity and vanquished his enemies and he gave him a tithe of everything. And Abraham refused to take anything from him (20) and said unto him, "Give me the souls and take the goods to thyself." P. 84. (21) And Abraham said unto the king of Sodom, "I consider all the goods of Sodom like ban, and for that reason I cannot take anything from a thread to a shoelatchet. Save only those who have gone with me, Aneram, Eshkol and Mamre, let them take their portion."

(22) And it came to pass in the month of Nisan that the angel of the Lord appeared unto Abraham and told him four things, and that was in the dream of the night. The first thing which he told him was, "I am thy shield and thy reward is exceeding great." (23) The second message was when he took him outside and said to him, P. 85. "Behold! Look now toward heaven, and tell the stars, if thou be able to tell them." And he said unto him, "So shall thy seed be." The third was that He counted it to him for righteousness, and He told him that he was one of those who will in future inhabit the Garden Eden. And

9. And these are the first to start wars which led to their death, viz: — Lehadim, Eynamim, Lahabim, Nafthim, Patrosim, Kaftorim, Kaslhim.

10. And they placed above them to be the head over them the first born of Lehadim whose name was Giṭṭ and they were called by his name Gibṭai.

11. And the men of the Philistines came out and made the first war upon the Canaanites and the Zṭoṭai. And they took away the kingdom from Nimrod. And the Philistines ruled from Egypt to the river of Kush.

of the holy days in the hymn for the Day of Atonement, Cowley p. 634. (probably fourteenth Century.) which means: wars which led to the complete destruction of seven and survival of one. See Introduction These obscure verses may mean that the "seven" were the seven nations descending from Canaan, who were to be destroyed by Joshua, and the "one for the living" being the Israelites. Something to this effect may be gathered from Meshalma, fol. 174b, who dilates on this genealogical portion in the Bible. Altogether the whole passage seems to be very corrupt, and to contain vague reminiscences of wars, traces of which are found in Methodius. Sibylline Oracles, III, 152 ff., etc., see Introd. and Gruppe. Die Griechischen Cnlte and Mythen etc. Leipzig 1887, I. 679/80.—Josephus Antiq. I. 62. 136. 137 gives eight children of whom seven have disappeared and one is retained. The whole passage seems to have preserved a similar tradition.—Jubilees XI.

2: "The sons of Noah began to war on each other." Fully elaborated.—Beginning of wars; Ethiop. Adam Malan p. 173.— Yashar XI, 9: War of children of Ham.—Koran Sure 41. 15: 46. 23 ff. Total destruction of these generations. See Geiger, Mohammed p. 116.—About the war of nations see also Methodius Ch. III. IV. in Sackur (Sibyll. Texte) p. 20 ff.

(10) צבמאי i. e. Egyptians. Josephus I. 6. 2.130 gives a peculiar description of the countries occupied by Ḥam.— Schatzhöhle p. 30: mentions the first king of Egypt calls him Puntos and connects him with Nimrod as Asatir.— Yuhasin Ch. V: The Pharaoh in the time of Abraham was called Tuṭis.

(11) See V. 14.— Josephus I. 6. 2. 131 tells about the reign of Chus.—Clements Recognitions I. 31: Ham attacking Shem and driving him to the east.—Kebra Ch.9 and 12.—Methodius Ch. III and IV, p. 65 ff.

the fourth was, (Gen. 15. 7) "And he said unto him, I am the Lord that brought thee out of Ur of the Chaldees, to give thee this land to inherit it." And all this great honour was given to our master Abraham because of the strength and greatness of his faith and because of the excellence of his merit and because of his obedience to the command of the Lord,—exalted be He!

The first elements of faith are fear, merit and repentance; and it says in the book Asatir, (24) "The first principles of faith are fear P. 86. merit and repentance." (25) And all this happened to our father Abraham in one year in twenty-two days. (26) And when the Lord spake unto him these words, he was ninety and nine years old, before the circumcision. And in that year He commanded him to circumcise himself and made with him a covenant of circumcision and said unto him, (Gen. 17. 14.) "And the uncircumcised male who is not circumcised in the flesh of his foreskin on the eighth day, that soul shall be cut off." (27) And the making of the covenant took place on the Sabbath; and on the fifth day of that week came to him the three men. P. 87. One of them gave him the message about Isaac and said unto him, (Gen. 18. 10.) "And he said, I will certainly return unto thee when the season cometh round; and lo, Sarah, thy wife, shall have a son. And thou shalt call his name Isaac." And the two men who were with him, were for the destruction of Sodom and Gomorrah, and after the one who had delivered the message to our master Abraham about Isaac had gone away, the two men who remained went to the cities of Sodom and Gomorrah, and slept in the house of Lot. (28) And on that day Sodom and Gomorrah were burned and the Lord brought down from Heaven upon them brimstone and fire. And the Lord overthrew these cities and all the plain and the inhabitants of the cities, and Lot was saved P. 88. and his wife and two daughters.

12. And Nimrod came and he encamped against them (i. e. Giṭṭ), and he asked of them (i. e. Joktanites) to help against Egypt.

13. And the children of Joktan started and turned away and went out and they dwelt from Mesha unto Sifra unto Tmnta, a country called the towns of Yemen.

14. And Giṭṭ the head of Egypt died and Nimrod returned to Ashur and ruled there.

15. And when he became king there he made war with Nahor.

16. And he did unto Arpachshad just as Pharaoh did afterwards to the Hebrews, for he saw in the Book of Signs that there would come from Arpachshad a mighty man who would smite all the worshippers and destroy all the idols.

(12) This passage is evidently corrupt.

(13) Meshalma f. 177a: Children of Joktan. They were living in a country called Msḥ, from the name Mŝa, son of Aram until it reaches Sichem, the blessed mountain, and this Har Kedem, which is an appellation for Mt. Garizim, in accordance with the statement in Gen. X. 30. For Sifra is Sichem.—Josephus Antiq. I. 6. 3. 147: "from Cophen, an Indian river." תמנח Gen. XXXVIII, 12. The author of the Asatir identified the place with Yemen:—Meshalma says: "This seems to be the Temanya built by Noah and his three sons or his four sons and their wives,— being called the Town of Eight— in memory of the 4 pairs which came out of the Ark." This explanation is evidently the result of popular etymology.

(15) Meshalma f. 182b: mentions only the wars of Nimrod with Nahor after the birth of Terah, for the birth of Arpachshad, he since knew that a man would arise from among them who would destroy the idols.—Palestinian Targum to Genesis X.11: Nimrod fighting Ashur.

(16) Legends concerning Abraham see Jeraḥmeel ch. XXXIII—XXXV and Introd., p. LXXVIII, Gaster, Exempla IIa, p. 185 where the whole literature is given.— Malif. Q. 88: Wizards foretelling the birth of Abraham. Chs. of Rabbi Eliazer. ch. XXVI: Magicians seek to kill Abraham at birth.— Schatzhöhle p. 3: Nimrod taught by Jonithon knowledge of the oracle.

(29) And it came to pass after the lapse of one year that our master Isaac was born on the Sabbath. And in all probability he was born in the seventh month on the Sabbath. This is proved from the statement in the Asatir, "Listen to the commandments concerning the day of Sabbath, for the announcement of the men they heard on the fifth day, (on Thursday) on the sixth day (Friday) Sodom was burned, and on the seventh day (Sabbath) Isaac was born."

Chapter VIII. [Birth of Moses.]

(1) And it came to pass after the death of our master Abraham—on whom be peace—that Ishmael reigned as king for twenty seven years. (2) And all the children of Ishmael, P. 89. who are of the seed of his first born, Nebut, ruled one year in Ishmael's lifetime (3) and for thirty years after his death; (and they ruled) from the river of Egypt to the great river, the river Euphrates. And they built Bakh; (4) and therefore it is said in Genesis 25. 18, "As thou goest toward Assyria: he abode in the presence of all his brethren."

(5) And it came to pass in those days that Elifaz came and waged war against the children of Ishmael; and when Elifaz came and waged war with the children of Ishmael, they brought forth the documents (6) and they saw in them the division into which Noah had divided the land, and they found that Esau and Ishmael were placed together, and that the sons of Maḥalat joined the children of Ishmael P. 90 (7) That is the word which is said, "And he (Ishmael) shall be an associate of Edom" (Gen. 16. 16.) and "Esau is Edom." And the children of Adah and Aholibamah of Esau, who were from the Canaanites, (8) went and ruled over them with uplifted hands, and Bela, the son of Joktan and Jobab of the sons of Ketura gathered themselves together and went out of the way of Abraham, they and all the children of Ishmael and Esau.

16*

17. And he gathered all the wise men that were among Japhet and Ham, and he asked them that they should inform him when this one would be born.

18. [So they told him] within forty days the mother will be pregnant with him.

19. And Nimrod commanded that the sons of Arpachshad should not be allowed to approach their wives for forty days.

20. And he commanded that they should imprison the men in one place and the women in another place.

21. And after thirty days a sign was seen in the land of Shinear, a pillar of fire.

22. And all the men were frightened with a great fear and they prayed in the houses of worship and they dwelt outside in the open field for three days and three nights.

23. And Terah went and approached his wife.

24. And when he had approached her, the sign was removed and they said: "The child will be born."

(21) Malif. Q. 89.—In Yashar VIII. 2: the sign seen was a star swallowing other stars.—Bahya Commentary to Pentateuch Venice 1566 f. 22a. Abraham born in Aram, thrown into the furnace by Nimrod. Another version mentioned there in the name of Maimonides' Guide of the Perplexed, according to which Abraham was driven away by Nimrod.

(23) Mother of Abraham Amtlai daughter of Ḳrubo; T. B. Baba Bathra (fol. 91). Algazi ibid.: Name of Terah's wife Edna daughter of Abrnhu.—In Samaritan Book of Joshua, reference to Terah (ch. XXII) as idol-worshipper missing, thus proving very old Samaritan tradition (cf. my edition of the Sam. Arabic Book of Joshua p. 17).—Koran 6. 74. 74. 19. 42—57: agrees more with Samaritan, inasmuch as neither consider Terah idolator. Contrary to Jewish tradition.—Jubilees XII. 1—14: Terah idol-worshipper.—Kebra Chs. 12 and 13: Terah idolator.—Maimonides' "Holy Names" (ed. Gaster in Debir vol. I., Berlin). Nahor and his father idol-worshippers.

And it came to pass after these words that Abraham heard that the sons of Ashur and Joktan had grown very mighty; then he was sorely frightened at the wickedness of their deeds before the Lord, and he feared lest out of the wickedness some trouble might arise to him. And this is proved P. 91. from his saying in the Asatir. (9) "After these words Abraham heard that the children of Ashur and Joktan had grown very mighty and he feared a great fear." And he (the author of the Asatir) refers to this after his mentioning Elifaz, the son of Esau, and after he had mentioned Maḥalat and the children of Adah and Aholibamah; and we see that he mentions it after the death of Abraham, saying, "And these are the children of Maḥalat, Adah and Aholibamah." And know that Abraham is mentioned again when he refers to the kings of Moab where he first mentioned the two, Bela and Jobab, "and then Abraham heard it." This proves thereby that these had been born during the lifetime of Abraham—on whom be peace—and as the children of Ashur were the sons of Shem and those of Joktan the sons of Eber, they were thus the descendants of Shem and Eber, but that they had strayed from the way of life and therefore he was seized with fear. And about Jobab, it says in the book Asatir, that he came of the sons of Keturah, but God alone knows whether that tradition is correct, for it is difficult to prove seeing that Jobab was the son of Joktan, the son of Eber, the son of Shelah. And this is seen from Genesis 10. 20 ff. and whoever looks there will be able to ascertain the truth of this statement. But the Lord alone knows. And Husham was (10) from Moab P. 93. and Shamlah from 'Elam and Shaul from the sons of Nahor, Baal (11) Hanan from 'Elam, Hadad from the children of Elifaz, who lived in Beth Pau, and the name of his wife was Mitabel, daughter of Matred from Jefet Kittin. These are the genealogies of the kings who reigned in the land of Edom before a king was appointed over the children of Israel.

25. And Nimrod commanded that each man should return to his place.

26. And after that Abraham was born with mighty glory.

27. And Nimrod took him and threw him into the fire because he has said "The world has a God."

28. And when Haran was wroth with Abraham and said he was a wizard the fire came out and consumed him "and Haran died in the presence of his father Terah in Ur Kasdim." After seven years he (Nimrod) died.

Chapter VI. [Abraham in Egypt.]

1. With him came to an end the Kingdom of Ham: with a Nimrod it began and with a Nimrod it came to an end.

(26) Malif.Q.90.—Arabic Jewish parallel in the Geniza fragment. My Cod. 1328. f. 17 ff., is ascribed to Kab el Akhbar, probably due to Samaritan influences.

(27) Malif. Q. 90 idem.—Palestinian Targum to Genesis XI, 28: Nimrod threw Abraham into the fire because Abraham refused to worship Nimrod's gods. The fire did not burn.—Josephus I. 7. 1. 155: Abraham the first to proclaim one God.

(28) Meshalma f. 183b: describes Haran as an idol-worshipper acting against the teaching of his father. He merely says "God destroyed him."—Palestinian Targum to Gen. XI. 28: Fire from Heaven destroys Haran, who is believed to be a wizard, and thereby protected Abraham from the fire.—Jubilees Ch. XII. 14: Haran dies trying to save idols from fire.—Gen. Rabba to Gen. 11. 28. Horowitz Likute Agadot p. 40.—Jerahmeel 35. 1. Different account of Haran's death. Yashar XII. 26: Haran dies in furnace.—Clement's Recognitions I. 30: Nimrod worshipping fire.— Further literature concerning early legends of Abraham see G. H. Box Apocalyse of Abraham (London 1919, p. 88 ff.)—According to Ephraim Syrus and other Syriac writers, Haran dies in the Temple of Idols burned by Abraham; See Grünbaum, Neue Beitr. 94.

Ch. VI.

(1) Story of Abraham and his descent to Egypt, the close parallelism with Eupolemos and partly with Josephus has been treated fully

(12) When Jacob our master was eighty years old he went down to Haran, (13) and when our master Joseph—on whom be peace—was seventeen years and eight months he went down to Egypt. P. 94. (14) The Pharaoh who was in the time of our master Joseph was of the seed of Ishmael, and the Pharaoh who was in the time of our master Moses was of the seed of Jefet Kittin. In his days Moses was born; and it is said about him in the Asatir. "And the slave Rodanim became Pharaoh." (15) And these are the generations of Pharaoh, the son of Guṭis, the son of Aṭiss, the son Rbṭṭ, the son of Guṭsis, the son of Rims, the son of Kittin, the son of Javan, (16) who had learned in the Book of Signs in the town of Babel the Great. And he came out of Ṣion and he wandered to Nineveh. (17) And when our master Joseph—on whom be peace—was thirty years old, he became king over the land of Egypt. And he was second Pharaoh, P. 95. besides the first mentioned above, and he had gone to Nineveh (18) and had stayed there three years and one month; and after that he went to Damascus and to Kruzh, that is the town of Kush. And he stayed there sixty three years. (19) And Joseph died and all his brothers and all the men of his generation and the kingdom of Ishmael was changed; as it is said in the Book Asatir, (20) "And the kingdom of Ishmael was changed and Amalek became powerful and he ruled over the land of Egypt." (21) And when the second Pharaoh who was in Nineveh, heard of the death of the king of Egypt and that Amalek had gained possession of it, he came down with evil [intent] and ruled over it one year. And he stayed P. 96. and held Egypt by force and there was tribulation in its midst, (22) and the destruction lasted three years. And the king of Egypt died, (23) and there came another king in the land of Egypt and his name was Pharaoh III. And he gathered a large force of Ḳṭpai and he reigned sixty years. And thus the number of kings who ruled over Egypt in the time from Joseph

2. And from the first Nimrod to the second Nimrod there were one thousand and twenty years.

3. The first Nimrod was from Kush and the second Nimrod was from the Kaftorim.

4. And when Nimrod had died Terah started to go into the land of Canaan to establish his kingdom.

5. His son Nahor dwelt with Kedar Laomer and Tidal king of Goyim and they robbed him of his kingdom.

6. And Kedar Laomer went on plundering and they sent and imprisoned Terah in Haran.

7. Then Abraham came out to meet Kedar Laomer in Ur Kasdim.

8. There God called him and he came to the land of Canaan and they dwelt in the plain of Glory and he built up the altar of Adam and Noah.

9. And afterwards he went up Mount Garizim to the east of Bethel.

in the Introd. pp. 32—39; 69—70. Meshalma f. 193 b ff. gives the story in full in accordance with the Asatir.
—Methodius Ch. 3 (Sackur p. 65).
(2) In Eupolemos we find Belus twice: Belus-Nimrod, and this Bel who is then identical with in Belshazzar. This explains also the identification of Amrafel, with Nimrod in P. T. I (Gen. XIV. 1) last syllable being read Bel (Pel) hence Nimrod see Introd. p. 29.
(4) Josephus I. 7. 2. 159 in the name of Nicolaus of Damascus, says, "Abraham ruled at Damascus;" so also from Hekatäus ibid.—Abraham born in כותא and driven out from Babylon. Bahya Commentary, end of section Noah

(ed. Venice 1566, fol. 22. col. 2) quoted from Maimonides' Morêh Nebuḥim.
(5) Algazi ibid.: Name of Nahor's wife Isgb, daughter of Isḥob.
(7) Josephus Antiq. I. 9. 1. 174: "Offspring of the Giants." Eupolemos: Giants scattered throughout the land.
(8) See above Ch. I. 7: compare lit.—Schatzhöhle p. 34: "When he returned from the battle of Kings, then God called him, and he went up to the Mount of Jabos." This evidently confused from the passage here since Kedar Laomer appears here and later on in both encounters with Abraham.

to Moses, [until the one] who was drowned in the Sea of Reeds was four. For from the time when our master Joseph died unto the day when Moses the messenger was born sixty three years had elapsed. This is the absolute truth and there is no difference of opinion about it. P. 97. On the day when our Master returned from Midian to the land of Egypt, he was eighty years old, so the sum total of these years is one hundred and forty three. The Pharaoh in whose time our Master Moses was born, is the one who ruled for sixty years, and of him it is said, "and he died."

And the children of Israel multiplied and became very powerful. The women used at that time to give birth to two or three children at once: and God knows. And Pharaoh commanded all his people, saying. "All the male children ye shall throw into the river." P. 98. And the men and women were frightened of him, for the people of Pharaoh used to throw all the male children that were born into the river. And the woman whose child was thrown into the river killed herself after it. And the children of Israel kept to their faith and not one of their sons was thrown into the water, for the women of Israel used to pray to Him who knows the feelings of the heart. When they knew that the time had come when they should give birth to children, they used to go out into the field and give birth there, and then they asked those who stood by as witnesses, to which sex the child belonged, and when it happened to be a male, they left it in the field in the charge of the Creator. And the Lord, P. 99. may He be exalted, made them suck honey and milk from the flint of the rock according to His statement in His mighty writ, "And he suckled him with honey from the rock and fatness from the flinty rock." (Deut. 32.13.) When it was a girl, the mother brought it home. And the command, therefore, to throw the male children into the river became a source of destruction to his own people, the Egyptians.

For the continuation of this chapter see XII, 5.

10. And then he started going down to Egypt.

11. And when he reached the boundaries of Egypt, shakings seized all the idols and trembling fell upon all the dwellers in the houses of worship.

12. For Abraham dwelt in Rifon (field?) close to Ṭks (border?) of Egypt which is called Alrif, and they came to a palmgrove in the valley.

13. And there they (the Egyptians) saw Sarah and the women praised her to their husbands and

(11) Meshalma 196 b: says "When Abraham reached the border of Egypt a sign was seen in all the places and those who lived in that generation were seized with a great fear, and it is said that the place is known to this very day." Same happened when Abraham came to Nimrod; See Introd. p. 25.—Fall of idols: Meshalma f. 197b. In the Hebrew Romance of Abraham by Eliah de Vidas in Shebet Musar (Amsterdam 1732) fol. 193a the idols fall down when Abraham proclaims his faith before Nimrod. This is precisely the same situation as found in the Asatir.—The falling of idols when Jesus reached Egypt: Hofman, Leben Jesu nach den Apocryphen, Leipzig 1851, p. 148. Hennecke, Handbuch der N.T. Apokryphen, Tübingen 1914 p. 101: refers to Ps. Malthäus, and mentions generally Eusebius, Athanasius, Sozomenius.—Evang. inf. Arab. Ch. X.—Historia de nativitate Mariae Cap. 22—24.

(12) Kaldebak occurs here and VII. 14: The Arabic paraphrast and the Pitron do not explain the meaning of it. It may be an abreviation for Hakal (or grove) de Bikah = a plantation in the valley, and I translated it accordingly. In the P.T. Deutr. I. 7 "Kaldohi" is mentioned as a place not far from Lebanon. But no explanation is forthcoming for this term.—Meshalma 196b, writes: "And Abraham dwelt in a place called "the Field of Tfoš תפוש" near פישרן (i. e. the Nile) which is said to be known to this very day." He evidently has taken the word literally בקל = בחקל especially as ח and ק are not differentiated in Samaritan pronunciation: then the word would mean "field" דבק·שדה is taken in this meaning: "to seize," "to capture." I have taken it to stand for בקעה for the same reason since they are not differentiated in the pronunciation. The Samaritans would read these two words: b'al edbaa: see the pronunciation of קול היה as oliya in the transliterated specimen to Ch. XI.17.—Sepher Hayashar XV. 2: "He dwelt at the river of Egypt some time."—Pal. Targ. to Gen. XII. 11: Abraham came to the borders of Egypt and they came to the river.

(13) Meshalma 196b idem.—Jo-

Chapter IX. [Moses.]

Blessed by He, who does what He wills and grants salvation! (1) And by the power of the Righteous Judge, there was born the mighty prophet—may he be remembered for good for ever—our Master Moses, upon whom be peace. And his birth was in the month of Nisan, on the fifteenth day thereof, P. 100. on the Sabbath. And his mother hid him for three months, 71 days, for it is said in the Asatir, (2) that on the fifteenth day of Sivan, he was thrown into the river. And when they threw the Prince of Creatures, Moses, into the river, the water stopped still by the power of God—my He be exalted—and its flow abated beyond measure, and the waters began to diminish. (3) And the women of Egypt came out to see the diminution of the river of Egypt, for that was at the time when the river used to swell. (4) And among the women who went down to see the river, was the P. 101. daughter of Pharaoh. And with every day that passed the waters grew less, according to the statement in the Asatir, (5) "And every day that passed, the waters grew less." And the child was in that ark which was daubed over with slime and pitch, floating by the border of the river; and when the waters of the river stopped from flowing below the normal, (6) then all the wizards and magicians gathered themselves together and took counsel together; and they searched and they examined and they discussed and disputed, and sought with their sorcery for the reason of the stopping of the waters of the river. (7) And among them was a magician whose name was Plti, and he looked into and searched and he consulted the Book of Signs, P. 102. for he was the chief of them. And he became dumbfounded and lifted up his head and said, "The child of which we said before, that his death would be through water, his ark is now in the Sea of Reeds." He did not say in the sea of the river, the men to Pharaoh and she was taken to the house of Pharaoh. And to Abraham he did good for her sake.

14. And when Sarah was staying in the palace of Pharaoh, many wonders were seen.

15. And the princes began to be plagued privily and openly and Pharaoh became like a stone as one who has been smitten by sorcery.

16. And they said "Let there not be left out any magician or sorcerer."

17. And all the magicians and soothsayers gathered together and they were in great tribulation.

18. And there was among them a sorcerer called Turṭs who had learned the Book of Signs in Ḥanoḥiah.

19. And he was wroth and said "He who worships the God of the whole world is here, and all this distress is for his sake."

sephus I. 8. 1. 163: fame of his wife's beauty was talked of."

(14) From here Ps. Eupolemos agrees in the main. See Introd. —Kebra Ch. 82: An angel pursuing Pharaoh.

(15) Stone: Meshalma adds: "And the men were like a stone and the women were like a wall (f. 196b) and the whole kingdom suffered likewise and no man could approach his wife and their faces were troubled."

(16) Seder Hadorot p. 32: A wizard called Anoki interpreting a dream to Nimrod regarding Abraham.

(17) Meshalma 197b: "And Pharaoh called all the soothsayers, and he asked them for the truth about it, and they could not answer him. And they said, "We have no power over this, nor do we know any way to remove it," and then all the soothsayers gathered together."—Josephus Antiq. I. 8. 1. 164: He enquired from the priests."—Eupolemos Eus. Prep. Evang. IX. 17: "The priests whom he consulted, etc." see Introduction.

(18) Asatir alone and Meshalma have the name of the soothsayer. Meshalma 196b: "Turss" from the House of Enoch."

(19) Meshalma fol. 197a: "And they asked him about this happening and he said, "Woe unto you for what you have done to your souls, for this plague has

he only said, "the child is there, and the ark is now among the reeds." And that was through a vision from God—may He be exalted—for the sea is greater than the river, and when Plti said, "he is among the reeds," they said, "No doubt the child has died." And for this reason, they did not search for it. They neither went nor looked for the ark in which he was. And that was a great miracle—may the Lord be praised, the All-Powerful, the High One, P. 103. who does what He wills and brings deliverance! (8) And when the daughter of Pharaoh saw the ark in the midst of the sea, (9) she sent her maid who brought her the ark. And then she opened it and saw in it a beautiful, holy child, and the sore disease which was on her disappeared and she was filled with desire for its holy soul; and the child was crying inside the ark. And the daughter of Pharaoh took pity on it, (10) and she conceived for it an exceeding great love. And she said, "This is one of the children of the Hebrews." And she commanded her servants that no one was to speak to anyone about the child, P. 104. and all her maids and servants who stood about and saw the child with her, swore it unto her.

(11) And the Mistress Miriam, the sister of our Master Moses stood afar off to see what would happen to it at the hand of the stranger. And when she saw that the daughter of Pharaoh had taken it and loved it and had pity on it, she went quickly and stood before her and said, "Shall I go and call for thee a Jewish woman to suckle the child?" (12) And the daughter of Pharaoh said unto her, "Go!" And the young woman went and called the mother of the child. (13) And the daughter of Pharaoh said unto her, "Take this child and suckle it for me and I will give thee thy wages." And the woman took the child and suckled it. And the child grew up and was weaned, and she brought it to the daughter of Pharaoh, who paid her her wages, P. 105. as it is seen in the Holy Law in the second book (Exod. II.

20. And when Abraham heard mention of the God of the whole world, then he quickly turned with prayers as towards heaven.

21. Then they were freed (from the plague) and the whole palace was lit up by the sight of the glory of the face of Sarah and there (fell) upon them great fear.

22. Then it became known that Sarah was the wife of Abraham, and Pharaoh's tongue was set free and he began to speak and Abraham proclaimed and prayed for the loosening of the bonds.

23. And this is the first proclamation (of faith) for Abraham said: "O, Lord! God of heaven and Earth, all merciful, be merciful."

24. And the house(hold) of Pharaoh began to be healed and all the houses of worship were destroyed and the objects of worship in them fell down and could not be raised up.

25. And the magician Ṭurṭs went up from there to Hebron.

26. And Pharaoh appointed men, and he sent him (Abraham) away and his wife and Lot who was with him.

been sent by God upon you by your wrongdoing to that man who has come to dwell here with his wife. And he worships the God of Heaven and Earth who cannot be seen, and He is a shield unto him and helps him." And thereby made known that Sarah was his wife."
(21) Josephus I. 8. 1. 165: "he then out of fear, asked..."

(24) —This proclamation of God as the only ruler of Heaven and earth was afterwards interpreted as meaning that Abraham taught the knowledge of the ruler and of the rule (science, astronomy etc.) of heaven and earth. So Eupolemus Artapanors, Josephus, etc. See Introd.
(24) see v. 11.
(25) See above VI. 18.

v. 9). And after he was brought to the daughter of Pharaoh, she called his name Moses, and she said, "He has been saved and drawn out of the water and the fire."

As we have mentioned before, he was born on the fifteenth day of Nisan, on the Sabbath. And on the Sabbath, the fifteenth day of Sivan, he was thrown into the water, and he was taken out of the water also on the same Sabbath in the fifth hour.

(14) And Moses grew up in the house of the enemy, in strength honour and might, until he grew to manhood. P. 106. And he was with the governors who were appointed overseers over the children of Israel, and he went out in those days and looked on their burden. (15) And he saw an Egyptian smiting a Hebrew of his kinsmen. And he looked this way and that way, and when he saw that there was no man, he smote the Egyptian and hid him in the sand. (16) And behold, on the second day, two men of the Hebrews strove together, and he said to him that did wrong, "Wherefore smitest thou thy fellow?" And the wicked man said, "Who made thee a prince and a judge over us? Thinkest thou to kill me as thou killedst the Egyptian yesterday?" And Moses feared and said, "Surely the thing is known," for the deed had evidently become known. P. 107. And when Pharaoh heard of this thing, he sought to slay Moses. (17) But Moses fled from the face of Pharaoh and dwelt in the land of Midian. And he remained there sixty full years. And he was a shepherd to Jethro, his father-in-law. (18) And then there was great oppression against the children of Israel and great tribulation during the absence of the messenger in the land of Midian. And Guṭs (19) the king of Egypt died, and he was the one who was called Pharaoh. And before another king was appointed in Egypt, the children of Israel despaired of the time [of deliverance] (?) and they gathered themselves together. P. 108. And the children of Israel sighed by reason of

27. And they came to the place of the first altar and they raised it up again. And he brought thankofferings and praise offerings.

Chapter VII. [Abraham and Battle of Kings.]

1. And Amrafel was king twelve years, and Abraham and Lot tarried in the land of Canaan one year.
2. In the month of Nisan Abraham came from Haran and in Iyar he went to Egypt.
3. And in Nisan Lot separated himself from him and dwelt in Sodom one year.
4. In that year in which they came, Ṭurṭs went from Hebron to Shinear and he told Amrafel and Kedar Laomer that there would be much killing, and he studied the Book of Signs and foretold to them what to do.
5. And Kedar Laomer knew Abraham and he would not listen to his sorceries.
6. But he started killing all the people that were against him and he went and laid waste a town called Ḳdsh.
7. And these were the last kings of the land from the children of Ḥam.
8. And Lot was captured by them and he sent for counsel to his uncle Abraham.
9. And 'Aniram, Eshkol and Mamre were those who had made the covenant with Abraham.
10. And he said "O my brothers, let us go to meet them in order to save them."

Ch. VII.
(6) Josephus I. 9. 1. 174: "Laid waste all Syria."

their bondage and they cried and the cry came to God by reason of the bondage. And God heard their groaning, and God remembered His covenant with Abraham with Isaac and with Jacob. And God saw the children of Israel, and God took knowledge of them. "And God saw" means, He saw the oppression in which they were, on account of the Egyptians; and "God took knowledge of them" means, "I will requite the Egyptians for all that they have done." For the Lord knew the secret meaning of the revelation which He had made to our master Abraham, P. 109. for its fulfilment had now drawn nigh. And that is what is said in Gen. XV. 13, "and they will cause them to serve them and they will afflict them."

And it came to pass after these things that a new king arose in Egypt and his name was Pharaoh from the Kiṭṭim, and he was 'Aṭirt. And this is the third king who ruled over Egypt from the Pharaoh who had ruled in the time of Joseph. (21) And it came to pass on the fifteenth day of the third lunar month, on the fourth day, that there came our Master Moses the Messenger—upon whom be peace— P. 110. (20) with the sheep of his father-in-law, Jethro quite unexpectedly to the mountain of God, Horeb. And on the fifteenth, on the selfsame day the Lord fulfilled his covenant with the Meritorious Ones, (22) and the staff of Adam and his clothes, namely the clothes of light, that were upon Adam when he was in the Garden, were given to Moses on that day. (23) And the proof of it is the word which he spake before anything else where he said, "and this shall be a token unto thee; this has been given as a sign that I have sent thee." (24) And the Lord appeared unto Moses on the third day of the month which was a Wednesday, (25) and on the first day (Sunday), Moses went down to Egypt. P. 111. And the Lord said unto Aaron, "Go into the wilderness to meet Moses." (26) And he went and met him at the mountain of God, and kissed him. And both went up to Egypt and performed

11. For in the fourteenth year Kedar Laomer had come and made war with the Amorites.

12. And again Nahor the brother of Abraham then sent and informed Abraham what he (Kedar Laomer) had done in his country in Ur of the Chaldees.

13. And the messengers found Abraham who had started to pursue the kings who had taken Lot captive and they encamped in a plain (?) which is called Ṭbriṣ of Kinnereth.

14. And it was at the going out of the Sabbath (i. e. Sunday) that Abraham came to a palmgrove in the valley.

15. And on the second (Monday) he found them at the rising of the moon in the valley (Emek).

16. And in the month of Elul on the twenty first of the month in the valley of Ḥobah a place which is now called Amr.

17. On the fifth Abraham came to Shalem the Great and the King of Sodom and the King Nahor came to Abraham to Shalem the Great.

(13) Ṭbriṣ. This may mean a mountain near the lake of Genezareth; for this location there is no justification in the Bible. See Introduction. Gen. XIV, 14. ד The S T mentions here כזיאם instead. Pal. Targum: "Kaisarin."

(14) See note to VI. 12.

(15) Josephus Antiq. I. 10. 1. 178: "The second day he drove them in a body unto Hoba." Evidently means the second day of the week i. e. Monday.

(16) Fight of Abraham with the kings takes place on the night of Pesaḥ (cf. Ch. I. 8) as to events that happened on the night of Pesaḥ).—Pal. Targ. to Gen. XIV. 15: The fight the same night as the smiting of the first-born.—Meḥilta p. 13a.—Pirke de Rabbi Eliezer Ch. 27.—Genesis Rabba et XLIII, 3. S T has מאוני which is a translation of the word meaning pain or guilt.

(17) Josephus Antiq. I.10.1.177: "He fell upon the enemy . . ." The date given by Josephus is the date here given for the entry in Shalem; evidently a confusion by

the wonders in the sight of the children of Israel. And the people believed. (27) On the third day, they went up and stood before Pharaoh and told him all the words of God; (28) on the fifth day was the miracle of the blood. (29) In nine months, all the great and wonderful miracles were enacted in Egypt. (30) In the sixth hour of the night of the fifth day the children of Israel went out of Egypt with uplifted arm. (31) On the night of the first day they passed the dry land through the midst P. 112. of the sea; according to the words of the Asatir, the Feast of the Pesach was the night of the fifth, for God has said in the Holy Law, "on the morrow after the Passover the children of Israel went out with an high hand in the sight of all the Egyptians." And the sacrifice of the Pesach was from the evening until the break of the first dawn. And the festival is from the break of the first dawn to the setting of the sun, although our master Markah, in his exalted poem, said that the feast in Egypt was on the second day, (Monday) for he said, "Thus have they made the Passover; then they journeyed to Rameses, and they travelled P. 113. three days until they came to the Sea of Reeds; and in the night of the second day of the festival, when it was morning, they came to the sea." But according to the true tradition, their entry into the Sea of Reeds was on the night of the first day, (Sunday). For we have the remembrance of it unto this very day, as we call it, "The night of Sunday," but according to the statement of our master Markah, the first day of the festival would be on the Monday and the last day on the Sunday. But God knows. But I believe that the statement of our master Markah is a true one, and may the Lord forgive every sin and trespass! (32) And on the third day, they came to Elim and the bitter waters were made sweet unto them. P. 114. And the Lord showed them a bitter tree and they put twigs into the water so that it became sweet, and this is a well known and wonderful tree which even to this day, if put

18. And when he saw Abraham he prostrated himself and bowed down and he praised the Lord the High God.

19. Then Melchizedek after the feasting called upon the name of him who had granted victory and he gave him the tithe of everything, but he (Abraham) refused to take.

20. And then he said, "Give me the souls, and the wealth thou mayest take."

21. And Abraham said to the King of Sodom, "The wealth of Sodom is considered by me as banned." (haram)

22. And in Nisan God revealed himself to Abraham and he spoke to him on the fourth (Wednesday), and he said unto him "I am a shield to thee," in the dream of the night.

23. And he took him outside and said "Look at the heaven and count the stars." Great was this event: there was none like it.

24. The principles of faith are fear, merit and repentance.

25. All this happened in one year: but up to the twenty-second God had not yet spoken to him.

26. When he was ninety nine years old he accepted (the covenant of) circumcision.

Josephus.—Abraham going to Mt. Garizim, "Mount of the Most High one" to meet Melchizedek. Eupolemos; Eusebius, Prep. Evang. Bk. 9. Ch. 17. 481cff.

(19) Meshalma ff. 214a and 215b: Melchizedek offering gifts to Abraham as the priest of the High God.

(22) Gen. XV, 1. "on the fourth." Date here may refer to the date of the month: it is often very difficult to distinguih between the two dates before the 7th.

into bitter water, turns it sweet. (33) And on the sixth day (Friday), which is the fifth day after the morning of the second festival, Amalek came upon them and he fought them, and they weakened him and they wiped out his name from under the heavens. And the children of Israel were victorious over him by the help of God—may He be exalted! (34) And on the third day of the third month on the fourth day (Wednesday), the Lord called from Mount Sinai.

(35) There are three memorable mornings of the world and they have no equals. P. 115. (36) The first is the morning of the first day of the creation of the world. (37) The second is the morning of the fourth day (Wednesday) on which was the standing (Maamad) before Mount Sinai. And the third is the morning of the day of requital. And know there is a proof for my explanation of these three mornings, for on these three mornings there was neither the sun nor the moon nor the stars, as for of all of them that of the fourth day is proved by the Holy Law in His word in Deut. 4. 12. "And the Lord spake unto you out of the midst of fire: ye heard the voice of words, but ye saw no form, only a voice." The meaning of which is, "ye saw none of the heavenly forms." The third morning is the Day of Judgment; on it there will be neither sun, nor moon nor stars, for they are required only for the necessities of the world, but on the Day of Judgment there is no necessity for them. And it is also said about it in the book Asatir, that latter day will be on the sixth day—that is proved by his statement, "the morning of the Creation on the first, the morning of Mount Sinai on the fourth (Wednesday), the morning of the Day of Judgment on the sixth."

On the first day of the first month of the second year of their going out of Egypt was the tabernacle established. In the third month they journeyed forth from Mount Sinai. P. 117. (39) On the fourth died the master Aaron. (40) On the seventh month was the war between the children of

27. On the seventh his people accepted it.
28. On the sixth Sodom was burnt.
29. On the seventh Isaac was born.

Chapter VIII. [Birth of Moses.]

1. And after the death of Abraham, Ishmael reigned twenty seven years
2. And all the children of Nebaot ruled for one year in the lifetime of Ishmael,
3. And for thirty years after his death from the river of Egypt to the river Euphrates; and they built Mecca.
4. For thus it is said "As thou goest towards Ashur before all his brethren he lay."
5. Elifas the son of Esau fought with the children of Ishmael and they produced their

(27) In the Asatir חוה (Gen. XVII, 23) is taken as numerical = 7 th, the word probably written ח as before in connection with the flood (IV. 10). Jubilees XIV. 20: On the first.

(28) Genesis Rabba Ch. L. Urim ve Tumim: Sodom and Gomorrah destroyed on the 17th day of the month.

(29) Tanḥuma Exod. Pekude: Isaac born 1st Nisan.—Seder Hadorot p. 36: Isaac born on 15th Nisan.—Urim ve Tumim: Isaac blessed Jacob on the 20th day of month and Esau on 21st.—Kabasi fol. 103: Isaac 70 years old when taken to be sacrificed.

Ch. VIII.

(2) Yashar Ch. XXV. 16 ff: A list of the descendents of Ishmael, with many Arabic names of tribes.

(3) Josephus I. 12. 3. 221: "These inhabited all the countries from Euphrates to the Red Sea, and called it Nabatene."—Gen. 25. 18. Pal.Targ.: "And they dwelled from Hindikia (Indian Ocean) to Palusa (Pelusiumt which is before Egypt as thou goest to Atur (Assyria).—In Kebra Ch. 83: many countries are enumerated over which Ishmael ruled.—"Built Mecca." Already known to Ptolemy as Makoraba. Pitron has preservad the original neading באכה (ibid) Which they nead Baka and took it to mean a local name. Hence מכה into which it was afterwards changed.

(5) See the story of the death of Jacob and the attempt of the children of Esau to prevent the burial of Jacob in Hebron. Naphthali ran back to Egypt and

Israel and the King of Arad, and he captured captivity from them. And they, the children of Israel, returned a second time and waged war with him, and they banned him and everything that belonged to him.

Chapter X. [Bileam.]

(1) And in that time there was a wizard whose name was M'artis, and his dwelling place was in the town 'Arad. And when he heard of the children of Israel coming to the town, he fled from there to Midian. And there was Pe'or who was asked by the children of Moab to call Bileam, the son of Beor, the son of Gdiṭis, the son of Paṭh, P. 118. the son of 'Amingf, the son of Laban, (2) the owner of the Terafim, who was from the town of Ṣ'ar.; for he had these Terafim from Ksht, the king of Moab, from Ḳain the murderer: and God knows! (3) And Balak the king of Moab sent messengers to Bileam, to Petor, which is on the river of the land of the of the children of Ammon, to summon him with these words, "Come and curse for me the people of Israel." (4) And this happened in the sixth month. (5) And Bileam understood and knew the Book of Signs (6) and he worshipped these seven angels viz: the god of fire, the god of the firmament, the god of water, the god of the heavenly luminaries, the god of holiness, P. 119. the god of the winds and the god of the corners of the heaven. (7) And he used to call them by the following names, and such are their names. 1, Hlm, Hml, 2, Hhml Haml, 3, H'amal Hmnal, 4, Hṣprh Hsmim, 5, Hlk Lil Ḥlḳ Lb, 6, Hlin Hntr, 7, Hlpgr.

(8) These are the seven angels whom Bileam served and worshipped. And when Bileam consented to go with the princes of Balak and he rode on his ass, he boasted and said, "Behold, this ass will go which ever way I wish it without anyone showing it the way." P. 120. And when he said these words, an angel of the Lord (the holy god) stood in the road with a sword drawn in his hand, and the

genealogical claim to the kingdom and the division (made) by Noah.

6. And they found that Esau was associated with Ishmael, and they put the sons of Mahlat on the same level as the sons of Ishmael.

7. And this is the word which has been spoken, "And he will be 'fari Edom'" and Esau is Edom. And the children of Adah and Aholibamah belonged to the generation of Canaan.

8. And there came and ruled over them with might Bela the son of Joktan, Jobab of the sons of Ketura.

9. And after all these words, when Abraham heard that there was war between the people of Ashur and Joktan, he was seized with a great fear.

10. (And after that ruled) Husham from Moab and Shamlah of Elam, and Saul from the sons of Nahor, Baalhanan from Elam.

brought the documents to prove their own claim, Esau having given up his birthright to Jacob. Midrash.

(7) The Samaritans pronounce Fari Edom, which pronunciation I have retained, and in conversation they call the Mahommedans by this name, meaning thereby "Kinsmen of Edom."—Malif. Q. 117 reads: "farah haadamah," "the wild man of the earth," or rather "ruthless warrior" who lives upon his sword.

(8) Jubilees XXXVIII. 15 ff.: Gives a list of the kings of Edom following the M.T. (Gen. XXXVI. 31 ff)—The Pal. Targ. and Samaritan Targ. agree also, with one exception. In all of these the names of the are retained, whilst corresponding names in the Asatir are all changed and to each of the kings, another genealogy is given. This is another proof of the independence of the Asatir from Samaritan Targ. and high antiquity.

(10) In all the other Jewish versions it is Bileam who is the sorcerer and chief adviser of Pharaoh for the destruction of the children of Israel. Chronicle of Moses (Jellinek II. 1—11) and Introd. to Jerahmeel p. 87 ff. Yashar Ch. 67, differs from Samaritan version.

ass strayed from the way and went into a field, and Bileam smote the ass to turn it back on to the road; and then the ass lay down under Bileam and the wrath of Bileam was kindled, and he smote the ass with his rod. And the Lord opened the mouth of the ass and the Lord opened the eyes of Bileam, and he saw the angel of the Lord standing in the way, and he bowed himself down and he prostrated himself. And the angel said, "Beware that thou dost not turn aside from the word which I will speak unto thee." And Bileam went with the princes of Balak. The angel who commanded him to build the first seven altars [was Hanhl.] P. 121. Three times he built the altars, and afterwards he told us the origin of Bileam, that he was from Aram Naharaim, which is the town of Nahor, and is proved by Holy Writ that this was the town of Nahor, (Gen. XXIV. 10) where it is said, "Aram Naharaim (Mesopotamia) which is the city of Nahor." And in the Asatir it is said that his genealogy (chain) was from Aram. (10) When he stood before the altars, the first angel came and told him what he was to say, (11) and then came the god of fire; and then Bileam refused to curse the people and said, "I will not curse for the Lord has not cursed them. P. 122. And I will not execrate whom God hath not execrated!" (Numb. XXIII. 8.) And he blessed them. (12) And afterwards there came to him the god of the firmament, who changed his vision so that he saw Israel in Paradise. When he saw these sights, he said, (Numb. XXIII. 10.) "Let me die the death of the righteous and let my last end be like it." And when Balak the son of Ṣippor heard his words, he said, "What hast thou done with me? I took thee to curse mine enemies, and behold, thou hast blessed them altogether." (Numb. XXIII. 11.) And he answered and said unto him, "Whatsoever the Lord putteth into my mouth, I must take heed to speak." And Balak said, "Come with me to another place; perchance it might be found right in the eyes of the Lord, and curse them for

11. Hadad of the sons of Eliezer and his dwelling place was Betad which is Forikh. And the name of his wife was Mehetabel daughter of Matred of Japhet of the Kittim.

12. Jacob was eighty years old when he went to Haran.

13. Joseph was seventeen years and eight months old when he went down to Egypt.

14. The Pharaoh of Joseph was of Ishmael and the Pharaoh of Moses was from Japhet of the Kittim the servant of the Rodanim.

15. Pharaoh the son of Goṭis the son of Aṭiss son of Rbṭṭ son of Gosis son of Rims son of Kṭim son of Javan,

(12) Jacob 77 years old when going to Haran; Demetrius (v. Freudenthal, Hellenistische Studien, p. 39).—Schatzhöhle 39: Jacob 77 when Isaac blessed him.—Seder Olam Ch. II: 63 when blessed by Isaac and 77 years when he reached the fountain (in Haran).—Seder Hadorot p. 41: Jacob 84 years of age when he married.—Urim ve Tumim: Jacob born on the 18th of the month.

(13) Schatzhöhle p. 39: Twenty-three years after return of Jacob Joseph was sold to Egypt.—Urim ve Tumim: Joseph born on 22nd day of the month.

(14) Samaritan legends of the birth of Moses, see Introduction For other literature see Freudenthal, Hellenistische Studien, p. 169 ff.—The remarkable parallelism between the Samaritan legends of the Birth of Moses and the Christian legends about the birth and childhood of Jesus must be reserved for separate treatment. The relation of the Asatir to Josephus has been dealt with fully. Introduction and Jeraḥmeel (Gaster) Ch. XLII. Introd. LXXXVII and Index S.V. Moses.—Josippon (ed. F. J. Breithaupt, Gotha 1707) I. 2. p. 13: A long history about Sefo and the King of the Kittim, and the wars between them may have some connection with the brief allusion here.—Urim ve Tumim: Pharaoh born on the 24th day of the month.—Some confused notions about the beginnings of the Pharaohs; Adam and Eve Malan. Bk. III, Ch. XXIV, p. 174.

(15) Meshalma fol. 231a says: "Guṭsis... son of Japhet, son of Noah."—*New* Dinasty Josephus Ant. II. 9. 1 (202), cf. T. B. Sota IIa.—Long genealogical lists not uncommon in later Arabic literature are also found in Palmyrene Inscriptions (v. Lidzbarski, Hand-

me thence." (13) And it came to pass when he stood at the altars, P. 123. there came unto him the god of water who said unto him, "Thou art not able to see but hear." The explanation of it is, "Thou art not able to see but only to hear what is said unto thee," that "the Lord God is not a man that he should lie, neither the son of man that he should repent. He hath said and shall He not do it?" (Numb. XXIII. 19.) "Know that I am giving to the Children of Israel the blessing and the Garden of Eden and I will not withold my gift from them." (15) Then there came to him the god of the corners of the heaven and said unto him, "Surely there is no enchantment with Jacob." (Numb. XXIII. 23.) "Glory ect." And the explanation of it is this: This people doth not listen to enchantment, nor doth it rely upon it, and it is glorified by the angels and the light, which is resting upon it." (17) And afterwards there came to him the god of holiness, who said unto him, P. 124. "The Lord his God is with him, and the shout of a king is among them." (Numb. XXIII. 21.) And the explanation of it is, that the Lord helps him, and his great angel Kbla waits in his midst. And then Bileam stood up for a third time and blessed Israel, and he did not according to the wish of Balak, but said unto him, "Come, I will advise thee what this people will do to thy people in the latter days." (Numb. XXIV. 14.) And before he said anything to them, there came to him the god of the luminaries and said to him, "I see him but not now, I behold him but not nigh: a star rises from Jacob and the destruction of thy people shall be through his hand." (16) And then there came the god of the winds, who said unto him, "And Israel doeth valiantly." (Numb. XXIV. 18.) P. 125. And the explanation is that "this will happen at the end of days when Israel shall grow mightier than all the nations of the world." And afterwards he said unto him, "Harken unto this and take heed of it. A star will arise, i. e., a man, who will smite all the corners of Moab." And that is his

16. Who learnt the Book of Signs in Great Babylon, and he came from Gifna and went to Niniveh.

17. And he heard that Joseph was king of Egypt.

18. And he (Pharaoh?) dwelt there three years and a month and then he went to Damascus, and from Damascus to Gezurah and that is 'Akushim and he tarried there sixty three years.

19. And Joseph and all his brothers died.

20. And the kingdom of Ishmael was changed and that of Amalek began to take its place.

buch der Nordsemitischen Epigraphie, Weimar 1898, p. 133. See also A. Cook, Text Book of North Semitic Inscriptions, Oxford 1903) Lidzbarski traces them back to Arabic influences, but genuine Jewish genealogies are much older, found already in Ezra, Nehemiah, and Chronicles. Later on in the genealogy of the Karaite leader: (see Dod Mordecai ed. J. C. Wolfius. Hamburgi et Lipsiae 1714 and S. Pinsker. Likute Kadmoniot. Wien 1860 p. 53) and also in that of the Exilarch, Bostanai (Seder Olam Zuṭṭah). Fictitous genealogies, however, are found already in the Palestinian Targum, and in Targum II to Esther. (Introd. p. 154 —155). Another series of genealogies is found in Ps. Philo XV. 3. of Joshua and Caleb. Mention may be made also here of the long lists of Babylonian Kings found in Babylonian records and curiously enough, a "Gentium" appears among the Kings of Agade (see Johns in P. S. B. A. 1916, p. 199). Altogether this tracing of pedigrees in order to prove a pure or noble lineage seems to be a very ancient practice which has been afterwards dropped. On the other hand, this very practice of making out a noble pedigree led to the parody of making up a pedigree with fictitious names all having a bad character of doubtful reputation. In the case o Haman's pedigree Targum II t Esther II. 1. Cassel has shown tha the names in this pedigree of Haman are slightly corrupted names of procurators and governors of Palestine known as enemies of the Jews, though anachronistic. This pedigree characterizes Haman as descendent of wicked ancestors. So probably is the case here with Pharaoh, later on Bileam X,1) The wicked men have wicked ancestors.

ושחו So in MS.: must be ושעי Gesira: probably the Gesira from above (IV, 30).

saying, "And a sceptre shall rise out of Israel and smite through the corners of Moab." (Numb.XXIV.17.) And here Bileam refers to the time of God's Favour and the Taheb. This is not mentioned in the Asatir, for it is mentioned in the Holy Law.

(18) And when Bileam heard all these words from the angels, then he thought an evil thought and he said in his heart, "The God of Israel hates defilement." And he said to Balak, P. 126. "If thy desire is to destroy the people of God, you can do it quickly by fornication," and he told him what he was to do. And Bileam returned empty to his place. And after Bileam had left, then Balak and his company did what Bileam had told them, and they gathered from their daughters 120,000, and clothed them in beautiful robes and sent them to the borders of the camp of the Israelites. (19) And they reached that place in the third hour of the Sabbath Day, for the people of Moab said, that the fornication with their daughters would be better if it took place on the Sabbath that their sin should grow great, for the sin would grow greater having been committed on the Sabbath P. 127. (20) And the covenant with Pineḥas was made on that day, with him and his seed after him. Happy are those who love God, but woe unto them that hate Him! And it was at the third hour of the Sabbath, (21) that the elders of the children of Israel gathered themselves together at the gate of the tent of the covenant in the south corner; (22) and the flag of the camp of Reuben was also on the south side. And the holy priests stood there on the east side and the tribe of Simeon was with the flag of Reuben. Reuben was on its left and the tribe of Gad on its right hand. And the tribe of Gad knew all the hymns of praise, and it is the first who established hymns of praise. And that is made manifest from his statement in the Asatir, (25) "and with the harp and the cither, and timbals and drum and musical instruments." (27) And when the daughters of fornication came

21. And Pharaoh came to Egypt in the first year and he dwelt there, and he kept Egypt by force.

22. And through him there was tribulation in the land for three years and the king of Egypt died.

23. And then Pharaoh arose and gathered large armies from the Kfṭeim and he reigned afterwards there for sixty years.

24. And in Egypt there was a wizard whose name was Plti and he saw the greatness of Israel.

25. And he saw Levi going up to Pharaoh in a chariot with great honour and he came out with great honour.

26. And he said "Who is this man" and they told him that he was a Hebrew.

27. And he said: "Great is the honour of this man and of that which is hidden in his loins, and what will come out of it."

(21) The text here is somewhat confused. Evidently reference is made to some wars of Pharaoh with other nations. Jubilees XLVI. 9, contains a description of such wars of Pharaoh with the Canaanites.

(24) "Plti." So Meshalma 231 a: This name is mentioned as the wizard of the time of Moses and also in other Samaritan literature, see Introd.—Josephus II. 9. 2. 205: A scribe . . . who foretells the future. —Palestinian Targum Exod. I. 15: Janis and Jambris the sons of Bileam are the wizards consulted by Pharaoh to interpret the dream, and they advise the killing of the male children.—In the Book of the Bee Ch. XXX p. 51: the name of the sorcerer is Posdi probably a corruption from Plti.—A similar name in Numb. XIII. 9, and in the Aramaic papyri (see Introduction).—The daughter of Lot is called Paltia, or Pleṭith feminine form. Pal. Targ. Gen. XVIII. 21.—Pirke de Rabbi Eliezer Ch. 25.—T. B. Sanhedrin, 109b.—Gen. Rabba XLIX. 6. Yashar XIX, 24, etc.

(25) Josephus II. 9. 3. 210: "Amram. one of the nobler sort of Hebrews." Probably means Amram son of Levi, and therefore Josephus says "Amram."—Amram man of nobility; T. B. Sota 12a.

(27) Josephus II. 9. 3. 212: Through dream of Amram birth of Moses is foretold.—"Great is the glory of this man." Prediction of birth in a somewhat different form; Mehilta ed. J. H. Weiss Wien 1865 p. 52.

the daughter of Ṣur was in their midst: she travelled in a chariot, of wood [driven] by the wind from all sides, and she travelled in it whither soever she wished. (28) At that time there came a voice from the clouds saying, "Slay ye every one his men that have joined themselves unto Baal-peor." (Numb.XXV.5.) (29) And the judges of the children of Israel had come together for the Sabbath midday prayer, and after the end of the prayer the judges rose up quickly and did not do as Moses had commanded them; and those who took first the daugthers of fornication were of the tribe of Simeon, and his word, "behold the judges" means those who were the first to take from the daughters of fornication were judges. (30) And after them the foolish youths took [the women] "and there went into the pavilion Zimri and Cozbi, (Numb. XXV. 8.) and this their abomination became revealed before the whole people. (31) And the cloud removed and a plague came instead; (32) and then there arose a zealous man, the well-known master, the high priest Pineḥas, from the midst of the community. And he took a spear in his hand (33) and performed the two miracles: one with the living and one with the dead. The cloud of plague brought plague (34) and Pineḥas brought the cloud of mercy, which carried away the plague which oppressed all the sinners. And the miracle for the living was that Pineḥas, by his zeal, saved allt he pure ones. P. 130. And he did good unto them by the deed which he performed. (35) And the miracle concerning the dead was that when he had the spear in his hand, not one drop of the blood of the harlots fell on him, for a burning fire came down from heaven and stood between the blood and the hand of Pineḥas, and all the blood came down on it and burned it away. And the Lord—may He be exalted—rewarded him for his zeal by the seven gifts especially granted to him and to his seed after him: the sacrifices, the spices of incense, the new offerings and the sin offering, burnt offering, peace offering, and the

28. And his speech reached Pharaoh and he sent and called the wizard.

29. And he said unto him, "Truly out of the loins of this man will come one who will be mighty in faith, in knowledge, and the heaven and earth will hearken to his word; and by his hands will come the destruction of Egypt."

30. And Pharaoh commanded they should separate the women from the men forty days and when they separated from one another nineteen days,

31. A man of the house of Levi went: mighty is the tree from which Moses was plucked.

32. And the wizard saw in his enchantment that Israel's star was in the ascendant and he saw that the mother was pregnant with him.

33. So he said to the king, "Thy intention has now been frustrated."

34. Pharaoh said to him, "What shall be done?"

35. And the wizard replied, "His death will be through water."

36. And Pharaoh commanded the Egyptians saying, "No Hebrew male child shall be left."

(29) I Enoch X. 16 and XCIII. 5 and 10.—Palest. Targ. to Exod. 1. 14.". . . and by his hand will be destruction of Egypt.

(30) Amram keeping away from Jochebed until told by an angel; Poem of Abdalla ben Jacob, Cowley, Liturgy 626, exactly like Josephus.—Malif. Q. 139: Pharaoh prevented the men from approaching their wives.—Amram and the people separated from their wives; T. B. f. Sota 12a.—Ps. Philo. IX. 2 ff.

(31) "Glorious is the tree from which Moses has been plucked." Same phrase referring to Moses occurs in Markah (see Introduction).

(32) Appearance of star in connection with birth; v. Dieterich, Zeitschrift für die Neutestamentliche Wissenschaft III, Giessen 1902, p. 1 ff.: Die Weisen aus dem Morgenlande.

oil of ointment. And He completed them by an eighth, namely, the high priesthood. P. 131 And He made the covenant of peace with him according to his statement in Holy Writ, "Behold, I give unto him my covenant of peace: and it shall be unto him and to his seed after him the covenant of an everlasting priesthood." (Numb. XXV 12 and 13.) And it is said in the Book Asatir, (36) "Those who keep the faith have been guided in the establishment of all the prayers by the numbers seven and eight." The explanation of it is that all the Jewish laws are connected with seven: seven days, seven purities; the Ancients have also said that every seventh thing is holy. But also the eighth is connected with the Law: as, the eight days of circumcision; but if we were to enumerate here all the sevens, then the number would be too long, P. 132. while we are anxious to write as briefly as possible, and not to expand it. And God knows.

(37) And know that on the new moon of the eighth month was the coming of the daughters of the harlots into the camp of Israel, and in the tenth month the Lord said unto Moses: "Avenge the vengeance of the children of Israel on the Midianites, and afterwards thou shalt be gathered unto thy people." (38) And the messenger of God—may the peace of the Lord be upon him—selected 12,000 men of war; (39) and when they went up to the war, the Lord said unto Moses that he should go with them and do to them as he had done in the war against Amalek, and he should stand on the top of the mountain with the rod of the Lord in his hand. And he fell on his face and prayed P. 133. and he called the children of Israel. (40) And it came to pass when they went to Midian, our Master Moses the Messenger—upon whom be peace—gave the trumpets unto Pineḥas, and he commanded him to go before the army and (41) "they made war against the Midianites as the Lord had commanded Moses." But before they reached them on the fourth day, there came spies

37. And he put Shifrah and Puah over the birth of the Hebrew women and Pharaoh said to them "Every male child shall be killed and every female child shall be kept alive."

38. And Amram was a good physician trusted in Egypt and Shifrah was showing lovingkindness to the Levites and Puah showed loving-kindness to the Hebrews.

39. And the fear of God dwelt in their hearts and they did not as they were told.

40. And the people multipled and waxed very mighty.

41. And Pharaoh commanded his people that they should throw the children into the river.

42. And the fathers and mothers were frightened and the women acted in faith and the women destroyed themselves with their children.

Chapter IX. [Moses.]

1. And the great prophet—may he be remembered for good forever—was born in the month of Nisan on the fifth of it on the Sabbath.

(42) Pitron: children born in the fields and miraculously fed underground. cf. T. B. Sota f. 11b. Jerahmeel Ch. XLII. 4.—Josephus II. 9. 2. (207), says: "They and their families would be destroyed." Here it says; They did destroy themselves.—Ps. Philo IX, 2 ff. (see James' notes in loc).

Ch. IX.

(1) Birth of Moses 7th hour, 7th day (Sabbath), 7th month (Nisan); Poem by Abdalla ben Shalma (Cowley p. 747).—The story of Moses, etc.; Jerahmeel 43.—Seder Hadorot p. 77: Born on Wednesday 7th Adar, 3rd hour of the day. Other dates are also given there, among them that he was born on the Sabbath.—Josephus Ant. II.9. 3. 216: "His memory will last forever." The very same words: Sanhedrin, 101b.

who told the Midianites that the children of Israel were coming to wage war against them. And they sent men to Bileam and said unto him: (42) "O thou who art the head of the sorcerers, arise against this community which does not believe in thee and does not hearken unto thee. In a short while some people [of the tribe of Dan] came from the side of Edom." (43) And that is the word which P. 134. our master Jacob—upon whom be peace—had said, "Dan shall be a serpent in the way, an adder in the path." (Gen. XLIX. 17.) (44) And Bileam hastened to come to Midian, and he came to the city of Ṣur, south of Midian. And he lifted his eyes towards the East and he saw the tribe of Gad facing them all, and this is the word whic is said, "As for Gad, a troop shall press him." (Gen. XLIX. 19.) And the interpretation of it is that the tribe of Gad shall always be in the front of the war. (45) And as the angel had furthermore said to Bileam son of Beor, "A star has arisen from Jacob and a rod from Israel." This star was our master Pineḥas, "and the rod which has arisen from Israel was our master Joshua, the successor of the Messenger of God. (46) And all were shouting, P. 135. "The Lord is our God, the Lord is One, separate, always segregated, with Him is no other God like Him, nor has He substance nor any form."

(47) And when Bileam saw these great sights and the torches of the angels round them and the holy Kbla round about them, then Bileam was frightened and he fled before them seeking safety and peace. And the Lord—may He be exalted—gave him neither safety nor peace. And Zered, the son of Ḳmual, the son of the brother of Kaleb, who was of the tribe of Judah, caught him and brought him before Pineḥas, the son of Elazar, the high priest, and before Joshua, the son of Nun. And he talked to them, but they did not understand what he was saying P. 136. (48) and Rdit, the son of Ṣuriel, the son of Salu, of the tribe of Simeon, rose up and killed him, for he had

2. And on the tenth of Sivan he was thrown into the river and when he was thrown into the river the waters subsided.

3. And all the women went out to look at it.

4. And when all the women went down, the daughter of Pharaoh also went down.

5. And (with every day) that passed the water decreased.

6. And all the wizards and sorcerers came together and they were in great tribulation.

7. And Plti the wizard found by the secret of the Book of Signs that the child had gone down.

8. And the ark was in the flags and the daughter of Pharaoh saw it in the fifth hour on the seventh (Sabbath).

9. And she sent her maid and she took it and opened it and she saw the child and behold the child wept loudly and the daughter of Pharaoh had compassion on it.

10. And being filled with love for it she commanded her maids that no word should be spoken about it.

11. And Miriam who stood close by when she saw it rejoiced and ran to her and said, "Shall I go and call (etc.)."

(2) Moses hidden unscathed in furnace; Poem of Abraham b. Jacob (Cowley p.626). Poem by Abdallah b. Shalma Cowley p. 747.— On the 6th Sivan; Seder Hadorot p. 77.—Molad: The waters subsided.

(4) Pharaoh's daughter healed of skin-disease by the touch of the child. Pitron. So Molad f. 13a.— Poem by Abdalla b. Shalma (Cowley p. 747).—Maif.l Q. 139: Pharaoh's daughter cured from sickness.—Pal. Targum Exod. II. 5.

(11) cf. Exodus III, 7.

caused the abomination to be practised in Israel, and this had happened among the tribe of Simeon. And the number of the tribe of Simeon was in the beginning 59,300, and after Zimri and the daughters of fornication had performed that deed and brought the wrath of the Lord upon them, then he reduced their number to 22,200, for those of this tribe who had died of the plague on the first and second occasions were 37,100, although the evil deed of this tribe had only been made manifest on the latter occasion. Behold, O my brother, search and investigate and ask, and open thine eyes, and see that the plague of Korah and all his company came, when they spoke against Moses and Aaron—may the peace of the Lord be upon them. Then the plague came swiftly upon the people, and those who died by it were 24,700 (14,700) according to his saying in the Holy Law, "And those who died of the plague were 14,700." Since he says that in the later plague 24,700 died, P. 138. that means that those who died in these two plagues together were 38,700, and the tribe of Simeon was reduced by 37,100. And then the above mentioned Zered smote him (Bileam) in the presence of Pineḥas and Joshua, (49) and Joshua was frightened at him, and shouted at him to bring him (Bileam) near to smite Bileam before him and before Pineḥas, the priest. The chief of those who died in the war was Bileam, and this is made manifest from what is stated in the Asatir, "the heart of the avenger of the blood grew hot at the sight of him (Bileam.)"

(50) On the fourth day (Wednesday) they returned from the war, and on the fifth P. 139. the overseers over the thousands of the army brought the spoil from those who had gone out to the war, from everyone, whatever he had found, gold, bangles, chains, bracelets, signet rings, earrings and armlets. They placed it in the tent of the covenant as a memorial of that war in which 12,000 men smote five kings with their camp and their host and

12. And she said unto her, "Go." And she went and called its mother Jochebed.

13. And she said to her "Nurse this child for me and I will give thee the money of thy milk." And she suckled him with undefiled milk and he grew up and she brought him to the daughter of Pharaoh and she called his name Moses.

14. And after this Moses grew in strength and he was appointed with the chiefs of Pharaoh over the Hebrews.

15. And he saw an Egyptian smiting an Hebrew man and he killed him and hid him in the sand.

16. And on the second day he saw two men striving and he said unto him that did the wrong, "O thou wicked one." And the Hebrew was angered and he said unto Moses, "O thou murderer."

17. And he fled to Midian and he tarried there sixty years.

18. And after that there came oppression upon Israel and Goṭs (Pharaoh) died.

19. And Israel sighed and their groaning went up. And there arose a Pharaoh from Kittim whose name was 'Aṭirṭ.

20. And Moses kept the flock of Jethro and he came to Mount Horeb.

21. On the fifteenth day of the third month on the fourth (Wednesday) God fulfilled the covenant which he made with the Meritorious Ones.

---

(13) Moses refusing to suck defiled milk of heathen women; Pitron so Molad f. 13a and 13b.—Poem of Abraham b. Jacob (Cowley p. 626, § 5).—Malif. Q. 139.—Josephus II. 9. 5. 226.—Exod. Rabba I. 27.—

destroyed them and spoiled them and took them captive, while of themselves not one man was missing. And this is made manifest from his word in the Holy Law, "and there lacketh not one man of us." (Numb. XXXI. 49.)

(51) And after all these words, there came forth P. 140. a voice from the Lord, saying, "No Ammonite or Moabite shall come into the congregation of the Lord." (Deut. 23. 3.)

(52) And furthermore the Lord said, "Now, therefore, kill every male among the little ones, and kill every woman that hath known man by lying with him. But all the women children, that have not known man by lying with him, keep alive for yourselves." (Numb. XXXI. 17 and 18.) And they did as the Lord commanded them. And the word which says "they who did not lie with man," means the virgins who had not been married. "Smite all the males" refers to the young boys whom they had brought captive with them: and those who were suckling were to be killed with their mothers, P. 141. for anyone who has reached the age of manhood he is no longer a child and he is counted among the men of war. And God knows.

Chapter XI. [Death of Moses and Prophecy.]

(1) And after this war, the Lord said unto Moses—may the peace of the Lord be upon him "Take thee Joshua, the son of Nun, a man in whom is the spirit, and lay thine hand upon him; and set him before Elazar the priest and before all the congregation." (Numb. XXVI. 18 and 19.)

And this happened in the fortieth year of the going out of the children of Israel from Egypt in the eleventh month. And Moses did as the Lord commanded him with great joy and pleasure, as is evidenced from what is stated in the Asatir, P. 142. (2) "thus did Moses with great rejoicing and pleasure, as if he were of his sons. May they never be lacking in happiness and faith." And the explanation of it is this, that none of the sons of our

22. The rod of Adam and his clothes were given to Moses on that day.

23. And this is the word which is said, "And this is a sign to thee."

24. On the fourth (Wednesday) He showed himself to Moses.

25. On the first (Sunday) he went down to Egypt and God said to Aaron, "Go and meet thy brother."

26. He went and met him and they both went up to Egypt and they made the signs before the Israelites.

27. On the third (Tuesday) they went to Pharaoh.

28. On the fifth (Thursday) they smote the river.

29. All the judgments were enacted within nine months.

30. On the fifth (Thursday) they went out of Egypt at the sixth hour; they went out in the sight of all Egypt.

31. At the going out of the Sabbath (they passed) through the divided Sea.

(22) See III. 25: It is not stated here who gave Moses the rod of Adam and the clothes. According to Jewish tradition, the rod was in the house of Pharaoh left by Joseph, taken by Jethro and planted in his garden where Moses found it. See above literature on rod of Moses. As for the clothes, Adam gave them to Enoch. Noah; then they came to Ham and from him to Nimrod. Thus far Pirke de R. Eliezer XXIV. Zohar II. 39a. Esau killed Nimrod and took the clothes, Gen. Rabba Ch. 68, similarly Yashar VII. 24 ff.— Book of the Bee p. 55.

(24) Chs. of Rabbi Eliezer, Ch. 8: God appears to Moses on the New Moon of Nisan.

(25) cf. Exodus III, 12.

(28) Seder Olam Ch. V. Ratner ad loc. Note 10: The whole Rabbinic literature.

(29) Mishnah Edujoth II. 10 cf. Jalkut Machiri to Isajah f.105b. —Seder Olam Ch. III, Ratner ad loc, note 20.—Urim ve Tumim Plagues began on the 25th day of the month.

(30) Malif. 145 and 198.

(31) Urim ve Tumim: On the 26th Moses cleft the waters of the Red Sea. Seder Olam Ch.

Master Moses,—upon whom be peace—was with him on the day of his death, for he, at the time of his death, remembered them and prayed for grace for them, and sent them "greetings of peace everlasting," for there is be no other peace besides his—may the peace of God be upon him. And our master Markah—upon whom be the favour of the Lord—said in his well—known writing that Moses, at the time of his departure called the congregation of Israel and said, P. 143. "Oh Gershom and Eleazar, ye are the two sons, upon whom I command the peace." And the meaning of this "peace" has been, that they shall never be in any trouble. Their father, the Master of the flesh, and the Lord—may He be exalted—shall befriend them through the prayer of their father. And their father testified about them in the Book Asatir wherein he says, "May they never be lacking in happiness and faith."

(3) And afterwards there came the priests and elders of the children of Israel, and he commanded them to keep the Law of the Lord, which he had brought down with his hand. And he told them that, except for the Law, the world could not exist; and behold, P. 144. there is proof for my word that our Master Moses the Messenger—upon whom be the peace—took the Law from the hand of Glory, for no man could speak about that Book, no man could describe its true form, whether it be of skin or light, nor of its grand appearance, nor of the greatness of its majesty; and no man could touch it save Moses alone, our Master,—upon whom be peace; and from this he copied the book which he wrote down. And now we shall bring one proof out ot many proofs for the justification of our statement that God gave to our Master Moses with the first two tablets upon which He had written P. 145. the ten words, also the book of the Law; and this proof is the word which Moses spake in his prayer to the Lord at the time when the children of Israel made the calf; "For their

32. On the third (Tuesday) the waters of Marah were sweetened. And God showed him that rod by which he smites and heals.

33. On the sixth (Friday) they gained the victory over Amalek.

34. On the fourth (Wednesday) God called him up to Mount Sinai.

35. There are three mornings in the world, one is the morning of creation on the first (Sunday).

36. Another the morning of Mount Sinai on the fourth (Wednesday).

37. Another the morning of the day of vengeance on the sixth (Friday).

38. On the first the Tabernacle was set up; on the third they went away from Mount Sinai. On the third Miriam died.

V. On Friday night they entered the sea. See Ratner note 15 ad loc.

(32) According to Pitron.

(34) According to Samaritan tradition and practice, the day of the Giving of the Law was on the 3rd of the month (Ex. XIX. 11). It is kept independently of the Feast of Weeks, which is always on a Sunday, with special services arranged for each of these occasions. v. Cowley, Sam. Liturgy and Codd. Gaster Samaritan Prayer Books. — Seder Olam Ch. V: All the five days: that means from Sunday to Thursday, and on Friday the Law was given, but in T. B. Sabbat f. 88a Moses came down on Wednesday. See Ratner notes 46—51.—Mechilta Exod. Beshallah, sect. 4. 1.—Pirke de Rabbi Eliezer Ch. 41.

(35) "Day of Vengeance" (Pitron no stars visible). Book of Laws and Ceremonies: Last Chapter contains full description of Sam. eschatology. See also Pinehas son of Amram, Yom al Din, where all the passages of the Pentateuch referring to Judgment are collected. Sibyl. Or. VIII. 337 ff.—Pal. Targum Exodus XII. 42: There are four nights prepared by God, the Night of Creation, the Night of Covenant with Abraham, the Night of going out of Egypt, the Night of Redemption from Exile.—Sibyll. Oracles. Book II. 185.— See Charles Eschatology on general happiness at the end of days.

(37) David Apocalypse in Merx. Archiv II. p. 21: Light of Creation to reappear at the Advent of the Messiah.

(38) Miriam died. 10th of

own sake, now if thou wilt, forgive their sin, and if not, blot me out from thy book which thou hast written." And if we should say that this was referring to the two tablets, we find that there was no mention of Moses to be found on the Tablets.—(Woe unto those who forsake the Law of Moses for there is no salvation for them!) (For verse 4—18 see XII. 5).

(20) Then afterwards he began to speak about what was going to happen in the remaining 3,204 years of the 6,000 P. 146. since the Creation of the world until the Advent of the Taheb. For from Adam until the death of our master Moses were 276 (2,796) years, so that all these together make 6,000 years. And then he began to speak the words "when ye will beget children and children's children, etc." (Deut. IV. 25), for this section contains everything that will happen at the end of days. And there in is a prophecy foretelling the Advent of the Favour and of the Mercy after the end of the days of the Fanuta, according to His word—may He be exalted— P. 147. "when all these things come upon thee, in the latter days thou shalt return to the Lord thy God, and hearken unto His voice; for the Lord thy God is a merciful God; he will not fail thee, nor forget the covenant of thy fathers, which he sware unto them." (Deut. IV. 30, 31.) And the explanation of it is this: That the Lord,—may He be exalted—if ye turn unto Him with repentance, will establish His covenant with you and He will do unto you as He did in the time of Favour; and this He will do and still more, and this is a true thing and there is no falsehood in it. And concerning this there is a large amount of matter handed down from our fathers the patriarchs, and therefore, our Master Moses began his words in this section and everything that they mention is deduced from it, for therein is included the teaching and the future; and furthermore he said P. 148. "The beginning of the Fanuta, the gate of the back-sliding" and furthermore,

39. On the fourth Aaron died.

40. On the seventh the King of Arad fought against them and took from them captives and afterwards the Israelites utterly destroyed him and his possessions.

Chapter X. [Bileam.]

1. M'rṭis the wizard fled from Arad to Midian. This was Peor whom Balak son of Zippor, King of the Moabites, sent to call Bileam son of Beor son of Gdiṭṭ son of P'ṭ'h son of 'Amingf son of Laban.

Nisan.—Seder Olam Ch. X.— Jeraḥmeel 48. 17.—Cod. Gaster 97 a.f. 11a: On the 10th of Nisan. —Pirke Rabbenu Hakkadosh. (Eisenstein, Ozar, p. 505 ff.)— Albiruni (Sachau) p. 274: Fast day of the Jews on 10th of the month of Nisan, and according to some on the Monday.—Seder Hadorot p. 90: On the 10th of Nisan Miriam died.

Ch. X.

(1) מערטים unquestionably a mistake. It is the result of double correction. ערטים for טרטים and טרטים for טרטים. The last copyist combined both. Pitron follows Asatir.—MS reads דאשלו׳instead of דאשלחו Either scribe's error or has fallen out owing to its not being pronounced by the Samaritans.— The whole episode of Bileam as described here, especially his worship of idols, may have formed part of a book of magic, ascribed to Bileam. It differs considerably from the text of the Bible, and contains a large amount of legendary matter to which no direct parallel can be found. Much ancient material, hitherto unknown, seems to have been preserved here. In the Introduction. I have dealt more fully with the legends of Bileam, and the cycle of legends, which has gathered round him.—The story of Bileam from here to his death is given in full in the Arabic Book of Joshua ed. Joynboll, Chs. 3—5. Much better in Cod. Gaster 1140, p. 14— 22. The description of the deities worshipped by Bileam as well as the words of blessing and their interpretation are missing in this description, but the temptation by the Midianite women and especially the death of Bileam are described in greater detail, as it were, interpreting more fully the brief references in Asatir. See below. v. 45.— Bileam identified with Laban. Tabyah (Ghazal) el Doweik in his commentary to the blessings of Bileam says: "According to tradition Bileam was the son of Laban" and he promises to explain it more fully in its place, probably referring to a commentary to Numbers which he intended

he—upon whom be peace—said, (21) "A Levite will arise and his name will be Ezra, the son of Fani. And the beginning of strife will be by his hand. (22) He will add a sanctuary in his days (23) and he will exchange the sanctuary of the Hebrews for a strange sanctuary. He will throw division in the midst of the assembly. (24) The order of turning away and arbitrariness Ḳrṭm of Benjamin will establish among them." All this refers to Ezra, for he was the first who turned the letters of the Law from the Hebrew language in to the language of Assur, which is now in the hands of the Community of the Jews, and he established the work of Shelah (Solomon) by saying that the chosen place was Zion P. 149. And he expunged from the Law the fourth* paragraph from the Ten Commandments, and he did with the Book of the Law according to his desire. And he added to it and took away from it many things which have been preserved by us, and he was the father of everything that is between us and the Jews; and though the wrong had already happened before the advent of Ezra, through him, however, it increased and was added to, but no error will remain when the Taheb will return to us; and the deeds of this man are all recorded in our book of Chronicles (Sefer Hayamim). And should we wish to give it in detail, the tale would become too long.

(25) And after that, the Messenger Moses—upon whom be peace—said, P. 150. "In the world by the power of the House of Judah, divers statutes will be annulled." And the explanation of the word עולם "world" is found in the numerical value of its letters, i. e., 4367; and the reason for it is because the tribe of Judah changed the commands of God. And the matter is further alluded to in his words, (26) "Hear, oh Lord, the voice of Judah." (Deut. XXXIII. 7.) And God alone knows whether this interpretation agrees with what our master Jacob—upon whom be peace—said, "The

* This refers to the additional 10th Commandment of the Samaritan recension. See Gaster, Samaritans (Schweich Lectures) p. 185ff.

2. He grieved and did not grieve over what happened to him. He (did not) grieve for the trust (honour) [shown] to him by the King of Moab, but came to grief through his empty vanity.

3. For he had sent messengers to Bileam and he had asked him that he should come and curse Israel.

4. On the sixth month messengers went to Bileam.

5. And Bileam knew the Book of Signs and enquired therein.

6. And he worshipped the god of fire, god of the firmament, the god of waters, the god of heavenly lights and the holy god.

7. Hlm, Hml, Ihml, Vhml, Haml, H'amal, Gmgal, Hṣrfh, Hsmikm, Hld, Lil, Ḥlḳ-lb, Ḥlk, L'el Elyon, Hlyn, Hntr, Hlgfr.

ed to write.—This is a very obscure passage. Maybe that it is intended to explain the word קֹסְמִים (Numb. XXII. 7) which they read קֹסְמִים i. e. wizards and thus introduced the otherwise unknown figure of the wizard Martis differing here also from the Sam. Targ. Further also it is meant to explain somehow the mention of Midianites in connection with Balak, King of Moab. Josephus IV, 6, 2, 103 tries to explain it in a roundabout way, and Palest. Targ. to Numbers XXII. 4. makes Balak a Midianite.—Genealogy of derogatory names Ch. VIII. 15 f. Bileam son of Laban as an ancient tradition by Tabyah el Doweik, who refers to the oath made by Laban not to cross the stone of witness (Gen. XXXI. 45) which Bileam did, and thereby incurred God's wrath.—Bileam = Laban; Pal. Targ. to Numb. XXII. 5; XXXII. 8.—Tanhuma, Gen.: End of Vayeṣe. Bileam same as Laban.—Numb. Rab. to Numb. XXII.

(2) The passage is corrupt, and has been translated as best possible.—Josephus IV 6. 2. 105: He wanted to go but God opposed to his intentions.—Numbers Rabba XX.—Pal. Targ. XXII. 5: Interprets Beor as the man who became foolish through the greatness of his knowledge.—Tanḥuma to Numbers XXII. 20.

(7) These names differ slightly in the Arabic paraphrase, probably due to scribe's error. The narmes are the permutations of the letters of the names presumed to be those of the gods worshipped

sceptre shall not depart from Judah, nor the rulers's staff from among his flags until Shelah come." (Gen. XLIX. 10.) And Shelah is he who was before the advent of Ezra. P. 151. And the tribe of Judah remained protected and favoured until the turning away of Judah when Shelah came, and committed all those wicked deeds which the congregation of the Jews acknowledge, and they recount it in their chronicles and in spite of all that they call him a prophet.

Furthermore, he—upon whom be peace—said, (27) "The tower of shame He will build with might. The congregation which will be praying for truth, will be oppressed by a son born of a harlot, rebellious, he will be like the enchanter Bileam. In his days the worship of strange gods will be established." All this refers to the advent of Jesus, the son of Miriam; and as for his statement, "the tower of shame will be built," the explanation of it is, the faith of the world in Zion will grow. "בעטם with might." The explanation is to be found in its numerical value of 1472 from the establishment of the kingdom of the children of Israel, i. e., the year in which that man will be born. (28) And his statement, "the congregation will pray for maintaining the truth" means "up to the time of his advent, the congregation of the Israelites will be searching for the truth," And because of the desire for preserving the truth, they wished to kill him; for his killing was for the sake of the truth, as the Holy Law says, "And that prophet shall die:" (Deut. XVIII. 20.) (29) And as for his word, "the son born of a harlot and by fornication," the explanation is, that he was the child of a harlot; and of "fornication and rebellious;" the explanation is that he was rebellious and straying from the way of truth. P. 153. (30) The explanation of, "he will be like unto the wizard Bileam is that he will be a sorcerer like Bileam and he will perform miracles and wonders by way of sorcery, so that the world should believe. (31) And that is followed

8. These are the seven angels whom Bileam worshipped.

9. The holy god is the angel that met Bileam.

10. The god of the winds (El Harukot) is the angel who gave him the words at the first altars: three were his speeches.

11. The god of fire was he who rebuked Bileam that he should not curse the people.

12. The god of firmament obscured his sight.

13. The god of water was he who said, "Thou who canst not see but hearest."

14. The god of the luminaries said to him, "But not now."

15. The god of the corners of the heaven said to him, "There is no sorcery in Jacob."

16. Hdr, the God of winds said unto him, "And Israel is doing valiantly."

ped by Bileam; or possibly a methatesis of divine names written here in order to avert the influence of these heathen gods as the author is doing on other occasions. They occur also in the astronomical poem of Jacob ha-Rabban (v. Introd.) and in the Samaritan phylacteries. ed. Gaster ("Studies and Texts" p. 388 ff.) where their high antiquity has been shown. Angels appointed over various elements Book of Enoch, Hebrew Apocalypse of Moses("Studies and Texts" p. 125 ff.) and a complete hierarchy of angels is found in the Pirke Hekhalot. As for the mystical use of the names of angels see "The Sword of Moses" ed. Gaster "Studies and Texts" p. 288 ff. together with a very long list of angels, culled from the Sefer Raziel.

(10) נשלשה: So in MS. letter and word.

(12) The word אודם is nothing but a Samaritan transliteration of the Hebrew word סתם in Samaritan Targum to Numbers XXIX, 13. This word was not properly understood by the Samaritans; for how could Bileam see when his eye were "closed." The maning "wicked" or "froward" eye may have been suggested by the root.

(13) cf. Numbers XXIV, 3.
(14) cf. Numbers XXIV, 16.
(15) cf. Numbers XXIII, 23.
(16) cf. Numbers XXIV, 18.

up by the word, that "in his days the worship of strange Gods will be established;" which means that in his days, "the worship of strange gods will grow mighty and he will call himself God," and so it happened.

(32) After that, Moses—upon whom be peace—said (31) that in a short time the strange sanctuary would be destroyed by a people of hard face (33) and those of the house of Shhamh (God ?) and those of the house of Fanai, (i. e., turning away, rebellious) would be scattered throughout the earth. The explanation of it is this, that a short time after P. 154. the days of Jesus the sanctuary of falsehood and vanity would be destroyed through a hard-faced people, and the houses of worship which had been erected by the community of Jesus would be scattered which had remained still under their sway, in the year 2,127 from the time of the kingdom of Israel. And that refers to the advent of Mohammed who came in that generation. And then again he—upon whom be peace—said, "And because of the wickedness of the congregation, the latter will dwell in their stead in great arrogance." And the explanation is because of the multitude of the sins of the children of Israel, the Lord will annihilate them in the land, and other strange people will dwell in the land and rule over it. P. 155. Furthermore, he—upon whom be peace—said, (34) "The community in turning to strife will persist, and the land will be inherited by the chosen ones of Alinis." And the explanation of it is this: that Israel will be lead astray, but the law will be saved and the land will be ruled by the good community of Alinis. (35) And after that, he—upon whom be peace—said, "There will be in the world peace, freedom, might, honour and a life of happiness." And the explanation of it is this: He will bring upon them a time in which they will be resting in joy and pleasure safe from violence and from the rule of oppression, in glory, in happiness and in lovingkindness. And again he—upon whom be peace—said: (36) "After

17. Hazin the holy god said unto him, "The Lord God is with him and the trumpeting of a king is among them."

18. And when Bileam heard that, he hatched an evil plan for he saw (knew) that the God of Israel hated defilement, and he advised Balak concerning adultery, and the Moabites commenced to practise it.

19. On the Sabbath the harlots came out.

20. The covenant with Pineḥas was established by the Seven for him and his seed after him. Great is the loving mercy of God. On the seventh the harlots came out at the third hour.

21. And the heads of the community were congregated at the South before the Tent of the Covenant.

22. And Reuben was encamped there in the West.

23. And Simeon in the middle.

24. And Gad in the East.

25. With harps, zithers, cymbals, timbals and musical instruments.

26. And facing Simeon were about 120,000 harlots.

27. And the daughter of Ṣur was in the middle on a wooden chariot driven by the wind in whichever direction she wished it to go.

---

(17) cf. Numbers XXIII, 21.

(18) Evil advice concerning the daughters of Moab; Josephus IV. 6. 6. 129.—Ps. Philo Ch. XVIII. 13.— Sin through the daughters of Moab; Palestinian Targum to Numbers XXIV. 14. The evil counsel agreeing very closely with the text in Asatir.—Sifrei, par. 131, ed. Friedman. p. 47b.—T. B. Sanhedrin 106a.—Chs. of R. Eliezer XLVII —Tanḥuma to Numbers XXIV. 25.—Jeraḥmeel LV. 10.—Yashar LXXXV, 54ff. Story of the daughters of Moab.—Petrus Comestor to Numb. XXXIV.—Slavonic "Palaea" (first version, p. 106).

(27) No parallel to this except in the Samaritan Book of Joshua,

that, P. 156. the writing will be changed (37) and a new wording they will produce out of the old." The explanation of it is this: after these words there will be a complete change in the world, and new things will come out of the old; that is, a book full of lies and frowardness will be made manifest, and it will take as its basis the Holy Law and the words of the ancients.

(38) And after that he—upon whom be peace—fell upon his face and said, "And the Lord thy God will bring thee up into the land which thy fathers inherited (39) and Luzah will be rebuilt." He said this referring to their return from the great Exile, for at the time when they will come back from the Exile P. 157. to the Holy Land, they will go up to Mount Garizim, which is Luzah. Those days will be like unto the days of the Divine Favour.

Behold, O my brother, in this word there is something put before and something put after (not chronologically) for first he mentioned Jesus and Mohammed, the prophet of the Ishmaelites, whilst the above-mentioned exile was before their appearance. (40) He follows up the matter in his statement, "There will be a Jubilee in rejoicing." And this refers to the remnant he saved from persecution and from great oppression. And after that, he— upon whom be peace—said, P. 158. "A second turning away in error. At the end of days*..." And the explanation of this is, that after that Jubilee there will be for a second time error and turning away from the good path. (41) And in the community of the pure, whose root is from Isaac, in the year 5,237 [corresponding to the numerical value of עלבן] since the creation of the world, there will be great oppression. And he said again, (42) "On the holy hill, he will destroy the images and he will break the idols." And the explanation of it is this: on Mount Garizim in those days, the image and idol will

---

* He divides the text differently from the Asatir, and he confuses the real meaning of עלבין which he takes as a numerical cryptogram.

28. And a voice of the Living came from the cloud of glory and gave the command that those who went after Baal Peor should be killed.

29. After this the judges rose up and they returned quickly, and they did not perform the will of Moses.

30. And then Zimri and Kosbi went into the tent and the abomination was made manifest in the eyes of the whole people.

31. And then the cloud began to remove and the plague descended upon them.

32. And Pinehas rose up and took a spear in his hand.

33. And two wonders happened, one for the living and one for the dead: the cloud of the plague and Pinehas.

34. The cloud of the plague removed all the defiled, but did good unto the pure.

35. And the sign for the dead was [that from] the spear in his hand not one single drop of the blood of the harlot fell on him, but it was burned away (congealed?) on the spear at a distance of seven knots (handbreaths) between the blood and his hand.

Ch. IV, probably borrowed from here. Turning by the wind.—Moving by the wind see above III. 26.

(28) Voice of the Living see X, 50 and XI. 17. For Mandaean parallels see Introduction.

(30) Zimri's sin more fully elaborated in Samaritan Book of Joshua p. 59 ff.

(33) Pal. Targ. to Numbers XXV. 7. 12: miracles happened to Pinḥas. So also Numbers Rabba XX. 25.—Book of the Bee Ch.

30, p. 63. He lifted both on his spear.—See Ginzberg, Legends of the Jews, Vol. III. p. 387.

(34) דכים probably another form for גבאים—אפק: variant is אבק. —"And on his prayer the plague was stayed;" Pal. Targ. to Numb. XXV. 8.

(35) Blood congealed; Pal. Targ. to Numb. XXV. 8: One of the twelve miracles. "Their blood thickened so as not to flow upon him."—cf. T. B. Sanhedrin 52 b.

be broken; and the explanation of the word יריר means that there will be there [destruction] of the images; P. 159. and the darkness will be removed and illuminated by the breaking of the idols. And God knows.

Chapter XII [Oracle.]

And after he—upon whom be peace—had finished these words, he mentioned the kings who will arise in the time of the Fanuta, and he completed them (i. e., the list of kings) with the mention of the Taheb. And he mentioned two things as already afore-mentioned, and he mentioned another twenty-four each one separately. "A prince will arise with a strong hand for ten years. The proud nation Nds will come in his days." And the explanation of it is this: A prince will arise with a mighty hand; P. 160. and for ten years he will rule with honour and glory, and afterwards the mighty and exalted nation Nds will appear in his days." And they will wrest the kingdom from him. And God knows.

And the word "Kli" means exalted beyond degree; and there is another and fuller explanation of this in the statement of the men of understanding, like their expression, "Kli ledinih"—worthy of being a judge, or, worthy of judgment.

(2) "A prince will arise with might from his people for five years and he will not be exalted." And the explanation of it is that a prince will arise with great power; he will appear among them for five (years) and he will not be exalted. And God knows whether this interpretation is correct: or whether it means that enmity will arise among his people against him, or from himself, after five years of his reign. But for all that, the people will not overpower him, neither will they remove him from his kingdom.

(3) "A crowned prince will arise of evil repute. In his days they will be destroyed through the hand of strangers." The explanation of it is: P. 161. A prince will arise who

36. And thus it is said by those who keep the faith that all the fulfillments of the commands were connected with seven and eight.

37. At the beginning of the eighth month came the harlots, and in the tenth month the Lord said unto the prophet, "Avenge the children of Israel, and after that thou wilt be gathered unto thy people."

38. Twelve thousand were armed as men for war.

39. And it was after the men had gone that God said unto Moses that they should go to the war.

40. And when the armed spies went to Midian he gave to Pineḥas before the people the trumpet in his hand and they made war with Midian as God had commanded.

41. On the fourth the people came unto Midian and the Israelites captured it.

42. [And (the Midianites) said], "O! thou chief of the sorcerers. Arise for those who believe in thee!" In the twinkling of an eye there came a small troop [of Dan] from the direction of Edom.

43. And that is the word which Jacob had said "Dan shall be a serpent by the way, an adder in the path."

44. And Bileam hastened to return to Midian to Shur in the South. He lifted up his eye to the East and beheld there a troop of Gaddites.

---

(42) Josephus IV. 7. 1. 160: "Would suddenly be upon them."

(43) The interpretation of Bileam's prophecy in accordance with the Asatir is found in El Doweik.

(44) נדאח Exactly so in El Doweik Commentary on Bileam's prophecy.—Another reading נויח.

will speak falsehood. In his days they will die through the hand of a stranger. And God knows whether the meaning is so. In the days of this king falsehood will increase and he will be the leader of it. And afterwards will appear a people who will be strange unto him and to his people.

(4) "A prince will arise strong in truth. In his days the salvation of the community will be great." And the explanation of it is this: There will arise a prince very strong in truth. In his days the salvation of the congregation will be great. And the explanation of it is that there will arise a prince very strong in truth. In his days Israel will be in peace, and he will love those who are of the truth. And God knows.

(5) "A crowned prince will arise. In his days, the yoke of iron will return." This is the king of Egypt and the children of Israel groaned from servitude. And I will now refer again to what happened under that king, and will tell it as it is told in the Asatir of Moses.

To VIII. (24) In his time there was a wizard in Egypt and his P. 162. name was Plti. And he saw the might of the children of Israel. (25) And he saw Amram going up to Pharaoh in a very great chariot, coming and going with great honour. (26) And he asked, "Who is that man?" And he said to him: "It is a Hebrew man." (27) And he said, "Great is the honour of that man for that which is hidden within him and what will happen to him." (28) And this word reached Pharaoh and he sent for him and Plti was brought before him. And Pharaoh asked him about the words which he had spoken (29) and he answered, "It is so." He said that out of the loins of that man there would come forth a great man, who would shine in faith and wisdom. And the heaven of the heaven would be under his hand and the destruction of Egypt would come through him. Within forty days he would be in his mother's womb.

And that is the word that was said "Gad's troop shall overcome him."

45. And what the angel had said unto Bileam "A star will arise from Jacob," this refers to Pineḥas: "And a sceptre shall come from Israel." This refers to Joshua.

46. And their battle-cry was "The Lord is our God the Lord is One."

47. And Bileam fled and he was caught by Zrd son of Kmuel son of the brother of Caleb of the tribe of Judah; and he brought him before Pineḥas, Joshua, and Caleb: and they did not pay heed to his speech.

48. Then arose Rdyh son of Ṣuriel son of Slua and he strengthened himself against him and killed him by the sword.

49. Then Joshua said: "The heart of the avenger of the blood grew hot at the sight of him (Bileam).

(45) At a later period the Samaritans also refer this prophecy to the Taheb, like the Jews. So Tabyah el Doweik, in his commentary to the blessings of Bileam where he says, that this prophecy may be interpreted as referring to the Taheb, but preferably to Pineḥas. Similarly he explains this passage in his treatise on the 2nd kingdom —This application of the verse is very significant. There is no trace of Messianic prophecy in it, as found already in the N. T. story of the star of Magi as later on. See Introduction.

(47—48) Identical story in Samaritan Arab: Joshua, p. 63, and ed. Joynboll. Ch. 5.—In Arab. Book of Joshua: no name is mentioned except the fact that he who killed Bileam is described as belonging to the tribe of Simeon, which had been decimated through action with Midianite women. This explains words of Joshua in v. 49.—Pitron agrees more closely with P.T.—Palest. Targ. to Numb. XXI 8: close parallel, but Pineḥas is the one who kills Bileam.—A much closer parallel is found in the Zohar II. 21B: to the effect that man who captured Bileam was a certain Iliḥ of the tribe of Dan. He brought him before him and killed him there in order to avenge the death of the 24,000 who were, killed in consequence of Bileam's evil advice.—In Pal. Targ. also reference to the confused speech of Bileam.—T. B. Sanhedrin 106a.

(30) Thereupon Pharaoh commanded quickly that the men should separate from the women for forty days P. 163. And they imprisoned the men in one place and the women in another according to his command. (31) And it came to pass after seventeen days of the forty had passed, that a man from the house of Levi went and took the daughter of Levi, the son of Jacob, and she became pregnant with the Master of all flesh, the Master of all mankind, as it is mentioned in the Book Asatir, "Mighty is the tree from which Moses was plucked." (32) And when Jochebed became pregnant with the Master of the flesh, then Plti saw the star of Israel in the ascendant and knew that the mother of the child was pregnant with him. (34) And he said unto Pharaoh, "Thy deed and thy plans which thou hast made have this day become void." So Pharaoh said, "What shall we do?" (35) Plti said to Pharaoh, that he would die through water. And that is evidenced from his statement in the Asatir: "His death will be through water." (36) Then Pharaoh commanded the Egyptians P. 164. that no male child of the Hebrews should remain alive. (37) And he sent the overseers to the midwives, namely, Shifrah and Puah, who attended upon the Hebrew women, and Pharaoh had them brought before him; and he said unto them, that every male child which would be born to the Hebrews, should be killed but that every female child should be kept alive. (38) But Amram was wise and known for his wisdom and intelligence, and he was overseer in the land of Egypt, and did good unto all the people. And Shifrah was the midwife appointed to attend to the tribe of Levi, and Puah was appointed as midwife to the congregation of Israel. (39) And the fear of the Lord entered their hearts, and they did not do as the king of Egypt had commanded them, for there is no peace like the peace of the Messenger—upon whom the peace of God is. And our master Markaḥ—upon whom be the favour of the Lord—

50. On the fourth (Wednesday) they came from the war, on the fifth (Thursday) the elders of the assembly brought the offering of gold, and it was brought up to the Tent of the Assembly.

51. And there came a voice of the Living [saying] "No Moabite nor Ammonite shall enter the community of God."

52. And the women that were taken captive were killed.

Chapter XI. [Death of Moses and Prophecy.]

1. And God said unto Moses, "Take to thyself Joshua the son of Nun, a man in whom there is the spirit and set him before Eleazar the priest and before all the congregation in the fortieth year in the tenth month."

(51) See above X. 28 and below XI. 17.

XI.

(1) "May they never be lacking etc..." This phrase is probably one of the many pious exclamations inserted by the author of the Asatir; unless it is to be taken as one made by Moses concerning his children. This passage, moreover, is open to a different interpretation. It agrees curiously with Josephus IV. 8. 2. 180: "There is one source of happiness, the favour of God." cf Sibyl. II. 170—171.—Already 4 Ezra, XIII. 40ff. mentions the ten tribes hidden away in distant lands.—Midrash of the 10 Exiles (Jellinek IV, 133 ff.).—Bousset, The Antichrist Legend London 1896 p. 103.

—Here is evidently a reference to the old legend according to which the children of Moses were then separated from the rest of the Israelites and sent away to a distant country in the desert to live there a pure life. They will emerge thence at the end of days, and come with the Taheb or Moses Redivivus at their head to revive the time of God's favour. Thus runs the Sam. Legend. The Jewish counterpart is found in the story of Eldad, the Danaite (ed. Abraham Epstein, Pressburg 1891, p. 42 ff.) a host of other legends which have appeared round the story of the disappearance of the children of Moses. (Jellinek, Beth Hamidrash, II. 10 ff. and VI. 102 ff.)

said in his exalted saying, that the Messenger said unto the children P. 165. of Israel before he died, "O Gershom and Eleazar, ye are the two sons upon whom I have commanded peace." And the Lord knows that from this day to the last day, they are happy believers in the Holy Law. And the Lord—may He be exalted—is favourable unto them through the prayer of their father, according to his word in the Asatir, "May they never be lacking in happinees and faith!"

And the Taheb will only arise from among them. And know that the cause of their being hidden away from the sight of the creatures and their absence from among the children of Israel was only in consequence of the request of their father to the Lord God,—may He be exalted. For he—upon whom be peace—saw all the creatures and the generations from the Day of Creation until the last Day of Requital, and he saw the days of the Fanuta. P. 166. And he saw also everything that would happen to Israel and all the great oppression which would come upon them, and he asked of the Lord that his children should be exempted from all this, and that nothing should happen to them of that which would happen to the children of Israel. And the Lord did according to his request and he hid them until the day of the advent of the Taheb, who will arise from among them. And he will come with a mighty host from the eastern side.

O, may mine eye behold them when they will come with the Taheb among them, and the pillar and cloud covering them and the angels with them! I pray of the Lord that he may cause this time to draw near and that the day be not distant but nigh! And of this there are many things to be told which would be too long here. And God knows. P. 167.

(to Chapter XI.)

(4) And after that came the command to the Master of the flesh, Moses, that he was to write the scroll of the Holy

2. And Moses did so with great joy and delight, as if he had been one of his sons—may they never be lacking in happiness and faith!

3. And Moses began to copy out the Holy Law.

4. And God said to him: "Go up the Mount Abarim and see the land of Canaan and fix its boundaries round about. And this is the beginning of the boundary.

5. In the East from Ḳori to Ivai, and the boundary of the land in the South from the shore of the Salt Sea eastward.

6. Ascending into the midst of the land: because he said that the Valley was within the boundary from Akrabim passing on to Ṣin; and now it is in the middle of the land and it continues unto the town which is called today El Ḳdr.

7. The boundary of Paran is from the side of 'Aṣmonah until the river of Egypt going on to Sukkoth passing on inside the boundary until Shaḳi of Egypt.

8. Going down to the sea and then going up to Ṭrss. It turns towards the mountain and ye shall espy unto yourself [the mountain of God] in the midst of the land.

(4) The following geographical description of the boundaries is based on Numb. XXXIV. 4—12, but the author has taken great liberties, the same way as he did with the kings of Edom above Ch. VIII, 7 ff. He has, moreover, substituted new names for old and the text has suffered also in the hands of copyists, so that in many places it is quite unintelligible. The P.T. ad. loc. offers a close parallel and also in P. T. Deut. I, 7a similar tracing of the boundaries of Palestine with the substitution of new names for old is found.—See brief description of boundaries Josephus Antiq. V. 1. 22 (80) ff. and Sam. Book of Joshua ed. Gaster ch. XIV, 1 which agrees in the main with Josephus.

Law and he was to read it before the whole congregation of Israel. Then He said unto him, "Get thee upon this Mount Abarim and behold the land of Canaan, and its boundaries all around." And Moses went up and beheld the land of Canaan and its corners and its boundaries, as is mentioned in the Book of Numbers, Ch. XXXIV, "And the mighty prophet went down with joy because he beheld the Mount Garizim Bethel, the most Holy of all the places of the land." And he was in great sorrow because he could not go up to it.

(15) And after that, on the third day, he began to copy the Holy Law and he finished it on the fourth. (16) And he brought it to P. 168. the tent of the Covenant on the fifth day. (17) And the voice of the Living came down from the cloud of glory, saying, (18) "Completed is thy work, O perfect One. This is thy last day." And the explanation of this is: The word of proclamation came out of the cloud of glory, that is the glory of the Lord, "O thou hast performed perfectly thy good deed. This is thy last day." Make known to the generations what has been revealedto Moses, the mighty prophet, even what his master had told him. And nothing of this is found in the Law. (Up to v. 26 there is no commentary. The author merely repeats the words of the original text.)

26. Twenty six corresponding to twenty six! May He be praised, He, Who sees all that is hidden and revealed! May He be exalted, Adam, Noah, Abraham, Moses. Upon them be peace for ever!

Know that just as there were from Adam unto Moses twenty six prophets, so also from the beginning of the Fanuta to the time of the Taheb will arise twenty five kings and the Taheb will be the twenty sixth. Praised be He, Who is Omnipotent, and may His name be sanctified!

9. In the North Ḥmṭ on the river of Ḥanoḥiah which is Zifronah, and goes on to Hazar 'Enan.

10. And from Ḥazar 'Enan to Shefamah which is Askofiah unto the Arbelah.

11. And its borders go down and reach unto the eastern shore of the sea of Kinnereth.

12. And the mountain (Ṭbris) in the west which can be seen from all the four sides.

13. And the prophet went down in joy and in grief.

14. He rejoiced because he had seen the beauty of the land, but he grieved because he was not allowed to enter.

15. And he began to copy out the Law on the third (Tuesday) and he finished it on the fourth (Wednesday).

16. And he went into the Tent on the fifth (Thursday).

17. And there came down the voice of the Living from the cloud of glory.

(15—16) Tabaḥ: Moses copied the Law on the 3rd and went up on the 4th. (This may mean either Tuesday—Wednesday, or 3rd and 4th of the month. —Arab. Book of Joshua p. 8: Many more details are given like in "Death of Moses" further on.— Josephus Antiq. IV. 8. 49 (327): Moses died on the 1st of Adar.— On the 7th day of Adar Moses was born and died; Pal. Targ. Deut. XXXIV. 5.—Seder Olam Rabba. Ch. 10 (p. 41—42, ed. Ratner) interpreted: "the Law for 36 days from 1st Shebat, to 6th Adar, on which day he is ordered to go up the Mount and on the 7th Adar he died." The Hebrew word באר is translated by Samaritans as "copying," by Jews as "interpreting" (as in Deuteronomy I, 5).— Moses died on the 7th day of the month of Adar; T. B. Kiddoushin 38a, T. B. Megilla 13b.—Jeraḥmeel 48. 17: Moses dies 7th Adar.—Diḳduke Hatamim ed. S. Baer and H. L. Strack Leipzig 1879 § 70, p. 58: Moses died 7th Adar, on the Sabbath.—Moses died 7th Adar; Albiruni p. 273.—Died on Sabbath afternoon: Seder Hadorot p. 92. —v. Baer Abodoth Israel p. 265.

(17) See Ch. X. 28. 51 and Introd. for Mandaean parallel 1 f.—Pal. Targ.

SAMARITAN STORY
OF THE DEATH OF MOSES.

The Samaritan story of the Death of Moses (from the Samaritan Chronicle in my Cod. 1168 f. 1 b—8 b).

For the literature referring to this chapter, the parallelism with Josephus and its relation to the pseudepigraphic literature, see Introduction where this has been treated fully. Various details in the beginning are found in the Asatir Ch. XI, such as the writing of the Law, the taking leave of the people, and the Prophecy. The phrase of approval by God, and the announcement of Moses' last day have been referred to in connection with Markah. The last sentence in which Moses is lifted up and sees the whole world, as it were, under his feet, is strongly reminiscent of the wonderful vision of the Hellenist poet Ezekiel (see above).

1732 A.

Chapter concerning the Death of our Master Moses, son of Amram, upon whom be prayer and peace.

In the year two thousand and seven hundred and ninety four years from the creation of the world, and in the fortieth year of the going out of the children of Israel from the land of Egypt, in the eleventh month on the first day of the month, began our Master Moses,—upon whom be the peace of God,—to copy out the holy Torah from the book which was written by the finger of God; perfectly he copied it, rolled it into a scroll, and divided it into sections (Ḳiṣṣim) and portions (Parashot) by the holy spirit: for thus it was (found) in the above mentioned book. And he finished the copy of this holy Torah from the above mentioned original book in thirty days, and he read it in the sight and hearing of the Elders of his community and of the priests, the sons of Levi, and he gave it unto them. And after that he went to the Tent of Assembly and opened the Ark of Testimony and he placed the Book of the Law which was written by the finger of God in it,

18. "Completed is thy work O Perfect One. This is thy last day (that which God has allowed), thou who beholdest the generations·" (i. e.) that which Moses the great Prophet had revealed by the permission of his Master.

19. Therefore it is said "And he beholds the vision of God."

20. And he foretold what would happen in the next three thousand two hundred and four years, as is told in (the section) which begins "When ye beget children and children's children," the beginning of the Fanuta, the gate of the backsliding.

XXXIV. 5: The berath kola; (i. e. bath kol) Fell down from Heaven.—cf. X. 28; X. 51.

(18) This sentence is quoted verbatim in poem of Jacob ha Rabban. See Introduction.

(20) Arabic Book of Joshua p. 22. 23, refers to the Song of Moses Deut. XXXII. and suggests that it contains revelations of future events, but gives none of the details found here: So Abul Hassan al Suri (ca. 1030) in his Al Tabah., and other Samaritan Commentators on the blessings of Jacob and of Moses. None, however, contain this Prophecy found in the Asatir, although they seem to hint at it, for they say Moses revealed the time of "Favour," and the day of exile, and also foretells the flood of fire and day of requital and reward, and the happiness when God returns back to them. This entirely corresponds with the general outline of future events, for which the Asatir gives definite details.—3,204 years. This corresponds to the year 2,796 from Creation. Samaritan date.—The confusion of the dates concerning Biblical chronology and the differences are so profound that only a few examples are mentioned to show the utter impossibility to harmonise them. Book of Jubilees: 2,450; Book of the Bee ch. XXX p. 65: (30): 3,860; Josephus 2,550 (2,530); LXX. 3,859; T. 2,706.— In the Assumption of Moses the date is given 2,500 or "according to Eastern reckoning" 2,700, and 200 since Exodus from Phoenicia. The last figure but one approximates to the Samaritan calculation.—Apoc. of Baruch: Hebrew calculation of 2,700 seems to be the nearest. This calculation of the Asatir differs from Sam. Chronology and rests upon another text or another calculation.— For the form and contents of this Prophecy see the Aramaic prophecy ascribed to the high priest Ishmael, best preserved in the Pirke Hechalot ch. VI. 4. ed. S. A. Wertheimer Jerusalem 1910.

by the side of the two Tablets upon which were engraven the Ten Words, and placed upon the Ark the covering (kaporet) which no one could lift from the Ark up to this very day. There he bowed down and worshipped before the Lord in front of the Ark of Testimony. And the Lord whose holy name be praised, spake unto him, from between the two Cherubim.

[f. 2 a] "O Thou whose work has been perfect, nigh is now the last day," and thus He informed him, that the day of his death had arrived. This happened on the morning of the fifth day, the day of the New Moon of the twelfth month of the above-mentioned year. Then the exalted prophet went to his tent, which he had set up outside the camp; his tongue was praising in hymns his Master and saying: "Unto Thee, O Lord, belong the righteousness and the judgment. Thou who dost not show favour, either to a prophet or to those who are meritorious before Thee? O Thou who art wise; thou art righteous and just, a faithful God."

And after that stood up the exalted prophet—upon whom be the peace of God—and prayed to his Master. When he had finished his prayer, he called Joshua his servant and told him all the words which the Lord had spoken to him; and he said unto him "O my servant, go to the house of the priethood and tell them of this, and tell Eleazar, Ithamar and Pinehas that they come hither quickly so that I may be able to see them." And when the master Joshua son of Nun heard from the prophet these words at the door of the Tent of Assembly (f. 2b), he went forth quickly to the holy sanctuary, and stood before it weeping and called the three priests. And they heard his call; they came out of it quickly, and they beheld our master Joshua standing there weeping and the tears of his eyes washing his face. So they said unto him: "O thou Minister of the Excellence of the children of Eber, what is the matter and wherefore art thou weeping? and why is thy heart

21. There will arise a man from the Levites; his name will be 'Azrz son of Fani and the beginning of the strife will be by his hand.
22. And he will add a sanctuary in his days.
23. He will exchange the sanctuary of the Hebrews for a rebellious (strange) sanctuary. He will throw division in the midst of the assembly.

Another one similar in character, also in Aramaic short sentences ascribed to Rabban Gamliel is fully discussed in the Introd. p. 93. Other forms of such Aramaic prophecies connected with the High priests Simon the Pious and Johanan, see Megillath Taanith ch. XI and T. B. Sotah f. 33a. T. J. Sotah IX. f. 24b. these are similar to the Asatir in their syntactical construction and in the use of Aramaic.—If Charles' hypothesis is correct, then rhymed prophecies were in the original of the Book of Enoch. Their real form would be similar to that found in the Prophecy.—The Pal. Targ. I Deut. XXXIV. 1—3. contains a succinct history beginning with Jephtah continuing without historical sequence to the time of Gog and Armilos and the Angel Michael who will redeem the people. The same survey is found here from the point of view of the Samaritans. They run on parallel lines each leading to the same final redemption, and period of freedom (Introd.)—Moses ordered to write down this eschatology in the Apocalypse of Abraham XXIII. 32. Similar eschatological pronouncement Jubilees XXIII. 18 ff.—Ezekiel the poet. The vision of Moses sitting on the throne and with his view encompassing the world rolling under his feet. F. Delitzsch, zur Geschichte der jüdischen Poesie etc. Leipzig 1836. p. 211 ff.

(21) The Prophecy starts with the beginning of the Fanuta, the hiding of the temple vessels, in the time of the high priest Uzi. The Levite referred to here, under the name of Azrz, as the head of the Rebellion, is none other than Eli. The Samaritans write his name איילי for which the cryptogiam עזרן nd has been substituted by way of the permutation of the letters. This method is already known in the Talmud and probably also in the Sibylline, and above all in the Samaritan Philacteries v. Gaster Studies and Texts p. 387 ff. This procedure is already used by Aquila and the LXX to Jeremiah 25. 6 and 51. 7. etc. (see Dornseif, das Alphabet in Mystik and Magie, Leipzig 1922, p. 136 f.) and so also in the Targum ad. loc.—With slight variations this passage occurs also in Sifre to Deut. XXXIV. 1. Others surveys are those in Ps. Philo, Jubilees, Ch. 15. Assumption of Moses. See references in Introduction.

(23) This refers to the establishment of the sanctuary in Shiloh, which the Samaritans describe as a heretical and vile sanctuary.

broken?" And he answered them and said in a mournful voice: "My Master the prophet Moses, the exalted Messenger, is going to die this day: and this thing is bitter unto us and hard to bear and surely not pleasing to your souls nor to mine." And when the priests had heard this of Joshua, they grieved and they went to Moses with their faces troubled and their hearts broken. And when they came near to him they quickly bowed down before him. And Pineḥas the son of Eleazar—upon whom be the peace of God—held the trumpet in his right hand and stood weeping before him. Then he told him. "Go thou and thy uncle (f. 3a) Ithamar to the gate of the Tent of Assembly, and blow the trumpets, so that all the people should hear and come hither and stand before me, so that they obtain (the greeting of) peace from me."

And when these pious ones had heard this, they went quickly to the door of the Sanctuary, and blew the trumpets according to his holy command. And when the people heard the sound of the trumpets they trembled and were frightened and said: "What is this sound of trumpets which is so loud? It is neither the time of the sacrifice, nor is it the time for journeying." And they rose all up quickly in fear and after enquiry were told the reason of this ocurrence.

Bitter was the hour when they learned of it and when it was told to them, that the exalted prophet Moses, son of Amram, of the highest rank was going to die. They all gathered themselves together and went out and came to the door of the prophet's tent, the heads of the people and the judges and overseers and the priests and the seventy elders, and stood before the mighty prophet, they stood in proper order and in perfect reverence. And the mighty Messenger stood up and he told them distinctly what the Lord had told him (f. 3b). And he made a high throne and mounted upon it, so that he might see all the people which had gathered there before

24. The order of turning away and arbitrariness Kṛṭm (of) Benjamin will be established among them.

25. "In the world" through the power of the house of Judah diverse statutes will be annulled.

26. Hear O Lord the voice of Judah.

27. He will build the tower of shame with might.

28. The people will be praying for Truth.

29. Will be oppressed through the son who is born of a harlot.

30. He will be ... like the enchanter Bileam.

31. In his days the worship of strange gods will be established.

32. And within a short time the unholy sanctuary will be destroyed by the hand of a nation of a hard face.

33. And those of the house of Shmh (God ?) and of the house of Fanyh (i. e. turning away, rebellious) will be scattered throughout the earth. And because the congregation is guilty, they (the conquerers) will dwell in their place in great arrogance.

(24) Kṛṭm evidently refers to Shemuel or, much more likely, Saul, as he is described as of the tribe of Benjamin.—The name of Kṛṭm is a cryptogram like Azrz.

(25) Refers to David. See also Assumption of Moses II. 3.

(27) Refers to the building of the Temple of Ṣion cf. above ch. III. v. 13, where Sion is called Shame (Gifna).

(29) This refers to Solomon born of Bathsheba, whom they describe as a harlot.

(30) The witchcraft of Bileam refers to Solomon whose great wisdom is described in the Bible and is explained by them as the result of sorcery. Solomon also built temples for the idol-worship of his heathen wives. The word בראה is obscure. Abisha skipped it when reading. See above in the Transliteration. In the Pitron מורר is substituted, i. e. rebellious. It may mean, "the soothsayer," or misspelt for ברה=son of.

(32) Refers to the destruction of the Temple trough the Chaldeans. The words "A nation of hard face" are taken from Deut. XXVIII. 50.—V. Jubilees XXIII. 23.

(33) Refers to the evil deeds both of Judah and Israel and the occupation of the land by foreign

him. They were looking at him. He—upon whom be the peace of God—was weeping and the tears rolled down from his eyes to his loins like dew upon the seed. And he showed them the glory of the Commandments and the high station of the faith and its decrees and statutes. And everyone of them heard his voice and hearkened to his speech.

And the master Joshua listened to everything that came out of his exalted mouth and he, may the peace of the Lord be upon him, stood there like the moon in its fulness, instructing and teaching his people the children of Israel. And his weeping went up to the heart of the heavens and he cried with a loud voice: "O ye dwellers of the cave, O ye the meritorious ones of the world! Does your spirit know what is in store for your children?

"Oh thou son of Terah, thou the root of the Perfect and Meritorious Ones! Dost thou know that the plants of thy garden which thou hast planted are being spoilt through sins and rebellion?

"Oh thou Isaac, the sacrificed and sanctified (f. 4a) whose blood had not been spilt! Doth thy spirit know that thy inheritance which has been established through thy merit, is going to destruction through sin?

"Oh thou Jacob, father of the favoured tribes! Doth thy spirit, the purified one, know that the tribes which issued from thee and were saved through me from Egypt by the power of my Maker and heard His voice crying out from the midst of fire the Ten Words, and which saw all that had been done for them and how the mouth of Bileam was changed so that he said: How goodly are thy tents. O Jacob, thy dwelling places, oh Israel! that all these good things will be covered up by the curse; and that the Favour will become hidden, and the sanctuary of the Lord will be hidden away, and Mount Garizim will be defiled and the Fanuta spread everywhere, and that no one will be found zealous for God?"—And he—the peace of God be upon him—testified against the people with his words

34. The community in turning to strife will persist and the land will be inherited by the chosen ones of Alinis.

35. There will be peace in the world, freedom, might, honour, and a life of happiness.

36. And after that a change in the Writing will be made.

37. And a new wording they will produce out of the old.

38. And the Lord thy God will bring thee up into the land which thy fathers have inherited and thou shalt inherit it.

39. And Luzah will be rebuilt.

40. There will be a Jubilee in rejoicing and (after that) there will be a second turning away.

41. And transgression will be seen among the pure people, but at the end of days

42. On the holy hill he will destroy the images and he will break the idols.

armies. All these names are probably cryptograms as the result of a peculiar permutation of letters.

(34) This refers to the first return under the priests who came back from Babylon.

(35) Referring to the same period probably; See XII. 24.—Jubilees XXIII. 28 ff.—Agrees with Sibyl. Or. III. 573 ff. and 657 f. A more materialistic view, ibid. V. 281 ff. V. XII. 24.

(36) Refers to Ezra who changed the script.

(37) In A the words מלין חדתן (B, Pitron—)have been corrupted into מלית עדתן.—A altered the text so as to differ from and contradict the Samaritan contention.

(38) This probably refers to the 2nd return under Abdiel when a large number returned from the exile.

(39) Rebuilding of Sichem and of the temple on Mount Garizim.

(40) The author referring to the time of a Jubilee being re-established by the second return of Abdiel after which again another turning away will come to pass (v. 41).

(42) It is very difficult to refer to any definite period when such

and began rebuking, them saying "Ye have been rebellious with God and still more so [you will be] after my death. And thou whom I have brought (f. 4b) out of Egypt, my strength and my song, let not my good actions for thee be lost, so that thou perishest after my death; for I am going the way of man, and my heart is frightened of that which I have seen concerning thee: I am now standing in the position of a prophet and I behold what will happen unto thee and unto the generations after thee. Happy shalt thou be Israel if thou hearkenest unto me and what I now speak unto thee by my mouth and my tongue. And know that three times did the Lord say unto me "Come up to me," and I went up, and I came down with the Law and with the Tablets; and at this time now my burden is being taken off me, which I have inherited from the Father of all flesh; but ye shall not doubt my return; and now before my death I will bless you with a pious (beautiful) blessing founded upon the Name of the Lord thy God."

And all the people were standing and kept in perfect order in front of him; and he looked at them and blessed them each tribe separately, and he began to command them saying: the commandments and statutes of God ye shall keep, and ye shall not change it (p. 5a) lest there should happen to come upon you the Fanuta, and destruction should seize you.

Then he turned towards Eleazar the priest the son of his brother who was standing at his right hand, and he said unto him "O my brother's son; O thou who art the "Khalif" of God; O thou who art the heir to the high priesthood; now thou hast been placed in this position where the Lord is thy possession; keep it fully." Then he turned from him to his brother's son Ithamar, and he said unto him "O thou in whose hands is the keeping of the watch of the Levites, and all the goodly vessels, keep thy priesthood and the holy vessels which are in thy hand and make thyself worthy before the Judge of judges."

Chapter XII. [Oracle.]

1. A prince will arise with a strong hand for ten [years], and the proud nation Nds (or Aminds) will come in his days.

2. A prince will arise with might from his people for five [years] and he will not be exalted.

3. A crowned prince will arise, of evil repute: in his days they (he) will be destroyed through the hand of strangers.

images on the Holy Mountain have been destroyed or whether the text should not be differently translated.

(42) Concerning the cult of Zeus and temples and statues in on Mt. Garizim, see. A. B. Cook Zeus vol. II, 2. p. 888 ff.

XII. Ch.

(1) See Introduction, where the history of the Oracles has been dealt with fully from the oldest form found in the book of Daniel down to the latest of mediaeval oracles in connection with the Sibyl of Tibur. Reference has also been made there between this set of Oracles and especially the final portion with the various Messianic traditions and their relation to the Bileam saga and its further development. It is a hopeless task to identify these names with any historical personage. The Samaritans themselves have failed to find a satisfactory interpretation of this oracle. As the parallelism between the Asatir and the Sibyl of Tibur is so remarkable, I have limited myself to refer to it here almost exclusively. It may be mentioned that at the same time, the Samaritan writers seem fully conversant with this oracle as shown in Introduction.—In the Asumption of Moses (ed. Ferrar 1917) Ch. II. there is a list of kings of Judah and Israel and the action of the latter is similar to that given in the following oracle. But this may either refer to the one or they other, both being held in abhorrence by the Samaritans, with rare exceptions; for they considered them to be wicked and idolaters.—Josephus Antiq. X. 8. 4. 143 reckons 21 Kings from David to Captivity.—Assumption of Moses II. 316, mentions 19 and 20 (?) kings of Israel and Judah up to the destruction of the Temple.—The Samaritans themselves no longer understand the meaning of כלי. It could also mean: complete, or the whole of. Aminds, interpreted by the Samaritans, as "abominable nation," a metaphor probably for "Greeks" a cryptogram for יון (?)

(3) Tiburtine 4: According to Paris recension of Matthew where "barbarian nations" are mentioned missing in Sackur.

His eye lit upon the master Pineḥas who was standing at his left, and he said unto him, "Thy zeal has been manifest when thou didst behold a man turning away from the way of truth and sinning, thou didst rise and smite him according to thy excellent habit." Then he turned his eyes which were not dimmed to the master Joshua son of Nun his servant and he said unto him: "Be strong and of good courage (f. 5 b) for thou shalt bring this community into the land which is the most perfect of all the lands, which the Lord has sworn to give as an inheritance to the seed of the root of the Meritorious Ones; and may the Lord who prospers those who pray unto him assist thee and grant thee divine prosperity."

After that with his mighty countenance he turned towards the house of the priesthood the sons of Levi, and he said unto them: "Keep your priesthood and all the holy things which are in your hands; ye are taking the portions of God, and you eat them in those places where Israelites are found; and this is the reward of your service unto you and unto your seed after you; ye shall not defile the holy things so that Belial should cause you to act treacherously through his treachery." Then he turned with his word to the heads of the tribes, and he said unto them: "Beware lest ye turn away from the statutes which I have established; so that there shall not be destroyed that which has been built up by me through my holy teaching." And then he spoke to the judges to every one of them singly "Ye shall do no iniquity in judgment; and ye shall take no bribery; and judge righteously between every man and his neighbour."

And to the scribes he said: "Teach the community the laws and statutes and commandments with good care, as the righteous and the just has commanded, and each one of you shall watch carefully upon his station (f. 6 a) And this is the end of my presence with you, and ye shall not doubt that I will return from Mount Nebo unto you." Then he

4. A prince will arise strong in truth: in his days the salvation of the community will be great.

5. A crowned prince will arise: in his days the yoke of iron will return.

6. A prince will arise mighty in wealth: in his days the house of worship (?) will be built.

7. A prince will arise who will dwell in Luzah and Aminds will be in trouble.

8. A prince will arise mighty in the knowledge of the truth: the people will rejoice.

9. A crowned prince will arise: he will walk in darkness: his days will be of trouble.

10. A prince will arise mighty in wealth: rulers will perish in his days in secret. A hundred will flee to the borders of Sichem.

11. A prince will arise [Gog] (he) will perish in grief: in his days the people will turn back to sin and they will forsake the covenant (or, they will turn back and sin against the covenant and be punished).

12. A prince will arise: tribulation and weariness will be before this.

(4) Tiburtine 7.

(5) To this many parallels of wicked kings can be found. So ibid: 13 or 22.

(6) This passage may also be translated "the house of worship". —cf. Tibur 3.

(7) עמי נדם according to the Samaritans is interpreted "Abominable nation being a deliberate change for עמינדב n. pr. meaning "generous nation" probably a cryptic form.

(8) cf. Tibur 11.

(9) cf. Tibur 13.

(11) The nation Gog is taken as typical for froward, wicked or cruel. The word Gog is missing in Cod. B., but it inserts it in v. 13. —cf. Tibur 18. In addition to the remarks concerning Gog, Introd. should like to add that Esther, the Greek Lucian ed. (ed. Lagarde) instead of Agag in the Hebrew text there appears Gogos, i. e. Gog.

(12) Simple forms of Messianic Woes. More fully elaborated later

lifted up his voice and spoke with a high voice, O "Gershom and Eleazer my sons, unto you be the blessing of everlasting peace from me."

And all the people stood in front of him him and the tears were bedewing their faces, and his weeping was greater than theirs, for he saw what would happen unto them through their corruption.

And when he had finished speaking with them he, upon whom be the peace of the Lord, stood upon his feet and looked at them and repeated the greeting of Peace unto them. Then he hastened to go up to Mount Nebo to die there; and our master the priest Eleazar supported him on the right hand, for the Lord had exalted him, and his son Pineḥas supported him on the left side, and Ithamar and Joshua and the whole house of the priesthood walked with him weeping with a loud weeping. And when they reached the foot of Mount Nebo, then the heads of the tribes drew near together and kissed his hands, and the whole community of Israel were shouting "Peace unto him." And then Eleazar and Ithamar and Pineḥas drew near and fell down to his feet and kissed his right hand and his left hand. [f. 6 b] And after that his servant Joshua drew near and kissed his face and his right hand and his left hand; and then bowed down and knelt, and began to address him with "Peace" unto him.

"May peace by upon thee O thou who hast rent the heights. Peace unto thee thou who didst tread upon the fire. Peace unto thee O thou who didst draw near unto the thick cloud. Peace unto thee O thou who was clothed with light. Peace unto thee O thou who didst receive the Law. Peace unto thee O thou to whom the covenant was handed. Peace unto thee O thou whose hymns were so powerful. Peace unto the O thou to whom the Lord spake mouth to mouth. Peace unto thee O thou who art the essence of the Meritorious of the World. Peace unto thee O thou whose glory was not hidden. Bitter unto me is the hour of thy separation."

13. A prince will arise at the end of wickedness: in his days desolation from the land of the mighty a mighty force will bring.

14. A prince will arise who will increase the tribulation of the people.

15. A prince will arise through wickedness of sorcery: the Temple of Sichem will be burnt by his hand.

16. A prince will arise, Gog, after these.

17. A prince will arise with tribulation: the land of the Hebrews he will lay waste.

18. A prince will arise through modesty (prayer?): in his days he will be wise.

19. A prince will arise, the son of sin: in his days the false sanctuary will be established at the end because of his evil deeds it will be burned with fire and brimstone.

on in general eschatology see Charles Eschatology and Weber Eschatologie.—Tibur 22.

(13) cf. Tibur 13.—cf. Matthew Paris.

(14) cf. Tibur 13.

(15) cf. Tibur 17.

(16) The appearance of Gog here before the days of the Taheb, and the wars which will ensue, leading up to the final victory of Israel, have been fully treated (Introduction).

(17) The word פרוש does not occur in the Samaritan. It is probably a corruption from בדוש, i. e. violence, tribulation. The initial פ must have been read like ב as in v. 21 in the word פגמה = ביומיה and ד has easily been mistaken for ר.

(18) Tiburtine 23.

(19) Ab Ḥasda in Tabaḥ f. 508 interprets Deut. XXXII. 22 as follows: This verse refers to the two places on which the rebellious rely and seek them, and that is Jerusalem, towards which the Jews are turning and made it a place of worship. A fire will come out from before God against this city and brimstone and salt of which it is said: (Deut. 29. 23). "And that the whole land thereof is brimstone and salt and burning, that it is not sown nor beareth, nor any grass groweth therein." And is evident from his earlier saying (Deut. XXX. 22). "And shall consume the earth and its increase." The wording is absolutely identical

And when he finished these words, then the exalted prophet lifted up his beautiful voice to those who were surrounding him, and he said unto them: "Remain in peace, and from this day on I shall have no further intercourse with you."

And when the people heard this word then they felt sorely grieved, and they lifted up their voices and said: "By thy life, O thou O prince of the prophets, tarry with us an hour longer. By thy life, O thou Messenger of God, stay with us just for one short while." And the Lord proproclaimed unto him saying "Hasten." (f. 7 a.) And the people never ceased weeping, and shouting aloud they said "O thou glory of the prophets, tarry with us for one hour." And the angels of heaven shouted to him with loud shouting "Quicken thy step O Moses and come according to the command of the word of the God of Gods;" and when the people realised this word which caused them so much pain, and they knew that he was going away from them, then they said with one mouth "Go in peace O prophet; go in peace O thou the of the house of Levi, go in peace O thou to whom the Lord God hath revealed everything that was hidden and open."

And the prophet Moses, the son of Jochebed and Amram went up to Mount Nebo, with great honour crowned with light, and all the angels came to meet him. And in the hour when he became separated from the people and he hastened to go up to the top of the mountain, then the whole congregation of Israel shouted with a great and bitter shout which went up to the heart of heaven from the earth. And the Messenger—upon whom be the peace of the Lord— went up slowly, slowly, and he looked back to those whom he had left behind and the tears were trickling down from his eyes for his people when he separated himself from them. And he grieved in his heart (saying). "How will they fare after me." (f.7b) He was like a loving woman who leaves her suckling child. And he blessed them with a

20. A prince will arise, one who abolishes circumcision: in his days he will suck from the abundance of the sea.

21. A prince will arise: in his days the community of abomination (Aminds) will again be scattered in the land of Gb'alah while Israel does valiantly and the top of the hill will be in glory, and faith established.

22. A prince will arise from the section (portion) of the Lawgiver. From the West the messenger of peace (comes) to the gate of glory. The community will rejoice; for they will worship our Lord in peace.

23. A prince will arise who will spoil the [gentile] nation and "will come out of (rule from) Jacob and will destroy the remnant of the town."

24. A prince will arise who will write the Law in truth, the rod of miracles in his hand. There will be light and no darkness.

with the Oracle. Tabyah el Doweik in his treatise on the second Kingdom adduces the same argument as the VIth proof, but in a slightly different form and he does not mention distinctly the burning of the Temple. But on the other hand in Proof IV he interprets the prophecy of Bileam, Numb. XXII. 17 ff. in a manner which shows his dependence also on the Asatir XII. 21. See also Introduction concerning this portion of Bileam's prophecy.—Sibyl XII. 28 ff.

(20) Literal phrase taken from Hebrew text. Deut. XXXIII. 19, but the passage seems to be corrupt and the spelling is entirely phonetic e. g. בשפע = בשפה.

(21) This verse seems to reflect in a different form the same outlook as given in the Prophecy above XI. 41 42.—The word פינמיה has no meaning. Probably a corruption from ביומיה i. e. in his days, which occurs often in this Oracle. Initial פ was probably pronounced ב like פרוש = ברוש in v. 17.

(22) Deuter: XXXIII. 21.—It is noteworthy that both in the Asatir and in the Samaritan Targum, ed. Walton Hebrew words were retained untranslated. Brüll gives a translation.—In the P. T. it refers to Moses who is to come back and lead the people in the time to come.—Tibur 23.

(24) A full description of the Time of the Taheb and the signs of his advent in the poem of Abisha son

choice blessing, full of mysteries, rejoicing at the call of his Master and looking up to the top of Mount Nebo. There he beheld the rows of angels resting there, and the community of the children of Israel were standing at he foot of the mountain and they lifted up their eyes to look at him and he likewise—may peace be upon him—did also look at them. Bitter was the hour in which the prophet was covered up by a thick cloud and was lifted up beyond the ken of the eye. And the angels rejoiced and were delighted. They came down from heaven with hymns and they praised and thanked God, lauding and magnifying Him with honour. And the Lord opened the light of his eyes and he beheld the four corners of the world and he praised the Lord of the world.

Great was that hour in which Moses beheld the boundaries of the land, the inheritance of the people. And the Lord revealed unto him the ordinances of the day of requital and all that will happen [as described] in his mighty oration. He therefore did not fear death, which is the passing out of the soul from this world, and he lifted up his eyes (f. 8 a) and he beheld Mount Garizim Bethel Luzah. And he bowed down and prostrated himself on his face and he turned in his prostration towards it. And when he rose from the prostration, he beheld a cave with the door open. When he saw it open he praised the Merciful One and the Gracious One and he went into that cave and he turned his face towards Mount Sifra and he laid himself down to sleep upon the ground. And the Lord let fall upon him a deep sleep and his holy spirit went out with the breath; and the angels of the Lord were ordered to take it up, as befitted his greatness and his countenance. And the days of his life were-as is written in the holiest of teachings —one hundred and twenty years. Of these he spent in Egypt twenty, in Midian sixty, and forty in the wilderness, and all of them in great honour which cannot be surpassed, in prayers and fasting and in goodly knowledge.

25. May the Lord hasten this: and happy is he who will see it and will reach [that time] Blessed be our God forever, blessed be His name forever.

26. Twenty-six corresponding to twenty-six. Praised be He who knows the hidden and the revealed, may He be exalted, Adam, Noah, Abraham, Moses, upon them may peace be everlasting.

of Pineḥas (Cowley, pp. 511—519 and Merx, DerTaheb ef. my review in "Studies and Texts" p. 638 ff. — Concerning this rod and its Messianic significance see above note to Asatir III. 25.—The vague allusions to the future time of happiness and redemption agree with the Sibylline Oracles III. 282—285, 367—380, 573—595, 702—731, 740—760, 767—794. See also above XI. 35.

(25) In the colophon 26 is given as the final number: evidently these lines must be counted as the last of the 26 stanzas.

And at his death his eye had not grown dim nor had his sap vanished.

And as to our master Joshua his praise grew mighty and his throne became exalted, and he became filled with the spirit of wisdom; for he who was the flower of all that breathes, had placed his hand upon him; may the peace of the Lord be upon him.

And this is the end of all that we have found of the record of the death of the Messenger (f. 8 b) Moses, son of Amram. May the prayer and the peace be upon him and upon his forefathers.

LIST OF ABBREVIATIONS.

Albiruni: Ed. Sachau.
Algazi: Toledot Adam, Venice 1600.
Anonym. Chron.: Anonymi Chronologica, ed. B. G. Niebuhr, Bonn 1831.
Anon. Poem: Samaritan MS.
Aptowitzer: V. Aptowitzer, Kain und Abel, Wien-Leipzig 1922.
Armen. Adamschr.: Die Apocryphen Gnostischen Adamschriften aus dem Armenischen, übersetzt von E. Preuschen, Gießen 1900.
Assumptio Mosis:
— ed. R. H. Charles, London 1897 (see also Charles, Apocrypha and Pseudepigrapha of the Old Testament, Oxford 1913, Vol. II. p. 407ff.;
— ed. E. Kautzsch, Die Apogryphen und Pseudepigraphen des A. T., Tübingen 1900, Vol. II. p. 311ff.).

Bate. Sib. Or.: H. N. Bate, The Sibylline Oracles, Books III—V, London 1918.
Beer: Abraham Beer, Das Leben Abrahams, Leipzig 1859.
B. of Bee: E. A. Budge, The Book of the Bee, Oxford 1886.

Charles, Eschatology: R. H. Charles, A Critical History of the Doctrine of a Future Life. London 1899.
Chs. of Rabbi Eliezer: The Chapters of Rabbi Eliezer (Pirkê de Rabbi Eliezer);
— ed. pr. Constantinople 1514.
— Trsld. by G. Friedländer, London 1916.
Chron. Pasch.: Chronicon Paschale ed. B. G. Niebuhr, Bonn 1832.

Cowley, Liturgy: A. E. Cowley, The Samaritan Liturgy, Oxford 1909.

F. Delitzsch: Die Geschichte der Jüd. Poesie, Leipzig 1836.

Eisenstein Ozar: I. D. Eisenstein, Ozar Midrashim, New York 1915.

Eisler, Orpheus: R. Eisler, Orphisch-Dyonistische Mysteriengedanken in der Christlichen Antike. Berlin-Leipzig 1925.

Enoch: The Book of Enoch ed. R. H. Charles, Oxford 1912.

Ethiop. Adam: The Ethiopic Book of Adam and Eve ed. and trsld. by I. C. Malan, London 1882.

Fabricius: Codex Pseudepigraphus Veteris Testamenti ed. J. A. Fabricius, Hamburg and Leipzig 1713.

Frankel, Einfluss: Z. Frankel, Über den Einfluss der palästinischen Exegese auf die alexandrinische Hermeneutik. Leipzig 1851.

Freudenthal, Hell. Stud.: J. Freudenthal, Hellenistische Studien, Breslau 1874.

Gaster Exempla:
M. Gaster, The Exempla of the Rabbis, London-Leipzig 1924.
— The Chronicles of Jeraḥmeel, London 1899.
— Studies and Texts, London 1925.

Gedalyah Shalshelet: Gedalyah Aben Yaḥyah, Shalshelet Hakkabbalah, Ed. Pr. Venice 1587.

Geiger Mohammed: A. Geiger, Was hat Mohammed aus dem Judentum aufgenommen? Bonn 1833.

Geiger, Urschrift und Uebersetzungen der Bibel Breslau 1857.

Ginzburg Legends L. Ginzburg, The Legends of the Jews. Philadelphia 1909 ff.

Grünbaum, Neue Beitr.: M. Grünbaum, Neue Beiträge zur Semitischen Sagenkunde, Leiden 1893.
Gruppe, Griech. Myth.: O. Gruppe, Griechische Mythologie, Munich 1906.
Hastings Encycl.: Hasting's Encyclopedia of Religion and Ethics.
Jerahmeel vide Gaster.
Jew. Enc.: Jewish Encyclopedia.
J.R.A.S.: Journal of the Royal Asiatic Society.
Jellinek: A. Jellinek, Beth Hamidrash, Leipzig 1855.
Jubilees: The Book of Jubilees,
— ed. R. A. Charles, London 1902;
— ed. G. A. Ross, London 1917.

Kampers, Kaiseridee: F. Kampers, Die Deutsche Kaiseridee in Prophetie und Sage, Munich 1896.
Kampers, Werdegang: F. Kampers, Vom Werdegang der Abendländischen Kaisermystik, Berlin 1924.
Kebra: Kebra Nagast transld. by C. Bezold, Munich 1905.
[Budge, Queen of Sheba is the English Translation.]

Langlois: V. Langlois, Collection des Historiens de l'Armenie. Paris 1867.

Malif: Samaritan MS. Biblical Questions and Answers.
Mechilta, ed. pr. Constantinople 1515,
— ed. Friedmann, Vienna 1870.
Merx, Taheb: A. Merx, Der Messias oder der Ta'eb der Samaritaner. Gießen 1909.
Meshalma: Commentary to Genesis, Samaritan MS.
Methodius vide Sackur Sibyll. Texte.

Pauly-Wissowa. Enc. Klass. Alt: Pauly-Wissowa-(Kroll) Real-Encyclopädie der Klassischen Altertumswissenschaft, Stuttgart 1894ff.
Pesikta: Pesikta de Rabbi Kahana, ed Buber, Lyck 1868.

Pesikta Rab: Pesikta Rabbati,
— ed. pr. Prague 1656,
— ed. M. Friedmann, Vienna 1880.
Pseudo-Philo: The Biblical Antiquities of Philo trsld. by M. R. James, London 1917.

Sackur Sibyl. Texte: E. Sackur, Sibyllinische Texte und Forschungen, Halle a/S. 1898.
Samaritan Ar. Book of Joshua. ed. Joynboll, and different recension Sam. MSS.
Schatzhöhle: Carl Bezold, Die Schatzhöhle, Leipzig 1883. (Cave of Treasures.)
Schürer: Schürer, Geschichte des Jüdischen Volkes zur Zeit Jesu III.
Seder Hadoroth: Seder Hadoroth by Yehiel Heilprin,
— ed. pr., Carlsruhe 1769.
— Last edition by Naftali b. Abraham, Warsaw 1878.
Seder Olam. ed. pr. Mantua 1514.
— ed. B. Rathner, Wilna 1894.
— ed. A. Marx (Chs. I—X), Berliner Dissertation 1903.
Sib. Or.: Sibylline Oracles, various editions.

Tolidah: Chronique Samaritaine, ed A. Neubauer, Paris 1873.

Urim ve Tumim. by Abraham b. Abraham, Dyhernfurth 1700.

Vita Adae
— in Charles, Pseudepigrapha.
— A. Kautzsch, Pseudoepigraphen,

Weber, Eschatologie: in F. Weber, Jüdische Theologie, p. 332 ff.

Yashar: Sefer Hayashar
— ed. pr. Venice 1625. English translation by Donalson, New York 1840.

INDEX.

(Note.) Figures not preceded by a letter refer to the pages of the Introduction. Figures separated from these by a dash and preceded by the letters A, N, or P refer to the translation of the Asatir, the Notes and the Pitron respectively. These references are by Chapter and Verse, Roman figures being used to indicate the Chapters and Arabic figures for the Verse. References have been given to the Notes and Pitron when these give matter not found in the text and not merely comments on the latter. References preceded by M are to the Translation of the Death of Moses and give the page.

	page
Aaron:	
Death	A IX 39
Stones of breast-plate	P II 7
Ab Ḥasda, author of Tabah, borrowings from Asatir	58, 135
Ab Ḥasda, Samaritan High Priest, copies of Asatir made by	163, 173
Abdalla ben Shalma, date and dependence on Asatir	73, 139
Abimelech, theft of Sarah	34, 69
Abarim, Mount from which Moses see Holy Land	A XI 4
Abisha, Samaritan poet, dependence on Asatir	139
Abisha, Samaritan priest, aid to author 163, 164, 174, 176, 177	
	(footnote)
Abraham:	
Angels' message to	P VI 27
Asatir version of story	24, 33—34, 68—70
Assyrians, fight against	70
Astrology, supposed knowledge	31, 34—35, 41
Astronomy taught by, see Calendar below.	
Babel story connection	28, 39, 41
Birth:	
Omission in Josephus	66
Titan and Chronos legends, parallels	22—23, 25
Various versions	24—27
Calendar taught to Egyptians and others	31, 34—35
Chronological discrepancies in story	38
Circumcision accepted	A VII 26
Dwellings	A VI 8, 12 — A VII 2
in Egypt variants of story	32—35, 37, 40, 69 — A VI 10—26, VII 2
in Elijah de Vidas' version	26—27
Escape from fire	27, 69 — A V 27
Eusebius version of story	39
First prayer and proclamation of faith	A VI 20—23

	page
Abraham:	
Genizah version	25
Idols destroyed by	23, 34 — A VI 11
Josephus account	33—35, 66, 68—70
Melchizedek's gifts refused	A VII 19—20
in Meshalma's writings	37
at Mt. Garizim	A VI 9
in Phoenicia	18, 28, 41
Pirke de Rabbi Eliezer, version of story	27
and Philistines	34, 69
in Pseudo-Eupolemos' works	18—19, 27—28, 32—35, 37—39
Revelation to	A VI 8, VII 22—23
War with Kedar Laomer and others	A VII 8—21 — P VI 7
Zeus, identification with	26
Abraham ben Jacob, see Ibrahim ben Jacob.	
Abraham Ḳabaṣi, borrowings from Asatir	139
Abraham Sakuto, writer on chronology	145
Abraham, son of Pineḥas, copy of Asatir made by	163, 164
Abul Hassan, author of Tabah see Ab Ḥasda.	
Abydenos, history of Tower of Babel	13, 15
Adah, built by Lamech	A II 9
Adah, descendant of Canaan	A VIII 7
Adam:	
Age	146 — A I 24, III 1
Astronomy and the Calendar instituted by	35—36, 65, 85, 108, 137, 141 — A I 22
Book of Signs, source of his wisdom	35—36 — A II 7, 12, 37
Death and burial	A III 1—4
Dwellings	A I 19, 21, 23, II 11
Flood foretold	A II 17
in Garden eight days	A I 25
Hebel beloved by	A I 15
and Mt. Garizim	123
in Pseudepigraphic literature	5—6, 113—115
Rebukes sons of Ḳain	P II 12
Separation from Eve for century	A I 26
Teaches descendants in Book of Truth	A II 7, 12, 25—31 37
Adar Shgg, dwelling of Noah	148
Adrms, place of worship of Adam	148 — A III 14
Afrikia see Phrygia.	
Agag see Gog.	
Aḥidan:	
Builds Ṣion	A III 13, 19
Chief of Ḳainites	A II 35
Children of	A III 18
Idolatry set up by	100—101 — A III 14—16, 20—30
Taught by Adam	P II 31
Towns built by	A III 19

	page
Aholibamah, descendant of Canaan	A VIII 7
Akiba, Rabbi, new versions of Palestinian Targum and Pentateuch	82
Akushim see Gezurah.	
Al Doweik see Ghazal al Doweik.	
Al'alah, twin sister of Kain and Hebel's wife	A I 3
Albasra see Skips.	
Alexander, treatment of name Kamarine	30
Alexander Polyhistor see Polyhistor.	
Algezirah see Great Kutah.	
Alinis, promise of land to	A XI 34
Al'ns, site of Rechobot	P II 11
Alrif see Rifon.	
Altar, first, erection and restoration	A I 6, 7, VI 27
Amalek, defeat by Israel	A IX 33
Aminds, "proud nation" of Oracle	A XII, 1, 7, 21
Amr see Hobah.	
Amram, father of Moses:	
Plti's prophecy 73—74, 140 —	A VIII 25—29, P VIII 31
Saves Hebrew children	A VIII 38
Amraphel, king of Shinear:	
Identification with Nimrod	29
War against Abraham 28—29 —	A VII 1, 4
'Anah, built by Lamech	A II 9
'Aniram, covenant with Abraham	A VII 9
Antichrist legend:	
in Apocalyptic writings	51—52, 60
Development from Bileam legends	96, 104
in Mandean teaching	128
in Sibyl of Tibur	47
Antokia see Hanohiah.	
Apocalypse literature, meaning	4
See also Oracular writtings.	
Apocalypse of Daniel, see Daniel.	
Apocalypse of Moses:	
Asatir, comparison	115
Ascription to Moses, reason	6
Character and contents	5, 115
Apocryphal literature, meaning and origin	4, 83
Aquilas, Greek translation of Pentateuch	82, 83
Arabic, use in Asatir	150—153, 165
Arad, King of, wars with Israel	A IX 40
Aram:	
Land received from Shem	A IV 14, 30
War with giants	30
Aram Naharaim, dwelling of Bileam	P X 8
Aramaic, Jewish pronunciation	175
Ararat, Mt. in Asatir and Josephus	68
Arfat, dwelling of Kain	A I 17

	page
Argarizin, meaning	19

Ark:
- Accounts compared — 67
- Made by Noah — A IV 8

Armilos:
- Identity with Bileam — 93, 94—96
- Occurence of name in various works — 94—95

Arpachsad:
- Dwellings — A IV 14, 31
- Identification with Saturn — 25
- Persecution by Nimrod — 11, 24—25 — A V 16

Artapanos:
- and Asatir, divergence — 40, 42
- Date and nature of work — 40, 72
- and Josephus, relationship — 63, 71—72

Asatir Moshe:
- Anachronisms in legend of Nimrod — 38
- Anti-Jewish bias — 42, 128, 133
- Antiquity — 60—61
- Arabic glosses on names — 150—151, 165
- Arabic paraphrase:
  - Characteristics — 57—58, 168—170
  - Date — 170
  - Manuscripts and copies existing — 168
- Apocryphal literature, relationship to — 4, 42—43
- Authorship — 5—7
- Characteristics — 1, 39, 80, 84, 140
- Chronology, characteristics and objects 122, 141—147 — P XI 20
- Contents — 1—3, 11, 158—159, 121
- Date of composition — 9, 39, 79, 80, 109, 153, 158—160
- Discovery — 8
- Editing, method employed — 166—168
- Eschatology — 145
- Geographical names:
  - Forms used — 150—153
  - Identification difficulty — 147
- "He learned" characteristic phrase — 144
- and Josephus, parallels — 61—79, 122
- and Joshua, Arabic Samaritan version, correspondences 37, 77, 136, 171
- Language — 150, 151, 156—158, 160—161, 165
- and Mandaean writings, comparison — 127—134
- Manuscripts and copies, description — 163—166
- and Mosaic prophecy, place — 5, 86—87
- Oracle:
  - and Bileams prophecy, connection — 90
  - Contents — 42
  - Daniel's visions, comparison — 50

331

Asatir Moshe (contd.):
  Oracle:
    List of kings   45—46
    Omission from Arabic paraphrase   57—58
    Origin and antiquity   57—58
    Poetic form   58—59
  and Palestinian Targum parallels   80, 84—90
  Period covered by   5
  Personal names, treatment   154—156
  Prophecy, contents and characteristics   42, 46—47
    See also Oracle above.
  and Pseudepigraphic literature, relationship   8—9, 105, 120
  and Pseudo-Eupolemos, relationship   17—42
  Punctuation   163—165
  in Samaritan literature, references   5, 137, 140
  Samaritan view   3, 6—8
  and Sibyl of Tibur:
    Parallel passages   53—57
    Relationship   42—61
  and Sibylline oracles:
    Parallel passages   32, 45—46
    Relationship   19—42
  Sources in Midrash   98
  Title, meaning and origin   3—5
  Translation difficulties   167—168
  Transliteration   174
  Unique features   119, 121—124
  and Universal legends, connections traced   99—105
Asbolus see Chus.
Ascensio Jesaiae, use of name Beliar in   96
Ashur:
  Book of Wars given to   A IV 15
  Land allotted to   A IV 14, 27
  War with race of Joktan   A VIII 9
Assumption of Moses:
  Character and contents   5, 116
  and Hebrew legends, comparison   78
  Prophetic character, comparison with Asatir   43, 87
  and Samaritan Chronicle, comparison   180
Astrology: Abraham's supposed knowledge   34—35, 40, 41
Astronomy:
  Abraham as first teacher   31, 34—35
  Book given by Noah to Elam   A IV 15
  Origin   37
  Samaritan system   37
    See also Calendar.
Asur, birth   A III 18
'Aṭirṭ, name of Pharaoh   A IX 19

'Atrot Shafim, built by Kênân   A II 4
'Azrz see Eli.

Baalhanan, king of Edom   A VIII 10
Bab el Abwab, town of Gomer and Magog   A IV 27, 29
Babel, Tower of:
  Asatir version   20—21 — A IV 32 — V 3—5
  and Giants, stories linked by Sibyl   13
  in Sibylline Oracle, compared with other versions   12, 13—16
  Variants in different writers   12—15, 17—19, 21—22
  See also Nimrod.
Badan, dwelling of Adam   148 — A I 19, III 2 — P I 23
Balak, sends for Bileam to curse Israel   A X 1—3
Barah, built by Lamech   P II 9
Bel see Belus.
Bela, son of Joktan, king of Edom   A VIII 8
Beliar, evil spitit identified with Bileam   96—97
Belus:
  Builder of tower   41
  Identification with persons of Nimrod and Abraham legends
                                       15, 38
  Two persons so named   33, 38 — N VI 2
Bene Elohim, interpretation of name   17, 121
Berosian Sibyl, version of Titan legend   24
Berosus:
  Babel legend in works of   14
  Compiler of list of kings   141
Bet Ad, dwelling of Hadad   A VIII 11
Beth Maktash see Jerusalem.
Bible:
  and Asatir, relationship   61—62, 161
  Chronological system evolved from   141
  Literature of, debt to Josephus   61, 71, 105
  Samaritan recension, evidence of Asatir on date   161
  Ultimate source of legends   14, 19
Bileam:
  Advice to Balak to tempt Israel   A X 18
  in Al Doweik's work   137
  in Asatir   59, 76—77, 85, 88, 122, 130—132 — A X
  Ass frightened by Angel   P X 8
  in Bible, references   88
  Blesses Israel   P X 10—18
  Capture by Israelites   A X 47—49
  Demon worship attributed to   130—132
  Genealogy   154 — A X 1
  Gods of, names   A X 6—17
  Identification with Laban, Armilos and others 85, 88, 93, 94, 96, 97, 99

	page
Ass frightened by Angel	
in Josephus	76—77
Messianic development of story	88, 94, 95, 98—99
in Palestinian Targum	77, 88—89
Prophecy of, influence on Asatir Oracle	59
Source of Antichrist story	96
Bispara see Sifra.	
Book of Astronomy:	
Given by Noah to Elam	A IV 15
History of	N III 25
Book of Creation, learnt by Noah	A III 9
Book of Enoch, see Enoch, Book of.	
Book of Generations of Adam see Book of Wars.	
Book of Signs:	
Adam's wisdom derived from	34, 36, 37, 65
Authorship	37
Given to Arpachshad	IV 15
Parallel in Josephus	65
Prophecy of destruction of Nimrod	24 — N V 16
Taught by Adam to his sons	A II 7, 12, 35
Wizards using	A VI 18, VII 4, X 5
Book of Truth, taught by Adam to Lamech	A II 25
Book of Wars, given to Ashur	A I 21, IV 15
Book of Wonders, acc: of death of Moses	78
Bousset:	
on Antichrist	96, 97
on Worship of Elements	131
Brandt, W., work on Mandaean literature	125
Brktrs, dwelling of Arpachshad	A IV 31
Calah Rehoboth Ir, built by sons of Shem	A IV 35
Calendar:	
in Asatir, comparison with Bk. of Enoch	108
Festivals and fasts, how fixed	142, 143
Institution by Adam	35—36, 65, 85, 108, 137, 141
in Pirke de Rabbi Eliezer	117
Reformation, evidence in Book of Jubilees	110
Samaritan view, controversy with Jews 31 (footnote), 35—37, 111	
Taught by Abraham to Egyptians etc.	31, 34—35
See also Chronology.	
Cave of Treasures:	
and Asatir, comparison	113—114
Contents, comparison with Methodius	21
Chain of High Priests:	
Compiled to discredit Jewish claims	145
on Noah, agreement with Josephus	68
Chain of Tradition see Gedalyah aben Yahia.	

	page
Chaldaean Sibyl, ascription to, of Sibylline Oracles	12

Chanoch, see Enoch.
Charassan the Black see Great Kutah.

Chosroe, claims to worship	100—101

Chronica Maiora see Matthew of Paris.
Chronicles of Jeraḥmeel see Jeraḥmeel.

Chronicles of Moses, parallelism with Josephus	71

Chronology:
    in Asatir, peculiar features   122, 141—147
    Days of week given in dates A I 25, IV 8—12, VII 14—15, 22,
        25, 27, 29, IX 8, 21, 24, 25—37, X 50, XI, 15, 16
    Eras in use among Jews and Samaritans   111, 143
    First ten generations, table by Geiger   146—147
    Noah's calculations   A IV 19—22
    Rival Samaritans and Jewish compilations   144—145
    See also Calendar.

Chronos:
    and Abraham, connection of legends   23, 25
    Indentification with persons of Hebrew and Babylonian legends
        19, 31, 33
    in Sibylline Oracles, connection with Babel   15, 22—24

Chus, progenitor of Ethiopians	33
Circumcision instituted	A VII 26, 27
Constans, name of last king on list of Sibyl of Tibur	55
Cryptograms, use in Asatir	124
Damascus, built by Seth	A II 3

Daniel literature:
    Apocalypse of Daniel, character and contents   51
    Book of Daniel, comparison with Asatir   50, 56
    Seventh Vision of Daniel, Armenian version   51

Dates see Chronology.

Day of Punishment and Reward, in Asatir	145—146
Demetrius, book on Biblical chronology	122, 141

Divine Institutes see Lactantius.

Division of earth	A IV 13—26, 37

Doweik see Ghazal al Doweik.
Dumh see Ṭbris.

Ebal, Mt. burial place of Enoch	A II 39 — P II 39
Edom, identification with Esau and Rome	92—93, 97
Edom, kings of, names in Asatir	155 — A VIII 10—11

Egypt:
    Debt to Jews   34—35, 40
    First kingdom, origin of legend   19
    New dynasty   71 — A VIII 14—15
    Rise, in Sibylline oracles   12, 13—14, 19

Elam:
  Book of Astronomy given to   A IV 15
  Land given to by Shem   A IV 14, 27
Eleazar, priest, at death of Moses   M 305, 311, 315
Elements, origin of worship   131
Eli, schism of   47 — N XI 21—23
Elifas, fight with children of Ishmael   A VIII 5
Elijah de Vidas, on Nimrod-Abraham legend   26—27
Elon Moreh, dwelling of Abraham and Lot   P VI 8
Ennius, use of Titan story   23
Enoch:
  Age   147, II 31
  Astronomy first taught by   33, 37
  Birth   A II 6
  Learning of Book of Signs   A II 7
  Death and burial   68, 145 — A II 32—40
  Piety   A II 13—14
  Town built by   A II 1
  Translation, view of Meshalma   N II 32
Enoch, Book of:
  and Asatir, comparison   87, 107—109
  Date   107, 159
  Symbolism   45, 50
Enos, Mandaean name for Messias   128
Enosh:
  Age and birth   A II 2, 27
  at Burial of Enoch   A II 34
Era of Entry of Children of Israel see Calendar: Eras.
Erythraean Sibyl, authorship of Sibylline Oracles ascribed to 12, 23
Esau:
  Associated with Ishmael   A VIII 6
  Substitution for Seir in Samaritan writings   92, 97
Eschatology in Samaritan writings   145—146
Eshkol, covenant with Abraham   A VII 9
Essenes, rise of   127
Euhemeros:
  Sibylline Oracles used by   14
  Titan legend, version   23
Eupolemos see Pseudo-Eupolemos.
Eusebius:
  Collection of legends   13, 39
  Knowledge of Sibylline Oracles   12
Eve:
  Sojourn in Garden   A I 25
  Visit to Ḳain   A I 16—17
Exempla (Gaster) evidence on legend of Universal King 100—101
Eyul Mth see Machpelah.

	page
Ezekiel:	
David represented as expected Messiah	103
Source of Gog and Magog story	92
Ezra:	
Charges against in Asatir	47 — P XI 21, 24, 36
Influenced by Daniel	50
Fanuta:	
Duration foretold by Moses	A XI 20
Origin of belief	144
Fanyah, scattering foretold	A XI 33
Fate-willed child legend, in Asatir etc.	101—103
Flood:	
Announced to Noah	A IV 2
Duration and dates	144, IV 9—10
Foretold, by Adam	A II 17—18
Josephus' and Samaritan accounts, difference	67
Flores Historiarum, see Sibyl of Tibur: in European Literature.	
Forikh, see Bet 'Ad.	
Frankel:	
on Messianic idea in Septuagint	91
on Palestinian Targum	81
Freudenthal:	
on Artapanos, date	71—72
on Anonymous story of Abraham	41
Pseudo-Eupolemos distinguished from Eupolemos	17—18
Gabala, connection with Messianic idea	92—93
Gamaliel, Rabbi, prophecy on destruction of Gabala	93 (footnote)
Garizim, Mount:	
Abraham goes up to	A VI 9
Defilement	158 — M 305
First altar erected	A I 7
Holy Mountain of Samaritans	123—124
Identified with Luzah	P XI 39
Meridian used by Samaritans	37
Name in Asatir	66
Restoration foretold	A XI 39, 42, XII 7
Seen from Nebo by Moses	M 3
Gate of Heaven, name given to Mt. Garizim	123—124 — A II 40
Gedalyah aben Yaḥia, writer on chronology	145
Geiger:	
Chronological table of first ten generations	146—147
on Palestinian Targum	81, 82
Genealogies, fictitious, purpose	154—155 — N VIII 15
Genesis, story of giants	16—17
Genizah fragments in British Museum, contents	25, 27, 53
Genza of the Mandaeans:	
Characteristics	126
Publication	125

Geographical names:
in Asatir	66, 147—152
Modernisation in ancient authors, stages	149

Gezurah, dwelling of Pharaoh — A VIII 18

Ghazal al Doweik:
Asatir first mentioned by	137
Borrowings from Asatir	58, 136—137
on Prophecy of Bileam	90
on Second Kingdom	137

Giants, in Babel and Nimrod legends — 13, 16—17, 41

Gibeon, see Rifat.

Gibor, meaning — 16—17

Gibṭai, see Giṭṭ.

Gifna, dwelling of Javan — A VIII 16

Gifna, symbolical use of name in Asatir — 154

Gifna, wife of Asur, establishes idolatry — A III 20—30

Giṭṭ:
Death	A V 14
Head of Seven Nations	A V 10
War with Nimrod	A V 12

Gnosis, see Mandaeans: Doctrine.

God:
Mystical name in Asatir and Moses books	138
Name in Mandaean writings	129

Gog:
in Asatir	90—92 — A XII 11, 16
Greek Empire identified with	97
in Palestinian Targum	86

Gomer, receives land from Japhet — A IV 17, 29

Gomorrah, destruction — P VII 28

Gots, see Pharaoh (of Moses).

Great Kutah, dwelling of Ld and Aram — A IV 30

Greek language, excluded as language of sources of Jewish apocrypha — 156

Greek literature:
Jewish rivalry	141
Parallels to Jewish stories of Genesis	33

Hadad, king of Edom — A VII 11

Haggada, ref. to Laban (Bileam) — 95

Haig, counterpart of Abraham in Armenian legends — 29

Hakadosh, changes of meaning in Asatir and Mandaean writings — 130, 133

Ḥam:
Identification with Titan and Belus	16, 38
Kingdom of, end	A VI 1, VII 7
Marries Skh	A IV 6
Portion of earth alloted to	A IV, 13, 14, 17

Asatir. 22

	page
Haman, genealogy	154
Ḥanoḫiah:	
Built by Enoch	A II 1
Dwelling of Ḳain and his sons	152 — A III 9
Haran:	
Death of	102 — A V 28
Idol worshipper	N V 28
Haran, dwelling of Abraham and Jacob	A VII 2. VIII 12mmm
Haran, dwelling of Abraham and Jacob	A VII 2, VIII 12 — P VI 8
Hayya, see Voice of the Living.	
Hazin, "holy God" of Bileam	A X 17
Hebel:	
Marriage to Makeda	A I 3
Murder	A I 16—20
Sacrifice	A I 6—11
Twin sister	A I 3
Hebrew Sibyl, ascription to, of Sibylline oracles	12
Hebrews, land to be laid waste	A XII 17
Hebron:	
Dwelling of Aḥidan	A II 35
Identification with Eyul Mth	148
Hellenistic literature:	
and Asatir, relationship	9—42
Debt to Midrash	162—163
in Palestine, date	39
Hermes-Thoth, identification with Moses	72
Herod the Edomite, death of, in Bk. of Jubilees	110
Hiram, claim to worship	101
Ḥobaḥ, place of Abraham's meeting with kings	A VII 16
Hoḥmata, see Sifra.	
Holy Mountain, various identifications	123—124
See also Mt. Garizim.	
Horeb, Moses at	A IX 20
Husham, king of Edom	A VIII 10
Ibrahim ben Jacob, borrowings from Asatir	140
'Irad, birth	A II 8
Isaac, son of Abraham	A VII 29
Isaac, son of Amram, assistance in transliterating Asatir	174
Ishmael:	
Contest with Children of Esau	A VIII 5—6
Dwelling according to Josephus	70
Succeeds Abraham	A VIII 1
Ishmael Rumihi, borrowings from Asatir	74, 139
Israelites, escape from Egypt	A IX 30
'Ith, dwelling of Noah	A IV 12
Ithamar, priest, at death of Moses	M 305, 306, 311, 315
Itanu, son of Aḥidan and Gifna	A III 27—28

Ja'azer, built by Mahalalel	A II 5
Jabal, town built by	A II 23
Jacob, son of Isaac, age and dwelling	A VIII 12—18
Jacob, Samaritan High Priest, copies Asatir	168

Jacob ha-Rabban:
and Asatir, correspondence	137
Date	137
Place among pseudepigraphic writers	119

James, M. R., translation of Pseudo-Philo	112

Japhet:
Land given to	A IV 13, 14, 17, 37
Marries Mkisth	A IV 6
in Nimrod legend and parallel stories	16, 25

Jared:
Age	147, A II 30
at Burial of Enoch	A II 34

Javan:
Ancestor of Pharaoh	A VIII 15—16
Land given by Japhet	A IV, 17

Jeraḥmeel, Chronicle of:
Characteristics	71, 117—119

Jerusalem:
Abuse in Samaritan literature	128, 154
Built by Aḥidan	A III 13
Rock established by witchcraft of Na'amah	P II 24

Jesus:
Asatir prophecy applied to	P XI 27, 33
Birth, stories in Samaritan writings	172
Hayyah, use of word	129
Mandaean view	132—133

Jethro, flock kept by Moses	A IX 20
Jobab, ancestry	P VIII 9
Jochebed, mother of Moses	140, A IX 12—13
John the Baptist, Book of	125, 130

Joktan:
Dwelling of children of	66 — A V 13
Wars with Ashur	A VIII 9

Jonathan, Targum of, evidence on Bileam	94
Joseph in Egypt	A VIII 13

Josephus, Antiquities:
Anti-Samaritan bias	64, 67
and Asatir, parallels	61—79, 122
Character and aim of work	61—64, 79
Hellenistic literature neglected	63, 69
and Joshua, Samaritan book of, relationship	66—67, 77

	page
Josephus, Antiquities:	
Legendary matter in history, sources	64—65
on Passover	76
Place in Biblical literature	105
Joshua:	
Consecrated by Moses	A XI 1—2 — M 313, 320
at Death of Moses	M 305, 307, 315
Judgment on Bileam	A X 47, 49
Joshua, Samaritan Book of:	
and Asatir, relationship	37, 77, 136, 171
Date	171
and Josephus, relationship	66—67, 77
Hebrew version, genuineness	136 (footnote)
on Moses, correspondence with Markah etc.	179
Jskr, burial place of Enoch	A II 38
Jubal, town built by	A II 22
Jubilees, Book of:	
and Asatir, comparison	110—112, 142
Character and contents	110
Chronology	142
Geographical names in	148
Origin and date	110—112, 159
Judah, apostasy under Solomon	P XI 25, 26
Kabelhaber companion of Mohammed	25
Kadosh, destroyed by Kedar Laomer	A VII 5
Kain:	
Dwellings	A I 2, 17, II 2
Four years absence from Adam	A I 14
Killed by Lamech	A II 9, 21
Murder of Hebel	A I 18—20
Sacrifice	A I 8—13
Sons of, evil deeds	P II 8, 12
Twin sister	A I 3
Visited by Eve	A I 15—17
Kamarina, birthplace of Abraham	18, 28, 30—31
Karaites, genealogy of exiliarchs compiled by	155
Kênân:	
Birth and age	146 — A II 2—3, 28
at Burial of Enoch	A II 34
Dwelling	A II 4
Kenaz, built by Jabal	A II 23
Kedar Laomer, wars against Abraham's kindred	A VI 5—7, VII 4—16
Kings, lists of:	
in Asatir Oracle	A XII 1—24
Examples	45—46, 49—52
Purpose	60, 141

Kings paying tribute to Amraphel	P VII 7
Kinnereth	A VII 13, XI, 11
Kiṭṭim, ancestors of Pharaoh	A VIII, 15, IX, 19
Kadosh, see Hakadosh.	
Kohn, S., work on language of Samaritan Targum	150
Kol Hayyah, see voice of the Living.	
Koran, version of Abraham's story	26, 66
Kosbi, killed by Pineḥas	A X 32—35
Ḳrṭm, cryptogram for Saul	A XI 24 — P XI 24 — N XI 24
Kush, confusion with Nimrod	19, 22
Land given to by Ham	A IV 17
Ḳushṭa, meaning	130
Kutheans, see Samaritans.	
Laban, identified with Bileam	85, 95
Lactantius, acquaintance with Sibylline writings	12, 23
Lamech:	
Age	147 — A II 25
Ancestry	A II 8, 25
Images made by	A II 11 — P II 31
Murder of Ḳain	A II 9
Noah brought to Adam by	A II 19
Towns built by	A II 9—10
Law:	
Book written by God placed in Ark	M 305
Copy made by Moses	A XI 3, 15 — M 303
Lefehand, name of Lamech's image	A II 11
Lehaburatim, name of Lamech's image	A II 11
Lehadim, chief of seven Nations	A V 9—10
Leitner, Dr., translation of Arabic Asatir	170
Leo, Emperor, oracle	49
Levi:	
Blessing of Moses	M 313
Prophecied as ancester of Moses	A VIII 25—29
Lidzbarski, work on Mandaean literature	125, 127, 128
Logos Ebraikos, embodied in Book of Enoch	109
Lost hero legend, general account	103—104
Lot:	
in Canaan	A VII 1 — P VI 8
Capture by Amraphel	A VII 8, 13—20
Leaves Egypt with Abraham	A VI 26
in Sodom	A VII 3 — P VII 28
Ld, land received from Shem	A IV 14, 30
Luzah, see Garizim, Mt.	

Machpelah, burial place of Patriarchs, description 123 — A III 3—7, IV 38

	page
Mahalalel:	
Age	146 — A II 29
Birth	A II 4
at Burial of Enoch	A II 34
Mahlat, sone of associated with Ishmael	A VIII 6
Maimonides, references in Arabic Asatir	170
Makeda, twin sister of Hebel and wife of Ḳain	A II 3
Makṭash, Samaritan name for the Temple	154
Malif:	
Characteristics, borrowings from Asatir	140
Destruction of Tower of Babel described	21
Mamre, covenant with Abraham	A VII 9
Manda-de Ḥaya, see Mandaeans: Doctrine.	
Mandaeans:	
Anti-Jewish teaching	128, 133
Doctrines	126, 129
Language and terminology, affinity with Samaritan	126, 128—130
Literature:	
Comparison with Asatir	127—134
History of publication and bibliography	125 (footnote)
Manichaeans, similar in beliefs to Mandaeans	125, 127
Manetho, author of list of kings	141
Mar Apas Katina, versions of the Genesis stories	14—15, 29
Marah, waters sweetened by Moses	A IX 32
Marḳaḥ:	
Borrowings from Asatir	78, 135
on Passover	P IX 31
Poem on death of Moses	78, 178—179
on Sons of Moses	P VIII 39
Matthew of Paris, influenced by Sibyl of Tibur	48, 54 (footnote)
Matthew of Westminster, influenced by Sibyl of Tibur	48
Mecca, built by children of Nebaot	A VIII 3
Mehetabel, wife of Hadad	A VIII 11
Mehuyael, birth	A II 8
Melchizedek, offer of tithe to Abraham	A VII 19
Mertis, wizard, flight to Midian	A X 1
Meseda (Rabta) built by Jubal	A II 22
Mesha, dwelling of sons of Joktan	A V 13
Meshalma:	
Names, treatment by	149
Rejection of legends of Terah's idolatry	67
Asatir, early mention by	140
Flood, commentary of	67
Versions of Genesis stories	21, 27, 37
Messiah:	
Moses descendants to produce	P VIII 39
Twenty-sixth from Fanuta	P XII 26

Messianic idea:
  in Asatir   87, 92, 144
  in Ezekiel   103
  and Lost Hero Legend, connection   103
  in Palestinian Targum   92
  in Ghazal al Doweik   137
  in Bileam prophecies   88—92, 94, 95, 98, 99
  Oldest sources   87—88, 90, 93
  in Vision of Daniel   51—52
Mestraim:
  Ancestor of Egyptians   33
  Land given to   A IV 18
Methodius of Patara, Revelations:
  and Cave of Treasures, comparison   21
  Characteristics   114
  influenced by Sibyl of Tibur   48
Metushelah:
  Age   147
  Birth   A II 15
  at Burial of Enoch   A II 34
Midian:
  Dwelling of Moses   A IX 17
  Wars of Children of Israel against   A X 37—51
Midrash:
  Antiquity, evidence of Asatir   162
  Palestinian, use by Josephus   65
  Probable dates   118
  Source of Asatir and other writings   98
Miriam, sister of Moses   A IX 11—12, 38
Mkisth, wife of Japhet   A IV 7
Moabites, send women to tempt Israel   A X 18—37
Mohammed:
  Coming of   P XI 33
  in Daniel apocalypse   52
Mohammedans, identified with Edom by Samaritans   N VIII 7
Molad Moshe, two Samaritan poems agreeing with Asatir 73—74, 139
Monotheism, origin attributed to Abraham   69
Moriah, Mt. rival of Mt. Garizim   123, 124
Moses:
  Abraham ben Jacobs's account   140
  Address to Israelites before death   M 309—313
  Anonymous poem on, compared with Asatir   137—139
  Artapanos version   20, 40, 75
  Asatir version   72—75, 77, 122, 137
  Benefactor of Egypt   40
  Birth   24, 72—74, 140 — A VIII 22, IX 1
  Books ascribed to   3, 5—6, 7

Moses:
   Children, legends of seclusion   138 — P VIII 39, XI 2
   Death, various accounts   77, 97—98 — A XI 1—19
     See also Samaritan Chronicle, Death of Moses.
   in Egypt   24, 71, 74—75, 40 — A IX 14—17, 25—30
   Foretold by Adam   P II 22
   Heavy of tongue, origin of legend   75
   Hermes-Thoth, identified with   72
   Josephus' account   71, 72—75, 77, 179
   Length of life, Samaritan tradition   67
   in Palestinian Tragum   97—98
   Prophecies made by   86—87, 144 — A XI 20—42
   in Pseudo-Philo   87, 179
   Redivivus, Samaritan hopes   55, 60—61, 97—98, 103
   Rescue from river   IX 2—13
   Rod and clothes of Adam given to   A IX 22, 32
   in Samaritan literature (Codex Gaster)   73, 77
   Songs of, comparison with Asatir Oracle   46, 59
   Vision of Promised Land   A XI 4—14 — M 319
   Wars against Midian   A X 37—51
   in Wilderness   A IX 30—40
     See also Asatir: Authorship.
Moses of Chorene, version of legends   13, 24, 29
Mourning, Mount of see Ebal, Mount.

Na'amah, witch, sister of Tubal Ḳain   P II 24
Nabaoth, meaning of name   71
Nablus, substitution for Sichem in Arabic Asatir   149
Naḥman Ketufa, mystical oracle   52
Nahor, defended against Kedar Laomer by Abraham A VI 5 —
                                                        A VII 12, 17
Nbu-Mshiba, demon identified with Jesus   133
Nds, see Aminds.
Nebaot, children of   A VIII 2—3
Nebo, Mount, dying place of Moses   M 315, 317
Nigug, tower made by Aḥidan   A III 20—26
Nikl, city of Ḳain   A I 4
Nimrod:
   and Abraham, attempt to prevent birth   A V 19—25
   Asatir version of story   11, 20—21, 24, 27—28, 65
   Babel built by   12, 14, 22 — A IV 32
   Chronology of legends   11, 27, 29, 38
   Death   A V 28
   Elijah de Vidas' version   27
   Genizah version   25
   as Giant, growth of tradition   17—18 — A IV 32
   Josephus' account   19—20, 65

Nimrod:
  King of Ashur   A V 14
  Midrashic exegis based on name   16
  in Philo   17
  in Pirke de Rabbi Eliezer   27
  Ruler over children of Ḥam   IV 31
  Sibylline Oracle version   16—18, 22—24
  Titan legend, parallels   16—18, 22, 25
  Two persons in Asatir   38 — A VI 1—3
  and Universal kingship   100
  Variants of story, summary   31
  Wars against Philistines and Nahor   A V 11, 12, 15
  See also Babel and Abraham: Birth.
Nine Suns, vision, interpretation   48
Nineveh, built by sons of Shem   A IV 35
Nistarot, connection of word with name "Asatir"   5, 52
Nisah, built by Lamech   A II 9
Nisan, important events according to Samaritans   N IV 8—10
Nisbor, see Kenaz.
Niss see Book of Signs.
Nisus see Belus.
Noah:
  Age   147 — A IV 24, 33
  in Ark   A IV 8—11
  Asatir version of story   68
  Astronomical calculations   A IV 19—21
  Birth, signs in heaven   A II 15—16
  Books of Wisdom learnt and given to sons   A III 9 — A IV 15
  Calendar revealed to   37
  in Chain of High Priests   68
  Death and burial   A IV 36—38
  Dwelling   A IV, 12
  Earth divided by   A IV 13—26, 37
  Received by Adam   A II 19
  Teaches faith to children   A IV 12
Nöldeke, Th., Mandaean grammar   126

Onkelos:
  on Messianic prophecy   89
  Targum substituted for Palestinian Targum   82
Opsopeus, treatment of name Kamarine   30
Oracular writings:
  General character and range   43—45
  Recasting of old oracles   44
    See also Sibylline Oracles and Sibyl of Tibur.
Ourie see Kamarina.

	page
Padrai Tns:	
Built by Lamech	A II 10
Idolatrous place of worship	P II 10
Palestine, boundaries	148, 152, XI 4—14
Palestinian Targum:	
and Asatir, parallels	80, 84—90
Character and language	80—84
Date	81—82
New version of Rabbi Akiba	82
Prophecy of kings	51
Various texts	82
Plti, wizard:	
Counsels Pharaoh concerning Moses 74, 75 — A VIII 24—29, 32—33, 35, IX 7	
Occurrence of name in various works	138, 155
Parchment, used only for sacred books	7—8
Parker, Archbishop, use of Sibyl of Tibur	48
Passover:	
Institution	P IX 31
Samaritan and Jewish practices, divergence	76
Patriarchs:	
Ages	144, 146—147 — A II 25—31
Ten generations from Adam	A II 1—9
Pentateuch:	
and Asatir, relationship	1, 61
Greek translation of Akiba and Aquilas, purpose	82
Source of Messianic idea	87—88
Peor see Mertis.	
Peshitto, use of story of giants	17, 29
Peterman, H.:	
on Mandaean literature	125
Work on Samaritan Hebrew pronunciation	174
Pesiktot, meaning	83
Pharaoh (of Abraham):	
Detroys idols	P VI 24
Theft of Sarah from Abraham 32—34 — A VI 13—14, 26	
Pharaoh (of Moses):	
Attempts to destroy Moses	A VIII 28—37, 41
Death	A IX 18
Defiance by Moses	A 24, 40, 74 — A IX 27—30
Dwellings	A VIII 18, 21
Genealogy	121, 122, 154 — A VIII 14—15
Wars of	A VIII 21—23
Pharaoh's daughter cured of disease	P IX 9
Philistines:	
Take kingdom from Nimrod	A V 11
War against Canaanites	A V 11

	page
Philo, account of Nimrod and giants	17
See also Pseudo-Philo.	
Phoenicians, taught by Abraham	18, 28, 41
Phrygia, dwelling of Ld and Aram	A IV 30
Pilonah, built by Seth	A II 2
Pineḥas, son of Amram, translation of Malif	140
Pineḥas, son of Eleazar:	
at Death of Moses	M 313, 315
Kills Zimri and Kosbi	A X 32—35
Leader against Midian	A X 40
Seven gifts as reward of zeal	P X 35
Pirke de Rabbi Eliezer, contents	27, 117
Pitron to Asatir:	
Authorship problem	171
Characteristics and language	172
Manuscripts described	173
Place names see Geographical names.	
Planets, fight of seven	A I 22
Polyhistor, references to legends and Sibyl	12, 13, 17, 40
Praeparatio Evangelica of Eusebius	13—14, 17
Precious stones of Book of Signs, meaning	A. P. N II 7
Proper names, symbolical	154
Pseudepigraphic literature:	
Age, method of judging	106
and Asatir, relationship	5,. 8—9, 105—120
Classification into three groups	119
General characteristics	105—107
Jewish sources for Greek texts	118
Origins	83
Pseudo-Eupolemos:	
and Asatir, relationship	17—42
Date	17
Chronology of stories	28
on Giants, account quoted	18—19
and Josephus, comparison	63, 69
and Sibylline oracle, relationship	30—31
Pseudo-Philo, Biblical Antiquities:	
Character and contents	43, 87, 112
and Asatir, comparison	112—113
on Moses	87, 179
Puah, midwife, saves Hebrew children	A VIII 37—39
Puntos, king of Egypt	N V 10
Qolasta, Mandaean liturgy	125
"Questions" of Philo	17
Rabbot, meaning	83
Rabta, see Meseda.	

	page
Rdyh, kills Bileam	A X 48
Rechoboth 'Ir, dwelling of Adam	A II 11
Reitzenstein, work on Mandaean literature	125—126, 127, 128
Resen, built by sons of Shem	A IV 35

Resurrection of the dead:
    Omission of reference in Asatir   60, 158
    Recent element in apocalyptic writing   60
Return from exile, prophecy   A XI 34, 38
Revelation of Methodius, see Methodius.
Rifat, built by Lamech   A II 20
Rifon, dwelling of Abraham   A VI 12
Rod of Adam see Rod of Miracles.
Rod of Miracles:
    Delivered to Moses   A IX 22, 32
    Source whence Moses obtained it   N IX 22
    Test of genuine Messiah   55—56, 98 — A XII 24
Rome, destruction to precede advent of Messiah   97
Romi see Brktrs.
Ruḥa d'Ḳudsha, changes in meaning in Mandaean and other literature   130—133

Samaritan Chronicle, Death of Moses:
    and Asatir, comparison   182
    General account   77—78, 178—182
    Translation   303—321
Samaritan Targum:
    Geographical names, treatment   151
    Obsolete words replaced by Arabic glosses   150
Samaritans:
    and Asatir, views   3, 6—8
    Astronomical system   35—37
        See also Asatir: Chronology; and Calendar.
    Demonology   96—97, 130—131
    Eschatology   146
    and Mt. Garizim, claims   123—124
    Idolatry charge by Josephus   159
    and Jews, rival Targum and Midrash   81—84
    Language:
        Affinity with Mandaean   128—130
        Pronunciation   174
    Legends, oldest source of universal stories   100
    Literature:
        Antiquity   78
        Influence of Asatir   134—140
    and Mandaeans, relationship   127, 133—134
    Messianic expectations   91
    Moses chief national hero   55, 60—61, 71, 75, 103

Samaritans:
  Names, double forms 153
  Return of Moses, divergence from Jewish views 97—98, 103
  Song of Moses, views 46
Samlah, king of Edom A VIII 10
Sanchuniaton, author of list of kings 141
Sarah, taken by Pharaoh A VI 13—26
Saturn, identifications with Noah and Chronos 19, 23
Saul, king of Edom A VIII 10
Scheftolowitz, work on Manichaean writings 127
Script, change by Ezra 47 — A XI 36
Scroll of Fasting, Calendar 142
Second Kingdom, see Ghazal al Doweik.
Secrets of Moses, see Asatir Moshe, title.
Secrets of the Heart see Abraham Kabasi.
Secrets of Rabbi Simeon ben Yochai see Simeon ben Yochai.
Seder Hadorot see Yechiel Heilprin.
Seder Olam Rabba, oldest Jewish chronology 145
Sefer Zerubabel, oldest legends of Messiah 95
Seir see Gabala.
Septuagint:
  Messianic idea in 91
  Neglect by Josephus 62—63
Seth:
  Age 146 — A II 26
  "Image" of Adam P I 27
  Towns built by A II 2, 3
Sethians:
  Connection with Holy Mountain 123
  Legends of, absent in Asatir 121
Seven, sacred number in Jewish laws A X 36
Seven Kings see Seven Nations.
Seven Nations:
  Disappearance, various accounts 19—20
  Names A V 9
  Origin of story 48
  Sibylline oracle's version 16, 20
  See also War of the Nations.
Shalem the Great:
  Built by Jered A II 6
  Meeting place of Abraham and kings A VII 17
  Shalshelet Hakabalah see Gedalyah aben Yahia.
Shekina, meaning 129—130
Shelah see Solomon.
Shem:
  Identification with Zerouan 16
  Land given to 11 — A IV 13—14, 37

Shem
    Leadership given by Noah   A IV 34, 37, 38
    Towns built by   A IV 35
Shem Hamitfaresh, agreement with Asatir   138
Shemhazai and Azael, legend   121
Shifrah, midwife, saves Hebrew children   A VIII 37—39
Shinear:
    Dwelling of Noah's sons   A V 1
    Site of Padrai Tns, idol   P II 10
Shobakh, war with Joshua   30, 171
Shrit, wife of Shem   A IV 5
Shur, dwelling of Bileam   A X 44
Sibyl of Tibur:
    Antiquity   53
    and Asatir, parallels   42—61
    Contents   47—49
    Influence on subsequent European literature   48
    Oriental origin evidence   49, 52
    Slavonic and Rumanian versions   47
Sibylline Oracles:
    Apocalyptic character   43—44
    and Asatir, parallels   9—42, 45—46
    Book III, origin and contents   11—12
    Book VIII see List of Kings below.
    Book XII, authorship, date etc.   45—46
    Chronos and Titan legend, source of version   22—23
    Date   12
    Jewish elements   9—10, 12
    Kings, list, compared with Asatir Oracle   45—46
    and Moses of Chorene, relationship   24
    Place among pseudepigraphic writings   120
    Sources   10, 16, 17, 23, 30, 31
Sichem see Sifra.
Sifra:
    Dwelling of Adam and children of Joktan   A I 21, II 19, III 32—33, V 13
    Identification with Sichem   149 — P I 21
    Temple to be burnt   A XII 15
Sifre, commentary to Deuteronomy   86
Simeon ben Yochai, Rabbi apocalyptic writings   5, 52, 95
Simeon, tribe of, plagued for sin with women of Moab   P X 48
Simon Magus, identification with Beliar   96
Sinai, law given to Moses   A IX 34—36
Şion see Jerusalem.
Skips, built by Tubal Ḳain   A II 24
Skh, wife of Ḥam   A IV 6
Shmh, scattering of   A XI 33

Sodom:
    Destruction   A VII 28
    Dwelling of Lot   A VII 3
    Sodom, King of, meets Abraham   A VII 17, 21
Solomon:
    Samaritan charges against 99 — A XI 24—30 — N XI 29—31
    in Sibylline Oracles   12, 20
    Witchcraft, views of Jews and Samaritans   99
Star:
    Connection with Messiah   90, 137
    Prophecy of angel to Bileam, interpretation   A X 45
Sukkoth, poem on, by Abdalla ben Shalma   139
Ṣur, daughter of, leads Moabite women   A X 27
Sursan, built by Aḥidan   148 — A III 19
Symbolism in oracular writings   44

Tabaḥ, comparison with Asatir   58, 135
Taheb see Messiah and Messianic idea.
Targum, rival versions   81—83
Tefillath, see Simeon ben Yochai.
Ten kings, story based on Nimrod legends   100
Tenth generation, importance   48, 67, 68
Terah:
    Contest with Kedar Laomer   A VI 4—6
    Hatred of Chaldaea   68—69
    Father of Abraham   23—24
    Idol worship conflicting accounts   25, 26, 66—67
    Kingdom in Canaan   A VI 4—6
Testament of Moses see Assumption of Moses.
Testament of Twelve Patriarchs:
    Divergence from Asatir   113
    Use of word Beliar   97
Tharbis, wife of Moses   40
"Three mornings"   A IX 35—37
Tibris of Kinnereth, camp of kings   A VII 13
Tidal king of Goyim   A VI 5
Tmnta, name applied to Garizim   66 — A VI 13
Titan:
    and Abraham, parallels in story   22, 25
    in Euhemeros' version   23
    and Nimrod legend parallels   15—16, 17, 22, 25
    in Sibylline Oracles   12, 15, 22—23
Tolida:
    Borrowings from Asatir   135
    Identified with Book of Generations of Adam   P III 11
Torah, see Law.
Tower of Shame, name for Temple at Jerusalem   A XI 27

	page
Tubal Ḳain:	
Ḳain killed by	A II 21
Metal worker	A II 24
Taught Book of Signs by Adam	A II 36
Ṭurṭs Egyptian magician:	
Dwellings	A VI 25, VII 4
Explains plague upon Pharaoh	A VI 18—19
Wars of Kedar Laomer prophesied	A VII 4
Twenty-six, final number in Asatir Oracle	60 — A XII 26
Universal King, connected legends	100—101
Universal sagas	99—105
Ur, meaning of name	18 (footnote), 30
Ur Kasdim, dwelling of Elam, Ashur and Arpachshad	A IV 27, 31
"Urschrift" of Geiger quoted	81
Voice of the Living:	
Commands to Israelites	A X 28, 51, XI 17
Meaning	129
War of the Nations:	
and Egypt, connected in Sibyl's account	13, 19
Various versions	19—20, 28—29 — A V 8—9
Yakubi, commentary to Koran, on birth of Abraham	26
Yashar, Book of, description	118—119
Yechiel Heilprin, writer on chronology	145
Yemen, dwelling of children of Joktan	A V 13
Yemenite documents	94 175
Yuḥasin see Abraham Sakuto.	
Zimri, killed by Pineḥas	A X 32
Zered, captures Bileam	A X 47
Zotenberg, on Apocalypse of Daniel	52
Ẓṭoṭai, attacked by Canaanites	A V 11
Zunz, view on Palestinian Targum	80—81

D

ASATIR

SAMARITAN TEXT

זה אסטיר : אדונן משה שלום יה :. עליו :
בשם יהי נשרי

I

(1) ישתבח אלה דעבד עלמא : ואקים אדם ארש : ובניו קין
והבל כמהו : (2) ויהב לקין מערבה : ויהב להבל צפונה וימה :
(3) ויהב אלעלה תלימת קין להבל לאתה : ויהב מקדה תלימת
הבל לקין לאתה : (4) וישרה קין במיסםת מדי : מתקריה ניכל :
(5) ופלג ארעה לה ולבניו : בירח אב : (6) והוה מסכום יומים
איתי קין מנחה : והבל איתי קרבן : (7) וראשית מדבחיה הוה

פתרון

(בשם יהוה הרחום)

אמר אדונן משה שלום יהוה עליו מאהל בתהללות הרוממות
לאל שדי אשר ברא אדם מפני כל הבדראות : ושמו אב לכל
הבשר : יתהלל אלהים אשר עשה העלם ואקים את האדם שרש :
ואז דרש השם יתעלה התולדות מן אדם ברא לו את חוה אשה :
ונתן לו ממנה שני תאמים : כל אחד מהם זכר ונקבה : הבכור (קין :)
ועמו נקבה ושמה (מקדה ;) וזבב (2) אחות זה לזה : ויחלק
את הארץ עליהם : ונתן לקין ימה : ונתן אל הבל צפונה : ונגבה :
וזה הדבר מתודע מן מאמרו שלום יהוה עליו (ובניו קין והבל
כמהו) ויתן לקין ימה : ויתן אל הבל צפונה ונגבה : ויתן אלעלה
אחות קין אל הבל לאשה : . ויתן מקדה אחות הבל אל קין לאשה :
ויהי פלוג הארץ לו ואל בניו : בחדש אב : . (3) ואהל קין יבנת
מקום מתקרי שמו ניכל : וזה מתודע מן מאמרו עליו השלום
(ואהל קין יבנה מקום מתקרי ניכל :) ופלג את הארץ בחדש אב :
ויהי מקץ ימים ויבא קין מנחה : והבל הביא גם הוא קרבן : ובנא
מזבח בתחתית הר גריזיים הקדוש : בין לוזה והרנגריזים : וזה ראש
מזבח אתבנא : וזה מתודע מן מאמרו עליו השלום (ויהי מקץ ימים
ויבא קין מפרי האדמה מנחה ליהוה : והבל הביא קרבן :.) וראשית
המזבחות (4) היה בתחתית המקדש : בין לוזה והרנגריזים והיו שני
האחים מולים זה לזה : בעת עשו המנחה והקרבן : כפי מאמרו : (וזה
מול זה :) ואז קין והבל אקריבו היה הלוך עשרים יום מן חדש
האביב : כפי מאמרו (ואז אקריב קין והבל בעשרים יום בניסן הוה :)
ואז ראה קין מנחתו איננה מתקבלה כמה היה ידע סימת הקבול

חוה מלך מן אדם : דאזלת לידה : דהבל עמה : (17) ואשקחתה
עקיר לאתר מדו מתקרי אחריה ערפאת : (18) מלתה דאמירה
לקין ולידך עזרותה : וכל דבתרה נהך לבראה : ודמן תקנך
אדמה דהבל : (19) וכד השפך ארמה דהבל : אתעכרת
רוחיה : והות ארעה בקנאה : וימיה עבירין : ושמשה אשנתה
וזהרה בניושה : (20) ודחל אדם דחלה רבה : ביתה יומה :
היך יומה דלקטו פריה (21) וקעם אדם במדינה דחכמתה
דמתקריה ספרה דספר מלחמות יהוה : (22) ועמה נגימו
דיומיה : וז : . קרבי יתה (23) ועמה לית אחד מנון : ועקר

ואתה תמשל בו : ו) הפתרון לזה הוא אן זה מאום בידך : אם חפצת
טוב או רע : . ואחרי זה הדבר לא היה בלתי אמר קין להבל אחיד
קום אה אחי נלכה השדה : וילכו שניהם יחדו : ויהי בהיותם בשדה
ויקם קין אל הבל אחיו ויהרגנהו : ואז הרגו ושפך את דמו צררת רוחו
וצעקת הארץ ולא תתקבל את דם (10) הבל : אן תשתה אתו : אלא
על פי יהוה : ותחרד הארץ ואתכסף נור השמש : והירח : עת הרג קין
אל הבל : ויהי אדם שכון באלבאדאן : ואז ראה אדם מה אתעשה
בעולם : מן כמפות השמש והירח וחרדת הארץ ויירא מאד : בזה
היום : והיה היום הזה לו כמו יום מאכלו. הוא ואשתו מפרי העץ
אשר בתוך הגן : . ויעל אדם מן הבאדאן אל ספרה והיא
שכם : עד יראה ספר מלחמות (11) יהוה : ויירא העלות ימים
עד ידע נלל המתחוי בעלמה : וירא כי בניד השנים אין יש
אחד מהם מקים בארץ : ואן אחד חלל : והשני נפל מן חטאתו :
אשר נשא אתה : וידע אדם אן זה הוא הנלל : וישב ללבאדאן : .
ומיום בריאת אדם ואל יום הרג קין אל הבל שלשים שנה : ויהי
הרנות הבל ביום ששה עשר מן חדש טיבת : ברא אלהים אדם ביום
חשמי : בשעה הששית : ושכן (12) אדם וחוה אשתו בנן שמנת ימים :
ולא ידע חוה אשתו בדבר שכיבה בנן : ואתהפכת מדעיון במלת
הנחש : ואתגרשו מן הגן : בשעה אשר בה אתברא אדם : ויצא מן הגן
בשעה ההיא : .

ואחרי אן הרג קין הבל ואתגרש קין : ידע אדם בחטאתו ולא
נשאר לו זרע : לנחלות ה המיתובה : למחלפותו מצות אלהים : דרש
אדם השובה : ויעבד את יהוה : ואתנזר לו מאות שנה : ולא ידע
(13) את אשתו בזה העת : עד קבל יהוה שובתו : ואחר כן ידע אדם
את אשתו ותהר ותלד את שת : בעל המיתובה וירא את הצלם יניד

בשפול מקדשה: בין לוזה והרגריזים: אתה קעם אתה: (8) וכד
הקרב קין והבל בעשרים יום בניסן אבו: (9) וכד לא עמה
קין מנחתה מתקבלה הך דהוה אלוף: עמי: מנחתה דאבוה
ידע דו פסיל והדקריב אתעכר עלמה ורוחה: (10) וב: .
הקרב הבל: . .ב: (11) וב: . .ג שעין אתריחה והוה להבל ולמנחתה:
ולקין ולמנחתה לא אתריחה (12) דרוה: בשעתה קמאיתה
זלושה לא אתצטר: (13) ויחר לקין ועזר לארעה: (14) וכתר
ד: . שנין: דלא עמי לאדם ולא הבל: (15) והות חוה רחמה
לקין: ואדם רחם להבל: (16) וכד והו קין דלא אתי: נסבת

מן מנחות אביו אדם: כי אדם היה אקריב מנחה בראישונה
ואתלמדו בניו (5) ממנו: כפי מאמרו עליו השלום: (ואז לא ראה קין
מנחתו מתקבלה הך היה מתלמד וראה מנחת אביו) ואז אקריב ולא
יראה סימת הקבול ידע בנפשו כי הוא ריק: וחשכת עלמה
בפניו: ורוחו אתצררת: כפי מאמרו עליו השלום: (ידע כי הוא ריק:
ואז אקריב חשכת עלמה בפניו: ורוחו:) ופתרון אחר כי הוא אז
הקריב חשכת עלמה ורוחו: אי: אז הקריב חשכת עלמה (6) ורוחו: מזה
צררת: ויהוה ידע: . ובזים (הקריב הבל ב שעות ישע יהוה אל הבל
ואל מנחתו: ואל קין ואל מנחתו לא שעה:) וגם כי קין מן השעה
הראישונה ראה את מנחתו איננה מתקבלה: ויחר אפו ויתחזק: ולא
יוכל יכמנו: וישב אל ארצו ואקים ארבע שנים: ולא יראה לאביו
אדם: ולא אל אחיו הבל: כפי מאמר הנבי עליו השלום (עת ראה
בשעה הראישונה (7) והקבול לא אראה: ויחר לקין: וישב אל ארצו:
ואקים ד שנים: ולא ראה אל אדם ולא אל הבל:) והיתה חוה
תאהב קין: ואדם היה יאהב הבל: ואז חזת חוה כי קין בנה לא
יבוא אליה נכספת לו: ותקח צו מן אדם ותלך: ואז ראה אתה הבל
העלה והלכה לבדה: והמקום אשר היא הלכה אליו רחוק: קם
במהרה וילך עמה: ותמצאו הלוך מן המקום אשר היה ישב בו
בראישונה: (8) אל מקום יתקרא שמו אחר כן (ערפאת:) ואז
ראה קין את אחיו את הבל: חשב בלבו על הרנותו: והשם יתעלה
לא יכסה עליו כסי: וידע הבריו יתעלה יצר לבו הרע: ויאמר לו
כי הרנת את הבל אליך שובתו: וטעם כן אן הוא המדרש בדמו:
ויתנקם עליו: ראה מה בא בספר בראשית פרק ד: פסוק ו: .
(ויאמר יהוה לקין למה חרה לך: ולמה נפלו פניך הלוא אם
תטיב שאת: ואם (9) לא תטיב לפתח חטאת רבץ: ואליך תשוקתו

ה

(2) ואולד שת לאנוש: ובנא קריה ושמה פילונה על שם אנוש: (3) ואולד אנוש לקינן: ובנא שת מדינה ווקקה דמשק על שם קינן: (4) ואולד קינן למהללאל ובנא מדינה ושמה עטרות שפים: (5) ואולד מהללאל לירד: ובנא מדינה מתקריה יעזיר: (6) ואולד ירד לחנוך: ובנא מרינה ושמה שלם רבתה: בתר (7) יג:. שנה אלף חנוך בספר האותות דיתבנה לאדם: ואנין כד:. אבני שהם בי:. לרוחתה: בי:. לבחור כרניה בני יעקב: ולתולדות עבדיאל עליון: (8) ביתה עדנה אתילדו בני קין לאתרון

עיר חנוך: ובנה ענה זברה וניסה: ועדה: ערים קטנות זהרב לקין: ובנא דחלה: ופתרונה מעבד: שמה (פרדאי טנם) בארץ שנער ויהנה ידע:
(18) עבדי הצלמים: בעת ההיא עלה אדם מן הבאדאן אל רחבות: ויאמר אן הוא מדינה רבה ממצאת בערי אלענם: אשר יאמר עליה בספר בראשית פרק י׳: פסוק יא: (יצא אשור ויבן את נינוה ואת רחבות עיר ואת כלח ואת רסן:.)
ונלל מאמרו הצלמים הוא אן חנוך בן קין עשה בה שתי צלמים מן הזהב: ויאמר אן הוא קרא שמם אחד לפצעי: ואחד לחבורתי:. אמר אדנן משה שלום יהוה עליו בספר (19) אלאמטיר (קרו אדם ניסם קמי בניו:) אי קרא בספר האותות פני בניו אשר מן זרע קין: הזכיח אתם: מזאת המעשים: הרעות ולא אתוכחו:.
ודע אן גלל עלות אדם מן אלבאדאן אל רחבות עיר הוא בעת שמע בעוברי בניו אשר מן קין הלך אליהם למען יוכיח אתם: ויהי במשיתו אליהם קרא חלק מן ספר האותות: וטעם כן אן הוא פתח ספר האותות דאדידהם (20) ואמר להם: אם לא תשובו מן מעשיכם חרעות תמותו כלכם: ולא שמעו ממו ולא פחדו מדבריו: ויצא מאתם וישב למקומו בבאדאן: ויהי כשמע חנוך בן ירד במעשה בני קין יחר להם מאד: ואפרד לבדו: ויתהלך חנוך את האלהים: ובעת ההיא היו ימי שני חייו חמש וששים שנה ויתהלך ביראת השם ויבן חנוך מזבח סהבו אדם:. ואולד את מתושאל ומתושאל ילד את למך: (21) ולמך הולד את נח: ויהי מולד נח בחדש ניסן: ויהי ביום הרביעי מן מולדו אתגלי מופת בשמים: ואז ראו אתו בוראי עלמה ירדת עליהם חתת אלהים: ויבאו אל אדם ללבאדאן עד ישאלו אתו על זה המופת:

ושרה לגו באדן: (24) ומנה ר :. שנה עד קטל קין להבל
ליו :. עשר יומים בטיבית: (25) דאתברא אדם חרופתה:
ואשתחה אדם וחוה בגנתה: ח:. יומין דלא ידע חוה :וזנת
מרעיהון במלתה דנחשה : (26) ובתר קטלה דהבל :
אתנזר אדם ק:. שנה (27) ובתר חכם אתתה: והוליד ית
שת:

II

(1) ביומי שת אזל קין למרנחה: למדינה דבנא חנוך:
דשמה אנטכיה: ומלך קין ק:. שנה ימיה ויבשתה:

על פניה :ומזה ידע אדם כי הוא סוד השלשלה: והעד על כן ראה מה
אמר השם יתעלה בספר בראשית : פרק ה: פסוק ג: (ויחי אדם
שלשים ומאת שנה: ויולד בדמותו כצלמו: ויקרא את שמו שת:)
ראה אל הסוד אנה כי לא אמר עת (14) מולד קין דהבל: (בדמותו
כצלמו:) וזה הצלם הוא צלם נור משה שלום יהיה עליו: אשר
היה יתעתק מן גבר אל גבר :. ובימי חיי שת הלך קין לפאת
קדמה אל העיר אשר בנא אתה בנו חנוך: והיא אנטאכיה אשר שמה
בלשן הסריאני גם כן אנטאכיה: וימלך קין ההר והככר: והים: מאות
שנה :.

ויולד שת את אנוש: ובנא עיר ויקרא שמה פילותה על שם בנו
אנוש: ויולד אנוש את (15) קינן: ובנא שת מדינה: ויקרא שמה דמשק:
ויולד קינן את מהללאל: ובנא מדינה וקרא שמה עטירות שפים:.
ויולד מהללאל את ירד: ובנא מדינה: ויקרא שמה יעזיר :. ויולד
ירד את חנוך: ובנא מדינה ויקרא שמה שלם רבתה:.

ואז גדל חנוך והשיתו ימי חייו שלשה עשר שנה: אחל יתלמד
בספר האותות אשר אנתן לאדם: והיה זה הספר מתביאר על
ארבע (16) ועשרים אבן שהם: מהם שנים עשר לרחותה: ושנים
עשר לדמע המשפחות: בני יעקב: ולתולדות עבדי אל עליון: ויהוה
ידע: אן שנים עשר האבן אשר על חשן אהרן הכהן: הם אשר
יאמר עליהם לדמע המשפחות בני יעקב ולתולדות עבדי אל עליון:
והם מתבאר עליהם תולדות עבדי אל עליון :. ושנים עשר האבן
אשר אמר עליהם לרחותה הם סימה וסוד אל הדור אחרון:
ואתילדו בני (17) קין במושבותם: ושחתו בעולם מן קצהו עד אוליד
קין לחנוך: וחנוך לעירד :. ועירד למיחאל: ומיחאל למתושאל:
ומתושאל ילד את למך: ובשנת יד מן ימי חייו נסע מן חנוכיה

(16) בד: יומים מן מולדה: אתעמי סימן בממציע שומיה:
ורתתו כל דיארי עלמה: ואתו ליד אדם: (17) וקעם אדם
ברמות חכמתה: ובסר במבולה: ואמיר דאמר חנוך בחייה:
(18) ולא אתשקח: ואתפעם אדם: ד ו צפית נקמם: וחכם
בניו: (19) וכד הגמל נח אנדיה למך ליד אדם לביספרה:
ואמר אדם דן ינחמנו: דהוה טובה במולדה: (20) ובנא
למך קריה על שמה ושמה ריפת: והיא גבעון הדנון דרום
מקדשה הרנגריזים: (21) ואולד למך ששה בנים: תובל
קין אתילד דאקטל קין (22) יובל בנה מיסדה מת רבתה:

מוצא הנחשת והברזל וזהוא אשר ברא זאת המלאכה:. ואחת
תובל קין נעמה (26) להיותה מן אמו: כי למך אזדבן בשתי
נשים:. וזאת נעמה אשר אקימת הסלע בעיר ירושלים
בדרך הכשף:. ויהודה ידע:. ואלה אשר אתלמדז בספרי
דקשטח: אדם למד ק: ופ: את למך: שת בנו ה וק שתה: אנוש
ה שתה: וחק: שנה: קינן אתלמד י וטק שנה: מהללאל ה וצ וחק
שנה: ירד ז וכ וחק שנה: חנוך ה ום ונק שנה: ויהיו כל ימי
חנוך שלש מאות ולמך אשר בא זכרונו אנו הזא מבני קין: והעד
על כן כי אחידן אתלמד על אדם ככן למך סתב אחידן אתלמד
על אדם: וזה הזא האמת:.) (27) וחמשה וששים שנה: וימת: וזה מה
בא הזכרון עלין באלאסאטיר ביום מותו: ביום מות חנוך באו כל
בני אדם אל ספרה אז שמעו אדם יבכי עליו: ויהי מותו ביום
הרביעי בבאדאן: וישאו אתו אל ספרה אז שמעו אדם יבכי עליו:
והיו אדם ושת ואנוש זקינן ומהללאל וירד ומתושלח בנו אשר
היה שכון בבאדאן: ורבו מן הבכות עליו עד השיב מגידו אל
אחידן בן (28) תובל קין: אשר היה ישב בחברון: ויהי ראש יכול
ומתקדם על כל בני קין: אשר היה שם אתלמד ספר האותות על
אדם:.

ואן אתאספו הכל:. דרשו מן אדם אן יביאו לו נמים: ויבא
אדם: בו: ויקבר חנוך בו מול הרנגריזים בבטחה המתקריה מחנה:
ואתקרא שם ההר הר עיבל: כי קברו חנוך בו: ופתרון הר עיבל
הר האבל:.

ואתעשה בהר עיבל קברים רבים כאשר אמר חנוך (כי הזא
קברת אל העולם:) (29) וממפאת השמים אשר האש. לא תקרב סביב
ההר גריים ורחזקה מן המאמן בו מכל קצהו שנים אלף אמה: כי

וצעדו עלמה מן אצטרה׃ עד אולד קין לחנוך׃ וחנוך
לעירד׃ ועירד למחיאל׃ ומחיאל למתושאל׃ ומתושאל
לֹלמך׃ (9) ביד ׃. עשרה שנה׃ אזל למך מן חנוכיה׃ ובנא
ענה וניסה ועדה׃ (10) וקטל לקין׃ ובנא דחלה שמה
פאדראי טנם׃ (11) ובמיעול אדם ר'ע׃. אלצנגמין עביד סנט
דהב צלמים׃ לפצעי ולחבורתי (12) ב׃ הוו קרו אדם ניסם
קמי בניו׃ (13) וכד שמע חנוך בעו לאלה׃ בר ה׃. ום׃.
ואתהלך חנוך עם אלהה׃ (14) ובנא מרבח אדם סהבה׃
(15) ואולד למתשולח׃ ומתשולח לֹלמך׃ ולמך לנח׃ בניסן׃

אשר אתגלא בתוך השמים (ויקם אדם ברבות חכמתו ואדיע
אתם במבול׃) דיאמר להם אף כי חנוך ממצא בעלמה חי לא
יהיה המבול..

(22) ואחר כן ראה אדם עליו השלום ברוח הקדש באבדות כל
העולם ויהי עמו מגיד במובא משה עליו השלום׃ ואז אתילד נח
אנחם אדם בו ׃ וידע כי הוא בעל המיתובה ׃ ולא יתפלט מן
המבול בלתי נח׃ ובניז השלשה והודיע אדם לבניז בזה
הדבר׃ וזה מתודע מן מאמרז באלאסטיר (והנחם אדם כי הוא ראה
מראות׃ ואדיע לבניו בכן׃) (23) ואולי אן ימצא אנה רז על אברהם׃
כי קדקר (נקמס ובאברהם מספר אחד׃) ((נקמס ׃ 250׃ ׃ באברהם׃
250)) ויהי פנע אדם בזה אן השלום והפליטה באברהם׃ ואז גדל נח
עליו השלום הביאו אביז אל אדם עד ילמדה בכתבו׃ ויהי כראות
אדם לו אמר (זה ינחמנו ממעשינו ומעצבון ידינו׃ מן האדמה אשר
אררה יהוה׃) כי הטוב במולדו ומפתר כן כי האור אנגלא יזם
מולדו (24) אור גדול בתוך השמים׃ וזה מתודע מן מאמרז עליו
השלום (והיה הטוב במולדו׃) או אן היה הנור בפניו ׃. ויבן
למך עיר על שמו ויקרא את שמה ריפת׃ והיא גבעת׃ המטללה׃
והיא מפאת צפונה להרנגריזים.. ונשוב לזכרון למך אשר מבני
קין ונאמר אן הוא אתילד לו שלשה בנים ובתולה אחת׃
תלל זכרונו הבתולה באלאסאטיר הזא כי לעת אנגלא ממנה
(25) המעשה הרע׃ דעוד נאמר הנער הראש כאשר זכר אתם בספר
אלאסטיר תובל קין׃ וגלל קריאתו בזה השם הזא כי הוא אתילד
אל למך בעת הרנות קין ׃.

השני יובל בנא מיסדה מת הגדלה ׃. השלישי יבל בנא קנז׃ ותובל
קין בנא סכיפם ושמה אלבצרה ועשה בה בית מלאכה אל

וקינן ומהללאל וירד וברה מתושלח: דהוה דער בבאראן:
(35) וכתרו מבכין לה: עד אזל משמועה ליד אחידן בר
תובל קין: דהוה דער בחברון ריש חיל קינאי: (36) דהוה
תמן אלף ביספר האותות קמי אדם: (37) וכד אתו בעו
מן אדם דיקרי נימס: וקרא אדם בה: (38) וקביר חנוך בו
בגבון הרגריזים בבטי: די מתקריה יסכר: (39) ואתקרי
טברה הר עיבל: דהבחלו חנוך בה: והבנא בה קברים
סגי: (40) הך דאמר חנוך אדם דו שפך אל עלמה: ולעל
מנה תרח שומיה: (41) דלית אשתה קרבה ליד סהרת

---

(33) וישם צא עמו אבן מן הגן: ועשה מקום למעבדות חשם יתעלה:
האבן אשר צא עמו מן הגן בבית דמעבד אשר עשה: ויקרא את
שם המקום ההוא (אדרמם:) מתודע זה מן מאמרו באסאטיר משה
(כמה מדי המתקרא שמה אדרמס: אשר היא מבדת אדם בראישונה
אשר הוצאיאו מן הגן:) ומפתר אדרמס: מקום הבבות: דיהוה הידעיו
אשר היה יבכי בו אדם על מוצאו ופרקנו לגן: או יהי מפתרו
מקום המדרש והתלמוד אשר היה ילמד בו ספרי בריאתה: (34) ואמכ
באלאסאטיר על האבן אשר עשה אחידן והמעבד (צור חסיד בו:
בלא אשר כפרה בו: ואתרבת בישתה שש מאות שנה:) וזה אז עשה
אחידן האבן והמעבד אחלו העמים ידבקו ויאמנו בו: ואתרבת
הפשעות ואקימו על מעשה החטאות: שש מאות שנה:. ואחר כן
אמר: (וסרו אשר לא קעם:) ומפתרה אן עבדו אלוהים אחרים אין
לה אקר: ואז אגדלת עונותון עבד יהדה פנותה על אחר דור מהם:
(35) כי השם יתעלה בראישונה נשאם אולי ישובו: ולא שבד:.
רק רבו מן העונות: ותמלא הארץ חמם: ובזה העת אתילד
לאחידן בן זכר ויקרא את שמו אסר: ובנא עוד עיר צרוך
עיר מתקריה ציון תלה: והיא צהיון השחוקה: וישם האבן
אשר עשה בה: ואהב המושב בה: ושלח והביא נפנה בת
נעמה: מן בבל אשר היתה מן הרכילים מבקשה על למך והיתה
מכשפה ידועה בעבדת הכשף:. והיא (36) אשר יתבת בית מעבד
הרנן: ובעבור כן שלח והביאה אחידן: לביתו: נתתנה לבנו אשה עד
יתמעד בה על עבדת הכשף ואחרי מובא נפנה עשה (ניגוג נדולים)
ומפתרה צלם והיה על ארבע צלמים אחד מן זהב: ואחד מן הכסף:
ואחד מן הנחשת: ואחד מן עץ הזית: ועשה שמש וירח בתוך הארבע
לאהיר: וישם בתוך השמש גביע מן זהב מניר:. וישם בתוך

(23) יביל בנא קנז והיא ניסבור: (24) תובל קין בנא
סכיפס שמה אלבצרה: לארדאג כל אמן נחשה: (25) אלה
אלף אדם ק: : . ופ: : . אדם אלף למך ביספרה דקשטה:
(26) שת ברה אלף ה:. וק: . שתה: (27) אנוש ה:. שתה וחק: .
שתה: (28) קינן אלף י: . שנין וטק: שתה: (29) מהללאל
אלף ה:. וץ:. וחק:. שתה: (30) ירד אלף ז:. ום:. וחק:. שנה:
(31) חנוך אלף ה:. ום:. וגק:. שנה: (32) ביום מת חנוך אתו
כל בני אדם לספרה: משמע אדם מבכי לה: (33) בד מית
חנוך והסתבל לספרה: (34) ובכותה אדם ושת ואנוש

הדא מקלט הגם מן עונו: צור הישועה: ופתרנן כן אן כל מן יהי
מאמן בהרגרי: ואקבר סביבו כברת שני אלפים אמה לא תקרבו
האש: השריפה:

וכמו זה קשטו אלה שני הזכאים: והם אבינו אדם וחנוך עליהם
השלום? ואתלמד מתושלח עשרים שנה ושבע מאות שנה: ואתלמד
למך שלשה (30) וחמשים שנה: ושש מאות שנה: ונח אתלמד וקרא
בספר אדם אשר אתלמדו שש מאות שנה:.

III ואז קרבו ימי אדם למות ואכבש במלת מות תמות: ואלה ימי
שני חיי אדם אשר חי: תשע מאות שנה ושלשים שנה ויבאו כל
בניז אל מקומו אל הבאדאן: ויצום ישאו אתו אל (עוזל מטה:) אשר
היא עמק חברון: כי ראה בבינתו אן היא אתבראת עד תקבץ
לדרי זכותה: ואתבראת בעת מברא עץ הדעת: ואתבנת (31) על
שלשה פלנים: (הראש:) ליוצאים מן הנן:.. (השני:) ליוצאים מן
התבה: (השלישי:) ליוצאים מן הגמילה: והיא מתקרא שמה המכפלה:
וימלך נח תחת אדם אחרי מות אדם: שבע שנים אתלמד נח
מפרי בריאתה: ספר האותות: וספר נגמות: וספר מלחמות: אלה הם
ספרי אדם:.

זה ספר תולדת אדם: (מי כמוך באילים יהוה מי כמוך אלהי
בראשית ושופט יום נקם: יהזה אחד:) מאמרו זה ספר תולדת
אדם הוא (32) על התולידה אשר אתקדם זכרונה:.

ואחרי אקבר אדם שב נח וכל בני האדם למקומם: וירבו העם
ויעצמו מאד: וילך אחידן בן ברד בן תובל קין: ויבן את ציון:
המתקרא שמה נפנה:. והיא בית מכתש:. ומפתר מכתש בלשן
העברי נגע: תעשה בה אבן שחוק: וקראו מעבד: מדמי במקום
המתקרי אדרמם: אשר היא סגדת אדם בראישונה: כי אדם היה

לדיארי זכותה: דדעת: (5) והיא למיעול מות תמות: (6) ובניאה
על תלתה חלוקין: לנפוקי גנה: ולנפוקי תיבותה: ולנפוקי
ערלת בסרה: (7) די זעיקה מכפלה: (8) ויתב נח על אתרה
דאדם בתר מות אדם: (9) בז:. שנין אלף תלתה ספרי בריתה:
ספר האותות וספר נגמות: וספר מלחמות: זה ספר תולדת
אדם: (10) מי כמוך באילים יהוה (11) מי כמוך אלהון
דקמאי: ואכשרון דתנינאי יהוה אחד: דעזר (12) נח
וכל בניו דאדם אסגו עמה ואתחילו: (13) ואהל אחידן
בר ברד בר תובל קין: ובנא ציון: די מתקריה גפנה: והיא

עוד מת אחר הצדיקים אשר הוא מתושלח: כי המבול לא היה אלא
אחרי מות כל הצדיקים: ויהי מתושלח איננו חי:. ומן התורה
הקדושה יתודע אן למך ומתושלח מתו בשנה אחת: ויהודה ידע אן
למך מת בראישונה: ואחרי מות מתושלח אשר היה מתו ביום
יד: מן חדש השני: רטבת הארץ: ואחרי שלשת ימים אחרים נבקעו
(42) כל מעינות תהום רבה: וארבות השמים נפתחו: ויהי הגשם על
הארץ: בחדש השני בשבעה עשר יום לחדש ביום השלישי: וזה
מתודע מן מאמר השליח באלאסאטר (בד: ארטיבת הארץ ויטמת:
ובב: נפתחו ארבי השמים): ויהי כלול ירדות הגשם ביום השבת
בשעה השישית מן הליל: וזה מתודע מן מאמרו (וז: קצ: כלל:
בג:. שעין מן הליל: ז השבת כלולה בזרה כללה) אן אכלל מורד
הגשם בו בששה (48) ונותרת הדבר גלי: ואני ראיתי מן
יפתר מפתר אחר ככה: (ובשבעה מאות ותשעים כללה: בשעה
השישית מן לילת השבת:) וסר מן מאמרו (וז: קץ:) ויהודה ידע אן
זה הפתרון איננו על האמת: וסר מן המדרש:.

ועתה נשוב לאשר אנחנו בזכרונו ונאמר כאשר אמר בעל
אלאסאטיר אן נח עליו השלום היה מוצאו מן התבה ביום השבת:
וביום השני והשלישי (44) בנא מזבח: ואקריב עליו מנחה ליהוה כפי
מאמרו אנה ז: (וא: יצא נח מן התבה וב: בנא מזבח ואקריב)
ואחרי כלול המבול ומות כל חי על פני האדמה: ולא נשאר כי אם
נח: ואשר אתו בתבה:. ויירא נח וחשב ואמר בלבו אן ישוב
המבול שנית על הארץ: וידע יהוה מה חשב ויאמר אל לבו לא
אוסף עוד להכות את כל חי: ויכרת עמו ברית הקשת: ויתן
לו אמונה (45) לאחר הדורות: ויהי כריתות זה הברית עמו בחדש
השביעי:. וישב נח באחילה מפאת קדמה בעיר בבל: ולמד

הרגריזים ב:.. אלפים:.. דאמין בו קרי מקלט לערוק צור ישועה:.. (42) ואלף מתושלח כ:. שנה וזק:. שנה:(43) ואלף למך ג:. ון:. שנה וזק:. שנה:(44) ונח אלף וק:. שנה קרי בספר אדם דאלפו:

III

(1) וכד קרב יום מות אדם: ואכבש במות תמות: ואלין שני חיי אדם: טק:.. שנה ול:.. שנה: (2) וכל בניו אתו לידה לבאדאן: (3) ופקדון דיסבלונה לעיול מטה דהיא עמק חברון: חבר:.. (4) דעמה בנעירותה: די עבידה מכנשה

הירח אבן (37) שהם: ואמר לנפנה זאת המנורה הראישונה אשר אתעשת בעלמה ואקימת נפנה בחיל ארבע מאות עבד ועשרים סרים: היו בתשמישותה אמר אנה באלאסטיר (עצומה קדושה הדברים אשר היו על מטה אדם) אשר היא מטה האלהים מפתר זה הדבר ויהזה הידעיו אן הטעם בו המעשים אשר אתנלת מן הרשעים האלה: כתוב על מטה אדם הראיה עליה: ואחר כן עבדת נפנה ניבנ נשאת אתו ברוח (38) יתקרא פינדאל מזל הרוח מכל פאתיו והוא את יעבר הרוח בו יצא ממו קול ואקימו. מאה ועשר שנים: ויזלד לאמור בן מן נפנה ויקרא את שמו (איתנו) ויזלד אל איתנו בן ויקרא את שמו שריקה: והיתה נפנה תקרא להשמש והירח אשר עשה אתם אחדן והם הלכים עמה כמה תרצי: ואז ראו כל העולם זאת המעשים צחקו ודרשו ישתחוו להם: והיו כלם ישתחוו ויעבדו להם: (39) ותמלא הארץ חמס ורעות: ויהי האדון נח יזרי וילמד בעולם: ולא שמע ממנו אחד: וירא כי כל הבוראים סרו מן הדרך וכי המושב בתוך הרשעים לא תצליח: ויצא מן ריפת אל ההר אשר שמו (עדר שנב:.) אשר עשה בו התבה: ואדיעו שת במובא המבול ואקים נח יראה בסודי ספר האותות וירא צפינת אדם וימצא בה ראיה על התבה: ולעת מוצאו מן ריפת נלא יהזה מופת גדול במקום (40) אשר הוא חנה בו: וירא נח יראה גדולה: ואקים נח בתפלות ותהללות מאות שנה: אחרי מולדו את שם ואת חם ואת יפת: ובנות לא אתילד לו: רחמות לו: כי יהדה ידע במובא המבול: ויקח שם (שרית בת שת לו לאשה:) ויקח חם (מכה בת ירד) ויקח יפת (מקיסתה בת למך): ויהי בעת תמו עונות הבוראים והשיבו אל המאבד: אמר יהוה אל נח יעשה את התבה: ועשה אתה וכלל עשותה בעשרה (41) ימים מן חדש השני: ואחרי ארבע ימים

IV

(21) והוה על ד' :. צלמים :. אחד דהב : ואחד כסף : ואחד
נחשת : ואחד קיצם זית : (22) ועבד שמש וזהר דזגוג :
ויהב לגו שמשה עצוץ : דדהב מניר : (23) ויהב לגו זהרה
אבן שהם :. (24) ואמר לגפנה הא עבדת ארשה מלי נדנה :
(25) וקעמת נפנה בעזז ד' :. ק' :. עבד וכ' :. שמהן רום קדש
כריזתה : דהות על אטר אדם : דו מתקרי אתו האלהים :
(26) ועבדת ניגוג דרוח' מתקרי פיננגאל נגד קל ברוח מכל
רבעתה (27) וכתרו ק' :. וי' :. שנין ואולד אסור בר מגפנה
ושמה איתנו : (28) ואולד איתנו בר וזעק שמה שריקה

(וילך עילם ואשור לצפון אור כשדים : אשר הוא בדידון עיר
מתקרא שמה שער השערים :) ויהי שם על שפת שער השערים
גמר זמנונ' : (וילך לד וארם וישכנו בעיר הכותה : והיא עיר
(50) גדולה תתקרא השדים החשכה המתקריה הגבירה באפריקיה :
וארפכשד שכן באור כשדים : ברקטרס אשר יתקרא שמה רומיה :.)
וִיְלֶד כוש את נמרוד · ויהי כי נדל : מלך על בני חם :. ויהי איש
גבור בארץ ויאסף אתם על בניאן בבל הגדלה ויבנו אתה לו יראה
ממנו :.
ואהל נמרוד גבור בארץ : וזה הוא ראש כל גבור אתגלא בארץ :
אחרי המבול :.
ואז היה ימי שני חיי נח (51) תשע מאות שנה : וחמשה וארבעים
שנה אתגלא הנמרוד : וישמע בו ובמעשיו הרעות :. (ושם בנו אשר
היה מיתב בידו על דרג הממלכה : בעבור כי היה בכור :.) ומפתר
זה הוא : שם בנו היה פוקד בריתו : ואז נדל נח אביו הפקידו על
הממלכה :. ובזאת הימים שלח שם אל חמשת בניו (עילם ואשור
וארפכשד ולד וארם) ויביאהם אל אצלו : ויבאו אליו : ויבנו (52) את
נינוה ואת רחבות עיר : ואת כלח : ואת רסן : ורסן היא עיר גדלה בין
נינוה ובין כלח : ואמר עליה בתורה הקדושה : (היא העיר הגדלה :.)
ויהי כי קרבו ימי האדון נח למות שלח ויקרא לבניו השלשה
ויבאו אליו אל שלם רבתה : ויבנו מזבח :. (ויעלו עליו אודואן :)
ותהללות ורוממות לאלהים החי דלא ימות :. ויהי! האדון נח
בראישון פלג הארץ על שנים ועשרים חלק ושיאר לו שני חלקים
ולעת מותו נתן (53) לשם חלק :. ואל יפת חלק : ופלג עוד כל אשר
לו מן ממלכת עלמה להם : ואבדיל שם על יפת : יתר כי הוא
הבכור : והוא חליפתו : ובעל השלשה הקדושם :. ולבני חם לא נתן

בית מכתש: (14) ועבד לגבה[א]בו רימת דחלה: כות מדי
דמתקריה אדרמס: דהי מעקודית אדם קמאיתה דהפכו
מן גנה: (15) והיא צור חסיו בו: גלה דשדרכו (16) בה
וסגת בישתה ו: . ק: . דשתה ' ופנו דלא קעם עבד אלה
פנותה: (17) דעל עקב דרי פנותה ומתנאתה אסגה: ומלא
עלמה מן אנשה: (18) ואולד אחידן בר וזעק שמה אסור:
(19) ובנא צורן מדי מתקריה ציון תלה ויהבה לנבה:
(20) ושלח ואנדה לנפנה ברת נעמה: מן בבל דהות מן
מזידי דחלת למך: ויהבה לאסור לאתה: ועבד ניגוג ראס

בניו וראש מה למד אתם הסדרה ביחידאות השם: ואן יהודה אחד:
פרד: אין לו שני: מתודע זה מן מאמר בעל אלאסאטיר (ולמד
בניו אקר המאמן והיא הסדרה) ואחרי שנים וששים שנה מן
המבול פלג את הארץ על בניו: וישם (לשם שלשה חלקים: וליפת
ארבע: ולחם ארבע (46) ועילם: ולד וארם: ואשור ארבע חלקים:
וארפכשד חלק:) אלה חמשת הבנים בני שם: (ויתן ספר האותות
לארפכשד: ויתן ספר נבמות אל עילם: ויתן ספר מלחמות אל
אשור:) ושם ארפכשד ועילם ואשור בדולים וקדשים והגבישים על
כל בניו: (ועשה ליפת ארבע חלקים והם נמר ומגנ מדי ייון
תובל ומושך: . . ותירם חלק:) ועשה אל חם ארבע חלקים: וכוש
חלק: ומצרים חלק: ופוט חלק: (47) והכל מהם שנים ועשרים חלק:
ואבדיל בני שם במתנו להם ספרי בריאתה: כי הוא הבכור: ושיאר
לו שני חלקים: עת מותו נבוא ובזכרונם ופלותם: ואז כלל נח מן
מלאכתו ופלונו: קם על (ענימות הימים מספר ארבע אלפים
ושלש מאות שנה: . תמו שבע שנים אחרי המבול וראש יומי
בריאתן ששה אלפים:) ומפתר כן הוא מן אדם אל התהב
ששת אלפים שנה: והאלף השביעית יוביל: (48) ומיום ברא
אלהים את האדם עד היה המבול אלף ושלש מאות ושבע
שנים: ומיום פלג נח על בניו אל יום בניאן בבל: והפיצם יהוה על
פני כל הארץ: שלשה ותשעים שנה וארבע מאות שנה: וזה מתודע
מן מאמרו באלאסאטיר (ומיום פלג נח בניו עד היום אשר פקדון
דר הדור: דק עד וב: שנים:) ופלג נח עליז השלום מלכותה על בניו:
השלשה: אחרי המבול (בשלש מאות שנה ועשרים שנה:) (49) ויהי
נח ביום פלג נדולי בניו בן תשע מאות ושלשים שנה: ופלג הארץ
על בני השלשה ביום העשירי מן ירח אילול: ועבר קראים בתוך
בניו ילך כל איש למקומו: ונפצו מעמו: .

יה

רבה:. ואקים קנומה בצלו ותשבחן מאה שתה בתר דאולד
שם וחם ויפת:. (5) ונסב שם שרית ברת שת לאתה
(6) נסב חם סכה ברת ירד אתה:. (7) ונסב יפת מקיסתה
ברת למך:. (8) וכד אמר אלה מעבד תיבו עבדה וסכמה
בי:. יומין (9) בירח תנינה:. בד:. ארטיבת ארעה ומית (10) וג:.
אפתחו ארכי שומיה:. ז:. קץ:. גזרה בששה שעין מן ליליה ז:.
וא:. נפק נח מן תיבותה:. וב:. (11) בנא מדבחא ואקרב:.
(12) ואקים אלה קיאם עמה:. קיאמה דקשתה:. בז:. ושרה נח
בעטה מדנח שמש בבל:. ואלף בניו ריש כרי זיתי:. וסהדותה
(13) בתד ס:. וב:. שנין אתפלגת ארעה לבניו שם וחם ויפת:.

באש:. ויקחו ממנו את שרה אשתו שני פעמים:. ויהי עליו גם
כן מלחמות זכירים בספר התורה הקדושה:. דע אן כל אחד
מן הזכאים היה לו בימי חייו חזקות רבות והיא נסות מיהוה:. עד
יטהר אתם מן עונות עלמא:. וישא את (58) מיתוביתהם וינדילם
בעלמא ואחרית ואולי יהיה אות (57):. מן (זכרון) עד יהי להם דעות
ושם:. ואמר אדונן מרקה רצון יה:. עליה על הזכאים (מיתין
כקעימין):. והוא מאמרו (דכר לנך. קיאם:. מיתיך כקעימין:) ויהוה
הידעת:.

ומפתר עוד:. באות ז:. הנה היא שבעה:. והשבת שביעי:. ושמרו
יטהרו מן עונותו:. ואולי אן יהיו דרש יספר המלחמת אשר באו
בימי הזכאים:. והצרירות אשר היתה תהי עליהם:. היא היתה תטהר
אתם (59) כמה יטהר השבת לשמודיד:. ויהוה הידעיד:. ולזה המפתר
דבר יתורך:. ידעו לו בעלי המדעות:. אמר בספר אלאסאטיר
(ראש מלחמות המיתים קמאי ראש המלחמות היה נללו להדים
וענמים:. ולהבים ונפתחים ופתרסים וכסלחים אתאספו איש לרעהו:.
ובחרו להם שר שמו ניטט בכור להדים אשר אתקראו על שמו
ניבטאי:. ויצאו מן פלשתים ועשו המלחמה בראישונה את הכנעני
והפרזי:. ויקחו הממלכה מיד הנמרוד וימלכו מן ארץ (60) מצרים
אל נהר כוש:. וילך הנמרוד ויחן לפני ניטט:. ודרש מן בני
יקטן יסעדו אתו על בני מצרים:. וזרעו:. ולא שמעו אליו בני
יקטן:. רק אז השיבו חנו במקום יתאמר לו (ממשא באכה ספרה
הר הקדם) אל תמנתה המתקרא שמה עיר אלימן ספרה הר
הקדם אל תמנתה:. וימת ניטט שר המצרים:. ויהי כשמע הנמרוד

(29) והות גפנה זעיקה שמשה וזהרה: דעבד אחידן ואנון מהלכין עמה: (30) וכד עבדו הדה בעו אנשה סגדין לון: ואתעכר עלמה: וחבל כל בסד שבילה על ארעה:

IV

(1) וערק נח מן ריפת בטורה דשמה עדר שגג: דהוא אתר תיבותה: (2) ובסרה אלה במבולה: וקעם נח ברמי ספר האותות ועמה טמירת אדם: וסכו די לתיבותה: (3) והוה מפקאתה ואתחזי על אתרה סימן: (4) ודחל נח דחלה

בפעם ההוא. מאום: כי היה עשה מה בא זכרונו בתורה: וישמת נח יאמר (ארור כנען עבד עבדים יהיה לאחיו: וחם הוא אבי כנען:) ובדיל כן לא לקח מן ירשת אביו בפעם ההוא: ודע אן מזה אתודע אן הכפור לא (54) יירש המאמן: והמאמן לא יירש הכפור:.

וימת נח עליו השלום בן תשע מאות וחמשים שנה: וישאו אתו בניו: ויקברו אתו במערת המכפלה אשר אקבר בה אדם כאשר צדם:.

V וילכו כל איש אל מקומו: ויהי אחרי הארבע מאות ושלשה ותשעים שנה אשר אתנבא עליהם האדון נח היה קבוץ בעיר בבל במטלון ממדנח:. והא מקום יתקרא מטלון מקדם לבבל מצאו בקעה ארכה (55) בארץ שנער וישבו שם: והיא בקעה הך בקעת שכם: והא אלון מורא: ואצלה הר הך הרברייזים: ויאמרו איש לרעהו: נעלה לזה ההר: ונבנה לנו בניאן שחזק עיר ומגדל: פן נפוץ על פני כל הארץ: ויעלו אל ההר ויבנו עליו בראישונה מנורה: ויהי אורה יתגלי מן ארבע פאתי עלמה: ויקראו שמה שם: והיא המלה אשר אמר (נעשה לנו שם) וכללו מן הבניאן ולא (56) שלם להם השם בקשם: וינתק את בניאנה: ונפצו בני האדם על פני כל הארץ: ולא ידע איש מהם לשן רעהו:.

וזה הדבר היתה נלל המלחמות: כאשר אמר בספר אלאסאטיר: (וזאת היא אקר המלחמות אשר היתה למיתים והשביעית לחיים:) מאמרו דקרבים למאתיה: מלחמות המיתים איש לרעהו: והמיתים הם בעלי החטאות הריקים מן השלמות: יתאמר עליהם (קעימין כמיתים) ונמאמרו זז: לקעימיה אן המלחמות (57) אשר היתה בעת ההיא היו השלשלה הקדושה יתצרד ממנה: ויהי עליהם חזקות גדלות מן הנמרודים (תרח) קחו אתו ואסרו לו (אברהם) בנו השליכו אתו

בוראה דבראשית עד יום דפקדרון דר ודר : מיה אלף וג׃.
ק:. וז׃. שנין (22) ומיום פלוג נח בניו עד יומה דפקדרון דר
ודרור:דק:. וג:. שנין:. (23) ופלג מלכותה לג:. בניו:לג:.
ק:. וכ:. שנה:. (24) והוה נח יתה יומה:דפלג רבני בניו:דטק:.
ול:. שתה:. (25) ופלג ארעה לג:. בניו בי:. יומים מן ירח
חלול : (26) ועבד כרוזים לגו כל בניו ייזל כל אנש לאתרה :
(27) ואפטרו מקדמיה:ואזל עילם ואשור לצפון אור כשדים
הוא בדידון בדי מתמרה באב אלאבואב : (28) הוה על שפת

אמר הרן זה מכשף גדול וכשוופו מאן את האש תשרפו ותצא האש
בעת ההיא ותאכל (65) את הרן:. ראה מה אמר עליו בתורה הקדושה
(וימת הרן על פני תרח אביו בארץ מולדתו באור כשדים) ואז ראה
אתו הנמרוד ועדתו כי האש יצאת ואכלת את הרן ירדת עליהם
חתת אלהים וייראו אן תצא עליהם ותשרף אתם: ויצו הנמרוד במוצא
האדון אברהם: (ישתבח עבוד סימניה ופליאתה שמור הברית והחסד
לאתהיב:) ויהי אחרי שבע שנים מזה הדבר מת הנמרוד: ויהי כלל
המלכים (66) אשר מלכו מבני חם:.

על יד נמרוד אחלת: ועל יד נמרוד אתכללת: ומן הנמרוד הראישון
אל הנמרוד השני אלף שנה ועשרים שנה: הנמרוד הראישון מן
כוש: והנמרוד השני מן כפתרים:.

ויהי אחרי מות הנמרוד צא תרח להלך אל ארץ כנען כי היא
מחוץ לממלכת הנמרוד: כי ירא אן יתגלי עוד נמרודים: ויעשו בו
כאשר עשה הנמרוד הזוכיר:. ונחור בנו שכן בכדר לעמר: ותדחל
מלך גוים:. ויהי (67) כשמעם במוצא תרח: הוציאו אנשים לקראתו
עד ימנעו אתו מן המהלך ועלה נבז כדר לעמר: ושלח ואסר תרח
בחרן: ויצא אברם הלוך אל כדר לעמר לאור כשדים עד יתנפל
לפניו עד יצא לו תרח אביו מן בית הסחר:. שם קרא לו אלהים
ויצוהו במוצא מן חרן: ויבא אל ארץ כנען: ולוט בן אחיו עמו וישבו
באלון מורא:.

י ועתה ראה אה אחי מה רב משמע אדנינו אברהם לאלהיו: כי יצא
מארצו (68) וממולדתו ועזב אביו בבית הסחר יראה מן ממרות פי
יהוה:.

(טזבי אהבי יהודה וזה וילון משנאי יהוה:) ומזה הדבר אתדע אן
תרח מת ואברהם בנו איננו אצלו ונאמר אשר קבר אתו בנו נחור: וזה

(14) ויעבד שם ג: . חלקים: : ויפת ד: . וחמד : עילם ולד וארם ואשור : חלק ד: . ואפרכשד חלק (15) ויהב ספר האותת לארפכשד : וספר נגימות לעילם : וספר מלחמות לאשור : (16) ועבדון רברבין על כל בניו : (17) ועבד יפת ד: . חלקים גמר ומגוג מדי ויון תובל ומושך ותירס : חלק (18) ועבד חם ד: . חלקים כוש חלק ומצרים חלק ופוט חלק וכנען חלק: (19) וכד אסכם נח פלוגיה קעם על נגימות יומיה: ד: . אלפין ותלת מואן שנה: פרע ז:. שנין בתר מבולה : (20) וריש יומי בריתה ו: אלפין שנה (21) מיום

במות ניטט ויקם להלחם עם יושבי עיר אשור: והיא דמתקרא שמה אלמדצל וימלך אתה : ואז מלך אתה (61) קם ועשה מלחמה את נחור: ועשה הנמרוד עם ארפכשד הך מה עשה פרעה את העברים: כי הם בפעם ההוא ראו בספר האותות אשר אתעתק עמהם אן יקום איש מחי כל מן ישתחוי אל הצלמים ויתתק עוד להם: . ויאסף כל החכומים אשר היו בתוך בני חם: ובני יפת: דרש מהם יגידו לו על יום מולד זה האיש ויגידו לו ויאמרו לו אחרי ארבעים יום תהר אמו בו: ויצו הנמרוד אן יאסרו כל איש מעל אשתו מכל (62) בני ארפכשד: מספר ארבעים יום : ויהי כן : ויאסרו האנשים במקום : והנשים במקום לבדם: ויהי אחרי שלשים יום מן הימים הזכירה נלא יהוה מזפת בארץ שנער והוא עמוד אש ירד מן השמים לארץ: ויראו כל היושבים בה יראה גדלה: ויעשו תפלות בבית מעבדון פני הצלמים: ויצאו אל השדה אל מחוץ לעיר: . ואקימו שם שלשת ימים : והשם יתעלה: שם להם מלאכה ושכחו את האסורים: ובעת (63) הדיא הלך האדון תרח במראות מיהוה: וישכב את אשתו : ותהר : ואז שכב תרח את אשתו : ושב לבית הסאר. אתנשא המופת: מעל הנמרוד ועדתו: ויהי כי ראו המכשפים אן המופת אתנשא אמרו הילד השיב אל רחם אמו ויגידו אל הנמרוד בכן ויצו הנמרוד ויאמר הוציאו את כל האסרים אל מקומותם ויעשו כן : ויצא כל איש למקומו כאשר אמר: . ואחר כן אתילד אדנן אברהם עליו השלום ביכלות היכול העצום: . ויהי כי גדל לקחו (64) הנמרוד וישמו תחת ידו ויהי מן העמדים לפניו לראות : ואחר כן לקחו והשליכו בתוך האש : והאש לא תוכל תשרף אדנן אברהם כי היה יהוה עמו רעי בגלל אדון הבשר אשר יצא מחלציו וגם לרבות צדיקותו : ראה מה אמר לו יהוה (אני יהוה אשר הוצאתיך מאור כשדים) ואז ראו אן האש לא תוכל עליו

ברה: דהוה מתב בידה על דרג מלכותה בגלל דהוה
בכור: (35) וְשָׁלַח שֵׁם עוֹד לְעֵילָם וְאַשּׁוּר וְלַד וְאַרָם
וְאַרְפַּכְשַׁד וְאַתוּ וּבְנוּ נִינְוֵה וְכַלָּה וּרְחוֹבוֹת עִיר וְרֶסֶן הִיא קְרָתָה
רַבְּתָה: (36) וְקָרְבוּ יוֹמֵי נֹחַ לָמוּת: וְשָׁלַח וּזְעַק לְשֵׁם וְחָם וְיֶפֶת
וְאַתוּ לְיִדָהּ לְשָׁלַם רַבְּתָה: וּבְנוּ מִדְבַּח וְאַסְקוּ עֲלָיו אוּדָאוֹאָן
(37) וְאָקִים פְּלוּגְיָא יְהַב לְשֵׁם ו: וְיֶפֶת ו: . וְיַתֵּר שָׁם עַל יֶפֶת
סַגִּי (38) וְשָׁלַם נֹחַ וּמִית וְסַבְלוּתֵהּ בְּנָיו לְיַד עִיּוּל מַטָּה הִי

וִיהִי כְּשָׁמֹעַ הָאָדוֹן אַבְרָהָם עָלָיו הַשָּׁלוֹם בַּאֲשֶׁר הָיָה עַל פַּרְעֹה
וְעַל בֵּיתוֹ: קָם וְנָשָׂא פָּנָיו אֶל הַשָּׁמַיִם וְהִלֵּל לַיהוָֹה וְאוֹדִי לוֹ:
וְקִדַּמּוֹ עַל מַה עָשָׂה עִמּוֹ מִן הַטּוֹב: וְשָׁמַר לוֹ אֶת שָׂרָה אִשְׁתּוֹ
מִן הַטָּמֵא ..:
שָׁם אִתְקַשַּׁט וְאִתּוֹדַע לָהֶם אָן כָּל הַמַּעֲשִׂים אֲשֶׁר הָיְתָה מִן
(73) רְאוֹת פַּרְעֹה לְשָׂרַי: וְשָׂרַי לֹא יָכוֹל אִישׁ לִרְאוֹת פָּנֶיהָ: וְיְהִי עַל
פָּנֶיהָ אוֹר מֵנִיר רַב: מִתּוֹדַע זֶה מִן מַאַמָרוֹ (שָׁם אִתְהַפְּכוּ וְרָאוּ
אָן כָּל פְּעוּלָאתָה מִן הָאוֹת שָׂרָה עַל פָּנֶיהָ יְרָאָה רַבָּה.) וְשָׁם
אִתּוֹדְעַת שָׂרַי כִּי הִיא אֵשֶׁת אַבְרָהָם: דָּרַשׁ פַּרְעֹה הָרוּחַ
מִמֶּנּוּ: וַיִּתֵּן לוֹ אֶת שָׂרַי אִשְׁתּוֹ: וַיֵּצֵא מֵאִתּוֹ בְּשִׂמְחָה וּבְשָׁלוֹם:
בְּשַׁלְמוּת אִשְׁתּוֹ וְעָמַד לִפְנֵי יְהוָֹה: וַאִתְפַּלֵּל בַּעֲבוּר פַּרְעֹה וּבֵיתוֹ:
(74) וְזֹאת הִיא רֹאשׁ הַתְּפִלּוֹת אֲשֶׁר אִתְפַּלֵּל בָּהּ הָאָדוֹן אַבְרָהָם) וּמֶן
כְּלִיל מַה אָמַר בִּתְפִלּוֹתָיו (יְהוָֹה אֱלֹהֵי הַשָּׁמַיִם וֵאלֹהֵי הָאָרֶץ חָנֹן
חָנָן .): וַיִּרְפָּא אֱלֹהִים אֶת פַּרְעֹה וְאֶת בֵּיתוֹ: וְאָז אִתְקַשַּׁט פַּרְעֹה
בְּמַאֲמַן אַבְרָהָם וְכִי תְּפִלּוֹתוֹ מִתְקַבְּלָה: וְכִי אֱלֹהָיו הוּא אֱלֹהֵי
הָאֱלֹהִים וַאֲדוֹן הָאֲדוֹנִים: וְעָשָׂה הַמּוֹפְתִים בִּגְלָלוֹ: וְיָדַע כִּי הַתְּפִלָּה
פְּנֵי הַצְּלָמִים לֹא תִּרְפָּא אוֹתוֹ מִן הַנֶּגַע אֲשֶׁר הָיָה לוֹ: וְלֹא רִפְאוּ
אֶלָּא תְּפִלּוֹת אַבְרָהָם לֵאלֹהָיו: בְּעֵת הַהִיא צִוָּה בְּחָרְבוֹת בָּתֵּי
הַמַּעֲבָד אֲשֶׁר הַצְּלָמִים בָּהּ: . (75) וּשְׁבִירוֹת כָּל הַצְּלָמִים וּמְאַבֵּד כָּל
הַמַּצֵּבוֹת וְצִוָּה בַּחֲרָנוֹת כָּל הַמִּשְׁתַּחֲוִים לְהַצְּלָמִים: כִּי לֹא יֵשׁ לָהֶם
צוֹרֶךְ בָּהֶם: וְכָל מִן אִשְׁתַּחֲוָי לָהֶם יְהִי לוֹ מִנְגָע בָּעוֹלְמָא: וְחָטָא
בְּאַחֲרִית: וְכָל זֶה הַדָּבָר מִתּוֹדַע מִן מַאַמְרוֹ בָּאַלְאסאַטיר (וְכָל בֵּיתֵי
הַמַּעֲבָד אִתְלַחֲצוּ: וְכָל הַמִּשְׁתַּחֲוִים לוֹ נוֹפְלִים: וְלֹא מִתְנַשְּׂאִים .).
וְחַרְשָׁה טוֹרְטַם עָלָה מִשָּׁם אָז רָאָה מַה עָשָׂה פַּרְעֹה בְּבָתֵּי הַמַּעֲבָד:
וּבִצְלָמִים וְהַמַּצֵּבוֹת לֹא יָכוֹל לַעֲמֹד בְּמִצְרַיִם (76) וַיַּעַל מִמֶּנָּה וַיֵּלֶךְ
לְחֶבְרוֹן ..:
וְאַחַר כֵּן צִוָּה פַּרְעֹה אֲנָשִׁים מֵאֲנָשָׁיו וַאֲמַר לָהֶם לְכוּ עִם אַבְרָהָם

עילם ואשור : (29) ועל גמר ומגוג מן באב אלאבואב ולגו :
(30) ואזל לד וארם ושרו בכותה רבה דשמה הרסאן אלסואדא
די מתקריה אלגזירה היא באפריקיה : (31) וארפכשד
שרה באור כשדים ברקטרס דשמה רומי : ושרי מלך
נמרוד על כל בניו דהם (32) ובנה בבל רבתה : ואכנשו
כלה ונפקו למבני יתה : ושרי נמרוד למהך גבר בארעה :
(33) ונח ב טק :. ומ :. וה :. שנין ואיל משמועה ליד נח (34) ושם

מתודע מן מאמרו יתעלה (ויםת תרח בחרן :) ולא תתפני אל
מאמרו וימת תרח בחרן ואחר כן אמר (לך לך מארצך וממולדתך :)
זה כי אחל הדבר בקצת אברם עד יהי הדבר מתיתב : ויש כמו זה
בתורה רב עד מאד : וזה לא יהי מהפך ‏ אצל בעלי המדע
והבונה :.

ואז שכן אברהם באלון מורא במראות מיהוה יתעלה כי אמר
לו (אל הארץ אשר הראך) ויהי הראיזת לו עד השיג לאלון מורא ידע
כי שם המדרש : ויבן מזבח סהביו אדם ונח : ואחר כן עלה אל
הגרגרייזס מקדם לבית אל : ויקר וישתחוי שם ליהוה : ויעבדו וירד :.

ויהי אחר הדברים האלה היה רעב בארץ כנען וימע אברם זלוט
בן אחיו עמו מן אלון מורא (10) וירדו מצרימה : ואז השינו בנבול
מצרים היתה חרדה גדלה בכל בתי המעבד : אשר במצרים : ויראו
כל יושבי בתי המעבד :. ויחן אברהם במקום יתקרי הריף
ויהי בימים הרבים ההם יצאו נשי ארץ מצרים אל השדה למקום
הריף : וימצאו שרי אשת אברהם ויראו כי היא יפת תאר ויפת
מראה : ויהי במושבם מן השדה בערב הללו אתה פני בעליהם : עד
השיב הדבר אל משנה פרעה ויהללו אתה לפרעה : ויהי כשמע
במגידה (17) שלח והביאה לביתו : ויקח אתה : ואברהם הלוך עמה : ולא
יוכל לעשות דבר : ויתן לו פרעה מתנות רבה : וייטב לו בעבור
שרה : ויצא אברהם מאת פרעה שביר הלב בכי העץ : ויעתר
ליהוה במציל שרה אשתו מיד פרעה : ויעתר לו יהוה : וינגע
יהוה את פרעה נגעים גדלים ואת ביתו : ותהי הנגעות עליהם
מפאת ערותם : ופרעה היה הך אבן : וישלח פרעה ויקרא את כל
חרטמי מצרים ואת כל חכמיה : ויאסף אתם : והזה (17) בתוכם
חרש ושמו טדרים : מן המלמדים לספר האותות : ואתלמד זה
הספר מן חנוכיה מן חנוך בן קין : ויתחזק ויאמר יש בזה המקום
אשה מאמנה ביהוה וכל זאת החזקות היתה בעבורה :.

כא

(4) ובנו לון בניאן על טורה: על אפי כל ארעה:
ויהבו עליו היבוק והוה נורה מתעמי לד: רבעתה
(5) וזעקותה שם והי מלתה דאמירה ונעשה לנו
שם: (6) וקצו למבני ואתבדרו בניאנה ואבדרו בני אדם
על אפי ארעה: (7) ואחד מנון לא חכם לשן חברה:.
(8) והדה הי ניסס דקריביה: דקרבים למאתיה וא:
לקיעמיה: (9) ואהנו דיש קרבי מאתיה קמאי להדים

עמו: ויהי בעת השיב כדר לעמר אל מלכי האמרי עשה אתם
מלחמה: ויחלש אתם: ויבז אתם:. ויבז את נחור אחי אברם
עמהם: וישלח שלחים ינדיו לאחיו במה היה בנחזר: ויהי קרוב
מובא השבת: וילן הוא והאנשים אשר עמו לילת השבת בדומה
אשר היא טברים: ויהי במדצא השבת אחרי מובא (81) השמש
לילת חדה צא אברהם (לקל) (דבק) ובהים השני השיב להם טרם
מבוא השמש וימצאם חנים בעמק חזבה: ויהי זה ביום שנים
ועשרים מן חדש אילול: ויום אחד מן חדש הירח: בעמק חובה
אשר היא (ברזה) משמאל לדמשק:. והעד על כן: אן אברהם
השיב להם אחרי מבוא השמש: וילחם אתם בלילה: וישב את כל
הרכוש: ונם את לוט אחיו ורכושו השיב:. ראה מה בא בספר
בראשית פרק יד פסוק טז: אמר (ויחלק עליהם לילה הוא ועבדיו
(82) ויכם: וירדפם עד חובה אשר משמאל לדמשק) ובחמשה מן
חדש הירח בא לשלם רבתה: ויצאו לקראתו ולמוקרו יראה ממנו:
מלך סדם: וכל מלכי נחור באו לפניו אל שלם רבתה: ויביאו
מלך נחור עמם באמונה ואז ראו רבות האדון אברהם עליו
השלום: עקדו וישתחוו לפניו: ואחדה לאל עליון: ויהי אצלם
מניד במה עשה יהוה בפרעה בעבור שרה ויראו אתו יתפלל
אל האחד הפרד::. וירדף רב מן המלכים בשלש מאות איש:
(83) ולכן אתקשט אצלם אן לא יש אחד לו יכולה עליו: ואן
אלהיו בדול מכל האלהים: ויצאו לקראתו עד יבקשו ממנו שלום:
וראש מן אהל בכן מלכי צדק מלך שלם:. והוציא לחם ויין:
ויברך את אברם על מה עשה עמו מן הטובות והחסדות: כי
השיב לו את כל השבי ונצעו על שנאיו: ויתן לו מעשר מכל
ולא ירצי אברהם יקח ממנו: ושם אמר לו תנה לי הנפש והרכוש
קח לך:. (84) ויאמר אברם אל מלך סדם אני מתחשב אן אצלי
כל קניאן סדם הך חרם בעבור כן לא אוכל אקח ממנו מאומה:

חברון וקברותה בניו ליד עיול מטה: ואזלו כל אנש
לאתרה:

V

(1) ואתכנשו לבבל במטלון ממדינה אשבחו בקעה בארץ
שנער ודארו תמן (2) והי הך בקעת שכם שוי וטורא
הך הרגריזים (3) ואמרו דן לדן דחכים דאתרה נטעיל
לאכה: אלא אתו נבנה לנן בניאן ראס דלא נטלטל

וחשיבנו אתו אל המקום אשר יבחר לו: ולא תעזבנו אתו: וכל
מן עשה עמו או עם אשתו מאום מעט מות יומת ∙ ויעשו כאשר
צום: פרעה:. ויבאו בו ובלוט בן אחיו ובבל מקניהם: ובבל
אשר להם עד השיגנו בהם אל אלון מורא אל המזבח הראישון
ויבן אברהם את המזבח הזכיר (ויעל עליו עלות (77) ליהוה אשר
הצילו מיד מצרים:.) וישבו אברהם ולוט בארץ כנען שנה
אחת: בחדש ניסן בא אברהם מחרן: ובחדש איאר ירד מצרימה:
ובחדש ניסן הפרד לוט מעליו: ושכן בסדם שנה אחת:.

ויהי בימים ההם המלך בארץ שנער אמרפל:. בשנה ההיא
אשר שכן בה לוט בסדם: הלב טזרטם הזכיר מלעל מן חברון
לארץ שנער אל אמרפל וכדר לעמר ובשר אתם: אן הם יהרגו
אנשים (78) רבים: ואגיד להם את אשר יהיה להם באחרית
הומים:. וכדר לעמר היר ידע אברהם עליו השלום: ולא יתפני
אל דבר החרטמים: ואחל יהרג כל איש מפניו: ויבא אל חלל
השבאי מדינה תתקרא קדש:. ויהיו אלה אחר מלכי הארץ מן בני
חם:. ויהי אל אמרפל מלך שנער ואריוך מלך אלסר: וכדר
לעמר מלך עילם: ותדעל מלך גוים מום על ברע מלך סדם:
ועל ברשע מלך עמרה: ושנאב מלך אדמה ועל (79) שם אבר
מלך צבואים ומלך בלע אשר היא צער: ואקימו ארבע המלכים
האלה ישלחו הנזייה והמום אל אמרפל: ואל המלכים אשר אתו:
שנים עשר שנה:. ובשנת שלשה עשר הלכו ולא שלחו מאום:
ובארבע עשרה שנה בא כדר לעמר והמלכים אשר אתו: למען
ילחמו את מלכי סדב: ותהי המלחמה ביניהם: וישבו את לוט
ואת כל רכושו בן אחי אברם: וישלח לוט זינד לדו אברהם באשר
היה לו:.. זענירם ואשכול: וממרא (80) היו הם בעלי ברית אברם:
ויגד להם במה אתעשה: אל לוט בן אחיו: דרש מהם ילכו
עמו אל סדם: ויענו אתו על שיאלו וילך אל המלחמה והזכירים

מתקריה בלד אלימן : ‏(14) ומית גיטט ריש מצרים:ועזר
נמרוד לאשור ומלך : ‏(15) וכד מלך עבד קרב עם נחור :
‏(16) ועבד נמרוד לארפכשד הך דעבד פרעה לעבראי
דעמו בספר האותות : דעתיד קעם מן ארפכשד גבר :
מחי כל סנדיה:ומתבר כל צלמיה : ‏(17) וצמת כל חכימיה
דהוו לגו יפת : וחם בעי מנון מחכם אמת דו מתילד :
‏(18) ואמרו ליה למ:יום אמה בטנה בה : ‏(19) ופקד נמרוד

אחת אתילד האדון יצחק ביום השבת : ואולי היה מולדו בחדש
השביעי ביום השבת : וזה מתודע מן מאמר בעל אלאסאטיר (שמע
החקים ביום השבת ברים אנושיה שמעו ביום החמישי : וביום
VIII השׁשי אתוקדת סדם : ובז אתילד יצחק :) ויהי אחרי מות האדון
אברהם עליו השלום מלך ישמעאל שבע ועשרים שנה : וכל בני
ישמעאל ‏(89) אשר מן זרע בכורו נבאות מלכו בימי חיי
ישמעאל שנה אחת : ואחרי מותו מלכו שלשים שנה : מנהר
מצרים עד הנהר הגדול נהר פרת : ויבנו את באכה : ולכן
אמר בתורה הקדושה בספר בראשית פרק טז : פסוק יח (באכה
אשורה לפני כל אחיו נפל :) ויהי בעת ההוא מובא אליפז בן
עשו : וילחם את בני ישמעאל : וגם הוציאו וראו בפלוב הארץ
אשר פלנו נח מצאו עשו וישמעאל שניהם יחדו : ואתכנשו בני
מחלת ‏(90) עם בני ישמעאל והיא המלה אשר אתמרת : (והוא
יהיה פרה האדם : . ועשו הוא אדום :) ובני עדה ואהליבמה מך
עשו למין כנען:הלכו ומלכו עליהם ביד רמה:. בלע בן יקטן :
ויזבב מבני קיטורה אתאספו שניהם - יחדו והיו יוצאים מדרך
אברהם : כל בני ישמעאל ובני עשו : ואחרי כל הדברים האלה
שמע אברהם אן בני אשור ובני יקטן גדלו מאד ויירא יראה
בדלה מן רעות מעשיהם פני יהוה ויירא אן ישיב לו מן רעותם
צרר במאום : וזה מתודע מן מאמרו ‏(91) בספר אלאסאטיר :
(ואחרי כל הדברים האלה שמע אברהם כי אתגברו בני יקטן :
ואשור ויירא יראה גדולה :) וזכר זה אחרי זכרונו לאליפז בן
עשו :. דבר על בני מחלת ועל בני עדה ואהליבמה : ואנחנו
נראה כי הוא זכור מאום היה אחרי מות אברהם : וזהם בני
מחלת ועדה ואהליבמה:ודע אן זכרון אברהם הנה הוא אז בא
בזכרון מלכי ארץ מואב : זכר בראישון מהם שנים : והם בלע
ויזבב : ואחר כן שמע אברהם עד יורי הנה אן כל אלה

עינמים להבים נפתחים פתרסים כפהרים כסלחים (10) ויהבו
עליהון ריש מנון בכורה דלהדרים ושמה גיטט דאתקרו על
שמה גבטאי (11) ונפקו מיתי פלשתים ועברו קרבה קמאה
עם כנענאי וזטוטאי ונסבו מלכותה מן נמרוד ומלכו
פלשתים ממצרים לנהר כוש :. (12) ואזל נמרוד ושרה
קמיו בעי מנה סעד על מצרים (13) וזרעה ושבי נפקו
בני יקטן: ושרו ממשא באכה ספרה לתמנתה דמרי:

אם מחוט ועד שרוג נעל: רק אשר הלכו אתי ענירים ואשכול
וממרא הם יקחו חלקם:. ויהי אחר הדברים האלה בירח ניסן
אתחזי מלאך יהוה אל אברהם ביום הרביעי ובשר אתו בארבע
מאומות: ויהי זה בחלום הלילה:. הראש אמר לו (אנכי מגן
לך ושכרך ארבה מאד:) השני הוציאו אל מחוץ: ואמר לו (הבט נא
(85) השמים וספר הכוכבים אם תוכל לספר אתם: ויאמר לו כה
יהיה זרעך):. השלישי (ויחשבה לו צדיקה:) ובשר אתו אן
דזא מן שכתי בן עדן: (הרביעי) אמר לו (אני יהוה אשר
הוצאתיך מאור כשדים לתת לך את הארץ הזאת לרשתה:) וזה
המזקר הרב: כלז היה לאדונן אברהם לחזקות ורבות מאמנו ויתרות
זכותו ומשמעו למצות השם יתעלה: כי ראש המאמן הזכות: והיבראה
והשובה כאשר אמר בעל ספר אלאסאטיר: (ראש אימנותה היא
(86) היראה: והזכות: והשובה:) וכל זה היה לאדונן אברהם בשנה
אחת: בשנים ועשרים יום: ובימם דברו יהוה בזה הדבר היה בן
תשע ותשעים שנה: טרם הנמילה: ובשנה ההיא צודו בנמילה
וכרת עמו הברית על כן: ואמר לו (וערל זכר אשר לא ימול
את בשר ערלתו ביום השמיני ונכרתה הנפש ההיא:) ויהי זה
הדבר וכריתות עמו הברית ביום השבת: ויום החמישי בשבוע
ההוא באו עליו שלשה האנושים אשר מהם הגדול היחוד
בבשור (87) אברהם ביצחק: ואמר לו: (שוב אשוב אליך כעת
חיה והנה בן לשרה אשתך:) ואתקרא את שמו יצחק: ושני
האנושים אשר עמו הם להפיכות סדם ועמרה: ואחרי אן בשר
אחד מהם אדונן אברהם ביצחק הלך: הלכו השנים הנותרים
אל ערי סדם וילינו בבית לוט: ותשרפת סדם עמרה: ביום
ההוא:. ואורד יהוה עליהם נפרית ואש מן השמים: ויהפך
יהוה חמשת הערים האלה: את כל הככר ואת כל יושבי הערים:
ואתשלמו (88) לוט ואשתו ושתי בנותיו לבדם:. ויהי אחרי שנה

אברהם בחנו חיולה : (27) ונסבה נמרוד ורמתה לנורה :
בדיל דאמר דלעלמא אלה (28) וכד עצף הרן על אברהם
במימר דו חרש נפקת אשתה ואכלתה : ומת : ומית הרן
על פני תרח אביו באור כשדים ובתר ז: שנין מת .

VI

(1) ובעו עקב מלכות חם מן נמרד שריאת ועל נמרוד
חסלת (2) ומן נמרוד א :. אל נמרוד ב :. אלף וכ :

---

(96) בה שנה אחת : וכי עמלק מלך עליה : ירד ברעה ואקים
תמימה : ואחר כן קם במצרים בממציתה : ויהי בתוכה (עבור :)
והוא המשחית ארח שלשה שנים :. וימת מלך מצרים : ויקם
עוד מלך על ארץ מצרים ושמו גם כן פרעה השלישי : ויאסף
מחנה רב מן קטפאי ואקים מלך ששים שנה : ויהי מספר המלכים מן
פרעה אשר היה בימי יוסף אל פרעה אשר היה בימי משה : אשר
טבע בים סוף : ארבע מלכים : כי מיום מות האדון יוסף עד אתילד
אדונן משה השליח שלשה ושמים שנה : כמד זה מתקשט לא יש
בו מחלף :. (97) ויום שובת האדון השליח מן מדין לארץ מצרים
היה בן שמנים שנה ויהיו כל השנים האלה שלשה וארבעים שנה
ומאת שנה :. ופרעה אתילד בימי אדונן משה זה הוא אשר אקים
ששים שנה מלך ואמר עלו :. (וימת) :. ובני ישראל פרו וישרצו
וירבו ויעצמו במאד מאד :. כי היו הנשים יילדו בכל פעם שני
בנים או שלשה ויהוה ידע :. ויצו פרעה לכל עמו לאמר : כל
הבן הילד היאר תשליכון :. וייראו (98) ממנו האנשים והנשים :
והיו עם פרעה ישלי כו כל הבן הזכר הילד להם ביאר והיתה
האשה אשר יתשליך בנה ביאר תהרג נפשה אחריו :. ובני
ישראל היו באמונה : לא אתשליך להם בן אחד כי היו נשי
הישראלים שאלים ידעו יצר הלבבים אן אז תדע בנפשה כי
מדרשה תלד במהר תצא אל השדה : ותלד שם : ותרא האם
הילד זמה אתברא בו מן העדים ואן היה בן זכר תשלחו בשדה
לבריו הבוראים : והשם יתעלה (99) יתן לו מאום יינק ממנו חלב
ודבש מחלמיש צור : כפי מאמרו יתעלה בכתבו העויז : (ויניקהו
דבש מסלע ושמן מחלמיש צור :) ואם בת חיא תביאה עמה
אל ביתה : ולא היה הצו בהשליך הבנים ביאר אלא מאבד
לעםן : המצרים : יתהלל העשה למה יבחר יתריה : וביכלות
IX השם השופט הצדיק אתילד הנבי העצום ואדביר לטב עד לעלם

דלא־ישהבקון בני ארפכשד גבריה עם נשיה מ: יום (20) ושו
אתעבשו גבריה באתר ונשיה באחר : (21) ובתר שלשים
יום אתעמי סימן בארע שנער עמוד אש : (22) ורחלו כל
אנשה דחלה רבה : ועבדו בעוון בבתי דחלתה וכתרו בבראה
ג : . יומין וליליו : (23) ואזל תרח וקרב לאתתה (24) וכד
קרב לה : אסתלק סימנה : ואמרו דמולדה צעיר : (25) ופקד
נמרוד דיעזר כל אנש לאתרה (26) ובתר כן אתילד

---

(92) אתילדו בימי חיי אברהם עליו השלום : ואן בני אשור בן
שם : ויקטן בן עבר : וכי היה הם מן שם ומן עבר וסרו מן דרך
החיים : ולכן היה לו יראה : . ויובב יאמר עליו בספר אלאסאטיר
כי הוא מבני קיטורה יהודה ידע אן זה מתעתק איננו על האמת :
כי הוא איננו קרוב למדע : רק יובב הוא בן יקטן בן עבר : בן
שלח : ואשר יראה ויקרא בפרק י פסוק כ : מן ספר בראשית
יתגלי לו אמיתת זה הדבר : ויהוה הידעיו : . חשם מן מואב
(93) ושמלה מן עילם : ושאול מבני נחור בעל חנן מן עילם : .
הדד מבני אליפז : אשר היו יושבים בבית פעו : ושם אשתו
מיטאבאל בת מטרד : מן יפת כתים : . אלה תולדת המלכים
אשר מלכו בארץ אדום לפני מלך מלך לבני ישראל : אז היה
אדנו יעקב בן שמנים שנה ירד לחרן : והאדון יוסף עליו
השלום אז היה בן שבע עשרה שנה ושמנה ירחים ירד לארץ
מצרים : . פרעה אשר היה בימי יוסף הוא מן זרע ישמעאל : .
(94) ופרעה אשר היה בימי אדנו משה מן זרע יפת כתים : זה
אשר בימי אתילד משה : ואמר עליו באלאסאטיר (ועבד רודנים
פרעה .) ואלה תולדת פרעה בן גוטים בן אטיסם בן רבטט בן
גוטסיס : בן רימס : בן כתים : בן יון אשר אתלמד ספר האותות
בעיר בבל הגדלה : ויצא מציון ויבא אל נינוה : . ואז השיבנו
ימי שני חיי האדון יוסף עליו השלום שלשים שנה היה מלך
בארץ מצרים : ויהי פרעה השני (95) מלבד פרעה המתקדם זכרונו :
בא אל נינוה ואקים בה שלשה שנים : וירח ימים : וגם אחר כן
הלך אל דמשק אל כרוזה : והיא עיר בוש : . וישב שם שלשה
ושלשים שנה : . וימת יוסף וכל אחיו וכל הדור ההוא : ושנת
ממלכת ישמעאל כאשר אמר בספר אלאסאטיר (ושנת מלכות
ישמעאל : ואתגבר עמלק :) וימלך על ארץ מצרים : . ויהי
כשמע פרעה השני אשר היה בעיר נינוה במות מלך מצרים :

כן סלק להרגריזים: ממדנה לבית אל: (10) ושוי נחת
למצרים: (11) וכד שרה בתחום מצרים אתעמי זוען בכל
דחלתה: (12) ורתתו כל דיארי בתי סגדיה: דהוה
אברהם שרי בריפון כבון: טכם מצרים: דו מתקרי אלריף:
ונפקו לקלדבק (13) ותמן חזו שרה ושבחתה נשיה
לגברין וגבריה לפרעה: ואתנסבת אתתה לבית פרעה
ולאברם אתיטב בדילה: (14) ושוי דשרת שרה בבית

העברים זה: וצות כל אמתה אן לא ינידו לאחד במניד זה
הילד: וישבעו לה על כן כל אמתיה והעבדים הקעמים סביבותיה
אשר (104) ראו הילד עמה: . . והיתה אחותו האדונה מרים עמדה
מרחק לדעת מה יעשה לו: ביד הנכר: ואז חזת כי בת פרעה
לקחת אתו ואהבת אתו ורחמת לו אתקדמת במהרה לפני בת
פרעה ותאמר אלה האלך וקראתי ליך אשה מינקות מן העבריזת
ותינק ליך את הילד: ותאמר לה בת פרעה לכי: ותלך העלימה
ותקרא את אם הילד ותאמר לה בת פרעה הליכי את הילד הזה
והניקהו לי ואני אתן את שכריך: ותקח האשה את הילד
ותינקהו: ויגדל הנער וינמל ותביאו אל בת פרעה (105) ונתנת
לה שכרה: כמה זה מתודע בתורה הקדושה בספר משנה התורה
פרק ב: בפסוק השישי: . ואחר מובאו אל בת פרעה קראת
שמו משה: ואמרת כי מן המים והאש ותפלט והמשי: . ויהי
מולדו ביום השבת בחמשה עשר מן ירח ניסן: כאשר אמרנו
לעל: . . וביום השבת אתשליך ביאר: בחמשה עשר מן ירח
סיבן: ויהי מוצאו מן היאר ביום השבת הזכיר בשעה החמישית
ממנו ואתרבה משה בבית האויב בעז ואיקר וברבו עד כי
גדל (106): וקם עם שרי פרעה הפוקידים על העברים: ויצא בימים
ההם עד יראה בסבלותם וירא איש מצרי מכה איש עברי
מאחיו: ויפן כה וכה: וירא כי אין איש: ויך את המצרי ויטמנהו
בחול: . . ויצא עוד ביום השני מן הימים והנה שני אנשים
עברים נצים ויאמר לרשע למה תכה רעך ויען ויאמר לו הרשע
מי שמך לאיש שר ולשופט עלינו: הלהרגני אתה אמר כאשר
הרגת את המצרי אמש: . . וירא משה: ויאמר אכן
נדע הדבר: וכי (107) אתודע המעשה וישמע פרעה את הדבר
הזה ויבקש להרג את משה: ויברח משה מפני פרעה: וישב
בארץ מדין: . . ואקים ששים שנה תמימות: והוא רעה לצאן

שנה (3) נמרוד קמאה מן כוש: ונמרוד ב :. מן כפתרים:
(4) וכד מית נמרוד נפק תרח למיתי לארע כנען מקעמה
מלכותה (5) ונחור ברה כתר לכדר לעמר ותדעל מלך
גוים: ויהבו נבזים על מלכותה: (6) וסלק נבז כדר לעמר
ושלח ועבש לתרח בחרן: (7) ונפק אברם אתי לכדר
לעמר לאור כשדים: (8) תמן זעק לה אלהה ואתו לארע
כנען ושרו במישר חזוה ובנא מדבחה דאדם ונח (9) ובתר

אדונן משה בן עמרם עליו השלום) והזה מולדו בירח ניסן
בחמשה עשר יום ממנו   (100)   ביום השבת: ותצפינהו
אמו שלשה ירחים והזה מספרם אחד ושבעים יום: כי אמר
באלאסאטיר (ובחמשה עשר יום מן סיבן אתשליך ביאר:) ואז
אתשליך אדון הבוראים משה ביאר עמד מי היאר ביכולת
השם יתעלה: והלך עשנו: ולא אשתיאר בו מערך: ואחל מימיו
יגרע:. ויצאו בן נשי מצרים עד יראו מגרע נחל מצרים: כי
היה בימים ההם עת מוסף הנחל: ואז ירדו הנשים לראות את הנחל
היתה אתם בת פרעה: (101) ויהי כל מה עבר היום יתוסף מגרע
היאר: כפי מאמרו באלאסאטיר (והזה כל יומה דתלי פעת נהרה:)
ויהי הילד בתוך תבה מתחמרה בחימר ובזפת: האלכת על יד
היאר:. ואו עמד מי היאר מן המערך בלא הסכנת: אתאכפו
כל החרטמים וכל המכשפים והיו במלאכה גדולה ויבקרו: ויחפשו
ויחלקו ויקרו בחרטמיהם על גלל עמידות מי היאר: ויהי בתוך
החרטמים איש שמו פלטי והיה יראה ויחפש ויחקר (102) בספר
האותות: כי היה הזא הנשיא להם:. וידם: ונשא ראשו ואמר:
הילד אשר אמרנו עליו בראישונה גלל מותו יחי במים: ותיבתו
בים סוף:. ולא אמר בים הנחל: רק אמר (והילד בא והתבה
בחופה:) וזה היה במראה מיהזה יתעלה: כי הים רב מן הנחל:.
ואז אמר פלטי הא הזא בסופה אמרו בלא דבר הילד מת:
ובדיל כן לא שאלו עליז ולא הלכו ולא ראו אל תיבתו: אשר
הוא בתוכה: וזה מופת גדול יתהלל אלהים היכול הנשא
(103) העשה כל מה יבחר ויתריח:. ובת פרעה אז חזת התבה
בתוך הים שלחת את אמתה ויביאו לה את התבה: ותקחה
ותפתחה ותרא בה נער טוב קדוש:. וסר מעליה הנגע הרע
ודרשת נפשה הקדשה: ויהי בתוך התבה בכי: ותחמל עליה בת
פרעה: ואהבת לו מאהבה יתרה ורבה עד מאד: ותאמר מילדי

אלהה דכלה : עגל שוי לשומיה בבעואן : ‎(21) תמן אכפתו
ואניר כל פעלאתה מן חזוה דשרה על אפיה : דחלה
רבה ‎(22) תמן אתודעת דהי שרה די אתת אברהם ואשתרי
לשן פרעה ומלל ואכרז אברהם ואתבעי לפשר : ‎(23) והדה
היא ריש כריזאתה : דאמר אברהם יהי אלהי : השמים
ואלהי הארץ חנון חנן : . ‎(24) ושוי אתחסי פרעה : וכל
בית דחלה : אתלחצו וכל סנודיה נפלי ולא אסקפי :

הדם : בתשעה לחדש היתה כל האותות והמופתים הגדלים האלה
במצרים : בשעה הששית מן לילת החמישי יצאו בני ישראל
ביד רמה לעיני כל מצרים : . לילת חדה הלכו [112] ביבשה
בתוך הים : . ועל פי דבר ספר אלאסאטיר היה מועד הפסח
לילת החמישי : . . כי יהוה אמר בתורה הקדושה בספר במדבר
סיני פרק ל ג בפסוק ג : . ‏ (ממחרת הפסח יצאו בני ישראל
ביד רמה לעיני כל מצרים) וקרבן הפסח הוא מערב עד השחר
הראש : וזמן עלות השחר אל מבוא השמש הוא המועד : . אפס
על פי מאמר אדנן מרקה רצון יהוה עליו בצפינתו אמר
אן המועד היה במצרים ביום השני : כי יאמר ‏ (ככה פסחו : ואל
רעמסס נסעו ודרך שלשת ימים [113] הלכו עד באו אל ים סוף :
ובלילת המועד השני בחזית הבקר באו בימה :) ועל פי המעתק
האמת היה מובאם אל ים סוף לילת חדה : כי לנו זכרון על זה
עד היום הזה כל לילת חדה נקראו : . ויהיה על פי מאמר
אדנן מרקה מועד הפסח ביום השני : והמועד השני יום חדה :
ויהוה ידע : . ‏ והאמת אצלי הוא מאמר אדנן מרקה : ואכפר יהוה
מן החטא והשגג : . וביום השלישי באו אל אילים : ואמתק להם
מי מרה : . ‏ ויריאהם [114] יהוה עץ מרה : וישמו מקלות ממנו במים
עד אמתק : וזה העץ הוא עץ הדפלה : המתודע : ועד היום הזה
נראה אתו יֹמתק המים המרה עד מאד : . וביום הששי אשר
הוא חמש יום ממחרת המועד השני בא עליהם עמלק וילחם
אתם ויחלשו אתו ומחו שמו מתחת השמים : ונצע יהוה את
ישראל עליו ביכלותו יתעלה : ובשלישי מן חדש השלישי ביום
הרביעי קרא יהוה. על טור סיני : . ‏ (כל צפרי עלמה שלשה :)
אין להם דמות : ‏ (הראש מהם) [115] צפר יום חדח אשר הוא
ראש בריאת עלמה : ‏ (השני) צפר יום הרביעי אשר הוא יום
מעמד הר סיני : . ‏ (השלישי) צפר יום נקם : . ‏ ידע אה ראה

פרעה: אתעמי מופתים רברבים: (15) ושרו רבניה עלין
מקבל ומגלה ופרעו הך אבן חרשה מטלקה (16) ואמרו
לא ישתבק חרש ולא כקמאי הכה: (17) ואצטמדו
חרשיה וכל קסמיה וקעמו במרטוש רב: (18) והוה לגבון
חרש ושמה טורטס מן אלופי ספר האותות בחנוכיה
(19) עצף: ואמר סגודה דלאלהה דכלה באהן אתרה:
וכל הדה עקתה כגללה הות: (20) וכד שמע אברהם

יתרו חתנו. ואחר כן היה חזקות רבות על בני ישראל וצררות
גדולות בפרקן השליח בארץ מדין: וימת מלך מצרים גוטס:
והוא המתקרא פריגה זטרם אן יקום תחתיו מלך במצרים. בזזו
בני ישראל הזמן ואתאספו (108) וינחו בני ישראל מן העבדה:
ויצעקו: ותעל שועתם אל האלהים מן העבדה: וישמע אלהים
את נקאתם. ויזכר אלהים את בריתו את אברהם ואת יצחק
ואת יעקב: וירא אלהים את בני ישראל וידע אלהים:. מאמרו
(וירא אלהים) מפתרה ראה אל ענותם אשר היו בה: מן מצרים:.
ומאמרו (וידע אלהים:) מפתרה:) אני אנמיל המצרים במה עשו:
וגם אן השם ידע הסוד אשר אמר עליו לאדונן (109) אברהם:
כי היה קרוב כלולו וההוא מאמרו בספר בראשית פרק טז
פסוק יג (ועבדום וענו אתם:.) ויהי אחר הדברים האלה קם
מלך חדש על מצרים שמו פרעה מן כתים והוא (עטירת:) וזה
הוא המלך השלישי אשר מלך על ארץ מצרים: מן פרעה
אשר היה בימי יוסף:. ויהי בחמשה עשר יום מן חדש הירח
אשר הוא חדש השלישי ביום הרביעי בא אדונן משה השליח
עליו (110) השלום בצאן יתרו חתנו בלא צדיה אל הר האלהים
חורי ב. וזה: י ביום ההוא אקים השם בריתו את הזכאים: ומטה אדם
(ולבושיו) והם כסותיו אשר היו מן אור על אדם אז היה בנן
אנתנו למשה ביום ההוא: והעד על כן הוא מאמרו יתעלה לו
טרם כל דבר (וזה לך האות:) והיא נתנה לך סימה כי אנכי
שלחתיך:. בחדש השלישי בשלישי ממנו ביום הרביעי אתחזי
יהוה למשה:. ביום חדה ירד למצרים: ויאמר (111) יהוה אל
אהרן לך לקראת משה המדברה: וילך ויפגשהו בהר האלהים
וישק: לו:. ויעלו על מצרים שניהם ויעשו את האותות לעיני
בני ישראל ויאמנו העם:. ביום השלישי עלו ויעמדו לפני
פרעה ויגידו לו את כל דברי יהוה:. ביום החמישי היה מופת

B.

לא

מן חרן: ובאיאר נחת למצרים: (3) ובניסן אכרת לוט
מן עמה: ודאר בסדם שנה א::. (4) ביתה שנה אתו:.
ואהן טורטס אזי מן חברון לשנער ובסר לאמרפל
ולכדר לעמר כי קטיל קטלין סגי ואלף ספר האותות ועמה
לון מה מעבד (5) והוה כדו לעמר חכם אברהם: ולא צבי
מקבל מן חרשיו (6) ושרי קטל כל אנש דקדמיו ואתא
לחלל מדי מתקריה קדש: (7) והוו חראי מלכי ארעה

בזה השם הבאה לפניך: וההוא שמותם:. (א הלם המל:) ב
ההמל האמל (ג העמאל המנאל:) ד הצפרה הסמים: (ה תלך ליל
חלק לב:) ז הלין הנתר (ז הלפבר:) אלה הם שבעת המלאכים
אשר היה בלעם ישרת וישתחוי להם:. ואז אתיטב אל בלעם
ילך עם שרי בלק: וֹרכב על אתונו וילך מתפחר בה אמור
ראד כי האתון תלך בי לכל מקום אבחר לו בלא מורי יורי
לה: על הדרך:. ויהי (120) וההוא ידבר בזה הדבר והנה מלאך
יהוה (אל הקדוש) נצב בדרך וחרבו שלופה בידו ותט האתון
מן הדרך ותלך בשדה ויך בלעם את האתון להטותה הדרך:.
ותרבץ תחת בלעם ויחר אף בלעם ויך את האתון במקל:.
ויפתח יהוה את פי האתון: ויגל יהוה את עיני בלעם וירא את
מלאך יהוה נצב בדרך: ויקד וישתחוי לאפיו: ויאמר לו מלאך
יהוה השמר לך לא תסור מן הדבר אשר אדבר אליך: וילך
בלעם עם שרי בלק:. המלאך אשר צוהו על בניאן שבעת
(121) המזבחות הראישונים:. שלשה פעמים בנא המזבחות ואחר
כן אודיענו דגה אן בלעם תולדזותו מן ארם נהרים אשר היא עיר
נחור: כמה גלי זה כי היא עיר נחור בתורה הקדושה בספר
בראשית פרק כד: בפסוק י: וההוא מאמרו (אל ארם נהרים אל
עיר נחור:) ובמספר אלאסמאתיר אמר (שלשלה הוד מן ארם:.)
ויהי בעמדו לפני המזחזת בא אליו המלאך הראישון ואודיעו מה
ידבר: ואחר כן בא לו (אל האור:.) ומאן בלעם יאר את העם
ואמר בלעם (מה אקב לא קבו אל (122) ומה אזעם לא זעמו יהוה:.)
זברך אתו: ואחר כן בא לו (אל הרקיע) הפיך חזותו עד
ראה ישראל בנן עדן: ואז ראה זאת המראות אמר (תמות נפשי
מות ישירים ותהי אחריתי כמהו:.) ויהי כשמע בלק בן צפור זה
הדבר אמר מה עשית לי לקב איבי לקחתיך והנה ברכת ברוך:
ויען ויאמר הלוא את אשר ישים יהוה בפי אתו אשמר לדבר:

(25) וחרשה טורטס סלק מתמן לחברון : (26) ופקד פרעה
אנשים ושלחו יתה ואתה ולוט עמה : (27) ואתו לאתר
מרבחה קדמאה וקוממה ואסק אורואון ותשבחן :

VII

(1) בי : . שנה מלך אמרפל : וכתרו : אברהם ולוט
שנה א : בערע כנען : (2) בירח ניסן אתא אברהם

לדברי אן המפתר בכן אן שלשה הצפרים האלה לא יש בהם
שמש ולא ירח ולא כוכבים : . כי מן כלילון צפר יום הרביעי
בא עליו העד בתורה הקדושה במאמרו בספר דברים פרק ד :
פסוק יב (וידבר יהוה אליכם מתוך האש קול דברים אתם
שמעים ותמונה אינכם ראים זולתי קול :) והיא מפתרה לא תראו
(116) בשמים תמונה מן התמונות : . (והשלישי צפר יום נקם) לא
יהי בו לא שמש ולא ירח : ולא כוכב : כי ממצאם הוא מן צורך
עלמה : וביום נקם לא יש להם צורך : . ונם אמר עליו בספר
אלאסאטיר זה הזום. הוא יום הששי : מתודע זה מן מאמרו
בהם : (צפרה דבריאתה ב א : . צפרה דטור סיני ב ד : . צפרה
דיום נקם ב ו :) באחד לחדש הראישון בשנה השנית לצאתם
מארץ מצרים אתקומם משכנה : . בחדש השלישי נסעו מהר
סיני : . (117) בחדש השלישי היה מות מרים : . בחדש הרביעי מת
האדון אהרן : . בחדש השביעי היתה המלחמה בין בני ישראל
ומלך ערד : וישבי ממנו שבי : ונם עזרו עליו בני ישראל שנית וילחמו
לו : ויחרמו אתו ואת כל אשר לו : . ויהי בעת ההיא נחש שמו
מערטים : ויהי מושבו בעיר ערד : ויהי. כשמעו בבוא בני ישראל
אל עיר ערד נם משם אל מדין ויהי שם פעור אשר שאלו
אתו אנשי מואב יקרא אל בלעם בן בעור בן נדיטים בן
(118) פעטה : בן עמיננף בן לבן בעל התרפים אשר חזא מן עיר
X צער : כי השיב לו זה התרפים מן קשט מלך מואב מן קין
המכה ויהוה ידע : . וישלח בלק מלאכים אל בלעם בן בעור
פתרה אשר על הנהר ארץ בני עמון לקרא לו לאמר לכה נא
ארה לי את עם ישראל : ויהי זה הדבר בחדש הששי : ויהי
בלעם נבון וידעיו בספר האותות : ויהי ישתחוי לשבעת המלאכים
האלה והם (אל האור : ואל הרקיע ואל המים : ואל המאזרות ואל
(119) הקדוש : ואל הרוחות : ואל הכתפות :) והוה יקרא להם תמיד

בדימה דשמה טבריים מכנרת : (14) במפוק שבתה נפק
אברהם לקל דבק (15) : וב אמטה בון מסוק זעדה
בעמק בירח חלול (16) בכ : וא : לידחה בעמק חובה
מדי מתקרה כון אמר : . (17) בחמשתה אתא אברהם
לשלם רבתה מלך סדם ומלכו נחור אתו ליד אברהם
לשלם רבתה (18) כד עמו אברהם עקד וסגד לאפיו
ואודה לאלהה אל עליון : (19) תמן זעקה מלכי צדק
עקובה חדתה על שמה דפצנה ויהב לה עסור מכלה :
ולא צבה מקבל : (20) ותמן אמר לה הב לי נפשהתה
ועותרה סב לך : (21) ואמר אברהם למלך סדם חשיב
הוא עותרה דסדם לי הך חרם : (22) ובניסן אתגלי אלה
לאברהם ומלל עמה ממללה בד : ואמר לה אנא מגן לך
בחלם לילה (23) ואפקה לבראה ואמר הבט נא השמים
וספר הכוכבים : . רב הוא פסוקה דלית כותה : . (24) ריש

מבנותם מאות דעשרים אלף זאלבישו אתם הבגדים הטובים :
ושלחז אתם אל נבול מחנה בני ישראל ויהי משיגם לו בשעה
השלישית מן יום השבת כי אנשי מואב אמרו הטוב הוא יהי
מובא בנות הזנות ביום השבת עד יהי חטאון מתרברב כי העון
הרב המתעשה ביום השבת : . (127) וברית פינחס קם בזה היום :
לו זלזרעו אחריו טבזיון אהבי יהוה ואוי להם משנאיו : ויהי
ביום השבת בשעה השלישית היו זקני העם מתאספים פתח אהל
מועד מפאת נגבה : ויהי דגל מחנה ראובן גם כן מפאת נגבה
והכהנים הקדושים עמדים שם מפאת קדמה : ושבט שמעון עם
דגל ראובן : ויהי שבט ראובן על שמאלו : ושבטו גד על ימינו :
ושבט גד היה ידע כל הרננות : והוא ראש מן יתב הרנן : וזה
מתודע מן מאמרו (128) באלאסאטיר (בדייך וקיתרה ובצנצלך
ובטופה ובזמרין) ואז באו בנות הזנות ובת צור בתוכם הלבה
על ענלות מן עין ברוח : מכל פאתיה ותלך בה כפי מדרשה
בעת החיא צא קול מתוך הענן אמור (והרגו איש את אנשיו
הנצמדים לבעל פעור) והיו שופטי העם מתאספים אל תפלות
יום השבת צהרים : ואחרי כלול התפלה קמו חשופטים במהרה :
ולא עשו כאשר דבר משה : ואשר לקח מבנות הזנות בראישון

מן בני הם: (8) וקנא לוט בון: ושוי שלח ליד אברהם עביבה ממלך בה: (9) וענורם ואשכול וממרא: הוו מסחני קיאם אברם ואמר אה אחי לון: נחת לקדמאי לסעדון (11) בד:. י:. שנה בא כדר לעמר ואגחי עם מלכי אמראי: (12) וחורי נחור אחי אברהם שלח ואודע לאברם במה דעבד באתרה באור כשדים: (13) ואשקחו שליחיה לאברהם נפק רדף בתר מלכיה דשבו ללוט ושרו

ויאמר אליו בלק לך נא אתי אל מקום אחר אולי יישר בעיני האלהים וקבתו לי משם..
(ז) יהי בעמידתו על המזבחות (123) בא לו (אל המים) אמר לו (לית יכל עמי שמע:) ומפתרה לא ישעמי אחד שמיע מה אמר אליך: כי (לא איש אל ויכזב ובן האדם ויתנחם: ההוא אמר ולא יעשה:) ודע כי אני נתן לבני ישראל הברכה: וגן עדן: ולא אשוב במתנתי:. ואחר כן בא לו (אל הכתפות) אמר לו (לא נחש ביעקב הדר) ומפתרה זה עם לא ישמע לנחש ולא יתמעד בו: ואן זה עם חדר במלאכים והאור החנים עליו..
ואחר כן בא לו (אל הק דוש) אמר לו: יהיה אלהיו (124) עמו (ותרועת מלך בו:) ומפתר זה אן יהוה מסעד לו: וישב מלאכו הגדול כבלע בקרבו:. ויעמד בלעם פעם שלישית וברך את ישראל ולא עשה כפי מדרש בלק: ויאמר אליו בלעם לך ואעיצך את אשר יעשה העם הזה לעמך באחרית הימים: וטרם ידבר לו דבר בא אליו (אל המאורות) אמר לו (ולא עתה אשורנו ולא קרוב: דרך כוכב מיעקב:) ויהי מת עמך על ידו:. ואחר כן בא (אל הרוחות) אמר לו (וישראל עשה חיל:) ומפתר כן הוא באחרית הימים (125) ישראל ינדל על כל אמי עלמה:. ואחר הדברים האלה אמר לו (האזין לבן ואשמרה:) כוכב יקום איש יחרב כל פאתי מואב זהוא מאמרו (וקם שבט מישראל: ומחין פאתי מואב:) ושם זכר בלעם מאזם יזרי בו על מובא הרצון והתהב: ולא זכר אתו באלאסאטיר כי בא זכרונו בתורה הקדושה:..
ויהי כשמע בלעם מן המלאכים את כל הדברים האלה חשב חשבן רע ואמר בלבי אלהי ישראל ישנא הטמא: ואמר אל בלק אן הדית מדרשך (126) תאבד עם יהוה במהרה עליך בזנות: ואודיע אתו איך יעשה: וישב בלעם ריק למקומו: ואחרי הלכות בלעם עשה בלק וכל עדתו כאשר אמר להם בלעם: ויאספו

(8) אזלו ומלכו עליון בריאם : בלע בר יקטן יובב כנען
מן בני קטורה (9) ובתר כל אלין מליה שמע אברהם
דאתחילו אשוראה ויקטנאי ודחל דחלה רבה : חשם
(10) מן מואב : ושמלה מן עילם : ושאול מבני גחור :
בעל חנן (11) מן עילם : הדד מבני אליעזר דהות מדערתון
בית אד : והיא בית פוריך : ושם אתתה מהיטבאל
ברת מטרר מן יפת כתא : (12) בר שמנים שנה : אזל
יעקב לחרן (13) בר ז י : שנה וח : ירחין נחת יוסף
למצרים (14) פרעה דיוסף מן ישמעאל : פרעה דמשה מן יפת
כתים ועבד רודנים (15) פרעה בר גוטים בר אטיסם בר
רבטט בר גוסים בר רימם בר כתים בר יון (16) דאלף
ספר האותות בבבל רבתה ונפק מן גפנה ואתא לן ינוה
(17) ושמה דיוסף מלך מצרים (18) ושהו חמן ג : שנין
וירח : ואתו לדמשק : ומן דמשק לגזורה והי עכושים

(וכן אמרו מקוממי אימנותה כל מקעמין התפלות על ז : וח :)
ומפתר כן הוא כל משפט ישראל קשור בשבעה : . (והימים
שבעה : השהרה שבעה) והראישונים אמרו (כי כל שביעי קדש :)
וגם השמנה לה משפט : והוא כמו ימי הגמילה שמנה : ואן דרשנו
נספר כל השבעאות יתורך עמנו המספר : ואנחנו (12א) מדרשנו
קצירות הדבר : לא מורכו : ויהודה ידע : . דע אן בראש החדש
השמיני היה מובא הבנות הקדישים אל מחנה ישראל : . ובחדש
העשירי אמר יהוה אל משה (נקם נקמת בני ישראל מאת
המדינים ואחר תאסף אל עמך :) ויבחר השליח שלום יהוה
עליו שנים עשר אלף איש למלחמה : ואז הלכו עלים למלחמה :
אמר יהוה למשה ילך עמם : ויעשה כאשר עשה במלחמות
עמלק : . ויעמד על ראש ההר : . ומטה האלהום בידו : ויתנפל
ויתפלל (133) ויקרא לבני ישראל : . ויהי בעת הלכו אל מדין
נתן אדונן משה השליח עליו השלום אל פינחס השופרים וצוהו
ילך לפני המחנה (ויצבאו על מדין כאשר צוה יהוה : את משה :)
וטרם משיגם השיב גדים אל מדין ביום הרביעי ואמר להם אן
ישראל באים עליכם להלחם אתכם : וישלחו אנושים עוד אל
בלעם אמרים לו אה ראש החרטמים קום נא על העדה האלה

אימנותה היא דחלתה וזכותה ותוכבתה: (25) כל הדה
מיעלה בשנה א : בכ : וב : . . אדן לא ממללה אלה
(26) בר : ט : וצ : שנה קבל גזרתה (27) בז : קיאמה
אנושיה קבלון בה : (28) בו : . אתוקדת סדם : (29) בז :
אתילד יצחק :

VIII

(1) בתר מות אברהם מלך ישמעאל כ:ז:. שנה (2) וכל
בניו דנבאות מלכו ביומי ישמעאל שנה חדה (3) ובתר מותה
ל:. שנה מנהר מצרים עד נהר פרת: ובנו מכה (4) וכן
אמיר באכה אשורה על פני כל אחיו נפל: (5) אליפז
בן עשו אחי עם בני ישמעאל ואפקו גנים דמלכה ופלגיו
דנה (6) ואשקחו עשו שותף לישמעאל ואשוו בני מחלת
עם בני ישמעאל (7) והיא מלתה דאתאמרת והוא יהיה
פרה אדם ועשו הוא אדום: ובני עדה ואהליבמה לגנום

הוא שבט שמעון ומאמרו הנה השופטים: מפתרה אן ראש מן
לקח (129) מבנות הזנות: הם השופטים ואחריהם לקחו הנערים
הסכילים: ותבא קבתה וזמרי וכזבית אגלת תועבותם לעיני כל
העם: זמר הענן ויבא במנפה ושם קם בעל הקנאה המתודעה
אדנן הכהן הגדול (פינחם :) מתוך העדה : ויקח רמח בידו : ועשה
שני מופתים האחד להחיים והשני למיתים : . ענן המנפה הביא
את המנפה : ופינחם ענן הרחמים אשר נשא המנפה אשר היתה
אפך על כל החטאים : . ומופת החיים כי פינחם בקנאתו
(130) הציל לכל הטהורים : ואטיב להם במה עשה : . ומופת
המיתים היה הרמח בידו ודם הקדישים לא מתכרת עליו טפה.
אחת : כי ירדת אש שריפה מן השמים ועמדת בין הדם ויד
פינחם : ויהי כל הדם ירד עליה ותשרף אתו : . והשם יתעלה
אבטיל אתו תחת קנאתו בשבעה מאומות אסורים בו ובזרעו
אחריו : דם (הקרבנים : . וקטרת חמים ומנחה חדשה : .
החטאת : . והעלה : . והשלמים : ושמן המשחה : .) וכלל אתה
באחת שמינית : והיא הכהנה הגדלה : (131) וכרת עמו עליה ברית
שלום כפי מאמרו בספר התורה הקדושה (הנני נתן לו את בריתי
שלום: והיתה לו ולזרעו ברית כהנת עולם:) ואמר בספר אלאסאטיר

וחרבנה דמצרים על אדיו : (30) תמן פקד פרעה :
דיתפרשון נשיה מן גבריה מ : . יום ואתפרשו יט :
יום : . (31) ואזל גבר מבית לוי : רב הוא אילנה דמשה
זגול מנה : (32) ועמה חרשה בקסמיו דכוכבה דישראל
סליק : ואמה דילידה בטנה בה : (33) ואמר למלכה
בטלה היא חשבתך (34) ואמר לה פרעה מה מעבד :
(35) ואמר לה חרשה במיה הוא מותה : (36) ופקד
פרעה למצרים לא ישתבק יליד עבראיה זכר :
(37) ואתמני שפרה ופועה על מולד עבראתה : ואמר
לין פרעה כל דכר יתקטל : וכל נקבה תתחוי
(38) והוה עמרם אסאה טב מהימן במצרים : שפרה
קנת רחמות לואי ופועה קנת רחמות עבראיה :
(39) ושרת דחלת אלה בלבון : ולא עבדו כאשר אמר :
(40) וסגו עמה ואתחילו שריד (41) ופקד פרעה לכל

אתו : כי עשה נבלה בישראל : והיתה בשבט שמעון : . ושבט
שמעון היה מספרו בראישונה תשעה וחמשים אלף ושלש
מאות : ואחרי עשות זמרי ובנות הזנות זה המעשה ומובא הקצף
מלפני יהוה : הדמנפה אשר היתה להם צפר מספרם שנים ועשרים
אלף ומאתים : ויהיו המיתים במנפה מזה השבט שבעה ושלשים
אלף ומאות איש : . בראישון והשני (137) לא אתנבלא מעשה
הרע אלא מזה השבט : . ראה אה אחי ואדרש וחקר ושאל
ופקח עיניך : אז היתה מנפת קרח וכל עדתו : אחריה דברו
העדה על אדנן משה יהוה עליו : ועל אחיו אהרן שלום
יהוה עליהם : במהרה היתה המנפה בהעם : ויהיו המיתים בה
ארבעה ועשרים אלף : ושבע מאות כפי מאמרו יתעלה בתורה
הקדושה (ויהיו המיתים במנפה ארבעה עשר אלף ושבע מאות : .)
והנה אמר : (ויהיו המיתים במנפה ארבעה ועשרים אלף : .)
(138) ויהיו המיתים בשני המנפיפות האלה (שמנה ושלשים אלף
ושבע מאות :) ויהי המנרע מן שבט שמעון (שבעה ושלשים
אלף ומאות נפש : .) ואז הכה זרד הזכיר לבלעם פני האדון
פינחס ויהושע אחרד יהושע ממנו וצעק עליו להנישו : והכותו
אל בלעם לפניו ולפני פינחס הכהן : . וראש מן מת בזאת

וכתר בה ס : .ו.ג : . שנים : (19) ומית יוסף וכל
אחיו : (20) ושנת מלכות ישמעאל : ואתחיל עמלק
שוי : . (21) ונחת פרעה למצרים שנה א . : . כתר בה :
ובתר כן קעם במצרים בממציתה (22) והוה גוה עכור
ארעה ג . : . שנין : ומית מלך מצרים : (23) וקעם פרעה
וצמת אכלסין רברבין מן קפטאי ומלך בתרה ס : .
שנה (24) יהוה במצרים : חרש ושמה פלטי : ועמה
רבות ישראל : (25) ועמה לוי עלל ליד פרעה במרכבה
רבה מותר ונפק ברבו רבה (26) ואמר מנו גברה
הדן ואתאמר לה : עבראה : (27) ואמר רבה רבותה
דאהן גברה ומה טמיר בחלציו ומה יהי לה
(28) ואתחוי ממללה לפרעה ושלח וזעק לחרשה :
(29) ואמר לה כן : דעתיד. קעם מן חלצין דאהן גברה :
רב באימנו ובמדע ושומיה וארעה שמעים למימרה :

אשר אינם מאמינים בך : ואינם שמעים לפיך טרם רגע אחת
יבאו עמים מעטים מפאת אדום : והיא מלה אחת אמרה
(134) האדון יעקב עליו השלום (דן נחש עלי דרך שפיפון עלי
ארח :) וימהר בלעם במהלך אל מדין אל עירו צור אשר מנגב
למדין : וישא עיניו לפאת קדמה וירא לשבט נד פני הכל : .
והיא המלה אשר אתמרת : (נגד גדוד יגודנו) ומפתרה הוא יהי
תמיד נד פני המלחמה וכאשר. אמר המלאך עוד אל
בלעם בן בעור (דרך כוכב מיעקב וקם שבט מישראל :) וזה
הכוכב הוא אדונן פינחס : (וקם שבט מישראל :) הוא אדונן
יהושע הליפת שליח יהוה : וכלם צעקים ואמרים (יהוה
(135) אלהינו יהוה אחד : .בדד פרד תמיד אין עמד אל אחר :.ולא
הך : ולא דמות :) ויהי כאשר ראה בלעם זאת המראות הנדלות
וראה לפידי המלאכים סוביבה בהם וזכבלע הקדש בתוכם : יירא
בלעם : ויברח מפניהם מבקש הפליטה והשלום : והשם יתעלה לא
פלטו ולא שלמו : וימשך אתו (זרד בן קמואל בן אחי כלב :)
אשר הוא משבט יהודה ויעמידהו לפני פינחס בן אלעזר הכהן :
ולפני יהושע בן נון : והוה ידבר בדבר והם לא ידעו (136) מה
יאמר : ויקם (ורדית בן צוריאל בן סלוא מן שבט שמעון) ויהרג

ורחמת עליו ברת פרעה מלה (10) גדילה רחמו ופקדת
רביאתה דלא תפק מלתה (11) ומרים קעמה לקבלה
וכד עמתה עזיזה בה: . רעטת ואמרת לה איזל
ואזעה (12) ואמרת לה אזלי : ואזלת : וזעקה יוכבד
אמה : (13) ואמרת לה אינקי ילידה הדן ואתן דמי
חלביך : ואינקתה חלב טהור ורבה : ואנדיתה ליד
ברת פרעה וזעקת ית שמה משה: . (14) ובתר כן
אתחיל משה באלימותה : וקעם עם קעומי פרעה על
עבראי : (15) ועמה גבר מצרי מחי גבר עברי: וקטלה
וטמרה בחלה : (16) וביומה ב : עמה תרין גברייֿ
נצין : ואוכח סרוחה ואמר אה רשע: ואתרגז עבראה :
ואמר למשה אה קטולה (17) וערק למדין וכתר לגוה
ס : . שנה:. (18) ובתר כן: אתת עקין על ישראל ומית
גוטם: פרעה (19) ואתנח ישראל וסלקת אשוהותה וקעם

יהוה עליו (קח לך את יהושע בן נון האיש אשר רוח בו וסמכת
את ידך עליו: והעמדת אתו לפני אלעזר הכהן ולפני כל העדה: .)
ויהי זה הדבר בשנת הארבעים לצאת בני ישראל מארץ מצרים
בעשתי עשר חדש: ויעש משה כאשר צוה יהוה בשמח וששון
רב עד מאד: כאשר זה מתודע מן מאמדו באלאסאטיר (142) (וכן
עבד משה בחדו וזהו רבה הך דאלו הזה אחד: . . ובניו לא טזב
שבק אימנותה : לעלם:) ומפתר כן אן אדונן משה עליו השלום
לא היה אחד מבניו ביזם מותו ממצא אתו: ולכן שלח להם
מאתו שלום כי הוא את מותו שלום יהוה עליו זכר להם
וחנן עליהם: ושלח להם שלום עד לעלם: . כי לא יש אחריו
שלום יהוה עליו שלום : . . ואדוננן מרקה רצון יהוה עליו אמר
בכתבו המתודע : אן משה עליו השלום את שלחותו אל קהל
ישראל קרא ואמר (143) (אה נרשם ואליעזר תרי בניה דממני
עליכון מני השלם:) וזמזה השלום המתעתק אתודע אן לא יהי
להם דבר מן הצרר: ואדון הבשר אביהם: והשם יתעלה יהי רעי
להם בתפלות אביהם: וסחד עליהם אביהם בספר אלאסאטיר זאמר
(לית טבה שבק אימנותה לעלם:) ואחר כן באו הכהנים חקני
העם ויצו אתם על משמר תורת יהוה: אשר אורידו על ידו :

עמה למרמי ילידיה לנהרה :. (42) ורתתי אבהתה
ואמהתה ועבדי עבראתה באימנו והוה נשיה מטלקי
גרמין : עם ילידין :

IX

(1) ואתילד נביה רבה : אדביר לטב עד לעלם משה :
בירח ניסן : בה :. יומים מנה : (2) בז : וב : י : מן
סיבן אתרמי בנהרה וכד אתרמי בנהרה פחת נהרה
(3) ונפקו כל נשיה דתלי למעמי : (4) כד נהתו כל
נשיה נחתת ברת פרעה (5) והוה כל יומה דתלי
פחת נהרה : (6) ואצטמתו חרשיה וקסמיה : וקמו
במרטוש רב : (7) וקעם פלטי הקסם ברימם ספר
האותות : ואמר דילידה נחת (8) ותיבותה בסופה וחזתה
ברת פרעה בשעתה ה : בז : (9) ושלחת ית אמתה
ונסבת ואפתחתה וחזת ית ילידה והא רבי בכי

המלחמה בלעם : מתודע זה מן מאמרו באלאסאטיר (ארתע לבה
דנאל הדה קמאה : .) ביום הרביעי באו מן המלחמה : וביום
החמישי (139) הביאו הפקדים אשר לאלפי הצבא פדיון מן
היוצאים למלחמה : איש אשר מצא כלי זהב אצדה וצמיד
טבעת עגיל וכומז וישמו אתו באהל מועד זכרון לזאת המלחמה
אשר בשנים עשר אלף איש הכו חמשת מלכים וכל צבאם
ומחניהם ואבדו להם : ובזזו להם : וישבו אתם ולא נפקד מהם
איש אחד : כאשר זה מתודע מן מאמרו יתעלה בתורה הקדושה
(ולא נפקד ממנו איש :) ואחרי כל הדברים האלה צא קול
מלפני (140) יהוה לאמר : (לא יבוא עמוני ומואבי בקהל יהוה :)
ואמר עוד (ועתה הרגו כל זכר בטף וכל אשה ידעת איש
למשכב זכר הרגו וכל הטף בנשים אשר לא ידעו משכב זכר
החיו לכם :) ויעשו כאשר צוה יהוה : . ומאמרו (אשר לא ידעו
משכב זכר) הם הבתולות אשר לא ידעו איש : . וראה הך אמר הנה
כל זכר בטף הוא על הנערים אשר הביאו אתם עמם עם השבי :
והבנים אשר היו יינקו הרגו כל אחד מהם הוא ואמו : ומן (141) היה
משיג דרך הנברים לא יתקרא לו טף : אך יהי מן אנשי המלחמה
XI ויהוה ידע : . ואחרי זאת המלחמה אמר יהוה אל משה שלום

(36) בא : ‏‎.‎‏ צפרה בטור סיני : (37) בד : ‏‎.‎‏ צפרה דיום נקם בו : ‏‎.‎‏ בא : ‏‎.‎‏ אתקומם משכנה : בג : ‏‎.‎‏ נטלו מן טור סיני : (38) בג : ‏‎.‎‏ מיתת מרים : (39) בד : ‏‎.‎‏ מית אהרן : (40) בז : אקרב מלך ערד : עם ישראל : וישבי ממנו שבי ובתר אעיק עליו ישראל וחרם חרמה וקניאנה : ‏‎.‎‏

X

(1) מערטים : חרשה ערק מן ערד למדין והוה פעור דאשלו בלק בן צפור מלך מואבאי מזעק לבלעם : בר בעור בר גדיטט בר פעטה בר עמינגף בר לבן : (2) דמצטער דלא מצער : כי מטי לה מצטוער מקשט מלך מואב אצטער מן קינה ריקנה : (3) ושלח שלחין אל בלעם בעי לה דייתי מלוט לישראל : (4) בירחה ו : אזלו מלאכיה לבלעם : (5) והוה בלעם חכים ספר האותות וידע (6) לה : וסגד לאל האור ולאל הרקיע : ולאל המים : ולאל המאורות : ולאל הקדוש : (7) הלם :

השנים ששת אלפים : ‏‎.‎‏ שנה : ‏‎.‎‏ ואז אחל בדבר אמר : (כי תולידו בנים ובני בנים) כי זאת הקצה אספת כל מה יהיה באחרית הימים : והנה בשור במובא הרצון והרחמים : אחרי כלות ימי פנותה כפי מאמרו יתעלה (ומצאוך כל הדברים האלה באחרית הימים : ושבת עד יהוה אלהיך ושמעת בקולו כי אל רחום (147) יהוה אלהיך לא ירפך ולא ישחיתך ולא ישכח את ברית אבותיך אשר נשבע להם :) ומפתר כן אן השם יתעלה עת תשוב אליו בשזבתך : יקים בריתו עמך ויעשה לך באשר עשה בימי רצונה כן יעשה לך : ורב ממנו : וזה דבר קשט אין בו שקר : ויש דבר רב בזה מן מאמר אבותינו הראישונים : ‏‎.‎‏ ובדיל כן שם אדונן משה פתח דברי הנה בזאת הקצה : וכל אשר זכרו מדצא ממנה כי היא קבצת האלוף והבאה ונם אמר הנה (148) (ריש פנותה תרח מבויאתה) ונם אמר עליו השלום : (קעם גבר לזאה : ושמה עזרה בן פאני : וריש אקנאותה באדה ומקדשה יוסף ביומיד מקדש זרז קדש עבראותה יחלף פלנה

פַרעה מן .כתים שמה עטירט (20) ומשה רעי עאן
יתרו: ואתא להר חוריב (21) בה:. י: יום לירחה ג:
בד: אקים קיאמון דזכאי (22) אטרה דאדם : ולבושיו
אתיהבו למשה ביתה יומה: (23) והיא מלתה דאתמרת:
וזה לך האות: (24) בד:. אתחזי למשה: (25) בא:.
נחת למצרים ואמר יהוה לאהרן: זיל לזימון אחוך
(26) ואזל ואפגעה ועלו למצרים תריהון ועבדו סימניה
לעיני ישראל: (27) בג : עלו קדם פרעה: (28) בה:
מחו נהרה (29) כל דיניה לגו ט:. ירחין: (30) בה:.
נפקו ממצרים בו:. שעין נפקו לעיני כל מצרים:
(31) במפקי שבתה געזו ימה (32) בג : אתחלה מי מרה
וחזיה יהוה אילן אטרה דבה מחי ומאסי: (33) בו :
אנצח עמלק : (34) בד : קרא אלה על טור סיני
(35) כל יומי צפרי עלמה: ג.. צפרים: צפרה דבריאתה

ואהדיעהם אן לו לא זאת התורה לא היה לעלמה יתוב:. ודע
אה ראה (144) לדברי אן התורה הקדושה לקח אתה אדונן משה
השליח עליה השלום מיד הכבוד : על ספר לא יוכל אנש ידבר
עליו הך הוא ומה היא תמונתו: הוא מן עור: או מן אור :
ויהי מראהו גדול מאד : ולרבות נוראותו לא יוכל אחד ינע בו
אלא אדונן משה שלום יהוה עליו: וממנו עתק וכתב הספר
אשר כתבו:. ועתה נביא עד אחד מן כליל העדים בצדיקות
דברינו אן השם יתעלה נתן אל אדונן משה עם שני הלוחות
(145) אשר כתוב· עליהם עשרת הדברים: את ספר התורה והעד
על כן הוא מאמר משה עת עשו עת בני ישראל את העגל אמר
בתפלותו ליהוה בעבורם (ועתה אם תשא חטאתם שא ואם אין
מחיני מספרך אשר כתבת:) ואן אמרנו מדרשו היה על שני
הלוחות נראה אן לא יש למשה על הלוחות זכרון בהם (אוי
להם עזובי תורת משה כי לית להם שם מושיע.:) ואחר כן
אחל יאמר על מה הוא אוער יהי בשלשת אלפים ושנים מאות
וארבע שנים וזאת השנים הם (146) הם מן נותרת הששת אלפים
אשר מן בריאת עלמה אל מובא התהב: כי מן אדם אל מות
אדונן משה עליה השלום ששה ושבעים ומאתים שנה: ויהיו כל

בז : אתין קדישאתה בג : שעין : (21) והוו רבני מהלה
קמי אהל מועד : מדרום : (22) והוה משרי ראובן תמן
ממערבה : (23) ושמעון בממצית : (24) ונגד ממדנחה
(25) בדיוך : וקיתרה ובצנצלן ובטפוח ובזמרין (26) ובית
שמעון קעמין כבון ק :. וכ :. אלפין דקדישן (27) וברת
צור בממצתין על עגלה דקיצם נגידה ברוח מכל אתר
להאן דיתובה בעי היא אזלה בה : (28) וקל חייה
מן ענן כבודה נפק ואמר אמר : ויתקטל כל דאזל
לבעל פעור : (29) בתר דקעמו דיאניה עזרו בזריזו :
ולא עבדו מלי משה : (30) ואתת קבתה וזמרי וכזבית
לגוה : תועבה גליה לעיני כל עמה : (31) ושוי נחת
עננה ושדת מגיפתה (32) וקעם פינחס : וסבל רמח
באדה : (33) ואתעבד ב :. . סימנים א :. . דקיעמין :
וא :. דמאתין : ענן מגיפתה : (34) ופינחס ענן מגיפתה
אבק על כל מסבון ומיטב לכל דכים : (35) וסימן
מאתיה : רמח באדה : ואדם קדישתה לא מטפטף

אן מדרשו בזה הדבר הוא עד יאמר כאשר אמר האדון יעקב
עליו השלום : (לא יסור שבט מיהודה : ומחזקק מבין דגלית : עד
כי יבוא שלה : .) ושלה הוא אשר בא טרם מובא עזרה
(151) ושבט יהודה אשתייאר משתמר ומתרעי לשובבת יהודה : עד
בא שלה : ועשה המעשים הרעות אשר כל עדת היוחדים עדים
בה : וביאדרו לה בספרי הימים : אשר להם : . ועם זה כלו יאמרד
עליו נביא : ועוד אמר עליו השלום (מגדל גפנה יבני בעמק :
קהל ידו בעי קשטה : יתלחצון בר מולד אקדשו מורר יהי קסמי
בלעם בימיד תשמיש אלהי נכראי תתקומם :) זה הדבר כלו על
מובא ישוע בן מרים : זמאמרו (מגדל גפנה יבני) מפתרה
(152) יגדיל מאמן העולם בציון : (בעמק) מפתרה שנת אלף וארבע
מאות זמנים ושבעים לממלכת בני. ישראל יתילד זה האיש :
ומאמרו (קהל ידו בעי קשטה) מפתרה הוא עד מובאו יהיד עדת
ישראל מבקשים : האמת : דהאמת הוא בקודשם : להרג את נפשו :
כי הרגותו אמת : כאשר אמר עליד בתורה הקדושה (ומת הנביא

הָמַל : יְהָמַל : וְהָמַל : הָאָמַל : הָעָמָאל : גְמָנָאֵל : הַצָרְפָה :
הַסְמִיכֶם הָלַן : לִיל :. חָלַק : לֵב : חָלַק לָאֵל עֶלְיוֹן הָלִין :
הַנָתָר : הַלְגָפָר : (8) אָלִין שָׁבְעָתִי מְלָאכָיָה דְהוָה בִלְעָם
סָגַד לוֹן (9) אֵל הַקָדוֹשׁ מְלָאכָה דְקָדָם לְבִלְעָם : (10) אֵל
הָרוּחוֹת מְלָאכָה דְהוּשָׁט לֵהּ מָלָיָא מְרַבְחֵיָה קַמָאיָה :
ג :. שְׁלֹשָׁה הֲווֹ מַאֲמַר : (11) אֵל הָאוֹר אָנוֹף בִלְעָם
דְלָא יָלְעַט קוֹם : (12) אֵל הָרָקִיעַ אָזְדָם חֲזוּתָה : (13) אֵל
הַמָיִם אָמַר לֵית יָכֵל עָמִי שָׁמַע : (14) אֵל הַמְאוֹרוֹת
אָמַר לֵהּ וְלֹא עָתָה : (15) אֵל הַכְּתָפוֹת אָמַר לֵהּ :
וְלֹא נָחָשׁ בְיַעֲקֹב : (16) הָדָר : אֵל הָרוּחוֹת : אָמַר לֵהּ :
וְיִשְׂרָאֵל עָשָׂה חָיִל : (17) הַאֲזִין : אֵל הַקָדוֹשׁ : אָמַר אֵל :
יה : אֱלֹהָיו עִמוֹ וּתְרוּעַת מֶלֶךְ בוֹ : (18) וְכַד שָׁמַע
בִלְעָם חָשַׁב חֶשְׁבָה בִישָׁה דְעָמָה אֱלָהָה : דְיִשְׂרָאֵל סָנֵי
טְמָאָתָה וַאֲמַלֵךְ לְבָלָק בְזָנוּתָה וְאַשְׁווּ מוֹאָבָאֵי מְעָבַד
כֵן : (19) בְשַׁבְתָה אַפְקוּ קְדִישָׁאתָה : (20) וּבְרִית פִינְחָס
בַזְ : אֶתְקוֹמֵם לָהּ : וְלוֹרָעָה בַתְרָהּ טוֹב רַחֲמָיו דְאֵלָה :

רָמֵי לָנוּ קְהָלָה סָדָר פְּנֵי וְרָשָׁז קָרְטָם בְּנִימִים בְּעַמוֹן יָבֵנִי :) כָל
זֶה הַדָבָר עַל עֶזְרָה כִי הוּא רֹאשׁ מִן הָפַךְ אוֹתוֹת הַתוֹרָה מִן
לְשׁוֹן הָעִבְרִי אֶל לְשׁוֹן אַשׁוּר : אֲשֶׁר בְיַד עֵדַת הַיְהוּדִים : וָאָקִים
מִלַת שָׁלֹה בְמַאֲמָרוֹ אַן הַמָקוֹם הַמֻבְחָר בָּעִיר צָהִיוֹן : (149) וְנֶרַע
מִן הַתוֹרָה הַקָצָה הָרְבִיעִית מִן עֲשָׂרַת הַדְבָרִים וְעָשָׂה בְסֵפֶר
הַתוֹרָה כְפִי מִדְרָשׁוֹ : וְאָסַף עָלֶיהָ וְנֶרַע מִמֶנָה דְבָרִים רַבִים
מִשְׁתַמְרָה עִמָנוּ : וְהוּא אֲשֶׁר הָיָה אָב לְכָל מַה הָיָה בֵינֵנוּ וּבֵין
עֵדַת הַיְהוּדִים וְהַחֲכָמִים הָיָה טֶרֶם מָבוֹא עֶזְרָה : רַק עַל יָדוֹ אִתְאַסַף
וְאִתְרַבָה : וְלֹא אִשְׁתְיָאֵר בָצַע בְשׁוּבָה אֶל יוֹם מָבוֹא הַתָב : .
וְעוֹבָד זֶה הָאִישׁ כָלָה מִתוּדָעָה בְּסֵפֶר הַיָמִים : וְאַן דְרַשְׁנוּ הִגָה
נִסְפַר מַה עָשָׂה יְתוֹרָךְ מִסַפְרוֹ : . וְאָחָר כֵן אָמַר הַשָלִיחַ מֹשֶׁה
עָלָיו הַשָלוֹם (150) (רָשׁוּת דְבֵית יְהוּדָה בְעוֹלָם בְזִירָאתָה יֶבְטְלָן (:
וּמְפָטֵר עוֹלָם הֹדָא אָרְבַע אָלְפִים וּשְׁלֹשׁ מֵאוֹת וּשְׁבַע וְשִׁשִׁים
שָׁנָה : וְהַלֵל אֲשֶׁר הָיָה לְהַפִיכוֹת מִצְוֹת יְהוָה הוּא שֵׁבֶט יְהוּדָה : .
וְאָסַף הַדָבָר בְּמַאֲמָרוֹ (שְׁמַע יְהוָה קוֹל יְהוּדָה :) וִיהוָה הוֹדִיעַ

מלאכה לבלעם: דרך כוכב מיעקב והו פינחס: וקם
שבט מישראל: . והו יהושע וקל (46) : כריזאתון
יהוה אלהינו יה אחד: . (47) וערק בלעם ואצעד ביד
זרד: בר קמואל בר אחי כלב: דמן שבט יהודה
ואנחה קמי פינחס: ויהושע וכלב ולא חכמו ממללה:
(48) וקעם רדיה בר צוריאל בר סלוא ואתחיל עליו
וקטלה בחרבה (49) תמן אמר יהושע ארתע לבה
דגאל הדם קמאה: . (50) בד: אתו מקרבה: בה:.
אנדו רבני קהלה סלוחה דדהבה ואתיעל לאהל
מועד: . (51) ונפק קל חייה: לא ייעל עמוני ומואבי
בקהל יה: . (52) וארקטלי נשיה שביאתה: .

XI

(1) ואמר אלה למשה קח לך את יהושע בן נון גברה
דרוח בה ואקימה לקדם אלעזר כהנה: וקמי כל
כנשתה: בשנת ם: בירחה י: (2) וכן עבד משה
בחדו וזהו: רבה הך דאלו הוה אחד מבניו לית

(155) ונם אמר וישכנו הארץ הקדושה אנשים זולתם וימלכו לה: .
עליה השלום (קהל יהי מגבי לאקנדהותה יתעבד ארע בחזריה
אליתים: יסחנון :) ומפתר כן אן יהי ישראל בתהות ויתנצל ממנו
הדת: וימלכו הארץ הטובים עדת אליתים: ואחר כן אמר עליה
השלום (שדך יהי בעלמה בחור: ואיקר וחיים בטב :) ומפתר
כן הוא יבא עליהם זמן יהיה בו חנים בששמח וששון אמנים מן
חמס משפט הקשים באיקר וטוב וחסד: ואמר עוד עליה השלום
(ובתר כן (156) חלוף כתב יתעבד מלין חדתן מלבו עתקן יבקן :)
ומפתר כן הוא אחר הדברים האלה והמחלף ההוא כלו יתחדש
בעולם דבר חדש מן ישן: (והוא יתנלי ספר כלו שקר וזד:
ולקח אקרו מן ספר התורה זמן דברי הראישונים: . ואחר כן
אתנפל עליה השלום ואמר (ויעלנם יהוה אלהיך אל הארץ אשר
ירשו אבותיך ולזזה תבנה:) אמר זה הדבר על אשר עזרו מן
תגלות הגדלה כי בעת באו מן הגלות אל הארץ (157) הקדושה
ויעלו אל הרנריזים אשר הוא לזוה: ויהיו הימים ההם הך ימי

עליו טפה :. אלא קעם על רמח שריף :. בין אדמה :.
ואדה דפינחס ז :. קטירין :. (36) וכן אמרו ממומי
אימנותה כל מהעמין דרצבען על ז :.. וח :. (37) כי
בריש ירחה ח :. אתיי קדישאתה :. וכירחה י :. אמר
אלה לנביה נקם נקמת בני ישראל ובתר כן תכנש
לעמך :. (38) בב :. י :. אלף אודיאנו עלולי קרבה
(39) ואמת דאזלו עלולי קרבה אמר אלה למשה
דילך על :. קר :. (40) ואמת דאזלו עלולי למדין
יהב לפינחס :. קמי קהלה חציצרתה באדה :. ויצבאו על
מדין כמד פקד יהוה :. (41) בד :. נפק קהל במדין
איד לה ישראל (42) אה ריש חרשיה קום על אילין
דמהימנין בך :. הך רגע עין אתת סיעה זעורה מקבל
ארום (43) והי מלתה דאמר יעקב דן נחש עלי דרך
שפפון עלי ארח :. (44) וזרז בלעם לכתל מדין לשור
דרומה :. תלא עיניה למדנחה :. ועמה סיעת גדאה והי :.
מלתה דאמר גד גדוד יגידנו :. (45) ומה דאמר

ההוא .) :. ומאמרו (כבר מולד אקדשו) מפתרה אן הזא בן זנות
ומן הזנות (ומזדה) מפתרה סודר וזמזדה מן דרך האמת :.
(153) ומאמרו (יהי קסמי בלעם בימיז :) מפתרה ידו מכשף כמו
בלעם ויעשה אותות ומופתים בדרך הקסם עד יאמנו העולם :.
וזדף הדבר במאמרו (בימיז תשמיש אלהי נכר :) מפתרה אן
בימיז תתרברב עבד"י אלהי הנכר :. וזהא יאמר על נפשו אל :.
ויהד כן :. ואחר כן אמר משה עליה השלום (כצי בער יומים
מקדש זרותה יתפנר ביד נוי עז פנים :. דבית שהמה דבית
פאניה בדור :. בארע :) מפתר כן אן אחרי ימים מעטים (154) מן
מות ישוע מקרש השקר הבטול יתחרב ביד עם עז פנים :.
וימלכו בתי המעבד אשר בנו אתה עדת ישוע ותהיה תחת ידם
בדור שבע ועשרים ומאה :. ושנים אלפים :. לממלכת ישראל :. וזה
הדבר על מזבא מחמד אשר היה מזבאו בדור ההוא :.. ושב
ואמר עליה השלום (קהל ואשמר דאר תחתיון באסכמו רזח)
מפתר כן אן מן רבות עונות בני ישראל ישמדם יהוה בארץ :.
c

(15) והוא משרי מבאר ארהותה דליתו עלל לה :. (16) ומעיל לה לגו משכנה בג : ומחסל לה בד :. (17) ונפק קל חייה מן ענן כבודה : (18) ישר בה :. פעלה כשירה : אהנו יומה עקבאה : מחכום דריה מה דגלה משה : נביה רבה ממה דארשה לה מרה (19) וכן אמר ותמונת יה יביט : (20) ואמר מה אתי עתיד לג : אלפין ור : וד : שנים כי תולידו בנים ובני בנים : ריש פנותה תרח מגויאתה (21) קעם גבר ליואה ושמה עזרז בר פאני : וריש אקנאותה באדה : (22) ומקרשה יוסף ביומיו : (23) מקדש זרו קדש עברותה יחלף פלגה רמי לגו קהלה סדר פנו (24) ורשו קרטם בנימים בעמון : יבנה :. (25) בעולם רשות דבית יהודה בחלוף גזיראתה : יבטלון : (26) שמע יהוה קול יהודה : (27) מגדל גפנה יבנה בעמק (28) קהל יהי בעי קשטה (29) יתלחצון בר מולד אקדשו : (30) בראה יהי קסמי בלעם (31) ביומיו תשמיש אלהי

יקום ביד תקיפה י :. כלי : עמי נדם ביומי ייתי :.) ומפתר כן הוא יקום נשיא ביד חזקה עשרה שנים : תהי ממלכתו באיקר (160) וברבבו : ואחר כן יתגלי ביומי רבות ואיקרות העם הדנם : ויקחז הממלכה ממנו ויזחח הדידעו : ומלת כלי : מפתרה נשא מן המעלות : וזלה בא מפתר אחר רב מזה מן מאמר הגבונים כמד מאמרם (וכלי לדיניה :. ב :. קדקד יקום בחיל מעמי מה בה ולא כלי :) ומפתר כן : יקום נשיא בכוח נדל : יתגלי מנה בחמשה : ולא יתנשא : יהוה ידע אן המפתר בכן יתגלי לזה שנא מעמד או ממנו אחרי חמש שנים מן מלכו :' ועם זה לא יגדל עליו : ולא ישאו מעל ממלכתו :. נ :. קעם קדקד נזיר : אמורי בישתה ביזמי ביד נכר יאבדון :.) ומפתר כן הוא יקום נשיא מתעור : (161) המדברים בשקר ביומי ביד נכרי ימתו : יהוה ידע אן טעם כן הוא ביומי זה יתרברב השקר : והוא יהי הנשיא לו : ואחר כן יתגלי ביומי עם נכרי יהרגנו לו ולכל עמו :.

(ד :. קעם קדקד עציף : בקשט : יהי פלטנה קהלה ביומי

טבה שבק אימנותה לעלם: (3) ואתרשי משה
מביארה ארהותה קדישתה: (4) ואמר לה אלה סך
לטור עבראי ועמי ארע כנען: ואקים תחומיה סחר:
והוא משרי בתחומיה (5) מקורי ליואי ממרנח ובתחומי
ארעה מדרומה: מיסטר ים מלחה מרנחה (6) מיעל
לה לגו ארעה בגלל דאמר בקעתה מסחר תחומה מן
עקרבים ועבר צנה: ועדן לגו ארעה נגד על מרי
מתמרה אלקדר: (7) תחום פראן: ומסחר עצמונה
עד נחל מצרים מעל סכותה לגו מן תחומה עד
שאקי מצרים: (8) נחת ימה מעאל טרסוס: ונגד טורה
מעאל הר אללוכם לגו ארע (9) מצפון חמת נחל
חנוכיה והיא זפרנה: נפק חצר עינן (10) ומן חצר
עינן שפמה והי אסקופיה עד הארבילה (11) ומחית
תחומה: ומקבע לגו כתף ים כנרת קדמה: (12) וטברים
מתחמה בימה מכל רבעתה: (13) ונחת נביה רבה
בחרו ובצוקה: (14) חדי עמי טובה דארעה: ומציק

הרצון: ראה אה אחי אנה הדבר יש בו דבר מתקדם ודבר
מתאחר: כי בראישונה דבר על ישמע: ועל מחמד נבי
הישמעאלים: והנלות הזכירה היתה טרם מובאם: . ודרף הדבר
במאמרו (יובל בחדז:) והוא פלימה מן האסור והחזקות הנדלה
ההיא: . ואחר כן אמר עליו השלום (פנו תניאני: תקום טעו
בעלבן (158 יומיה) ומפתר זה הדבר הוא יתנלי עד תהות ופנות
מן דרך הטוב שנית אחרי היזבל ההוא: בקהל הנקיא אשר
אקרז מן יצחק: בשנת לו ובך: וחמשה אלפים לבריאת עלמה:
ובשנה ההיא יראו חזקות נדלות: ואמר עוד (קדש בנעתה ידיר
צעורין וצלמין פרוק:) ומפתר כן הוא יהי בימים ההם בהרתריים
פסל: ותמונה תשבר: . ומפתר (ידיר) הוא יהי בו מן התמנות
(159) חשכה תתנשא זיאיר בשבירות הצלמים: ויהזה ידע: . . ואחר
כלולו עליו השלום מזה הדבר בא בזכרון המלכים אשר יקומו
בימי פנותה וכללם בזכרון תהבה: וזבר בדבר המתקדם שנים:
וזכר עוד ארבע ועשרים כל אחד זכרו לבד: (א: קרקד XII

XII

א :
(1) קדקד יקום ביד :
תקיפה י : . כלי :
עמינדם ביומיו :
ייתי : .

ב :
(2) קדקד יקום :
בחיל מעמי :
מנה בה : ולא :
כלי : .

ג :
(3) קעם קדקד נזיר
אמורי בישתה :
ביומיו ביד נכר
יאבדון : .

ד :
(4) קעם קדקד עציף
בקשט : יהי פלטענה
קהלה ביומיו
ראבי : .

ה :
(5) קעם קדקד נזיר
ניר ברזלח
ביומיו יעזר

ו :
(6) קעם קד : עזיז
בעותר בית מלחמיה
ביומיו יבנה

אלאסאטיר : (רב הוא אילנה דמשה בזול מנה : .) ואז הרת האדונה
יוכבד באדון הבשר : . ראה פלטי אל כוכב ישראל וירא
אתו עלה : . ואן אם היולד הרה בו : ויאמר אל פרעה עובדך
וחשבנך אשר עשיתי אתו הזם בטול : ויאמר לו פרעה מה
נעשה : ויען פלטי ויאמר לפרעה במים יהי מת : וזה מתודע מן
מאמרו במפר אלאסאטיר (במיה הוא מותה :) בעת חהיא צוה
פרעה המצרים אן (164) לא ישתיאר בן זכר עברי : והיו הפוקדים
על המילדות אשר היו לנשי העבריות הם שפרה ופועה : ויבא
אתם פרעה לפניו : ויאמר להם : כל הבן היולד לעבריים ימות :
וכל בת תחיה : ויהי עמרם חכום וידעיו בחכמתו רב עד מאד :
ופוקד בארץ מצרים : ומטיב לכל העמים : . ושפרה היתה
הפוקידה על המילדות אשר מן שבט לוי : ופועה היתה פוקדה
על המילדות אשר מן עדת ישראל : וירדת יראת יהוה בלבביהם :
ולא עשו כאשר דבר אליהן מלך מצרים : כי שלום השליח לא
יש שלום כמו : שלום יהוה עליו : ואדונן מרקה רצון יהוה עליו :
ואדונן מרקה רצון יהוה אמר עליו בצפיתתו אן השליח אמר אל

נכראי תתקומם (32) וציבעד יומים: מקרש זרוחה
יתפגר באד גוי עז פנים: (33) ודבית שהמה: ודבית
פאניה: בדור בארעה קהל ואשמו דאר תחתיון
באסכמו רבע (34) קהל יהי מנבי לאקנהותה יתעבד
ארע בחוריה אלינים: יסחנון (35) שדך יהי בעלמה
בחור חיל ואיקר וחיים בטב: (36) ובתר כן חלוף
כתב יתעבד (37) מלין חדתן מלנו עתק יפקן
(38) ויעלנך יהוה אלהיך לארעה דירתו אבהתך
ותירתנה: (39) ולווזה תבנה: (40) יובל בחדו פנו
תניתני תקום (41) טעו בעמי נקיא תתעמי בעלבן יומיה
(42) קרש גבעתה ידיר צעורין
וצלמין פרוק: .

ראבי :) ומפתר כן הוא יקום נשיא חזק מאד באמת: יהי בימיו
ישראל יהי בשלום: ויהי מהב לאשר יהב האמת ויהוה ידע.:

(ח:. קעם קדקד נזיר: ניד ברזל ביומיו יעזר:) זה הוא מלך
מצרים: ויחז בני ישראל מן העבדה: ונשוב לזכרון מה היה
ביומי זה המלך ונאמר כאשר בא בספר אסטיר משה: אן היה
ביומי בארץ מצרים איש (162) מנחש ושמו פלטי: וירא אל VIII
גדלות ורבות בני ישראל: וירא עמרם עלה לפני פרעה במרכבה
גדלה מאד: ויצא וראמר ברבות גדלה: ואמר מן הוא זה האיש ויאמר
לו זה איש עברי:. וען ויאמר גדולה היא רבות זה האיש:
ומה הוא מתכסי בו: ומה יהי לו:. וישנב זה הדבר אל פרעה
וישלח ויבא את פלטי: אליו: וישאלו על דבריו אשר דברו:
ויענו כן.:

הוא אמר אן יקום מחלצי זה האיש איש גדול יתגלי באימן
ובבונגה: והשמים ושמי השמים תחת ידו: ומחרבות מצרים תהי
על ידו: ובתר ארבעים יום יהי בקרב אמו:. בעת ההיא
במהרה צוה פרעה אן ירחקו האנשים מן הנשים מספר ארבעים
יום: (163) ויאסרו את האנשים במקום: והנשים במקום לבדם:
כפי מאמרו: ויהי אחרי שבע עשר יום מן הארבעים: הלך איש
מבית לוי: ויקח את בת לוי: בן יעקב: וישכב אתה ותהר
האשה באדון הבשר: אדון כל אשה ונבר: כאשר בא בספר

נא   51

יה :	יו :
(15) ק'ק' באפילה קסמים	(16) קעם קדקד
יהי איכלה דשכם	גג : בתר
יקד באדה : .	אהן : :

יז :	יח :
(17) קעם קדקד פרוש ארע	(18) קעם קדקד באד בענון
עבראותה יבטל : .	בחכמה ביומיו יהי : ·

יט :	כ :
(19) קעם קדקד פשע	(20) קעם קדקד
מקדש זרותה ביומיו	נגוד עדלתו
יוסף עקב בישיה	ביומיו בשפח
יתוקד באש וגפרי : .	ימה ילנק .

מיהוה אן יקריב זה ולא ישם זה היום רחוק רק קרוב :. ולזה
הדבר דברים רבים יתורך מספרה בזה המקום : ויה : ידע :.
(167) ואחר כן בא צו לאהרן הבשר משה עליו השלום אן יכתב
ספר התורה הקדושה ויקרא אתו פני כל קהל ישראל :. ויאמר
לו עוד עלה אל הר העברים הזה : וראה את ארץ כנען ואת
גבולתיה סביב :. ויעל משה וירא את כל ארץ כנען ופאתיה :
ונבולתיה כאשר בא בספר במדבר סיני פרק לד :. וירד הנבי
העצום בשמח :. מן ראותו להרצריזים בית אל הקדוש : מכל
המקומים בהארץ : והיה באבל רב כי לא יכל לעלות .אליו :.
ואחר כן אהל בביאור התורה הקדושה ביום השלישי : ובללה
ביום הרביעי :. והביא אתה אל (168) אהל מועד ביום החמישי :
ונפק קל חייה מן ענן כבדה :. ישר אה פעלה כשירה : אהן
יומה עקבאה :. ומפתר כן אן צא דבר תבריח מן ענן כבדה :
הא איקר השם :. השיבת אה עשה הטוב : זה הוא היום האחר :
מדיע הדורות מה נלא לו משה הנבי העצום : ומאשר אמרו לו
מרו : וכן על התורה אינו מוצא מן זולתה :.

נו :	קעם קדקד עזיז בעותר בית מלחמה בימיו יבנה :)
נז :	קעם קדקד דער בלזה ישרי : עמי נדם בעבר :.)
נח :	קעם קדקד עזיז במדע מקשט : קהלה יהי חדי :)
נט :	קעם קדקד נזיר (169) זאל בתנומי יומיה עבירין :)
ס :	קעם קדקד עזיז בעותר שליטים יאבדו בימיו בדמסין

ח:	ז:
(8) קעם קד'עיז במרע'	(7) קעם ק:ק'דער בלוה
מקשט קהלה יהי חדי	ישרי עמינדם בעבר :.

י:	ט:
(10) ק'מ'עיז בעותר	(9) משם קדקך
שליטים יאבדו	נזיר זאלה
ביומיו בדמסין : מיה	בתנומי יומיו
יגחון לחופת שכם :	עכירין'

יב:	יא:
(12) קעם כרקך	(11) ק'ק'בעכר יאבד
ברוש ולעיו	ביומיו עמה יעזור
כדם אהן .	בחטיה קיאמה ילקון

יד:	יג:
(14) קעם קדקך	(13) ק'ס'עקב בישיה
ברוש קהלה	ביומיו שמאם מן ארע
יוסף : .	חיולה חיול ימטי :.

בני ישראל (165) אז מת :. אה נרשם ואליעזר תרי בגיה דמני עליבון מני השלם: ויהוה ידע אן הם עד היום הזה וער יום אחרית על טוב מאמן בתורה הקדושה; והשם יתעלה רעי להם בתפלות אביהם ואביהם מהד עליהם במאמרו בספר אלאמאסתיר XI (לית' טבה שבק אימנותה לעלם :) ותתבה לא יקום אלא מהם :. ידע אן נלל כמותה מן ראות הבוראים וחמר קוממותה בתוך בני ישראל הזא היה כפי דרישות אביהם מן השם יתעלה: כי הזא שלום יהוה עליו ראה לכל הבוראים בכל הדורות מן יום בראשית ואחרי יום נקם: וראה אל יומי (166) פנותה: וראה לכל מה יהי בישראל: וכל החזקות הנדלות אשר תהי עליהם: ודרש מן השם יתעלה אן יהיו בגיד רחוקים מזה: ולא ידי לחם מה יהי על ישראל :. : והשם עשה לו כפי בקושו: ואסתיר אתם אל יום מובא תהבה : אשר הזא יקום מהם : ויבאו במחנה רב מאאת קדמה מזרחה : (הוא לו תצמי עתי אליהם : אז יבאו ותהבה בינהם: ועמוד עננה מכסה לון : והמלאכים בתוכם :) אדרש

נג

כו : קבל כו : . וברוך : אלהינו
ישתבח חכום כסיאתה לעולם : וברוד שמו לעולם:
וגליאתה : . יתרומם : אדם נח אברהם משה
עליון השלום לעולם : .

כד : וקדקד יקום בקשט : יכתב ארהזתה : ואטר פליאתה באדה :
אור ולא יהי חשך : (נוז) מרן יורז בכן : טוב דיעמי
וימטי : וברוך אלהינו לעולם וברוך שמו לעולם : .)

כו : קבל כו : ישתבח הכום כסיאתה וגליאתה יתרומם : (אדם :
נח : אברהם משה עליון השלום לעולם : .) דע אן כאשר
היה מן אדם אל אדון הנביאים משה ששה ועשרים
נביא : כן יהי עוד מן ראש פנותה עד אן יקום תהבה
חמשה ועשרים קדקד : ותהבה הוא ששה ועשרים יתהלל
היכול על כל כלום : ויתקדש שמו : .

כא : כב :
(21) ק"ק פיגמיה קהל (22) קעם קדקד חלקת
עמי נדם יעזר בכל אתר מחקק : מערב משלם
בדור בארץ גבעלה וישראל תרח דאיקר : קהלה
עשה חיל : ודיש גבעתה יהי חדי : אהן
בחזוה : ומטן כן : . משמש למרן בשלם : .

כג : כד :
(23) קעם קדקד' (24) וקד' יקום בקשט יכתב :
בזז גוי ארהותה : ואטר פליאתה
ירדי מיעקב באדה : אור ולא יהי
 חשך :
והאביד שריד מעיר : . מרן : יורז בכן : טוב
 דיעמי : וימטי :

ינחן לחופת שכם (:)

יא : קעם קדקד יאבד : בימי עמה יעזר בחטיה קיאמה ילקן : :
יב : קעם קדקד בדוש ולעיד קדם אהן :
יג : קעם קדקד נג עקב בישיה בימי שמאם מן ארע חזלה : חיל ימטי (:)
יד : קעם קדקד בדוש קהלה יוסיף (:)
יה : קעם קדקד באפולה קסמים יהי איכלה דשכם יקד באדה :
יו : קעם קדקד נג בתר אהן :
יז : קעם קדקד פרוש ארעה עבראתה יבטל :
(170) יח : קעם קדקד באד בענן בחכמה בימו יהי : .
יט : קעם קדקד בר פשע : מקדש זרותה בימי יוסף : עקב בישיה יתוקד באש מנפרית :
כ : קעם קדקד נגד ערלתה : בזמי בשפח ימה יינק : .
כא : קעם קדקד פתמיה : קהל עמי נדם יעזר : בכל אתר בדור בארץ הבעלה : וישראל עשה חיל : ודיש נבעתה בחזוה ומטן כל : .
כב : קעם קדקד חלקת מחזקק : מערב משלם תרח דאיקר : קהלה יהי חדי אהן משמש למרן בשלם :
כג : קעם קדקד בזז גוי ירדי מיעקב והאביד שריד מעיר :

APPENDIX

(Codex Gaster No. 1168, folios 1*b*–8*b*).

ספר הימים :

(fol. 1b) חלק בזכרון מות אדוננו משה בן עמרם עליו הצלות
והשלם.: בשנת שנים אלפים ושבע מאות. וארבע ותשעים
שנה מן בריאת עלמה: ובשנת הארבעים למוצא בני ישראל
מארץ מצרים בעשתה עשר חדש באחד לחדש החל
אדוננו משה שלום יהוה עליו במכתב התורה הקדושה על
הספר המתכתב באצבע אלהים בתמימו עתקו ונלהו ופלנו
לקצים ופרשות ברוח הקדש וזה כן בספר הזכיר : וכלול
מכתבו לזאת התורה הקדושה על הספר דאתקדם זכרו בשלשים
יום : וקרא אתה לעיני ומשמע זקיני עדתו והכהנים בני לוי
ונתנה להם: ואחר כן בא אל אהל מועד ופתח ארון העדות
ושם ספר ארדזתה המתכתב באצבע אלהים בו :. בצלע שני
הלוחת המתחזקק בדם עשרת הדברים: ושם עליו הכפרת אשר
לא אחד יוכל עוד משאו מעליו עד היום הזה :. שם עקד
ומבד בין ידי מרה פני ארון העדות :. דברה יהוה ישתבח שמו
הקדש מבין שני הכרובים : (fol. 2a) ישר אה פעלה כשירה אדנך
יום עקבאה: ובכן הדיעהו כי מטת ימי מותו: וזה היה בצפר יום
החמישי בראש חדש שנים עשר מן השנה הזכירה: שם יצא
הנבי הרם אל אהל אשר היה מנטע אתו מחוץ המחנה: והזה
לשונה מהלל בתשבחן מרה לאמר הצדיק המשפט לך אדני :
אה מן לא תשא פני לא לנבי ולא אל מני: זכותה דילך אה
חכם: אתוד הצדיק והישר אל אמונה :.

ואחר כן עמד הנבי הרם משה בן עמרם עליו השלם וצלא
בין ידי מרה: ובכלות צלותו קרא ליהושע משרתו ואניד לו כל
הדברים דבר יהוה אתו : ואמר לה אה משרתי הלך לבית
כתתה ודבר להם בכן : ואמר אל אלעזר ואיתמר ופינחס ייתו
לאנה במדר עד נתמלי מן חזיתם: וכד שמע האדון יהושע בן
נון מן הנבי זאת הדברים דהות בפתח אהל מועד (fol. 2b) משם
יצא ואתא בזרז ליד משכנה קדישה: ועמד פניז בבי לכהנים
השלשה: וכד שמעו מקראו: משם במהר צאו: וחזו אדונן יהושע
עמד בכי : ודמעות עיניז מטללה על פניו: ואמרו לה אה משרת
דמע בני עבר: מה הדבר: ועל מה אתה תבכי: ולבבך משתבר
ויען להם בקול אבל עני: משה הנבי אדני: השליח האנשיא

נג

כו : קבל כו : .
ישתבח חכום כסיאתה
וגליאתה : . יתרומם :

וברוך : אלהינו
לעולם : וברוך שמו לעולם :
אדם נח אברהם משה
עליון השלום לעולם : .

כד :   וקדקד יקום בקשט : יכתב ארהותה : ואטר פליאתה באדה :
אור ולא יהי חשך : (וגו׳) מרן יזרז בכן : טוב דיעמי
וימטי : וברוך אלהינו לעולם וברוך שמו לעולם : .

כו :   קבל כו : ישתבח חכום כסיאתה והליאתה יתרומם : (אדם
נח : אברהם משה עליון השלום לעולם : .) דע אן כאשר
היה מן אדם אל אדון הגביאים משה ששה ועשרים
נביא : כן יהי עוד מן ראש פנותה עד אן יקום תהבה
חמשה ועשרים קדקד : ותהבה הוא ששה ועשרים יתהלל
היכול על כל כלום : ויתקדש שמו : .

כב:	כא:
(22) קעם קדקד חלקת	(21) ק'ק פיגמיה קהל
מחקק: מערב משלם	עמי נדם יעזר בכל אתר
תרח דאיקר: קהלה	בדור בארץ גבעלה וישראל
יהי חדי: אהן	עשה חיל: וריש גבעתה
משמש למרן בשלם:.	בחזוה: וממן כן:.

כד:	כג:
(24) וקד'קום בקשט יכתב:	(23) קעם קדקד
ארהותה: ואטר פליאתה	בזז גוי
באדה: אור ולא יהי חשך:	ירדי מיעקב
מרן: יזרע בכן: טוב דיעמי: וימטי:	והאביד שריד מעיר:.

יתחזן לחזפת שכם (:)

יא: קעם קדקד יאבד: בימי עמה יעזר בחטיה קיאמה ילקן::
יב: קעם קדקד בדוש ולעיז קדם אהן:
יג: קעם קדקד נב עקב בישיה בימי שמאם מן ארע חזלה: חיזל ימטי (:)
יד: קעם קדקד בדוש קהלה יוסיף (:)
יה: קעם קדקד באפולה קסטים יהי איכלה דשכם יקד באדה:
יו: קעם קדקד נב בתר אהן:
יז: קעם קדקד פרוש ארעה עבראתה יבטל:
יח: קעם קדקד באד בענון בחכמה בימו יהי:.. (170)
יט: קעם קדקד בר פשע: מקדש זרותה בימי יוסף: עקב בישיה יתוקד באש מנפרית:
כ: קעם קדקד נגד ערלתה: ביזמי בשפח ימה ינק:.
כא: קעם קדקד פיתמיה: קהל עמי נדם יעזר: בכל אתר בדור בארץ הבעלה: וישראל עשה חיל: וריש גבעתה בחזוה וממן כל:.
כב: קעם קדקד חלקת מחוקק: מערב משלם תרח דאיקר: קהלה יהי חדי אהן משמש למרן בשלם:
כג: קעם קדקד בזז גוי ירדי מיעקב והאביד שריד מעיר:

APPENDIX

(Codex Gaster No. 1168, folios 1b–8b).

ספר הימים:

(fol. 1b) חלק בזכרון מות אדנן משה בן עמרם עליו הצלות
והשלם .. בשנת שנים אלפים ושבע מאות. וארבע ותשעים
שנה מן בריאת עלמה: ובשנת הארבעים למוצא בני ישראל
מארץ מצרים בעשתה עשר חדש באחד לחדש החל
אדנן משה שלום יהוה עליו במכתב התורה הקדושה על
הספר המתכתב באצבע אלהים בתמימו עתקו וגלהו ופלגו
לקצים ופרשות ברוח הקדש וזהה כן בספר הזכיר : וככלל
מכתבו לזאת התורה הקדושה על ההספר דאתקדם זכרו בשלשים
יום : וקרא אתה לעיני ומשמע זקני עדתו והכהנים בני לוי
ונתנה להם : ואחר כן בא אל אהל מועד ופתח ארון העדות
ושם ספר ארהתה המתכתב באצבע אלהים בו .. : בצלע שני
הלוחות המתחזקק בהם עשרת הדברים : ושם עליו הכפרת אשר
לא אחד יוכל עוד משאו מעליו עד היום הזה .. : שם עקד
וסבד בין ידי מרה פני ארון העדות .. : דברה יהוה ישתבח שמו
הקדוש מבין שני הכרובים : (fol. 2a) ישר אה פעלה כשירה אהך
יום עקבאה : ובכן הודיעהו כי מטת ימי מותו : וזה היה בצפר יום
החמישי בראש חדש שנים עשר מן השנה הזכירה : שם יצא
הנבי הרם אל אהלו אשר היה מנטע אתו מחוץ המחנה : וזהוה
לשונה מהלל בתשבחן מרה לאמר הצדיק והמשפט לך אדני :
אה מן לא תשא פני לא לנבי ולא אל מני : זכותה דילך אה
חכום : אתה הצדיק והישר אל אמונה .. :

ואחר כן עמד הנבי הרם משה בן עמרם עליו השלם וצלא
בין ידי מרה : ובכלות צלותו קרא ליהושע משרתו ואנגד לו כל
הדברים דדבר יהוה אתו : ואמר לה אה משרתי הלך לבית
כהנתה ודבר להם בכן : ואמר אל אלעזר ואיתמר ופינחם ייתו
לאנה במהר עד נתמלי מן חזהתם : וכד שמע האדנן יהושע בן
נון מן הנבי זאת הדברים דהות בפתח אהל מועד (fol. 2b) משם
יצא ואתא בזרז ליד משכנה קדישה : ועמד פניו בכי וקרא לכהנים
השלשה : וכד שמעו מקראו : משם במהר צאו : וחד אדנן יהושע
עמד בכי : ודמעות עינו מטללה על פניו : ואמרו לה אה משרת
דמע בני עבר : מה הדבר : ועל מה אתה תבכי : ולבבך משתבר
ויען להם בקול אבל עני : משה הנבי אדני : השליח האנשיא :

נז

והעיד שלום יהוה עליו: לקהל בממללו: והחל יוכיחם לאמר:
ממרים הייתם עם יהוה: ואף כי אחרי מותי: ואתך (fol. 4b) על ידי
אנפכך ממצרים עזי וזמרתי: חלילה יאבד כשרני בך: ותשחת
אחר מותי: לדרך אדם אני הלך: ולבי ירא ממה מנך ראיתי:
ועתה הנני עמד על מיתובת נביותה: ועמי מה יהיה מנך זמן
אחריתה.. אשרך ישראל תשמע מני: זמה עתה מדבר לך מן
פמי ולשני: דע כי שלשה פעמים דבר יהוה אלי עלה אלי:
וסלקתי ובתורה ובלחזת ירדתי ובזאת הפעם מתלקח משאתי:
דמן (מן)אב כל הבשר נחלתי: לא תפג לך עזרותי: ועתה קדם
מותי מברכך בברכה חסידה בשם יהוה אלהיך מתיסדה..:
וכל העם היו קדמיו נציבים: בטב יתוב מתיתבים: והוא להם
מהבט: וברך להם לכל שבט ושבט: ושרא יצוה להם במימרו:
מצוות וחקות אלה שמרו: ולא תמירז אתה: (fol. 5a) פן תקראנוכון
פנותה ותדבק בכם מנביאתה.:
ואתפני לפאת בן אחיו הכהן אלעזר: והזה עמד על ימינו:
ואמר לו אה בן אחי אה חליפת אלה: אה ידוש הכהנה הנדלה:
אתה מתקומם על זאת המיתובה דיהוה לך נחלה: הוי מנטר לה
במלא..:
ואתפני בעיני אל בן אחיו איתמר ואמר לו אה מן בידך
משמרת הלוים: וכל כלי הקדש הטבים: שמר כהנתך: וכלי
הקדש דבידך: וזכי קנומך לדיאן הדיאנים.:
ואעיר בעיני אל האדון פינחס: והוא עמד על שמאליו ואמר
לו קנאתך מתנליה: כד תעמי איש סר מדרך הקשט ונניה:
קום הכה אתו כסככנתך דטביה..:
ואתפני בעיני דלית כהתו: לאדון יהושע בן נון משרתו:
ואמר לו חזק ואמץ: כי אתה (fol. 5b) תביא את עדתה: אל חארץ
דמע ארעותה: דנשבע אלה בנחלתה לזרע אקרה זכותה: ומן
יצליח יהוה פללה יסעדו וימצא אצלחותה.:
ואחר כן במראהו הרבי: אתפני לבית כהנתה בני לוי: ואמר
להם שמרו כהנתכם: וכל הקדשים אשר בידיכם: חלקות אלה
אתם לקחים: ואכלים אתם במכונות דבהם ישראל נמצאים:
והיא חלף עבדתכם: לכם ולזרעבכם אחריכם..: הקדשים לא
תחללו: עד לא ימעלכם בליעל במעלו.:
ואתפני בממללה לראשי השבטים: ואמר להם השמרד מן
המחוקקים דנצבתי לכם תמורד: עד לא יתאבד מה אתבני על
ידי בקדש אלפני..: וגם אמר לשזפטים דכל מנון שזפט: לא
תעשו עול במשפט: ושחד לא תקחז ואשפטו בצדיק בין איש
ובין רעהו..:
ולספריה אמר: למדו הקהל התורות והחקים והמשפטים בטב

בזה היום מבקש ימות וזה הדבר מריר עלינו וקשה: אכן לא
תאוה לו נפשותיכון וכבן נפשי:. וכד שמעו כהניה מן יהושע
זה הדבר אתעצב עליהם ובאו ליד משה מזתעפפת פנידהם:
ומשתברה לבבם: ובעת אמטו לה מהרו וסבדו בין ידיו: ופתנחם
בן אלעזר הכהן עליו השלום השופר בימיניו ועמד בכו פניו:
שם אמר לה הלך את ועביבך (fol. 3a) איתמר לפתח אהל מועד:
ובחציצרת תקעו: למען כל העם ישמעו: ולאנה יבאו:. ויעמדו
פני: עד השיג יתון שלם מני וכד שמעו אהלין החסידים זה
הדבר הלכו במהר לתרח המשכן: ותקעו בתרזעה על פי דברה
הקדש: ובעת שמעו העם קול חצצירות מתתקע: אזדעו ופחדו
ואמרו מה זה המתקע: דקולתו עתה שחוקה: לא הוא עת קרבן:
ולא זבן מסע:. וצפרו כהלון דחלים: ואחר כן מנון חקר:
אתניד לו הדבר:.
מרירה השעה דהתשיב בה זה הדבר: ואתאמר להם כי הנבי
הרם: משה ברה דעמרם: דדרניו רמות: הלך למות: האספו
כהלון דצאו: ואל תרח אהל הנבי באו: ראשי העם והשומפטים
והשוטרים והכהנים: והשבעים הזקנים: ומול גדלות הנבי עמדו:
ואתיצבו בכשר: בתם איקר:. וקעם נדלות השליח: ועפל ידבר
להם מה ידעהו מרה: (fol. 3b) ועשה לו דרג ועלה עליו: עד יחזה
כל העם מתאספים פניו: והם עמיד אליו: והוא עליו השלום יבכי
והדמעות ירדו מן עיניו: כטל לזרע למתניד וחכם אתם אקרדות
המקרא: חדרג אימנותה וגזריה ופקדיה: והכל מנון שמיע לקולה:
ומצית לממללה:.
והאזרון יהושע מאזין לכל מה יצא מן פמה הרם: והוא שלום
יהוה עליו עמד מדמי לירח בעת תמימו: ומוכיח ומלמד לכל
קהל ישראל עמו: ובכותו הות סלקה אל לב שזמיה: והוא מצעק
בקולות רמיה: אה שכוני המערה: אה זכאי עלמה: אה תדע
רוחיכם במה יתקומם לבניכם:. אה בן תרח אה אקר חזוכאים
הטבים: אה תדע כי סתי פרדסך דנצבת מתרעים בחזביה
ומרדיה::
אה יצחק קרבנה ומקדש: (fol. 4a) דלא השפך לו דמי אה תדע
רוחך כי נחלתך דאתכוננת בזכותך אזלה לחרבנה בחזביה: אה
יעקב אבי השבטים דרחותה: אה תדע רוחך המדכיה: כי השבטים
דקמו ממך: ואתפרקו על ידי:. מן מצרימה ביכלות עבדי:
ושמעו קולו קרי מלנו אשתה בעשרת הדברים: וחז מה בדילון
אתעבד: ואיך אתהפך פם בלעם ואמר מה טבו אהליך יעקב
משכנותיך ישראל: כל זאת הטובות מקלעים בעללה: ורחותה
תתכסי: ומשכן יהוה יתסתיר: והרגריזים יטמא: ופנותה בכל
מכון תתשקף ולא ימצא מן יקנא ליהוה::

והשליח שלום יהוה עליו סלק מעם מעם: ומביט אל אחריו
לכרניז: והדמעות מנעתה: מן עיניו: על עמד בפרקניד: ויאמר
בלבה איך ידענו בתריו: כאשה הנונה עזבת מינקות (fol. 7b) בנה: וזזה
מברכם בברכה חסידה ורזה שמיח בקראת מרה ומביט לראש
חר נבא: ומחזה מזרי המלאכים שרים בה: ועדת קהל ישראל
עמדים בתחתית ההר: נשאים עיניון להחזות: וככן הוא עליו
השלום היה עמי אליחן: מרירה השעה דבה הנבי אתכמה בענן
עבי: זאתשנב ממראה העין: ומלאכיה זהים זחדים: ולנלונה
רדו מן השמים ולאלה משבחים ומודים: מרבין לה בנכבדים:
זנלה יהוה נור עיניו ועמה ארבעת רבעת עלמה ושבח למרה
דעלמה::
רבה היא שעתה דבה משה עמה נבולות הארץ נחלת עמה:
זאבלי לי מרה מחזקקות יזם נקמה זמה יהיה לו מן הנליתות
העצזמה: לכן לא דחל מן המות דבו הנועת נשמה מן עלמה ושא
עיניו (fol. 8a) וחזה הרנריזים בית אל לו זה: ועקד ומבד על פניו:
ואתפני במנדתו אליו: וכד קעם מן סנדתה עמה תרח המערה
מתפתח ובעת עמה אתו פתיח: שבח הרחום וזרתי ובא בזאת
המערה ואתפני בפני להר ספרה: ודמך על הארץ אברו: ואפל
יהוה עליו תרדימה: ויצאת רזח הקרשה באנשמה: ואתפקדת
מלאכי אלהים בנמי לאוי לנדלותה וטמיתנותה: והזז ימי חייו הך
מה מתביאר בקדש כל אלפני: מאה ועשרים שנה: ממנה
במצרים עשרים: ובמדין ששים: וארבעים במדבר: וכהלון באיקר
רב עד מותר: בצלאן וציאם: בטב מדעה ובמזתו לא כהתה
עיניו: ולא נס ליחה: והאדנן יהושע עדפת נליגאתו: ואתנשאת
דרנותו: ואמלא מן רוח החכמה: כי סמך ידו עליו קטף כל
נשמה: שלום יהוה עליו: וזה אחר מה נמצא בזכרון מות
השליח (fol. 8b).: משה בן עמרם: עליו ועל אבהתיו הצלות והשלם.:

משמר: כמה צוה הצדיק והישר: וכל מכם (fol. 6a) מיתוביתו: לה
יתר: וזאת כלות ממצאי אתכם: ולא תפנו אשוב מן הר נבא
אליכם: . ונשא בקולו ואמר בקול עלי: אה גרשם ואליעזר בני:
עליכם השלם לעלם ממני: .
והוו כל העם נציבים פניז: ודמעות עיניהם מטללה על פניהם:
ובכותו ערפה עליהם: כי היה חכם במה יקרא אתם: תחת
משחיתם: .
ובכלות דברו אתם: עמד על רגליו שלום יהודה עליו: ועמה
להם. . ואשני השלם עליהם: ועפל בעלותו אל הר נבא למען
ימות שם: והוה אדונן הכהן אלעזר תמוך בימינו דיהוה הגדילו:
ופינחם ילידו תמוך בשמאלו: ואיתמר ויהושע וכל בית כהנתה
הלכים אתו בבכות רמתה: וכד אמטה לתחתית הר נבא נגשו
ראשי השבטים יחדו: ונשקו ידו: וכל קהל ישראל בשלם עליו
צעקים: ונגשו אלעזר ואיתמר ופינחס וחתכו לרגליו ונשקו ימינו
ושמאליו (fol. 6b) ואחר כן נגש יהושע משרתו: ונשק פניו וימינו
ושמאליו: ועקד וסגד על רגליו והחל בשלם עליו: .
השלום עליך אה מן דקרע שנבותה: השלם עליך אה מן דרם
לנו אשתה השלם עליך אה מן נגש לערפלותה: השלם עליך
אה מן לבש מאורתה: השלם עליך אה מן דקבל ארהותה:
השלם עליך אה מן אנדי לו בריתה השלם עליך אה מן נלנץ
ערפה: השלם עליך אה מן דברך יה (וזה) פה לפה: השלם עליך
אה מן דמע זכאי העולם: השלם עליך אה מן איקרך לא נעלם:
מרירה עמי שעת פרקנך: .
ובכלות הדברים האלה שא הנבי הרב: קולו הטב: לכל עמו
המסתובב ואמר הוו בשלם: ומזם הזה הלאה אינני מסב ומתן
עמכם: .
וכד שמע העם זה הממלל אתעצב עליהם ובמימרון שאו
קולתם: בחייך אה נשיא הנביים קעם עמנו שעתה: בחייך אה
שליחה דאלהיך קעם עמנו יעביד: ואלה (fol. 7a) כרז לו ברז מהר:
והעם לא ימורו מן הבכות: ורבות הצעקים אמרים אה איקר
הצביים קעם עמנו שעה: ומלאכי שומיה צעקים לה ברב צעקיה:
זרז אה משה ובא על פי מימר אלה אלהיה: וכד אתקשט העם
זה המימר דכאב להם: ואתכירו במוצאו מעליהם: אמרו פם
אחד אזל בשלם אה הנבי: אזל בשלם אה יקיר בית לוי אזל
בשלם: אה מן מרה דאלהותה אנלנך על כסיאתה ונלאתה:
והוה הנבי הרם: משה בן יוכבד ועמרם סלק להר נבא: בכבדזת
רבה: מתנזר בנוד: וכל המלאכים מתכוננים לקראתו: ובשעתה
דבה אתפרד מבין העם: ועפל לעלות לראש ההר צעקו כל
קהל ישראל צעקה גדלה ומרה: סלקה אל לבב שומיה מן ארע:

www.ingramcontent.com/pod-product-compliance
Lightning Source LLC
Chambersburg PA
CBHW051623230426
43669CB00013B/2159